No Vote for Women

*Alice Paul, the National Woman's Party and the Vote:
The First Civil Rights Struggle of the 20th Century*
(McFarland, 2015)

No Vote for Women

The Denial of Suffrage in Reconstruction America

Bernadette Cahill

McFarland & Company, Inc., Publishers
Jefferson, North Carolina

LIBRARY OF CONGRESS CATALOGUING-IN-PUBLICATION DATA

Library of Congress Cataloging-in-Publication Data
Names: Cahill, Bernadette, author.
Title: No vote for women : the denial of suffrage in reconstruction America / Bernadette Cahill.
Description: Jefferson, North Carolina : McFarland & Company, Inc., Publishers, 2019. | Includes bibliographical references and index.
Identifiers: LCCN 2019018877 | ISBN 9781476673332 (paperback : acid free paper) ♾
Subjects: LCSH: Women—Suffrage—United States—History—19th century. | Women's rights—United States—History—19th century. | Reconstruction (U.S. history, 1865–1877)
Classification: LCC JK1896 C24 2019 | DDC 324.6/23097309034—dc23
LC record available at https://lccn.loc.gov/2019018877

BRITISH LIBRARY CATALOGUING DATA ARE AVAILABLE

ISBN (print) 978-1-4766-7333-2
ISBN (ebook) 978-1-4766-3594-1

Front cover: Elizabeth Cady Stanton (left) and Susan B. Anthony, photograph by Napoleon Sarony, circa 1870 (National Portrait Gallery)

Printed in the United States of America

McFarland & Company, Inc., Publishers
 Box 611, Jefferson, North Carolina 28640
  www.mcfarlandpub.com

For all those who fought so valiantly
for equal rights for all during Reconstruction
and were virulently attacked for doing so

Acknowledgments

This work has taken me six years, during which time my husband, Ron Davis, has helped me learn to walk again after I suffered a smashed leg and supported me when I had cancer and other difficulties. I have received terrific support from my sister, Dr. Catherine Smith, of Stirling, Scotland, and her husband, Cairns Mason. My husband's grandson, Trey Davis; my friend Kay Bennett of Vicksburg, Mississippi, who regularly drove me 80 miles and back for chemo treatments; my friend Becky Conley of Monroe, Louisiana; and Gloria and Mick Watts of Romance, Arkansas, also supported me wonderfully, as did an array of other friends and angels in the healing community who rallied around.

On a professional level there were many librarians at the following who helped me pin down particular documents: the Library of Congress; the libraries in Little Rock, Alysanne Crymes of the Butler Center in particular; and Lesa Foster of the Vicksburg, Mississippi, library. I must also thank Hannah Weinberg and the archivists of the research services of the Schlesinger Library, Radcliffe Institute, Harvard University, Cambridge, Massachusetts, for locating—and making readable while dealing with upheaval—a source that turned out to be critical to the solution of a mystery and for providing everything I needed for its inclusion in this book. Finally, I thank all the historians before me, from the writers of the *History of Woman Suffrage* on, who uncovered facts, told their tales, made me hunt answers to questions, and pointed the way.

We are all building a monument to the history of women. This book is yet another contribution to its construction.

Table of Contents

Introduction

This book tells of the first political campaigns to win votes for women in the United States, which took place during Reconstruction. They resulted in women's resounding defeat by a Congress intent on having male suffrage only—Republicans specifically, who aimed to cement their hold after the Civil War and secure military, political, social, and economic victory over the southern slave power. Based on their reform history, Republicans should have supported equal rights for all, but agitators and the Republican Party latched onto a male-only agenda, peddling the reforms they advocated both as anti-slavery after abolition and as race equality. Based on their slave history, Democrats acted as expected, opposing voting rights for black males. They generally also opposed women until a small number switched sides, some perhaps out of justice but others to undermine the Republicans and even others to try to resist, subvert, or compensate for black male voting rights. This book is the story of how this happened during a vicious period in American history, a period in which in most treatments—some monographs specifically about women are the exception—women largely appear in a few paragraphs. It reinterprets Reconstruction from a female civil rights perspective, relating how Reconstruction politicians built a massive bulwark against equality in the United States, even as many professed they were for equality. In this perspective, neither political party emerges as praiseworthy. Neither political party should be proud of this history. Only those women and reformers who led the struggle, some other individuals, Congressmen, and around 9,000 male voters with mixed motives could hold their heads high over these events.

Yet this is history. It is about people and events in the past. Attitudes and laws have evolved and changed since then, through women's own monumental struggles specifically for the vote—won by an amendment to the United States Constitution in 1920 that wiped out some of the effects of the Reconstruction word "male" in that document. The contrast between then and now is startling. The only thing regrettable is that knowledge of what used to be is largely ignored and forgotten, so that many consider perennial the situation that pertains today. Unfortunately, lack of knowledge also allows

1

the notion to take hold that nothing has changed, that reform today requires the same supreme effort demanded of women more than 150 years ago and that men are as blinkered as they were then. This story might help to change these false impressions and any actions based on them. Nevertheless, as of this writing, women in the United States still do not have equal rights in fundamental law, for the Equal Rights Amendment, introduced in 1923, still awaits full ratification. However, since my first book about the vote, *Alice Paul, the National Woman's Party and the Vote: The First Civil Rights Struggle of the 20th Century* (McFarland, 2015), two more states have ratified it, leaving the field open for one state to assume in American history the honored position of taking the ERA over the finish line—to face a final, likely contentious hurdle in Congress that no other amendment has had to deal with.

This book, therefore, relates the women's post–Civil War story nationally, in New York State, and in Kansas. It continues to the aftermath for women of the Reconstruction amendments through judicial decision. It pays close attention to the time line, weaving national, state, and reform politics together with the women's work for true equality. Epigraphs in chapters throughout the book give voice to those in favor of woman's suffrage and those opposed to it. A concluding series of epigraphs speaks to the devastation of defeat.

The book corrects some time-honored myths—about events as the women remembered them in New York in 1867; about Susan B. Anthony's contentious role in Kansas that same year; about some of the reforming "saints" of Reconstruction; and about the truth of the Reconstruction agenda and its devastating impact. The time line has never been accorded such detail before, and the dynamic of its separate strands makes comprehensible for the first time the evolving attitudes of the leading women, challenging history's verdict on them and their colleagues.

Throughout the book the terms "woman's suffrage," "female suffrage," and "woman's rights" are used unless "women's" appeared in a quote or title, in which case it was not changed. "Woman" was used by the women of the time for their organizations and for the title of the *History*. "Female suffrage" was the Kansas usage.

1. The Negro's Hour

Let us see to this, that no State shall make a distinction among its citizens either of race, color, or condition—Wendell Phillips,[1] May 9, 1865, "The Anniversaries: Important Session of the Anti-Slavery Society. Speeches of Wendell Phillips et al." *New York Times*, May 10, 1865.

Rain was pelting down in New York City on Tuesday, May 9, 1865, but the terrible weather failed to prevent a huge crowd from turning up for the Thirty-Second Annual Meeting of the American Anti-Slavery Society (AASS). Already by 9:30 that morning, hundreds had packed the Church of the Puritans on Union Square. The expansive interior *thrummed* with jubilation, sorrow, and anticipation—the mixed emotions arising from several causes. On the one hand, the Civil War—ultimately transformed from a war to preserve the union into a crusade against slavery—was now nearly a month behind them. On the other hand, the leader of the nation throughout the struggle, President Abraham Lincoln, had been killed by an assassin's bullet just a few weeks earlier. Equally important, a proposed amendment to the United States Constitution—the first since 1804—had been proceeding through state ratification since that February 1; the battle to abolish legal chattel slavery in the nation was all but won and the American Anti-Slavery Society (AASS) had achieved its aim.

Now, however, there was dissension in the ranks. Many reports said that William Lloyd Garrison, the president and founder of the AASS, wanted to disband it, but not every delegate or supporter agreed. Susan B. Anthony, one of the leading woman's rights activists and a longtime staunch abolitionist worker, was one of them. She believed dissolution was premature. "The disbanding of the American Antislavery Society is fully as untimely as General Grant's and Sherman's granting parole and pardon to the whole Rebel armies," she wrote in dismay in April.[2] Still, she seemed to have faith that if Garrison dropped the baton his leading cohort Wendell Phillips would pick it up and carry on the crusade. Anthony was in Kansas at the time of the AASS meeting, but major questions were uppermost in the minds of the expectant delegates and audience that day in New York. What would the society's future be? Did it even have one?

At 10:30 "the venerable Wm. Lloyd Garrison, the perpetual President of the Society," called the meeting to order and the crowd quieted down. The choir sang "The Battle Hymn of the Republic," "the vast audience joining in the 'glory' chorus with fine effect." The Rev. Samuel J. May offered thanksgiving for deliverance from the war and for the leadership of the late president and sought God's guidance in the work yet to come. Another hymn, "The Star of Liberty," concluded the opening and then the proceedings began. Wendell Phillips stood up to speak.

Phillips was an abolitionist as renowned as William Lloyd Garrison, a powerful orator and a newspaper publisher as well. A Harvard law graduate and an aristocrat from a rich Boston family, he became interested in antislavery, according to Anthony's colleague Elizabeth Cady Stanton several years later, "by cruelty and injustice to his *own sex and color,* and he learned to hate the spirit of slavery not from personal observation of its working on southern plantations, but through the persecutions, the political, religious and social ostracism which he suffered in his own person in common with all abolitionists. Mobbed, denied the right of free speech, denounced by the press, priests and politicians, his warfare became not so much one of pure philanthropy as personal defence and self-assertion."[3] Pop-

Susan B. Anthony, c. 1870, began teaching in 1840. When her family moved close to Rochester, New York, the home became a hive of reform activity when antislavery was strengthening. In 1846 she became headmistress of Canajoharie Academy and in 1849 started work in reform—first temperance and then woman's rights and abolition. She was an instigator of a "mammoth petition" in 1863 for legislation to ban slavery. This work ultimately triggered the introduction and passage of the 13th Amendment. The main organizer of the pro-woman campaigns beginning in 1865, in 1867 she campaigned with George Francis Train and was excoriated for doing so (Library of Congress).

ularly dubbed "abolitionists' golden trumpet," he had great "power of sarcasm and denunciation," Stanton wrote much later.[4] Antislavery Phillips argued that racism was the foundation of society's ills and—partnering with Garrison after publicly condemning the notorious murder of newspaper publisher Elijah P. Lovejoy on November 7, 1837, by a mob incensed by his publications— Phillips committed himself to the antislavery cause. This work, with the Civil War ending in 1865, was finally approaching the triumph of abolition.

Phillips was also known for years of support for woman's rights. In the 1840s he backed the aspirations of women's activist Lucy Stone, helping her with petitions for votes for women in Massachusetts. Attorney Phillips' 1851 speech to the Woman's Convention at Worcester, Massachusetts, became a pamphlet entitled *Freedom for Woman,* which women campaigners circulated for decades.[5] Phillips was so closely associated with woman's rights that late in 1858, when fellow Bostonian Francis Jackson anonymously established a trust fund for woman's rights advocacy, he was appointed main trustee along with Anthony and Stone.[6] The next year, when Charles Hovey, another Bostonian, bequeathed $50,000 for reforms, including woman's rights work, Phillips was again lead trustee.[7] Some women with experience could remember Phillips' words at the World's Anti-Slavery Convention in London, England, in 1840 after the defeat of his motion to seat America's women delegates, who were unacceptable to the stuffy and prejudiced Englishmen organizing the all-male conference. "I have no doubt the women will sit with as much interest behind the bar" as if the resolution had passed, he said— which was unacceptable to the women at the time.[8]

Yet 1840 was far from women's minds. Fresh in their thoughts were their abolition and war work and dreams of rewards as Phillips came forward to deliver the keynote speech at the American Anti-Slavery Annual Convention a month after the end of the Civil War. He had chosen to appear that wet day in New York despite a heavy cold, he said, because he was advertised as the keynote speaker. Given his feeble voice, he intended to make "not a speech, but a few suggestions, which seem to me pertinent to the occasion." The society's purpose was abolition and the expected ratification of the antislavery amendment to the Constitution would guarantee the liberty of the slave. Yet this was not enough, he continued, warming to his theme: equally important was what transpired "in regard to the next national step to secure to the colored man his new-found rights." As "no freedom is real or emancipation effectual unless we arrange the forces of society that underlie law, so that they may secure to the freedmen their rights now and for all time [he said] our duty as Americans and clear-sighted Abolitionists is in the re-formation of the elements of State, so that the great forces of society shall guarantee the right recognized by the [Constitution]." Rallying the audience behind him, he declared, "I want to have another amendment passed which shall read thus: no State shall at any time make a distinction of civil privileges between the children of parents living on or born on her soil, either of race, condition or color." The rafters of the Church of the Puritans rang with applause when Phillips made his stirring proposal with his compromised voice. This was what the audience wanted to hear. With the American Anti-Slavery Society having achieved abolition, it should now set its sights on an updated version of antislavery, reflecting a higher level of the cause: pursuing equal rights for former slaves.

But as the applause echoed, faded away, and died, it emerged that what Phillips was proposing would not actually reach a higher level, for he continued: "I hope some day to be bold enough to add 'sex.' However, my friends, we must take up but one question at a time, and this hour belongs exclusively to the negro." This statement seemed to pass quietly by. Phillips continued speaking uninterrupted for some few minutes more. His 2,000-word oration was extremely short for his era, likely taking only about 25 minutes to deliver. It was long enough, nevertheless, to make his point, to couch it in the rousing rhetoric and delivery for which he was renowned, and to carry his audience with him. It did much more, however. By the end of May 10 William Lloyd Garrison's resolution to dissolve the American Anti-Slavery Society because slavery was being abolished had failed; the "perpetual President" of the AASS had resigned, and Wendell Phillips had assumed the leadership. These changes in the organization, combined with the "exciting" and "spicy debate" in the most important antislavery group in the nation, caused a public sensation as the news spread. But the part of the proceedings that would leave a lasting impression was what Phillips said to the packed audience on May 9. He had succeeded in his goals. But his "few suggestions" were heavily loaded with import for the future.

2. Men Only

We have fought great battles for the principles of freedom, and every colored man and woman testifies to that purpose. I say we must now go on and make the colored man an equal citizen.—The Rev. Samuel J. May, "The Anti-Slavery Society; Exciting Debate and Final Action on Mr. Garrison's Resolution of Dissolution. The Society Votes to Live," *New York Times*, May 11, 1865.

Elizabeth Cady Stanton was one of the country's foremost woman's rights campaigners, the philosopher of the movement. The daughter of a New York State attorney, justice, and state legislator, in 1865 she was 50 and the mother of seven children, with the last of five sons born in 1859. Stanton was the woman most identified with the cutting-edge 1848 convention in Seneca Falls, whose *Declaration of Sentiments* replicated the structure and ideals of the Declaration of Independence, presenting American women's case against their political and civil oppression in a republic founded upon equality. Resolutions of that convention called for specific reforms in marriage and divorce laws, property ownership by married women, rights to children, education, and employment. But its most contentious—and nearly stillborn—resolution was Stanton's own: a demand for women of "the elective franchise." Stanton believed that women, like men, should be able to vote in all elections, including those for President of the United States.

In the seventeen years since that convention, women had networked consistently. Almost immediately after Seneca Falls in July 1848 they frequently initiated conventions at local, state, and national levels, and an extensive, though informally structured, movement of women had grown up. Phillips had very early on supported women in this developing movement, just as the women had for years supported and worked for abolition. Since those early days women had won some reforms in some states—even a measure of married women's property law reform in New York and Ohio[1]—but suffrage for women had gone nowhere. The meager results had involved a massive expenditure of women's restricted time, their limited money and control of finances, and their finite energy. More and more female campaigners had begun to conclude that winning political rights first would be the only way they could wrest civil equality from an entrenched establishment populated only by men.

Stanton knew Phillips well, partly through her support of antislavery and partly through his support of woman's rights—both through many years. Given the momentum that women gained for their cause in early 1860 after their property law reform victory in New York, Phillips' support of women's political aspirations at the May 1860 Tenth Woman's Rights Convention, held at Cooper Institute in New York, was auspicious. That year, pointing out the double standards in the treatment of women, he had proclaimed if "woman has brains enough to be hung, she has brains enough to go to the ballot-box; and not until you strike her name off the tax-list, and excuse her from penal legislation, will you be justified in keeping her name off the list of voters."[2]

Five years had passed since then, and Stanton believed even more that women were poised for a momentous breakthrough, for they had worked so hard and in so many ways for the cause of the Union

Elizabeth Cady Stanton and her daughter, Harriot, 1856. Stanton was an instigator of the Seneca Falls Convention of 1848, in which American women called for equal rights for the first time. Her resolution proposing female suffrage was met with protest and hilarity. The philosopher and a main organizer of the campaign for woman's rights, from 1865 she campaigned ceaselessly with Anthony and other supportive colleagues to prevent "that word male" entering the United States Constitution. She went to Kansas in 1867 "to hunt the white male citizen out of that region." Reformers and Republicans excoriated her for taking part in a post-campaign tour with George Francis Train and for her increasingly angry objections to amendments giving all males suffrage while excluding women (Library of Congress).

and antislavery during the war. Nursing and fund-raising were women's most conspicuous and celebrated activities, but less celebrated was an Anthony and Stanton initiative to promote true abolition after Lincoln's Emancipation Proclamation of January 1863, which accorded emancipation only to those slaves not under Union control, which seemed a travesty of justice. In the summer of 1863, therefore, Anthony and Stanton had launched a campaign for a "mammoth petition" demanding statutory emancipation of all slaves. Under the auspices of the first woman's organization in the era of woman's rights, which they called the Woman's National Loyal League (WNLL), Anthony and Stanton spearheaded the petition drive, roping in their extensive network of woman's rights and female abolitionist colleagues to gather signatures and adopting creative financing in the absence of adequate funding from any other quarters for the work. The women were so successful that by late 1863, congressional legislators had taken up the cause, utilizing the presentation of these petitions for a larger goal. By mid–1864, Anthony and Stanton, watching the impassioned congressional battle for passage, not for legislation to emancipate slaves properly but for a constitutional amendment to abolish slavery completely in the United States, and judging their initiative successful, they wound the WNLL up. Late that year the amendment wended it way through Congress, until it passed by the two-thirds majorities required in both House and Senate. On February 1, 1865, its progress through state ratifications began.[3] Meanwhile, the women's initiative that had jump-started the amendment, even though it was more successful than they had ever anticipated, was consigned to a footnote in history.[4]

In 1865, however, this momentous result of their work was still fresh in their own minds. Given all that women had done for emancipation and to support the Union's cause, it was natural for women such as Stanton and Anthony to expect a just reward for women. And so, even if the apparently uncontroversial addendum to Phillips' declaration on May 9 seems to have largely passed unnoticed that day, Stanton did not miss it. Equally obvious to her was the fact that the AASS was holding yet another annual meeting, just as it had done every year except for 1861 on the outbreak of war—while the annual woman's rights convention had not met, with abolitionist encouragement, since cancellation because of the war. And very likely she was now fuming. For what Phillips' pronouncements meant was perfectly clear: women were to be excluded from postwar reforms at the most auspicious moment for their inclusion.

Such a conclusion did not automatically leap out from Phillips' words, for not everyone was attuned to woman's rights. Besides, he was speaking of race—and race meant "black." If there were any doubt, he made it clear when he also spoke of "the Negro." And "black" included men and women. However, when he outlined what he excluded from his proposal, he said "sex";

and "sex" in this context could mean only women, white and black, because he had already accounted for men. This mental compartmentalization was central to Phillips' statement on May 9 and was beyond the notice of many. Stanton, however, finely attuned to woman's rights, heard Phillips' statement as clearly as if it was directed at her. For a woman primarily concerned with woman's rights, her thoughts on the matter would have led in only one direction—towards the inequality of women.

No woman had equality with men in the United States. That included not just freed female slaves and free black women. It also included all white women. This discrimination applied to about 50 percent of the population. The words of Phillips—and those of other venerable participants who spoke that May 9—clearly said "men." They were not thinking of men as a generic for "humanity" but men meaning "males," for this is what they always did. When and if they intended to include women, they said it specifically. American men had done so since the Revolution. In fact, even though the Declaration of Independence might declare that "all men are created equal"— supposedly meaning humanity—many laws, including federal laws applying to the United States and many state laws relating particularly to marriage, treated women unequally, while references to suffrage in state and federal statutes specified males.[5]

These facts in 1865 raised a major new issue: if all males were treated equally under the law, the position of former male slaves required attention, because even if they were soon to be emancipated, nothing would ensure that the states would treat them equally with white men. Consequently, Phillips proposed his amendment focused on black men. Ensuring that the intentions of the moment could not be misinterpreted, the men at the 1865 AASS gathering spoke often of "freedmen"—using the specific rather than a generic such as "freed slaves." Then Phillips went one giant step farther to secure his point and clearly and deliberately excluded "sex." Therefore, he quite clearly meant the exclusion of all women from the Reconstruction amendment he proposed. Women, in sum, were to be ignored in postwar reforms. If Stanton was indeed fuming after May 9, 1865, she had good reason to be.

Phillips, meanwhile, publicly had every reason to pat himself on the back after the AASS annual meeting in May 1865. He had kept the society going, pleasing many members who argued that abolition itself did not provide true freedom for the former slaves; according to republican ideals, along with freedom went equality. Bearing this in mind, Phillips had set a new goal for the society—one to establish equality, even if it would mean considerable badgering of Congress, for it involved amending a rarely amended Constitution. Yet, as his May 9 speech stated, this challenge was nothing compared with what the AASS had just achieved with abolition.

Phillips had also solved problems for many activist men. With the end of the Civil War and the abolition amendment proceeding through ratification, abolitionists at this point had an uncertain future. Even if they had been idealists pursuing a dream, with victory they faced losing their daily work, their source of income, their public prominence—in short, their raison d'être, in some cases the way of life of decades during a long, protracted crusade. For full-time abolitionists, this development represented both a stunning victory and a major change in prospects. To redirect the AASS towards a new crusade under the abolition rubric was a satisfying solution for many. Money and a job might not have motived the wealthy, professionally prominent attorney Phillips, but passion did, and so might the prospect of wielding power and imposing his own policy on the nation, for victory for a once-maligned organization, which the AASS had been for long, must already have tasted very sweet. This victory likely left Phillips hungry for more.

Further, Phillips had even satisfied the reservations of woman's rights advocates-cum-abolitionists such as Anthony about the premature dissolution of the AASS. But if publicly he had so many reasons to pat himself on the back, there was one problem: those woman's rights advocates. Phillips might feel sure in himself about the exclusion of women as the right way to proceed after abolition, but he could not be sure about women's response to having "sex" shelved for his proposal. For American woman's rights workers, it would surely be a huge disappointment and it might anger some. Many, he was certain, would fall into line. It nevertheless represented a problem, for two of those women—Stanton and Anthony—were some of the best reform organizers he had worked with for abolition. They would be invaluable in campaigning for his proposed amendment to give black men equality. He could not risk losing them. The question was, would they back him and would they work with him? And so, with such problems at the back of his mind, on May 10 he wrote to Elizabeth Cady Stanton.

Apart from these concerns, Phillips obviously felt somewhat uncomfortable about his about-face on women in his proposed amendment, for he tried to explain himself. Even if he was focusing on a new amendment to solve the race problem by giving freedmen equality—which included the vote—he could nevertheless still advocate for woman's rights, he wrote to Stanton. This was true, he said somewhat lamely, even if he "would not mix the movements"—those of equality of race and equality of sex. But the issue was only of minor moment to him, for after all, "the only point where you and I differ [is] in a matter of method, of expedient action." More important, commingling black man's and woman's suffrage, "would lose for the Negro far more than we should gain for the woman."[6] In other words, reforms for men came first. Women came afterwards—and no one knew when.

To the fiery Stanton, these words were downright insulting. For Phillips to write in such insensitive terms to her, a woman, he must have felt supremely confident about their relationship and his new position at the pinnacle of the antislavery firmament. Yet, if the relationship between Phillips and women such as Stanton and Anthony had seemed to withstand the Civil War well, the truth is that unsettling undercurrents had been flowing for many years. In fact, the stunning victory for married women's property rights in New York in March of 1860 had already turned out to be the high-water mark of the early woman's rights movement. Intent on building on their momentum at that time, Stanton called for divorce reform at the May 1860 National Woman's Rights Convention. This audacious move opened a hornet's nest: while divorce was of major importance to women forced to live in unhappy marriages—suffragist Clarina Nichols of Kansas was one activist who had had to divorce an undesirable husband—divorce represented a huge threat to men used to controlling their wives, their wives' earnings, and their wives' wealth. Phillips, who early on had forcefully supported woman's rights, was ostensibly at the time happily married; but he turned the subject upside-down and protested fiercely the talk of divorce in a mere *woman's* rights convention. He attempted to have the subject—about which women themselves were not necessarily in agreement—expunged from the record. Horace Greeley, founder and editor of the *New York Tribune*, also a long-time supporter of woman's rights and whose marriage was shaky, editorialized about women discussing divorce. The debate was significant because it brought to the fore the opposition between the respective interests of men and women in woman's rights advocacy. It soured Phillips and the influential Greeley to the women's cause. It raised—not for the first time—the stark question of the role that men should play in winning woman's rights, for at some point their interests became incompatible. One succeeding event in their treatment of women highlighted the inherent conflict. Men, including William Lloyd Garrison, publisher of *The Liberator,* excoriated Anthony for helping, at the individual's own request, the wife of a Massachusetts senator (and sister of a United States senator as well) when she was trying to leave her abusive husband with her child.[7] Meanwhile, they helped fugitive slaves.

Not only were there new signs that women could no longer rely on previously supportive men, but women could also see something similar about woman's rights and antislavery by just referring to their own history. There was nothing wrong with women per se backing and supporting antislavery. But when men objected to their official involvement simply because they were women—and this had occurred back in the 1830s, leading to a huge split in the AASS in 1840—then the question of the disabilities of women came to the fore. Further, former slave Frederick Douglass in 1855 proclaimed that the two battles—for freedom for slaves and woman's rights—had to be separate.[8] Moreover, the men who had cancelled the AASS meeting in 1861 may have pushed for the cancellation of the woman's rights convention then because they did not want women continuing to press their own cause uninhibited by antislavery men who were otherwise occupied.[9] Given the opposition to the divorce proposal in 1860, postponement to prevent further discussion of the matter was a possible additional, covert, reason for pressing for cancellation of the woman's meeting—and Phillips may have had a hand in it. Further, Phillips, as lead trustee of the two funds that allowed some financing of women's work—the anonymous Francis Jackson Fund and the Hovey Fund—allowed only reluctant miserly support for the WNLL from the latter even as he used its money to keep his antislavery publication, the *National Anti-Slavery Standard (NASS)* afloat during the war.[10]

In the war years, various speeches about postwar reconstruction indicated a developing wind against women. Early in 1864, for example, Frederick Douglass, speaking to the WNLL called for black suffrage, specifically for males. In those pre–abolition days he declared, "While the Democratic party is in existence as an organization, we are in danger of a slaveholding peace, and of Rebel rule. There is but one way to avert this calamity, and that is destroy Slavery and enfranchise the black man while we have the power."[11] This clear emphasis on men by Douglass was not new. Even though he had been a supporter of woman suffrage at Seneca Falls in 1848, since at least the mid-fifties women campaigning for their rights had felt his wrath when they didn't follow his line. Even as Douglass continued to support woman's rights in his newspaper, the *North Star*,[12] late in 1853 he furiously castigated Lucy Stone for a woman's rights lecture tour in Kentucky, Missouri, Indiana, and West Virginia, declaring she was sidelining her antislavery principles "to deal with truth less offensive."[13] The next year, though Stone called for a boycott of the hall in Philadelphia in which she was speaking for not allowing entry to a black woman guest, Douglass attacked Stone on the front page of his newspaper for not cancelling the lecture outright.[14] Douglass also had a personal beef: he too had turned up at the hall and was turned away. In 1855, speaking at the Ladies' Anti-Slavery Society of Rochester—an organization founded to help finance Douglass's newspaper—he excoriated Abby Kelley, blaming her for the 1840 AASS split. He condescendingly patronized woman's equality as a "very minor question": "Shall a woman be a member of a committee in company with men? ... How beautiful would it have been for that woman, how nobly would her name have come down to us in history, had she said: 'All things are lawful for me, but all are not expedient! While I see no objection to my occupying a place on your committee, I can for the slave's sake forego the privilege.'"[15]

This attack, as far as Kelley was concerned, terminated her friendship with Douglass. The incident clearly demonstrated that even in the mid–1850s, Douglass could not be trusted regarding woman's rights. In these exchanges he was demanding that women stand on principle, unless it was more expedient not to. The "slave's cause" was "already too heavily laden," Douglass stated. "The battle of Woman's Rights should be fought on its own ground."[16] In other words, he was jettisoning the cause of women he had given support to in 1848 to lighten his own load, which at the time of these words was anti-slavery. Yet he ignored the fact that, were they so inclined, women could take the same position regarding woman's rights, putting males on the back burner. Stone became the target of Douglass's thunderbolts again in 1859 over what appears to have been a hoax letter designed to discredit Stone, mixing up Frederick Douglass the ex-slave with Stephen A. Douglas the Democratic senator and Lincoln's adversary in slavery debates in 1858, over an appearance at a woman's rights convention in Chicago. Garrison's *Liberator* exposed the hoax, but Douglass fulminated against Stone's so-called compromise of "her anti-slavery principles by a feverish desire for prominence and popularity." Stone refused to be drawn into unedifying feuding.[17]

Douglass's WNLL speech in January 1864 was simply the latest example of his long-term position, established before slavery was abolished. Phillips' own views had been trending in the same direction. In December 1864 he declared that the ballot was necessary for black men in readmitted states after the war to guarantee their rights.[18] Stanton's response amounted almost to hero worship. "Dearest Susan,—Glorious, good Phillips! Have you read his speech?" she wrote on December 29, 1864. "During its delivery I sat close on his right, and at its close was the first to clasp his hand and catch the currents of his inspiration. His audience felt his magnetism." Obviously aware, however, that Douglass had long been compromised on woman's rights, she continued: "Keep him on the right track. Tell him in this revolution, he, Phillips, and you and I must hold the highest ground and truly represent the best type of the white man, the black man and the woman."[19] In sum, the position of the two men already defined more narrowly the application of rights that Stanton and Anthony envisaged. None of it appears, however, to have added up in the mind of either woman to the fact that the support they had received from such men seemed, for several reasons, to be solidifying against them.

If Stanton and Anthony did not wish to face the truth about their increasingly insecure position in the minds of abolitionist men, the ground was nevertheless well prepared for what Phillips did in his speech at the AASS on May 9 and his letter to Stanton the next day. If Stanton was already fuming about the abandonment of woman's rights when she received Phillips' May 10 letter, however, it is likely she was further outraged by Phillips' follow-up speech of May 13, when he reduced women to the category of a "what not" while reaffirming that discrimination on grounds of sex would be the criteria for reform even when it was presented in the guise of removing race discrimination. "Our duty is clear," he declared. "We must announce our purpose that no State comes back into the Union with a constitution that knows a distinction of races. No matter what other qualification there is—age, property, or what not—the one single point now is, that the color of a man's skin shall not affect his right to vote."[20] Here, Phillips stated his plan to consign voting restrictions by race to history, while recognizing remaining potential restrictions—education, left unspecified, being another possible "qualification." The thrust of his speech clearly demonstrates, however, that the primary "qualification" he intended was restriction or discrimination by sex, for everything he said is based in the masculine while he had said that only "some day" might discrimination by sex be removed. Even if other "qualifications" for the franchise excluded some men, therefore, the primary restriction would be that of sex, for no woman would be included in the first place and therefore could not be excluded for some other reason. If there had been any doubt as to Phillips' intentions earlier, they became clear during this speech—at the same time as he demeaned women further as a "what not." Phillips' proposal represented a fundamental shift in the founding philosophy of the United States. This was true not so much in how the United States operated, for it had excluded women all along. It was more because the exclusion along sex lines was now being spoken of openly, and the proposal was that such sex exclusion should in some way be made explicit where it had never been before—in the Constitution of the United States.

Stanton took her time to reply to Phillips' May 10 letter, for it required an apt response that needed careful thought, which had long been her modus operandi: "For Miss Anthony and myself, the English language had no words strong enough to express the indignation we felt in view of the prolonged injustice to woman. We found, however, that after expressing ourselves in the most vehement manner, and thus in a measure giving our feelings an outlet, we were reconciled to issue the documents at last in milder terms. If the men of the State could have known the stern rebukes, the denunciations, the wit, the irony, the sarcasm that were garnered there, and then judiciously pigeon-holed, and milder and more persuasive appeals substituted, they would have been truly thankful that they fared no worse."[21] This was good policy, if only to avoid confirming the stereotype in men's minds of women as emotional creatures. They had enough opposition to contend with without reinforcing that prejudice. Perhaps Stanton attempted several replies. For her to do so would have been understandable, because the issue is complex. It seems probable that she began one new draft after another, throwing many away between her receipt of Phillips' letter and May 25, when she finally answered.

Her reply reflected her astute understanding of Phillips' game. When Phillips talked of equality of race he meant his proposal would favor black people. It would, therefore, discriminate against white women. When he

referred to sex, he naturally excluded black men because they would be protected, for white men were already covered. His proposal would, therefore,
discriminate against all women regardless of color. Phillips did not bother to
explain this: in his postwar world men were now men regardless of color, a
simple fact justifying any reform. His position was an improvement; it would,
however, have been just if men had equaled humanity. But the latter was not,
it seems, in Phillips' thinking at this point for he was obviously willing to
prioritize equalities, with men's rights before everyone else's. To strengthen
his position, he combined it with his argument to Stanton that including
women at this point "would lose for the Negro far more than we should gain
for the woman,"[22] a position which incorporated the anti-black unrest in the
South following the collapse of the Confederacy. But this argument was spe-
cious, for while he spoke of rights for black men, he ignored the rights of
black women facing the same circumstances as black men. And whatever the
basis of his position, he advocated a measure that would institutionalize sex
discrimination. Phillips was aware that many women would support his proposal because they always put themselves last. He was also aware that his
proposal would annoy the many white women who had worked hard to free
the slaves and had suspended their own cause to help in the war. For these
additional reasons, it was convenient to emphasize race, hiding sex discrimination underneath it.

To Stanton, neither race nor sex distinctions were justified in a nation
of supposedly equal rights. After abolition, black women and men would be
on the same legal footing as white women—all without the rights that white
men had enjoyed in increasing numbers for years. In her view, all such
inequalities were insupportable. Yet Phillips' proposal dealt with only the
smallest section of these unequal citizens—conveniently, all men. The men's
propensity to mean men only when they said "men" meant that it was second
nature for such as Phillips to talk of race equality even though his proposal
not only did not include all black people, but its use also masked the real
meaning, which was discrimination against women. His whole proposal was
shot through with contradictions, double standards, injustices and dishon-
esties. This, again, was convenient for Phillips: it muddied the issues and
made the ramifications of his plan difficult to discern. The deep thinker Stanton was aware of all of this and knew that countering him was a tough proposition. If Phillips was going to emphasize race, she should tackle that head-
on. Yet, to do so did not deal with white women's inequality. Nevertheless,
the complex situation necessitated a sharp response from Stanton and what
she wrote demonstrated concerns for black women, most of whom could not
fight for themselves. She settled on a simple, telling point that highlighted
Phillips' now obvious hypocrisies. What she wrote clearly held powerful feelings in check yet communicated exactly what she thought of Phillips and his

proposal. Her short, incisive, sharp reply was as cold as an ice storm in a New York winter and must have pierced even Phillips' ego like a dagger. It may even have caused him some concern: "May I ask in reply to your fallacious letter just one question based on the apparent opposition in which you place the negro and woman? My question is this: Do you believe the African race is composed entirely of males?"[23]

3. Women Need Not Apply

The battle of Woman's Rights should be fought on its own ground.—Frederick Douglass, *The Anti-Slavery Movement* (1855), 29.

I am now engaged in abolishing slavery in a land where abolition of slavery means conferring or recognizing citizenship, and where citizenship supposes the ballot for all men.—Wendell Phillips to Elizabeth Cady Stanton, May 10, 1865, in Elizabeth Frost and Kathryn Cullen-DuPont, *Women's Suffrage in America* (1992), 179.

"This hour belongs exclusively to the Negro." "The color of a man's skin shall not affect his right to vote." "I hope some day to be bold enough to add 'sex.'" Phillips' words traveled by telegraph, newspaper, canal boat, riverboat, and railroad over high mountains, through dense forests, and across wide, deep rivers to the rolling hills at the edge of the Western plains. They traveled to Kansas, where Susan B. Anthony had been staying since January of 1865, having arrived in Leavenworth at her brother Daniel's home when the new amendment to the Constitution was sent to the states for ratification.[1]

The amendment signaled not only the culmination of years of antislavery agitation, in which Anthony had played her part, but, once ratified, it would mean a new beginning in which all Americans would, in theory, be equal. Yet, the facts did not synchronize with the theory. The approximately four million freed slaves in their new status would significantly swell the numbers of unequal citizens in the nation, adding a huge new group to the millions of citizens already unequal, of whom Anthony was only one of more than 15 million.[2] This milestone of the new amendment, therefore, also created a new political landscape. If previously slavery had been the number one issue in the nation, equality was now number one. Passage of the abolition amendment represented, therefore, a watershed in which ensuring equality of rights with the privileged class—currently mostly white men—assumed prime importance. Anthony arrived in Leavenworth at the birth of this new reality.

Anthony "possessed a figure of medium size, a firm but rather pleasing face, clear hazel eyes, and dark hair which she always wore combed smoothly over the ears and bound in a coil at the back. She paid much attention to dress and advised those associated in the movement for women suffrage to be punctilious in all matters pertaining to the toilet."[3] Aged 45 in 1865, she was what society at the time unfeelingly and pejoratively called an old maid. The alternative and less harsh term for a woman of her status was "spinster." No matter what such women were called, society looked on them as odd, denigrating them with the slur that no man would have them, for insults were a normal way of casting to the far fringes of society those people who failed to fit the norms. The insult blithely disregarded the possibility that some of these women might well have married, but tragedy befell before their wedding day—particularly with 600,000 men dead during the war. Anthony had had suitors, but through her work had concluded, a colleague said just a couple of years later, "that to marry, it was essential to find some decent man," who were extremely scarce.[4]

Anthony may have been—to use further pejoratives relying on the negative to describe such as her—unmarried and childless. But she was a unique among women of her era, including Elizabeth Cady Stanton, who was by this time a mother of seven, for to remain resolutely single in the society of her day meant being child-free. Anthony was born February 15, 1820, in Adams, Massachusetts, a second child with a Quaker upbringing that imparted strict morals and attitudes, including equality of women. In 1826 the family moved about forty miles to Battenville, New York, where her father became a successful mill manager, able to send Anthony to school in Philadelphia. But the depression of the late 1830s bankrupted her father. He had to sell their home and her brief education in Philadelphia was interrupted. Following the family's 1839 move to Center Falls, Anthony started work as a teacher in 1840 in New Rochelle. Five years later the family moved to a farm close to Rochester, and the home became a hive of reform activity when antislavery sentiment was growing. In 1846 Anthony became headmistress of Canajoharie Academy, where she stayed until 1849, when she returned home dissatisfied with teaching and soon began the reform work that now called her—first temperance and then woman's rights. From a highly encouraging family who were supportive of her aspirations but, unlike those of a wealthy background, unable to support her, by 1856 she had become an agent for the American Anti-Slavery Society for New York State. Yet, with woman's rights her primary interest, by the start of the war she was the main organizer of the annual Woman's Rights Conventions, and the leading objector to the cancellation of the women's campaign in 1861. During the war she was a prime mover behind the "mammoth petition" that had ultimately led to the amendment now passing through ratification by the states. With the women's annual conventions cancelled since 1861 and the WNLL disbanded in mid–1864, in January 1865 Anthony headed off to Leavenworth, Kansas, to help with the confinement of her brother's wife, for spinsters (who were a problem to a society with little idea of what to do with them but always found them useful when it suited) were expected to help during such crucial family events. Anthony, therefore, now took the trip west. It gave her a role when there seemed to be nothing much else to do.

Her brother Daniel was the former mayor of Leavenworth and publisher of the *Leavenworth Bulletin*. Susan Anthony worked on the newspaper, complaining that he restricted writing about politics, particularly on the rights of women or black people.[5] Yet, through newspaper correspondence, reporting, editorials, and picking up articles from other newspapers and agencies, her work kept her plugged into current events, while her brother's prominence in the town brought visitors also carrying news. In touch with what happened elsewhere, she could quickly find out what had transpired at the AASS meeting where dissolution of the society was threatened—prematurely, in her thinking. The continuation of the AASS, even with Garrison's retirement, was a relief. The proposed treatment of women was another matter.

According to his own words, Phillips intended for men to have equal rights, including the vote, and for women not to have equal rights or the vote. Thereby, he said, he would solve the race problem. What kind of mumbo-jumbo was that? It said one thing but meant something else. It caused confusion. It concealed the truth. Yet his words reverberated across the Union. While abolitionists readied for another fight, both men and women listened. But the men heard one thing and women another. Black men heard that they were going to get equality. The women heard they were going to get more inequality. Both heard Phillips correctly. Yet the truth was that even if the official message was that the proposed amendment would purportedly end the race problem, the dividing line was a citizen's sex. And both sexes comprised both main races. Yet Phillips, the man promulgating the plan and a key leader of those people who could influence national policy, had deemed now that the Civil War was over the experience of men and women in the nation founded on equality was going to be markedly different.

Anthony well understood that male suffrage only was nothing new: it had prevailed since before the Revolution. She also knew that even since then race had not universally constricted voting rights. In 1865 many black men in the North could vote. With black male voting well established historically, it represented a strong precedent that had existed through many decades to influence visions of a future non-slavery nation. On the other hand, few women or men in 1865 would have lived long enough to remember the time when women voted in New Jersey—the last state in the nation where women had possessed the right to vote and a sliver of practice in the union, which ended in 1807. Only when women began to remind the antislavery men of the women's anomalous position in a supposed republic did some begin to realize that the Founders and their successors had failed to allow equality not just for slaves, but also for women. Garrison's AASS very early took notice, espousing equality for all, including universal suffrage. Yet not everyone took this view and continuing controversy meant that two fundamental definitions of equality existed before the Civil War: male suffrage that included black men and universal suffrage, meaning the vote for all adult Americans without regard for race or sex.

Even with the war raging, however, Phillips began to talk of votes for black men. "[T]he moment a man becomes valuable or terrible to the politician, his rights will be respected," he declared at the 1863 Anniversary Meeting of the American Anti-Slavery Society. "Give the negro a vote in his hand, and there is not a politician, from Abraham Lincoln down to the laziest loafer in the lowest ward in this city, who would not do him honor."[6] That June, Frederick Douglass, the former slave and antislavery activist, called for "perfect civil and political equality" for freedmen,[7] his message winning grassroots support at a convention of free black men in Leavenworth that October that called for complete freedom and the right of suffrage.[8] Nevertheless, neither suffrage for men only nor universal suffrage was new in 1865 and, whatever the emphasis, no law said that in enacting new criteria for voting there had to be a choice between votes for men only to the exclusion of women and votes for all. This was a choice that was up to the reformers and politicians of the time, the latter all male.

A proposal to limit the franchise, however, was perhaps not surprising, for a restrictive franchise had always existed in the United States. Primarily based on sex, sometimes on race, sometimes, though decreasingly, on property qualifications, sometimes on education, a limited franchise was not new.[9] Nor were discussions about such suffrage new in 1865. President Lincoln, long before his death, for example, clearly accepted limitations on suffrage. In a letter to the new governor of Louisiana in 1864, he wrote, "Now you are about to have a convention, which, among other things, will probably define the elective franchise. I barely suggest, for your private consideration, whether some of the colored people may not be let in, as, for instance, the very intelligent, and especially those who have fought gallantly in our ranks."[10] Lincoln here encouraged enfranchising blacks but with restrictions. Significantly, his reference to soldiers shows he also clearly assumed that only males would vote.

When Phillips in May 1865 declared "the negro's hour" and deliberately excluded women, therefore, he was proposing nothing new. In fact, he was openly falling in line with what Douglass and black men had been calling for—with one major difference. Douglass, having often weighed in during the war on the postwar rights of black males, clearly called that May 9 in Boston at the Massachusetts Anti-Slavery Society Annual Meeting for "the 'immediate, unconditional, and universal' enfranchisement of the black man, in every State in the Union."[11] Phillips, a few days later, called only for suffrage for freedmen, who were not the same as free black men. He and Douglass were not united on this matter. However, when Phillips said that "some day" might be more appropriate for including "sex" in equal rights, he was finally falling in behind Douglass, who had declared many years before that rights for black males and all women should be dealt with as separate issues. Two leading abolitionist men, therefore, had unilaterally sidelined equal rights for women.

With Phillips having announced it, abolitionists began to jump on the bandwagon—disturbingly for women. What was worse, they now started to distort prewar terminology and use it for this plan based on sex discrimination. "Universal" suffrage, which before the war had applied to equal suffrage regardless of sex or race, was now co-opted to mean equal suffrage for former slaves. Phillips' agenda had already encountered criticism, with the *New York Times* commenting, "He treats this whole subject of reconstruction purely with reference to its effect, or what he considers to be its effect, on the negro. He makes no account of the white man."[12] This was true: just as reforms for women would impinge on the rights of men—which Phillips had already found discomfiting—he failed to acknowledge that many white men did not like his proposal, for black male voting would dilute their power and status. More to the point for nearly half the population, however, Phillips "made no account" of women either, whether white or black.

Already opposing Phillips, after his May 1865 speeches the *Times* also fulminated against Phillips personally:

> The fierce obloquy which Mr. PHILLIPS pours upon President JOHNSON for not conferring by a stroke of the pen, the right to vote upon all the negroes of the Southern States, is characteristic of his relentless and arrogant temper. He visited President LINCOLN with the same tempestuous wrath, as he does and will every public man, who fails to come up to his standard of public duty. No ability, no uprightness of character, no public service can shield from his voluble virulence any man who fails to comply with his demands in regard to the negro. And these demands just now, ignoring every consideration of justice and public policy, exact from President JOHNSON that he shall give the enfranchised slaves complete control of the rebel States.[13]

The *Times* was painting a picture of a highly complex situation with many competing interests and concerns. It also described an obdurate and dictatorial individual, given to fiery invective to win and impose his way—the very man now intending to exclude women from postwar reforms. The *Times* editorial concluded, not with opposition to an extended suffrage but advocating a judicious extension of suffrage:

> The day will come, we trust, when every man, black or white, in the whole country, fit to exercise the right of voting, will possess and enjoy that right. But we require of for-

eigners who come to our shores some years of instruction and preparation before they are admitted to its enjoyment. The same reasons which make this wise, would also require a similar probation from those who have but just escaped from the ignorance and degradation of slavery.[14]

This restricted suffrage, therefore, would be based largely on education. But not completely: not a word did it say about women. In fact, in almost all sources, the issue meant male and black voting rights, not women: women's aspirations hardly rated reporting, it seems, even though women were the largest minority group in the country, representing about 49 percent of the population.[15] Put simply, women did not count and in 1865 if women wanted inclusion in this debate they were going to have to do it for themselves.

As a longtime supporter of antislavery, an abolitionist worker, and a woman's rights activist, Anthony was thoroughly conversant with this long history and the inherent problems of reform, but unlike the male principals and key commentators she was one of the intended excluded. In Kansas, not only was she working on her brother's newspaper, which published the most up-to-date news, but she was also helping with refugees, organizing into an Equal Rights League black people flooding into the state[16] and often garnering from them information about local conditions as they crossed to prewar free Kansas from prewar slave Missouri through Leavenworth, right on the banks of the Missouri River. Aware, therefore, of the national political disaster that was unfolding for women and invited to speak on suffrage at the first Independence Day celebrations after the end of the Civil War in Ottumwa, Anthony stepped into the fray. She had supported black male suffrage ever since the subject had first arisen and the topic was central to her speech. Now, however, demonstrating to Phillips that he could not, without a fight, kick out of sight the can of worms that woman's rights now represented to him, Anthony pointedly argued that so-called universal suffrage in its new, contrived meaning of male suffrage only was unsustainable:

> When I speak of the inalienable rights of the negro, I do not forget that these belong equally to woman. Though the government shall be reconstructed on the basis of universal manhood suffrage, it yet will not be a true republic. Still one-half of the people will be in subjection to the other half, and the time will surely come when the whole question will have to be reopened and an accounting made with this other subject class. There will have to be virtually another reconstruction, based on the duty of the national government to guarantee to every citizen the right of self-protection, and this right, for woman as for man, is vested in the ballot.[17]

In her assault on Phillips' position and on that of members of Congress that July 4 she excoriated the "so-called superior 'white male' class" who "may not be trusted even to legislate for their own mothers, sisters, wives and daughters" and who "can not legislate justice even to those nearest and dearest in their own hearts and homes."[18] And in her stirring conclusion, Anthony, who resolutely backed reforms for blacks, emphasized that suffrage to her meant equality of both race and sex. "Our new Union," she said, should be founded "on the everlasting rock of republicanism—universal freedom and universal suffrage." Such words did not support any of the less than half-measures that the men were intent on providing.[19] Soon, in the speech's after-math, she encountered local rhetoricians akin to those in the East, equally determined to exclude women: when Leavenworth Republicans urged her to prepare her Ottumwa speech for printing, they also urged her to cut out what she said about woman suffrage, which was not on their radar. Nor did they intend it to be.[20]

Yet Anthony's arguments, though emanating from a woman, were the most statesmanlike of all.[21] They harked back to ringing phrases of long before, to the Declaration of Independence about "holding these truths to be self-evident" and all men being "created equal." Her argument for suffrage for all adult men and women rested on basic principles—the same as in 1776 but using the word "men" in the general sense, not utilizing it in the peculiar one of "male." With the whole nation in shambles after the end of the war, in Anthony's reasoning it was the time to start again and remake the nation's institutions to include the two main previously excluded groups—not just men of color but also women of every race—in order finally to form the "more perfect union" that had not been originally created. Kansas Republicans said to Anthony that she should not confuse the two issues, "to which Susan replied that it was they who confused the issues, and that in her speeches she ... [talked] not party politics but straight republicanism."[22] This anti-woman pressure from Republicans in Leavenworth clearly brought to the surface what women now faced in the wake of Phillips' May announcement.

Meanwhile, colleagues begged Anthony to return home. In mid–July, she recorded in her diary a message via Stanton from Phillips urging her to "come East; there is work for [you] to do."[23] The man, it appears, had no shame, for he seemed to expect work for others from the best organizer he knew, even if equal rights for women failed his agenda. Abolitionists Lydia Mott and Parker Pillsbury also wrote, pleading with her to come east.[24] For Anthony, meanwhile, the imperatives of the national political situation were growing, while those of Leavenworth were disappearing. Her sister-in-law's baby had arrived, and she was no longer needed on that account. Ensuring the accurate and safe publication of her whole July 4 speech and a commitment to delivering another, which she gave to a huge audience in a grove in Leavenworth early in August, held her back for the moment.[25] This Leavenworth speech may also have helped to galvanize Anthony into action, for local Republicans now ordered her not to mention women.[26]

But other pressures were brought to bear. Around this time, Anthony apparently learned the new amendment would include not just freedmen but also the word "male" to determine the right to vote. The word's first inclusion in the United States Constitution, when it defined citizens as male, would exclude women from civil rights. A frantic Stanton wrote, "I have argued constantly with Phillips and the whole fraternity, but I fear one and all will favor enfranchising the negro without us. Woman's cause is in deep water. With the League disbanded, there is pressing need of our Woman's Rights Convention. Come back and help. There will be a room for you. I seem to stand alone."[27] All this precipitated Anthony's departure homewards. Anguished by the men's betrayal, soon after her speech in Leavenworth Anthony was heading east, paying her way home in a speaking and subscription-raising tour for the *National Anti-Slavery Standard*.[28]

A noteworthy event during her trip was Missouri senator Benjamin Gratz Brown's speech in St. Louis about enfranchising freedmen in which he also said, "That the rights of women are intrinsically the same with those of men and may not be consistently denied."[29] Such sentiments must have felt good, even as working hard for the *NASS* on her journey home she was still as constrained about her true concerns as she had been in Leavenworth. In Chicago that August 29, for example, in a speech headlined "Universal Suffrage," she spoke only of black male suffrage.[30] She arrived home in Rochester, penniless, on September 23.[31] This harried, busy return journey for this hard-working woman who was forced to subordinate her own interests to those of others in order to work her passage home was the last time Anthony would talk of the rights of men without the rights of women. When she arrived at the end of her journey the key players in the women's battle for inclusion in Reconstruction had lined up readying for the fray.

4. On Their Own

[W]e ask that you extend the right of Suffrage to Woman—the only remaining class of disfranchised citizens—and thus fulfill your Constitutional obligation "to Guarantee to every state in the Union a Republican form of Government."—Elizabeth Cady Stanton, Susan B. Anthony and Lucy Stone, 1865, *History of Woman Suffrage II* (1887), 91.

Anthony took only a short break with her mother at the farm in Rochester she called home: she had too much to do to take a longer rest. Many forces countering an intransigent President Andrew Johnson, who refused to consider black suffrage in the South, were now aligning themselves to fight for it. More to the point for Anthony, the same forces were aligning themselves to fight against woman suffrage, at the very least by ignoring it. Early in October she was in New York meeting with Stanton, the two women quickly planning yet another petition to Congress to call for the inclusion of women in any new constitutional amendment. On October 11, heading out from Rochester, Anthony began a tour through New Jersey, to Boston and Massachusetts and several New York towns. She visited Martha Wright, Lydia Mott, Ernestine Rose,[1] Lucy Stone, Antoinette Brown Blackwell, Stephen and Abby Kelley, Caroline Healey Dall, Phillips, and Garrison—all key reformers of the era—to canvass their help against the pending legislation.[2]

It was a sobering trip, for Anthony found that while her colleagues may have wanted her return from Kansas it was not for woman suffrage. Underground Railroad activist and signatory of the 1848 Declaration of Sentiments, Martha Wright of Auburn, and a nearby colleague, Mrs. Worden, both were "very dubious about reviving interest in woman's rights at this critical moment."[3] Lucretia Mott was equally restrained. Writing to her sister, she said that Anthony "was full of [the suffrage debate] as well as of the Woman movement and brought an address by E.C. Stanton for us to endorse." But she did not align with the plan to petition Congress to include women in the new federal measures, for, Mott observed, "it would be in vain, while the all-absorbing negro question is up."[4] Mott's position was paradoxical. She thought of winning the vote for women only through state reforms, saying, it might be "well for [New York] to revive the question as the time for revising the Constitution is near"; but she seemed at the same time to accept establishing the citizenship and political rights of black men through federal reform.

Frances Dana Gage, however, protested the exclusion of female suffrage. In November, she challenged the *NASS* for its reporting of Senator Gratz Brown's September speech. The *NASS* had "justly decided that, though long, it was too good to be any of it omitted," but then it excluded his pro-woman statement, which she now included with her letter. The *NASS* finally printed the extract. Gage then had a question:

> And, by the way, can any one tell us why the great advocates of Human Equality, such men as Wendell Phillips and Wm. L. Garrison, who a few years ago were bold champions for equality before the law for women, and gave eloquent lectures in behalf of the … one-half of the people of the United States, oppressed by unjust laws and partial legislation—now wholly ignore that part of the subject, and forget that once when they were a weak party and needed all the womanly strength of the nation to help them on, they always united the words "without regard to sex, race, or color?" Who ever hears of sex now from any of these champions of freedom?[5]

Lucy Stone traveled in New York and New England, attracting "good audiences and good pay" promoting woman suffrage,[6] and Anthony met with her late that November to plan, for now not only was there the petition for women's inclusion in a federal amendment but another campaign for woman suffrage in Washington, D.C. Once more needing campaign funds, Anthony spoke with Phillips and came away with $500 from the "W.R. fund"[7]—likely from the 1858 fund for woman's rights work of the anonymous donor later revealed to be Francis Jackson.[8]

Rapid action by the women was essential, for the new Congress would focus primarily on Reconstruction. In fact, immediately, on December 4, Thaddeus Stevens and the House Radical Republicans limited opposition to their plans by refusing, under the Constitution's Article 1, Section 5, to seat southern members. Triggering this were the problems anticipated from the 13th Amendment, which Secretary of State William Seward certified on December 18, 1865, after it met ratification requirements on December 6.[9] With slavery in the United States now finally abolished under fundamental law, the rights of freed blacks became a major concern because of the Dred Scott decision of 1857, which declared blacks were not citizens. Equally important for party politicians, however, was the fact that, with former slaves now no longer counted as only three-fifths of a person, the defeated South's congressional representation would soon increase through the "increased" population. The South would benefit, challenging the Union victory. For Republicans, preventing their defeat in coming elections and guaranteeing triumph in elections after that was a huge priority. Enfranchising freedmen, therefore, had become a matter of raw power. In the debate, Republicans and key reformers never spoke as if "freedmen" meant other than males.

From its beginning, the nation had used male terminology for voting qualifications in state constitutions, specifically as "white male." At the federal level, Section 9 of the 1787 Northwest Ordinance specified males several times, both for electing representatives and as the basis of representation. Now the word "male" quickly became prominent as black suffrage support increased. The word appeared for the first time in a constitutional amendment proposal when, on the first day of the Reconstruction Congress, Republican senator Charles Sumner introduced Senate Resolution 1.[10] This joint resolution specified "male citizens" to determine representation. The rapid introduction of this proposal demonstrates how much had been happening behind the scenes, including work to exclude women. For woman's rights workers, it represented a frontal assault. It was a startling new departure.

Lucy Stone, with daughter Alice Stone Blackwell, c.1858, was an early woman's rights activist who overcame family obstacles to pursue her education. She became the first Massachusetts woman with a college degree. Later a highly paid orator for abolition and woman's rights, upon her marriage to Henry Brown Blackwell she largely withdrew until Stanton and Anthony called on her help in the 1865 woman's rights crisis. She and Blackwell were the first campaigners from the East in Kansas in 1867. After Kansas, the three women became increasingly estranged, leading to a split in 1869 and Stone's creation of the American Woman Suffrage Association in opposition to the National Woman Suffrage Association of Anthony and Stanton (Library of Congress).

As this proposal was likely only the first move, women had to campaign to forestall both this exclusion and its institutionalization in the Constitution. Stanton began drafting yet another petition, which asked the Senate and House of Representatives for "an amendment of the Constitution that shall prohibit the several States from disfranchising any of their citizens on the ground of sex"—the first attempt to counter sex exclusion in the franchise. That Christmas Anthony and Stanton focused on "writing letters and addressing appeals and petitions to every part of the country"[11] asking for signatures. Their covering letter dated December 26 and signed "on behalf of the National Woman's Rights Committee" by Stanton, Anthony, and Stone, said that congressional proposals for the new amendment "would turn the wheels of legislation backward." Echoing Phillips' slogan for blacks, they stated, "It is the hour for Woman to make her demand … and unitedly protest against such a desecration of the Constitution and petition for that right which is at the foundation of all Government, the right of representation."[12]

Separately, Anthony sent the petition to Massachusetts native Caroline Healey Dall, writing that Senator Gratz Brown "is probably our best man in the Senate."[13] Brown had been variously an Unconditional Unionist, a Radical Republican, a Democrat, and a Liberal Republican and after the war he split from Radical Republicans by advocating voting rights for all. As early as Christmas, therefore, if not as early as September 1865 when Brown spoke up for women in St. Louis, Anthony was thinking beyond mere Republicans about how to have women included in the proposed constitutional amendment. She may have begun thinking along these lines when Kansas Republicans opposed her inclusion of woman's suffrage in her speeches. In her letter to Dall, Anthony said that Republican representative Thomas Allen Jenckes of Rhode Island had introduced a bill that specified "male citizens,"[14] adding that she was less clear about Republican senator Charles Sumner, whose bills were "worded so as not to add any new limitations to suffrage." By "limitations" she meant the constitutional expansion to all women of restricted suffrage in the United States. Perhaps she had not seen Sumner's December 4 joint resolution specifying males, and if this is the case it shows how handicapped the women were, based in New York and barred from Washington's inner power circles.

On December 27 Anthony in her diary wrote that pro-woman's rights Theodore Tilton, abolitionist and editor of the *Independent,* the leading publication carrying the fiery sermons of the famous the Rev. Henry Ward Beecher of Brooklyn's Plymouth Church, had suggested the formation of a new organization dedicated to equal rights for all[15]—an idea that pro-woman's rights Henry Clarke Wright had proposed in *The Liberator* the previous April and May. Calling for true universal suffrage, he asked, "Cannot the Abolitionists start a new movement that will cover the whole ground? … Now, while reconstructing our national and State governments, is the time to discuss these questions. Abolitionists are the ones sent and commissioned of God to do it."[16] In addition to Stanton and Anthony, men such as Tilton and Samuel J. May had advocated at meetings or personally for comprehensive instead of special interest reform,[17] effectively challenging Phillips' narrow agenda. The notion of an inclusive organization instead of one focusing on creating male-exclusive voting privileges under the guise of protecting the rights of freed male slaves seemed more attractive to some reformers in the new reality, with that November a proposal arising to change the name of the Pennsylvania Anti-Slavery Society to the Pennsylvania Equal Rights Society.[18] By December, however, nothing had been achieved. In fact, the clarion calls for black male suffrage of Douglass, Phillips, and others regularly after April 1865 demonstrated that many prominent men—now with politicians in tow—were deliberately and increasingly marginalizing half of the American population. By December, many bills discriminating against women either by failure to include women or by emphasis on the masculine, had been introduced before Congress. The women's situation looked gloomier every day.[19]

All these factors constituted the background to Tilton's suggestion of an Equal Rights Society to Anthony on December 27, soon after Anthony raised the idea with pro-woman abolitionist Parker Pillsbury, for that day the Pennsylvania Anti-Slavery Society recorded a discussion of letters between those two on the topic.[20] To some, an Equal Rights Society's aim was to work for equal rights for black men, both freed and free, which would stretch even the current congressional proposals. Yet, only by including women could an equal rights society be true to its name. Tilton's plan would combine equal rights women—a group with no formal structure—with the AASS and create a new organization advocating equal rights for former male slaves, for free black men, and for all women. Tilton soon published a stirring editorial in the *Independent* attempting to raise the level of postwar debate and calling for "woman's claim to the ballot" and declaring, "No republic is republican that denies to half its citizens those rights which the Declaration of Independence and a true Christian democracy make equal to all."[21]

Meanwhile, with the situation critical, the petition was uppermost. On December 30 Stanton wrote Martha Wright asking, "Will you see if you can get our petition in your city and county papers? Sign it yourself and send it to your representatives in Senate and Congress, and then try to galvanize the women of your district into life. Some say: 'Be still; wait; this is the negro's hour.' We believe this is the hour for everybody to do the best thing for reconstruction."[22] That same day one of her letters appeared in the *Standard*, arguing that Reconstruction should not create more inequalities through cherry-picking from among all the nation's citizens only specific beneficiaries for citizenship and political rights, especially when the cherry-picking excluded the female half of the population. Rather, she argued, there existed an opportunity to bring women into a polity reformed to encompass all Americans according to republican principles of equality. Phillips disagreed in an editorial, saying that including women would kill the opportunities for freedmen. Specific, narrow, apparently attainable goals, even if they created new inequalities for an indefinite future, were more appropriate for the circumstances.[23]

It was not just Phillips who was negative. So was Martha Wright. Just over a week after writing to her, Stanton wrote again: "I have just read your letter, and it would have been a wet blanket to Susan and me were we not sure that we are right.... I thank God that *two* women of the nation felt the insult and decided to do their uttermost to rouse the rest.... If the petition goes with two names only, ours be the glory, and shame to all the rest.... We have had a thousand petitions printed.... But if they come back to us empty, Susan and I will sign every one.... Martha, what are you all thinking about that you propose to rest on your oars in such a crisis?"[24] With even the women's old guard reluctant to join and the battle to be heard an uphill struggle, a new organization combining their limited resources with those of the more secure and influential AASS was inviting, especially as the influential the Rev. Henry Ward Beecher backed the idea. Tilton also suggested that Phillips could be president, and the *Anti-Slavery Standard* the official publication.[25] To Anthony and Stanton the idea seemed ideal, faced as they were with monumental struggles and aware that they still had to work with Phillips to access such financing as was available to the women's struggle from the bequests that included them. They supported rights for black men, but they had great problems with women's exclusion, especially carved into the Constitution. To them, this was just another form of slavery. A new organization might benefit both causes and save the women from having to pit themselves against the powerful Phillips.

The importance of some sort of help emerged when Robert Dale Owen visited on December 31 and gave Stanton copies of "all the resolutions before Congress on suffrage." They were a bombshell. The next day, she wrote frantically and angrily to her cousin Gerrit Smith trying to get that venerable reformer of many decades to stir up some opposition: "Do you see what the sons of the Pilgrims are doing in Congress? Nothing less than trying to get the irrepressible 'male citizen' into our immortal Constitution.... What a shame it would be to mar that glorious bequest of the Fathers by introducing into it any word that would recognize a privileged order. As our Constitution now exists, there is nothing to prevent women or negroes from holding the ballot, but state legislation. If that word 'male' be inserted, it will take a century at least to get it out."[26]

5. That Word "Male"

The Constitution classes us as "free people," and counts us whole persons in the basis of representation; and yet are we governed without our consent, compelled to pay taxes without appeal, and punished for violations of law without choice of judge or juror.—Elizabeth Cady Stanton, Susan B. Anthony and Lucy Stone, 1865, *History of Woman Suffrage II* (1887), 91.

Gerrit Smith and his wife Ann were known throughout the reform community for their philanthropy and support of temperance, abolition, and—most important as far as Stanton was concerned—woman's rights. In fact, Smith, when nominated the Liberty Party's candidate for president in June 1848, in his convention speech called for "universal suffrage in its broadest sense, females as well as males being entitled to vote." It was while visiting her cousin at Smith's elegant columned mansion in Peterboro, New York, that Stanton—born Elizabeth Cady—met her future husband, renowned abolitionist speaker, Henry B. Stanton. Smith was known as one of six men who had financed John Brown's raid at Harpers Ferry in 1859—part of the volatile background to the Civil War. Given Smith's life-long connection to philanthropy and reform, his support of the marginalized, and her family relationship, it was natural for Stanton, immediately after reading the actual amendment proposals before Congress, to think of her cousin's helping to press for the women's cause.

Those congressional proposals were horrific for women. One word only defined the problem: "that word 'male.'" Stanton had reason to be concerned; concurrently in Washington, D.C., she said, men were creating a "National Equal Suffrage Association" calling for suffrage for "all men." To call such a creature "national" or "equal," said Stanton, was "impudence."[1] This dire situation demanded reinforcements—essential to prevent nothing less than the debasement of the United States Constitution, where all were said to be equal. Armed with the information from Owen, Stanton went on the offensive in a letter to the *Standard.* Four constitutional resolutions on suffrage were before the 39th Congress, she said, besides Charles Sumner's S.R. 1 joint resolution—all specifying males[2]: "Mr. Broomall proposes to amend by saying 'male electors,' Mr. Schenck 'male citizens,' Mr. Jenckes 'male citizens,' Mr. Stevens 'legal voters.'" The guilty parties were all Republican. "There is no objection to [Stevens'] amendment proposed ... as in process of time women may be made 'legal voters' in the several States, and would then meet that requirement of the Constitution." Defiantly, writing to Martha Wright, she said it was the woman's time: "When Andrew Johnson began the work of reconstruction, the negro's opportunity was lost. Politicians will wrangle over that question for a generation. Our time is now."[3] In her letter to the *NASS*, Stanton did not oppose votes for freedmen, but she wanted "that word 'male'" out, her objection being to the deliberate inclusion of males only and the congressional intention to exclude women in fundamental law. Women might later enter the electorate if they were not excluded through the word "male." But if sex exclusion were specified, a huge and impenetrable barrier would rise against them. If passed, it would have to be nullified, for "neither time, effort, nor State Constitutions could enable us to meet [the sex qualification] unless, by a liberal interpretation of the amendment, a coat of mail to be worn at the polls might be judged all-sufficient," she wrote.[4]

To Stanton, sex was as invidious as race was for exclusion. She was impatient with political games. "There is now no law favoring slavery," she wrote, "and as it is to the interest of the Republican party to give the black man the suffrage, reformers may as well pass on to some other position a round higher."[5] Politicians had begun to draw in Congress a thick black line between men and women, outlawing discrimination against men because of "previous condition of slavery or involuntary servitude."[6] At the same time, they were also discussing expressly *disfranchising* any men who had supported the Confederacy—yet another twist now emerging on restrictive franchise.[7] But, Stanton argued, abolitionists were not bound by Congressional politicking: working with other reformers such as women they could demand the higher principles of equal rights for all and ensure at the very least that no new exclusions—in this case sex—became part of the United States Constitution under the guise of removing racism. It was important to campaign against these proposed exclusionary measures and for all "disfranchised classes" to be secured the right to vote. In their late 1865 petitions, they called for this higher philosophy because "all partial application of republican principles must ever breed a complicated legislation as well as a discontented people ... [and] ... to simplify the machinery of Government and ensure domestic tranquillity," they advocated, "that you legislate hereafter for persons, citizens, tax-payers, and not for class or caste."[8] Quite simply, equality and not exclusion made for justice. It was plain common sense.

The women had embarked upon a major battle, representing nothing less than a crusade to save the union based on a reassertion of the founding principles of the republic now that the most blatant blot on its fundamental principle of freedom had been abolished. They were fighting against one word that would enshrine in the Constitution a warped interpretation of the Declaration of Independence, which declared—in the general, not in the specific, meaning of the term—that "all men are created equal" and would cut out the female half of the population from equal participation. Women wanted inclusion in the polity based on the Declaration of Independence and the Constitution and they now called on the founding philosophy to support their claims.

In their battle the women faced politicians—all of them male—and many reformers, their most outspoken leader also male, who all planned to protect the victory over the South by enfranchising former male slaves. This reform would give ex-slaves the power to protect themselves and, combined with possible disfranchisement of white men who had betrayed the Union by fighting for the Confederacy, would ensure that the old southern slave power could not rise again. Further, the new electors would likely vote for those who gave them the franchise and so Republicans would benefit from suffrage for freedmen. Instead of Democrats capitalizing on the increased representation caused by the demise of the Constitution's three-fifths clause following abolition, Republicans would win instead.

In 1865, women such as Anthony and Stanton felt keenly their right and need to be involved in ensuring good Reconstruction policies. Women largely had not been directly involved in the creation of the republic imperfect with slavery—even if they might have benefited from, supported, and were excluded from its operation or were enslaved by it. In the succeeding years, many of them had been active abolitionists. All women were swept up in the upheaval of the Civil War, but they still had little say in what happened. They did, nevertheless, make key contributions to its conduct[9] and the powers-that-be respected the women when they promoted the men's causes. "While the 13th Amendment was pending," the writers of women's history remembered years later, "Senator Sumner wrote many letters to the officers of the Loyal League, saying, 'Send on the petitions; they give me opportunity for speech.' 'You are doing a noble work.' 'I am grateful to your Association for what you have done to arouse the country to insist on the extinction of slavery.'"[10]

With the war over, the women felt they should now be coming into their own, with their own concerns met and their rights won. Yet, the war's end refocused the men's interests and they began to push women aside. Sumner, who effusively praised them for their abolition work, was the one who, on the first day of the 39th Congress, brought forward a proposal to introduce "that word 'male'" into the Constitution. Then "came some of the severest trials the women demanding the right of suffrage were ever called on to endure," recalled the women in their own history. When "the same women petitioned for their own civil and political rights, they received no letters of encouragement from Republicans nor Abolitionists."[11] Bluntly put, despite their sterling contributions to the war effort and their key role in abolition, in 1865 the men were throwing the women off the cliff.

The sudden realignment of the abolitionist forces in 1865 also hampered women. When Garrison retired so did the most influential abolitionist—the very man who had backed women in 1840 when the AASS had split over women's active involvement. Garrison's revolutionary newspaper, *The Liberator,* had always been a platform for women's views. With his departure the spirit and outlook of those old anti-woman forces of 1840 took over in the AASS. Those forces had continued into political abolitionism, later aligning with other groups and finally forming the Republican Party. And now, leading the AASS was another man who had supported women in the past—the arrogant, obdurate, and irascible Phillips. With the Republican Party—partly created from anti-woman former abolitionist forces—in power, Phillips pulled the AASS back to the bent of political abolitionism, which included the exclusion of women. Despite Stanton's view that politics and abolitionists were different, therefore, by mid–1865 they were effectively one, reviving an old stream of history. On December 29, 1865, with both reform and political forces arrayed against the women, Garrison published the last issue of *The Liberator,* and a major platform for women to get publicity went silent. That same day Garrison published Stanton's letter about the political rights of women:

> I must call your attention to the fact that [the negro] has been declared free ... has the most influential political party of the day demanding that the Constitution be so amended as to give the ballot to all his race—and that his right of suffrage is already conceded in several of the States; while women's right is ignored everywhere, and a proposition has actually been made, this session in Congress, to so amend the Constitution as to exclude her forever from all representation in the government. I feel that it is unsafe to sleep now. As there is some talk of opening the Constitutional door to one class of disfranchised citizens, I would advise women everywhere to have their lamps trimmed and burning, ready to walk in the first chance, without respect to "white or black male citizens...."[12]

The petition appeared alongside Stanton's words, garnering some publicity; but as *The Liberator* went silent the *Anti-Slavery Standard* became more important. The idea of an equal rights organization such as Tilton had suggested was not straightforward, however. While it appealed to the women and some abolitionists, many did not concur. A merger of the AASS with woman's rights workers would finally mean, after nearly 30 years of women's campaigning, inclusion of the "only remaining class of disfranchised citizens"[13] in a reform platform on the same terms as former male slaves.[14] But the proposal would require an about-face by Phillips on a policy he began actively to promote as president of the AASS for the first time only the previous May. Furthermore, reforms that included women amounted to fundamental change whereas enfranchising more males did not. The first opportunity to debate and decide on the idea would be on January 24 in Boston.

During the interim before this meeting, Reconstruction raised many problems for the few woman's rights workers. From early January1866 bickering and horse-trading went on in the Congress and the Joint Committee of Fifteen on Reconstruction—created the previous month—over the exact wording of the proposed constitutional amendment about the rights of freedmen. Some wording mentioned nothing about either sex, leaving the situation unclear at both state and federal level. Others included "male"—for the first time expressly allowing the exclusion of women or discrimination against them in both state and federal law. Yet no constitutional proposal involved a right to vote directly, for most congressmen—and most citizens, North and South—were unready and often unwilling to give the vote to black men. The proposals dealt with suffrage only indirectly, through a calculation of congressional representation based on an undecided criterion: voters, population, male voters, citizens, male citizens, property-holders, the educated, the literate, or a combination thereof. Heretofore, representation in Congress had always been calculated on the population of a state—both male and female. In addition, a reduction in representation as a penalty when freedmen were not allowed to vote, with several variations possible, was also under consideration. All debates dealt with a restrictive franchise presented as "universal suffrage." There was nothing proposed to induce states to enfranchise women to increase state representation in Congress, for no proposal suggested calculating representation on the number of female voters. None represented an attempt to raise the United States Constitution to a higher level of principle. What women saw was politicians tinkering with the nation's Constitution and making it worse. While purporting to remedy the original sin of slavery, the white male representatives, with the support of black men led by Frederick Douglass, seemed intent on committing yet another equally egregious sin directed against a much larger section of the population—women.

The women, nevertheless, pressed on. On January 21 Anthony, writing to the *Standard*, commented enthusiastically on the formation of a "N.Y. State Equal Rights Association" for "the time for Negro or Woman specialties is passed—and we proposed to step on the broad platform of equality and fraternity."[15] Meanwhile, the women were also discovering that submitting signatures to Congress was a great challenge. Democrat representative James Brooks of New York revealed this on January 23 during debate: "The whole object of this amendment is to obtain votes for the negroes. That is its purport, tendency and meaning; and it punishes those who will not give the vote to the negro in the Southern states of our Union ... but negroes are men and brothers and why not, in a resolution like this, include the fair sex too...?" Continuing, he said, "Many members [in the House had] petitions from [the nation's] fifteen million women, or a large portion of them, for representation, and for the right to vote, and equal right with the stronger sex, who they say are now depriving them of it." He submitted a letter from Anthony dated January 20, 1866, saying that Radical Republican Thaddeus Stevens had ignored a petition sent the previous week, hence her request to a Democrat to introduce the cause.[16] The letter was read into the record along with a copy of the petition with the names of Stanton, Anthony, Stone, Antoinette Brown Blackwell, Ernestine Rose, Joanna S. Morse, Elizabeth R. Tilton, and others. It seems that Anthony first submitted her petition in the second week of Congress in January, with this revelation occurring now in the fourth week. With such underhanded Republican behavior exposed, Stevens would finally present the original petition quietly on January 29.[17] Black suffrage and representation, including presentation of petitions for votes for freedmen, by contrast, appear often in the congressional debates. It is difficult to avoid them, whereas finding women's interests is a challenge. The women later complained that representatives were unceremoniously shelving their petitions and conveniently forgetting them. Ignoring the women's constitutional right of petitions, it seems, was another incidence of squalid less than honorable behavior by politicians facing women attempting to win equal rights during Reconstruction.

The next day, January 24, Senator Gratz Brown of Missouri[18]—living up to the sentiments he had expressed in his speech in St. Louis the previous September—presented another petition from "some of the most intelligent and accomplished women of our land."[19] In addition, the Joint Committee's report on part of the proposed amendment came before the House, reading in part, "Representatives and direct taxes shall be apportioned among the several states which may be included within this Union according to their respective numbers, counting the whole number of persons in each State, excluding Indians not taxed; PROVIDED, That whenever the elective franchise shall be denied or abridged in any State on account of race or color, all persons therein of such race or color shall be excluded from the basis of representation."[20] Intended to replace the infamous Article I, Section 2 of the Constitution whereby slaves were counted as three-fifths of a person in calculating representation, the women had the consolation at least that the word "male" did not appear. It had been bandied about, however, several times during the session already and immediately Representative William Lawrence (Republican) of Ohio moved to include it.[21]

That same day, Anthony was in Boston for the AASS meeting, "full of the new idea of consolidating the old Anti-Slavery and the Woman's Rights

Societies under one name, that of the Equal Rights Association."[22] With nothing about a merger on the agenda, Stephen Foster proposed it, saying that "it was highly desirable to connect the advocacy of the women's cause with that of the antislavery cause. He preferred this course as not only just, but as bringing up a larger force against the common enemy." Theodore Tilton argued, "It is the duty of this people to found its Government, in this formative period, upon a basis of political equality, making distinction neither between black and white, nor between women and men. [It] is the only true ground to be taken." He expressed regret there was nothing about woman's equality in the resolutions for the meeting. Stone hedged her bets, advocating both woman's rights and supporting work to "maintain the rights of the negro," for "neither the rights nor the safety of the Southern blacks were secured." Abby Kelley, however, said, "Whatever claims women's rights might have in another place, the attention of this Society should be concentrated solely upon the claims of the colored race." Charles Lenox Remond "thought it was … too much to ask that the difficulties of the women's rights question be incorporated with those necessarily belonging to the question of negro suffrage. He vindicated the character … of the colored people and thought their rights should now receive zealous and undivided attention."[23] Anthony's work was on the business and finance side of the meeting and she made no comment,[24] but when Phillips did he squashed the idea. The proposal required an amendment to the AASS constitution, which in turn required three months' notice.[25] Aaron Powell[26] was "deputized … to give the formal notice, in order that it might be acted upon at the coming May Anniversary."[27]

For AASS members in Boston who supported women—aware that the thrust of congressional work in D.C. that day favored abolitionist goals for men—the setback of Phillips' opposition to an equal rights association was reinforced when the word "male" again featured in the House of Representatives, even as they were trying to promote a new organization to prevent it. Phillips' obduracy was losing them valuable time. Anthony did express some satisfaction about the presentation of their petition in Congress at last— in both chambers, on succeeding days. She mentioned this triumph for women in a letter to Phillips on January 28, calling Brown's work "splendid" and Brooks' "skillful." Instead of expressing disappointment at the outcome of the Boston events for women, she said the AASS meeting and the next day's Massachusetts society meeting "were very refreshing to every abolitionist present." She was equally enthusiastic about having raised multiple subscriptions for the *Standard*—pointing out to Phillips the value of her work for the AASS. It also gave her the opportunity to request "another $100 of the W.R. Fund"[28] in a letter in which she also mentioned the Francis Jackson ("W.Rights") and the "Hovey Com." funds in the same sentence, while she registered "protest against spending either fund" inappropriately.[29]

The women's position, however, continued to be weak. Congressman Lawrence's move to include the word "male"—evidence of the huge struggle the women faced—highlighted the importance of the women's petitions. Also, while Brooks, a Democrat, did present their petition to Congress and recited the clause of the proposed amendment with the added word "sex," he nevertheless declined to move an amendment to the proposed amendment to have it included, arguing that a Republican could do so. He refused to attempt to ban sex discrimination along with race, now also failing the women.[30] The debate record gives the impression that Brooks may have introduced the women's petition to score political points. His move, however, had great historical importance: it ensured that a petition from women about votes for women had breached Congress's hallowed halls. The presentation of the woman suffrage petitions in the House on January 23 and in the Senate on January 24, 1866, are, significantly, the first times the question had edged into and was recorded for posterity in national discourse at the highest level. It could never forthwith be truthfully argued that women were not interested in the vote or that women never tried to get the vote or even that if women had asked politicians would have granted it. Their petitions, quite simply, showed the men up on all these counts. It also showed that some politicians, for whatever reason, would put forward the concerns of the people they represented, even if those people could not vote for them. Brooks' maneuver may have opened the door for succeeding petitions. This battle for inclusion of women at the lowest level also showed Reconstruction up for what it was: a raw power grab at the highest level under the guise of ensuring justice for freed male slaves that institutionalized a new exclusion—of the female half of the population. Brooks' introduction of the petition also signaled the first time that women had openly worked with a Democrat for woman's rights, a tactic that Anthony and Stanton had decided was necessary late in 1865 when the intransigence of the Republicans was transforming into a block of cold stone. The women beginning to rethink their relationship with the Republicans was not because the women had chosen to do so: it was because the Republicans were shoving them unceremoniously out.

At this point at the end of January in 1866, therefore, Anthony felt some progress had been made. This was true even if the American Anti-Slavery Society forced women to tread water about an equal rights society and even, as at the meeting of the Massachusetts Anti-Slavery Society on January 25, the very existence of antislavery societies in a post-slavery world was called into question.[31] It seems that at this point Anthony was still behind Phillips, anticipating reciprocity from him for the women's work. Given his imperious personality and the force behind his vision of black male suffrage, however, it is difficult to avoid the feeling that Phillips was toying with the women. He was at the center of Republican-Abolitionist politics and it is unlikely that he did not know that, on the very day the AASS was meeting in Boston, not only that part of the amendment was coming up for debate but also that a member of the House would propose adding the word "male" to guard the male agenda. He also probably knew about the progress of the Committee of Fifteen's work on the amendment and he was also possibly informed of the projected date for the introduction of the full amendment. Likely aware of the congressional timetable in tentative form, and against including women in the current franchise reform, the chances are that at the January meeting in Boston[32] Phillips was playing politics, aiming to keep the women anticipating that the united reform organization would soon be formed. Republicans would be pleased that he had kept the women quiet so that Congress could press ahead with its exclusionary agenda without having to deal with contentious troublemakers and extraneous matters in the shape of woman, particularly if the troublemakers might stir Democrats up. Hence, Phillips utilized the very plausible excuse of the requirement of notice of three months for a constitutional amendment for the AASS. The maneuver put everything regarding women as far as the AASS was concerned on the back burner and out of sight, while simultaneously dangling the possibility that when May came the women's proposal would bear fruit.

At this point, Anthony and Stanton seem to have chosen to suspend any disbelief about a future equal rights society, even though correspondence between Stanton and Phillips earlier in January demonstrate spirited if not antagonistic relations between them about the latter's intransigence on votes for freedmen only, for he then denigrated the women's petitions and turned down a request from Anthony to speak in New York.[33] Phillips' obduracy was clear. But if all Phillips allowed them to do was wait for the AASS they could still make their own separate plans, and they now set about organizing the first Woman's Rights Convention since 1861 for the same week in May as the annual convention of the AASS.[34]

6. Petitions, Obstruction and Reform

The whole female sex not only are not, but never have been, free women....—Senator Reverdy Johnson, *Congressional Globe*, Senate, 39th Congress, 1st Session, February 9, 1866, 768.

Anthony was soon back in New York staying with Stanton, nothing having changed with Phillips' postponement until May of 1866 of any decision on an equal rights organization. Yet she and Stanton could easily have been in Washington, D.C., haunting the halls of Congress for the stir they were causing with petitions. Had Anthony not circumvented Thaddeus Stevens' obvious distaste at presenting hers, which she did with the help of Brooks, it might have disappeared into oblivion. His underhand behavior exposed, Stevens finally did present the original quietly on January 29.[1] Yet he was not alone in this nefarious behavior. In the upper house, Senator Sumner, who at this period in 1866 presented several petitions in favor of black suffrage, submitted one by Lydia Maria Child, renowned author and founding editor of the *Standard,* declaring that to present it then was "most inopportune."[2] Historical confusion about this event[3] may actually be due to paraphrasing in secondary sources, for Sumner's bad grace was on show on February 14 when he said of a petition "from women of the United States" that he presented it "at this time because it has been sent to me for this purpose; but I take the liberty of saying that I do not think this is a proper time for the consideration of that question. I move its reference to the Joint Committee on Reconstruction."[4] He failed to identify the signatories or source of the petition—rendering it ever more anonymous. By contrast, the same day he presented without protest several petitions regarding the removal of discrimination against black men in voting. Making the blatant inequality of treatment of men and women worse, the women now found strong opposition from black men, who objected to white women working for the vote for all women.[5] Almost the whole of the political establishment and its male aspirants thereto were against the women.

Behavior unbecoming to members directed against women was not new. During the 1830s, when women flooded Congress with antislavery petitions, Democratic congressmen introduced what became known as the gag rules.[6] Lucretia Mott and Lydia Maria Child had experienced that infamous refusal to deal with the women's petitions 30 years before. By the end of January Anthony was protesting to Caroline Healey Dall: "There are petitions in the hands of several Republican members of the House from which the public hears not a word.... The Republicans are cowardly."[7] She was either being charitable or was still unwilling to consider their apparent determination to undermine any possibility of rights for women.

Reform women as a group were also conflicted. While Anthony, Stanton, and Stone were petitioning for woman's suffrage, Anthony was incensed to find out from Dall during the AASS meetings that Boston was circulating a petition that objected to the word "male" in the proposed amendment but failed to advocate woman suffrage.[8] Even the support of some of the stalwart woman's rights women was half-hearted. Although expressing support for woman suffrage, Child argued that freedman votes should precede women— or at least the latter should not now press their case.[9] Lucretia Mott was also lukewarm, writing in April to Phillips and promising to attend the upcoming AASS meeting in May, hoping he would give "presence and encouragement" to the women's new equal rights organization proposal but conceding her reluctance about woman's rights at this juncture. "It seemed unwise to urge these, just now—as this is emphatically the negro's hour," she wrote, admitting that she had refused early on to sign the women's petition. Stanton, however, "had reasoned" with her that "the negro's hour was decidedly the fitting time for woman to slip in [and so] what could we do, but sign & forward the Petitions?"[10]

Meanwhile, in the early months of 1866, the Joint Committee of Fifteen and both chambers of Congress, hammering out the wording of what Phillips had called for the year before—a proposed 14th Amendment—were now leaning towards specifying males for voting rights. Some objections to the proposed amendment were race-biased and others on a perceived and actual limitation on states' rights to determine voter qualifications that, Democrats argued, betrayed the Founders' intentions for the political structure of the country. Consequently, the original intent of the Founders was also hotly debated, each side arguing either that racism was inbuilt or that it was forbidden in the Constitution. Republicans supported the enfranchisement of blacks to increase their own support, decrease opposition, and hold onto power. Democrats supported rehabilitating southern whites, thereby enabling them to regain power and prevent black power in the region.

Yet, common ground existed between the two parties about amending what Elizabeth Cady Stanton called the "immortal"[11] Constitution and the decision to establish sex as the primary qualification of the right to vote. The debate brought out into the open how the politicians clearly conflated politics with masculinity and male bonding. Such ideas, current since the founding and describing the kind of behavior that 1860s congressmen perceived that the founders had relied on, were now spelled out and raised to a constitutional philosophy that served as the foundation for amending the Constitution to allow the nation to put the slavery debacle behind them. From this perspective there was no place for women; and when the men of the 39th Congress decided to convert the Constitution into their own image and likeness, it was logical and easy to exclude women and to define the vote overtly as a male-only activity.[12]

Sumner declared his intentions early. When promoting the offending word "male" with the early draft of the proposed amendment he introduced in the Senate on December 4, 1865,[13] Stone had gone to Washington to try to persuade him to remove it. Exclusion, however, was on the minds of congressmen at the time, for in December 1865, Republican Thaddeus Stevens unhesitatingly denied southern representation by refusing to seat the former Confederacy's representatives in the House. This paved the way for easy passage of the reforms a group of Republicans had contrived just a few days before,[14] which included the exclusion of women. To Stone's entreaties Sumner's "encouraging" reply was that he had spent a whole night trying out a variety of ways to avoid using "male," but he had failed.[15] Assuming that a republican government was male, there was no way for him to avoid using the word. Consequently, he must have intentionally excluded women and might never have planned to include them. The notion of "perfecting the Union" by excluding 50 percent of the population also excluded the possibility of any higher political philosophy of inclusion. Exclusion based on sex is what Sumner and most of his congressional colleagues upheld. While the men could see as progress, no matter how indirectly, the inclusion of freedmen in the vote, they refused to see that deliberately cutting women out was a larger move in the opposite direction.[16] Yet the 39th Congress's contrivances regarding the proposed amendment might have been worse than just questions of masculinity or preserving and strengthening congressional power: it might have been also intended to protect business. This possibility emerged years later when Roscoe Conkling, a member of the Committee of Fifteen in 1866, argued that not only were corporations allowed for the purposes of the law but also that it had been the intention of the Joint Committee to consider corporations as "persons" under Section 2 of the 14th Amendment.[17] Corporations, in this reasoning, rated higher than women.

Discussion on the proposed amendment moved into high gear in January 1866, with the Joint Committee of Fifteen and both chambers introducing several different versions of the contentious Section 2 aiming to refine the wording. Women meanwhile continued their petition drive, in February gaining another significant victory along the lines of the one of January 24 in the House—a win that laid down a paper trail for the scurrilous unhelpful behavior of Senator Sumner on February 14. On February 21, Senator John Brooks Henderson presented the petition "of Mrs. Gerrit Smith and twenty-seven other ladies of the United States ... praying that the right of suffrage be granted to women." The senator read out, without attribution to the writer, an accompanying letter mentioning Senator Sumner's recent presentation of a petition, "with an apology [for so doing], from the women of the Republic." The writer excoriates him for his lip service to a republican form of government and his failure to meet that standard. The letter concluded: "Remember, the right of petition is our only right in the Government: and when three joint resolutions are before the House to introduce the word 'male' into the Federal Constitution, 'it is the proper time' for the women of the nation to be heard, Mr. Sumner to the contrary notwithstanding."[18] At least 23 petitions for woman suffrage were presented to Congress, either to the House or to the Senate, from January 24, 1866, until March 26, 1866[19]—a remarkable achievement given the women's late start, their lack of money, the opposition from so many quarters, and the disruptive tactics they faced from members of Congress. This number does not include any "lost" petitions. The women recalled submitting 10,000 signatures before the close of the session on July 28, 1866.[20] Nevertheless, congressional plans were virtually unstoppable, for Congress had more options: legislation was easier to force through than a constitutional amendment.

The main example was the 1866 Civil Rights Act, introduced by Senator Lyman Trumbull on January 5, 1866. Described as "a bill (S. No. 61) to protect all persons in the United States in their Civil Rights and furnish the means of their vindication,"[21] it was an enforcement act pursuant to Section Two of the 13th Amendment intending to ensure that the defeated rebel states could not deny rights as equal citizens to former slaves by re-creating slavery for them through highly restrictive employer and employee laws that applied only to blacks. These infamous "black codes" angered the North. The proposed Civil Rights Act's main provision for federal law was that any free person, no matter their race or previous status as a slave, might enter into a contract with the same freedoms as white people. It provided for federal trials and penalties for those who broke the law. The bill's most noteworthy feature for women was its almost completely unbiased language. It used the words "persons," and "them," rarely used "he" and did not include the word "male"— demonstrating what the politicians could do if they wished. The pro–Equal Rights Association advocate Theodore Tilton influenced this measure.[22]

The debate questioned the power of Congress to pass such legislation, argued over differences between manumission and emancipation and discussed the enforcement clause of the 13th Amendment. Congressmen debated its intention: emancipation only or a broad range of measures to ensure the equalization of the status of the freed slaves with that of other citizens when a wide range of inequalities existed among citizens of all states. It examined whether equal citizenship conferred through a federal measure could or should guarantee equal citizenship rights and the right to enforcement through all the states. Finally, it was asked, did it apply to more than former slaves—to whites as well as blacks? Wide disagreement prevailed, with well-founded constitutional arguments from many quarters arrayed against practical, political, emotional, and moral arguments for passing the law. Constitutional arguments were usually summarized as "states' rights" at a time when the several states of the Union were still—as the Constitution intended—largely paramount and masters within their own jurisdictions. A measure that significantly extended federal power and diminished the powers of the individual states to operate their civil and criminal processes without federal interference was a legitimate concern. It left the individual states in the dark about the impact of the measure on their internal operations if passed, and it raised the further question of where federal encroachment on the states' powers would end. No answer emerged.

Despite the bill's almost unbiased language, as far as Congress was concerned the measure was intended to apply primarily to men. Congressmen constantly used the word "men" to mean men only in debate; and both senators and representatives singled women out as an example of their concerns about the scope of the potential law. Sex in relation to the civil rights bill leapt into prominence on February 27, when Republican Robert S. Hale asked an awkward question about married women: "Did any one ever assume that Congress was to be invested with the power to legislate on that subject, and to say that married women, in regard to their rights of property, should stand on the same footing with men and unmarried women?"[23] Hale was from New York State, where married women only a few years before had seen their 1860 property rights law rolled back after women stopped campaigning during the Civil War. Married women's legal disabilities existed in every state in the union, he argued, indicating the vast potential impact of the bill if passed. A stunned Thaddeus Stevens spluttered that it would apply only to classes of people based on race. No other distinction counted. Hale countered by pointing out that the bill's language "gives to all *persons* equal protection." It could apply just as much to women as to freedmen.[24] For congressmen, Hale's apparent bombshell revelation of the potential impact of the absence of the exclusionary sex terminology in the bill revealed worrying possibilities of new rights or freedoms for women, particularly those who were married.[25] Once raised, the matter had to be squashed.

On March 9 Representative Samuel Shellabarger, a Republican from

Ohio, attempted to limit the damage. He noted the bill prohibited "discrimination in securing the civil rights of citizens on account of race, color, or previous condition of slavery ... [and that] without regard to such race or condition, [such citizens] shall have the same right to contract, convey, sue, testify, inherit, and to claim benefit of the laws protecting person and property as white citizens."[26] He added that if it overtly included married women it would "invade the rights reserved to the States." He continued: "[But] it does nothing like that.... Its whole effect is to require that whatever rights as to each of these enumerated civil [rights] ... the States may confer upon one race or color of the citizens, shall be held by all races in equality." Explicating his point, he said, "Your State may deprive women of the right to sue or contract or testify.... But if you do so, or do not do so as to one race, you shall treat the other likewise ... [and] if you do discriminate, it must not be 'on account of race, color or former condition of slavery.'"[27] This was a very limited interpretation of a bill whose language was unbiased along sex lines, and this congressman argued clearly that discrimination on account of sex, if not required, was permitted, for the only discrimination not permitted was according to race, while the "race, color or former condition of slavery" terms clearly indicated that the clause referred to freed people, more specifically black men.

During debate after the president had vetoed the bill, Senator Edgar Cowan of Pennsylvania argued against Congress's power to pass it. Although it based its justification on the enforcement clause of the 13th Amendment, he said the bill went far beyond the reach of the amendment. Sloppy draftsmanship exacerbated the problem. Like Shellabarger, Cowan used married women to support his argument. Referring to the abolition amendment, Cowan wanted to know exactly "what was the slavery mentioned in there." Was it slavery defined narrowly, applying only to those held in bondage to an owner and master? Or, he asked, "was it the right the husband had to the services of his wife? ... [and did it] actually entitle the wife to be paid for her own services, that they should not go to the husband?" He said that no one had ever believed that the 13th Amendment applied to married women as such: it was known and accepted that the amendment referred to slaves and slaves alone. Yet, he protested, this bill "proposes to legislate for a very large number of persons who were not slaves, and who were not within its purview or its operation."[28] On this ground alone, the bill violated congressional jurisdiction. He emphasized the limited scope of the 13th Amendment by referencing the accepted legal disabilities of married women, using existing discrimination to advance his argument.

Meanwhile, while attacking the "artistic mode" and "incongruous" phrases used in the bill, which created further potential problems, he again highlighted married women's disabilities to press his concerns. Pointing out that "a married woman in no state that I know of has a right to make contracts generally" and that every state's laws were different, he asked if his senatorial colleagues were "willing to put ... in the power of the district court of the United States ... [the right] to interfere with regard to the contracts of married women."[29] According to the "grammatical construction" of the bill, it conferred "upon married women, upon minors, upon idiots, upon lunatics and upon everybody native born in all the States, the right to make and enforce contracts, because there is no qualification to the bill" by sex.[30] Yet, Cowan emphasized, "the subject-matters of the first section of this bill never have been within the jurisdiction or control of the United States Government."[31] Again, even with drafting that left a lot to be desired, in Cowan's mind it was clear that the bill should not benefit women—married women specifically.

As the debates demonstrated, the civil rights bill represented a constitutional can of worms. Cowan was a member of the Senate when states appointed them. When analyzing the civil rights bill in terms of jurisdiction, he was representing the interests of the states.[32] Later, when Congress focused on overriding the president's veto, Cowan essentially pointed out the problems the potential law could create, which he did because "a great many good people think that the bill has intrinsic merits which ought to override the provisions of the Constitution and ought to become a law, notwithstanding our want of power to pass it." Even without the word "male" in the bill, Cowan's arguments made it clear for the record—as did Shellabarger's in the House before him—that the Civil Rights Act would have a limited reach and refer to former slaves. Whether it applied equally to freed women and free men and women in general was another question entirely, but based upon Cowan's arguments about married women it should not.[33] It was, therefore, a seriously flawed bill for reasons other than questions of constitutionality and bad drafting, for it did not allow for the application of civil rights equally. In fact, as the debate made clear, it did not even apply to white men. The Civil Rights Act had originally passed the Senate and House on February 2 and March 13, 1866, respectively. President Johnson vetoed it on March 27 and the Senate overrode the veto on April 6. When the House passed it on April 9 it became law that day.[34]

These considerations of women in the debates in the House and the Senate preceding passage overtly enshrined in the legislative process attitudes and a political philosophy based on sex discrimination. Both Cowan and Shellabarger used the existing restrictions that married women faced by common and statute law in all the individual states of the nation to justify ensuring that the Civil Rights Act would have only narrow application, to freed slaves only, specifically the males. This position on women was acceptable to the men of Congress at the time and largely unquestioned. However, their use of preexisting discriminations to justify continuing discrimination is paradoxical when they furthered a bill purporting to end discrimination and equalize civil rights when denying the inherent contradiction in it.

Once again an opportunity for true equality in the nation was not only passed over but also deliberately sidelined. There was more: the incorporation of this restrictive, exclusionary, and discriminatory philosophical position into federal debate reinforced discriminatory attitudes to women. The only significant development in the question of woman's status since the Revolution, therefore, was that the situation had become worse, for if the white man of Congress had ensured through married women's disabilities that his own legal position in relation to his wife was secure, he had also confirmed for newly freed black men that their legal position in relation to their wives would be secure. This was an important development for black men who believed in and had asserted their personal legal superiority over their wives at the National Convention of Colored Men in October 1864 in Syracuse, New York, which founded the National Equal Rights League intending to create an organization in every state. This organization aimed for equality before the law and suffrage but focused only on black males.[35] In fact, in the convention's "Declaration of Wrongs and Rights," Section 4 began as follows: "As a people, we have been denied the ownership of our bodies, our wives, homes, children, and the products of our own labor."[36] The debate preceding the passage of the Civil Rights Act of 1866 reinforced black men's sense of ownership in women, of women as property, mirroring the legal relationship of white men with their wives. What happened in the debates leading to the passage of the dubiously constitutional Civil Rights Act of 1866 occurred with little fanfare: the women already had too much on their plate to tackle everything that was coming at them. These events, however, represented a circumstance when the two sides of the women's proposed organization to promote equal rights for women and black men were, like the San Andreas fault in California, moving in opposite directions. In total, the women had lost a battle in their struggle to win equal rights for all, while black men inched ahead.

In other matters, the 39th Congress was already halfway to enshrining the word "male" in law once again—this time relating to suffrage in the nation's capital, just as Congress had done in Section 9 of the Northwest Ordinance in 1787. This new measure was launched on December 4 with Sumner's introduction of Bill S. 1 "to regulate the elective franchise in the District of Columbia." The House of Representatives voted in mid–January in favor of a bill, originally introduced on December 5, 1865, and numbered H.R.1, that was for "extending the right of suffrage in the District of Columbia." This bill did not mention the word "male" and only proscribed excluding from the vote any person in a District of Columbia election "on account of color." After passage in the House, H.R.1 went to the Senate on January 19, 1866. The

Senate then produced S. 118 of January 31, 1866—again to include the word "male"—and it was still going through the machinations of debates and amendments that June 27.[37] This bill, along with the other measures, demonstrated the all-pervasiveness and complete inequality of the struggle the women faced in campaigning for equal rights for all. The D.C. suffrage bill represented just another front on which women had to fight in the anti-woman climate among the leaders of the 39th Congress. At least one other bill, proposed by the Joint Committee of Fifteen, attempted to include "male" in federal law. Intended to "restore full political rights to the states," it was introduced in both Senate and House for that end.[38]

Later in April 1866—a year after the Civil War ended and the death of President Lincoln—the women's friend Robert Dale Owen offered a completely reworked constitutional amendment proposal in which the unacceptable word "male" never appeared. However, he faced an apparent inexorable tide of congressional leaders' determination to institutionalize enfranchisement by sex restrictions in the new post-slavery world. The proposed 14th Amendment in its entirety after vetting by the Joint Committee of Fifteen was first introduced in Congress on April 30, 1866, complete with the abhorrent word "male" included three times in Section 2.

7. The American Equal Rights Association

What difference does it make to the negro that you ask for his rights singly or in company with the rights of others?—Stephen S. Foster, "The Anniversaries," *New York Tribune*, May 10, 1866.

Far removed from the political maneuverings of the East Coast, on the east bank of the Mississippi at Memphis, Tennessee, riots from April 30 to May 4, 1866, killed 46 black people, maimed 285 and destroyed property worth at least $100,000.[1] No arrests ensued. The horror enraged many observers, who described and protested the violence, while the *Independent* castigated the anti-black "Copperhead press of Memphis."[2]

In this charged atmosphere, on May 8 the AASS met in the Church of the Puritans in Union Square for its 33rd anniversary meeting. "The sacred edifice was filled, and though many well-known faces were missed" the attendance was still good.[3] The women were eagerly anticipating this moment, for they hoped for a new organization, merging the highly structured AASS and the more informal conventions of the women, creating one with an agenda for equal rights regardless of race or sex. Disappointment—even shock—took over when they discovered that among the resolutions introduced that morning none appeared about any merger.[4] "As Mr. Powell had been delegated the previous January to give [notice of the resolution], there could be no other conclusion than that he had refrained from doing so."[5] The idea did not arise that speech-filled day, for it was effectively dead by default. In the next day's business meeting, Stanton fought for women during debate on a resolution to exclude the word "white" from the New York constitution in its expected upcoming constitutional convention, by also proposing to exclude the word "male." Abby Kelley spoke resolutely against woman suffrage in any AASS campaign for black suffrage. Stephen Foster advocated it, raising the merger idea. "The question now arises, is there any common ground on which we can all stand and preserve our unity? My conviction is [yes]." He said that the society could demand "everything that goes to secure [negro] suffrage" and that woman had "a right to strike off the shackles of the slave by her vote, as well as by her tongue. I will fight to the death for it." He declared, "Until you admit woman to the ballot box, you are exercising a rank tyranny. The same despotism that tramples on the negro will trample on woman."[6]

Despite Foster's eloquence, Phillips and the AASS refused to entertain the idea of including women in the AASS agenda, resolutely hanging onto its antislavery name. The disappointing outcome was likely preordained. Powell had previously favored an equal rights society; Phillips had not and Phillips determined AASS policy. The previous week's violence in Tennessee added ammunition to Phillips' argument that former slaves were not safe without the vote. It also likely hardened his attitude—not that he needed much hardening. He had opposed the idea of woman suffrage all along and his determined intransigence was starkly highlighted during the second day's debate on stopping the discrimination of women in the New York constitution.[7] Phillips, as congressional work progressed, continued to push black men's rights while holding the women back. Once a male-only amendment had been introduced, he was even closer to success. What women thought or felt about it would matter even less than ever, and it would be more difficult for women to round up opposition. That pivotal moment occurred on April 30, 1866, with the introduction of the proposed 14th Amendment. By then, even if it wasn't enough for him, Phillips had contrived major victories, both with the Civil Rights Act and the proposed amendment. On May 9 there was no reason for him to take off in a direction that he believed would complicate his plans; there was no reason *not* to deny women the clout of the much larger and more influential AASS. Therefore, his January postponement till May of discussion of the proposed amalgamation and then the—probably deliberate—failure to include the merger resolution held the women down. In a Machiavellian sense, Phillips' behavior at this point was astute and successful, for he had postponed until as close as possible to too late for the women's aims, any idea of combining with them for a goal he did not want.

One impetus for doing so would have been to stop the women working with Democrats, whose help Anthony and Stanton had early started to solicit when Republican opposition to their aspirations had begun clearly to emerge in Congress in December 1865. The women were very aware of the disapproval that this new departure on their part provoked: "The Democrats had listened to all the glowing debates on these great principles of freedom until the argument was as familiar as a, b, c, and continually pressed the Republicans with their own weapons. Then those loyal women were taunted with having gone over to the Democrats and the Disunionists."[8] Phillips naturally wanted to stop them, to limit potential Democratic opposition to his—and therefore the Republicans'—plan for black rights in the South. Phillips likely also thought that he could kill the idea of woman suffrage by refusing to merge abolitionism with woman's rights. Because of Phillips' machinations, at the end of May 9, 1866, the women had no reinforcements. Meanwhile, the outlook for women in the political landscape had become gloomier. Not only was initial consideration given by Congress to the proposed 14th Amendment on April 30, but also—overlapping the timing of the AASS meeting in New York when Phillips resolutely blocked the formation of an umbrella equal rights organization—starting on May 8 debate opened in the House.

Not yet in final form, the amendment still had two shortcomings for reformers. The first was that it failed to give the vote outright to former slaves, conferring it only through penalties against the white electorate if black males were not allowed to vote. The second problem was that word "male," which appeared three times. This terminology was offensive to women, for, as they had feared for months, overt sex discrimination was now to be carved into the Constitution,[9] while the 14th Amendment drafters had taken the principles of the Revolution and the founding documents with their broadest sense of "men" meaning "human" and reduced them to the narrow meaning of "male."

On May 10, 1866, as the House of Representatives continued to debate the proposed amendment, which would put "male" for the first time in the United States Constitution, "at an early hour Dr. Cheever's church was well filled with an audience chiefly of ladies who received the officers and speakers of the Convention with hearty applause."[10] Stanton then called to order the Eleventh Woman's Rights Convention—the first since 1860. This convention, however, was never intended to be for women's interests only. Its aim was to create an organization to work for the kind of union that the idealism of the Declaration of Independence, in the women's view, had proclaimed—a union based on true equality, not a purported "equality" based on discrimination by race or, worse, discrimination by sex.

When the women wrote their convention call between late January and late March, slaves were being freed to live in the "Land of the Free" without the rights of full citizens. With chattel slavery abolished, the former slaves and women now essentially had the same legal status. Broad issues affecting both were taxation without representation, equality before the law, equal education, and for many working women just as for blacks, extreme poverty derived directly from job discrimination, lack of training, and poverty wages. The most significant difference between the two groups was that blacks, without the bounds of slavery and the protection of the laws, were facing racism now running rampant. Unheralded, however, except by women themselves and some men—and paralleling the racism—was the now more open climate of sex discrimination against women regardless of race, which Congress was overtly promoting. With the two groups in similar situations requiring political solutions, the idea that their interests should come under the umbrella of a new organization of equal rights appeared appropriate. Susan B. Anthony, the secretary, had sent out from New York on March 31, 1866, the call for the meeting on May 10 "on behalf of the National Woman's Rights Central Committee, Elizabeth Cady Stanton, President."[11] These two women were the standard-bearers of the cause.

Stanton spoke briefly. The times required women to focus on "woman's right and duty to claim and use the ballot" because their interests in such matters were equal with those of men. Ironically, right at this moment, the proposed amendment to exclude women was under debate in Congress. But, Stanton reminded listeners, there was also the state route to enfranchisement, and women could support not just removal of the word "white" from state constitutions they could also campaign to remove the word "male." She said, "This should be a year of great activity among the women of this State. As New York is to have a constitutional convention in '67, it behooves us now to make an earnest demand, by appeals and petitions, to have the word 'male' as well as 'white' stricken from our Constitution."[12]

Even if the AASS had sidelined the women, therefore, it had not silenced them or halted them in their stride. With Stanton's proposed agenda, it is almost as if she is staring Phillips down. At the very least, they ensured that women's aspirations appeared in the historical record, demonstrating that they disputed the Phillips and congressional approach to Reconstruction and that they wanted a more just solution. The convention authorized an "Address to Congress" to try to stop the inclusion of the word "male" during the congressional debate.[13] A later resolution called on the women of the states "to petition their Legislatures to take the necessary steps to so amend their constitutions as to secure the right of suffrage to every citizen, without distinction of race, color or sex; and especially in those States that are soon to hold their constitutional conventions."[14]

Yet, convention speeches revealed rifts. Anticipating a very different outcome of the AASS meeting, Stanton and Anthony had invited Theodore Tilton and the Rev. Henry Ward Beecher to speak. As was men's wont whenever they spoke at women's conventions, which they had done from the first of these events, their prolixity commandeered hours. Meanwhile, Tilton and Beecher, while exchanging personal barbs,[15] both supported woman suffrage. Tilton argued that "not for woman's sake, but for man's … we shall never have a government thoroughly noble, thoroughly trustworthy, until both men and women shall unite in forming the public sentiment, and in administering that sentiment through the government."[16] Beecher declared that woman's rights were women's duties—the double standard on which woman's rights had been based since the Founding. He also said that it was more important for women to vote than black men, because of women's virtues.[17] Neither argued that women should have the vote as of right. The organizers had also invited Phillips to speak and he turned up, despite his treatment of them at the AASS, to insult them. He called them creatures of fashion, put much of the blame for the Civil War on their shoulders, criticized them for their poverty and concluded that woman should "Go home and reform yourself."[18] This was typical: he became vindictive when others stood their ground. The attendance of Phillips and Tilton at this meeting indicates that Stanton and Anthony had not anticipated the result of the AASS meeting, while the men's performances highlighted their cavalier and dishonest attitude to the women's concerns.

Those days in May demonstrated that perhaps it was time for women to reassess their relationship with their so-called colleagues. Ernestine Rose left before the end of Phillips' speech, saying to Frances Dana Gage that the subject had been "exhausted." Rose, an atheist, had fought for woman's rights in Europe since her teens. "Perhaps she had had enough of pompous, religious men,"[19] and was giving up in disgust, believing that the women's struggle against overbearing, domineering, and dishonest males was too steeply uphill. She continued to work for woman's rights, but it seems that she at any rate was reaching the end of her tether. In the supposedly most revolutionary nation in the world, she saw not just the replay of the past but also its continuation into the future, for Phillips' speech revealed a man who was willing to yield nothing.

After the speakers, who had also included Gage and Frances Watkins Harper reporting on the problems that black women faced under Reconstruction and when excluded from the vote (their experiences during the Memphis riots were horrible),[20] Anthony presented a resolution to dissolve the Woman's Rights Convention and create the American Equal Rights Association (AERA) to demand true universal suffrage,[21] which the convention duly passed. Involving many men and women also still members of the AASS,[22] the AERA assembled at 4:00 p.m. to perfect the new organization, when Lucretia Mott, who was elected president, insisted that a preamble to their documents "should state the fact that the new organization was the outgrowth of the Woman's Rights movement."[23] This clearly differentiated it from the AASS and contrasted it with congressmen and abolitionists-turned-male-suffragists who were promoting and instituting reforms based on a philosophy of masculinity and male bonding.

Stanton's preamble expressed a philosophy and an interpretation of the events of the preceding years:

> Whereas, by the war, society is once more resolved into its original elements, and in the reconstruction of our government we again stand face to face with the broad question of natural rights, all associations based on special claims for special classes are too narrow and partial for the hour; Therefore, from the baptism of this second revolution

purified and exalted through suffering seeing with a holier vision that the peace, prosperity, and perpetuity of the Republic rest on EQUAL RIGHTS TO ALL, we, to-day, assembled in our Eleventh National Woman's Rights Convention, bury the woman in the citizen, and our organization in that of the American Equal Rights Association.[24]

The AERA, therefore, was deliberately created to work for reforms based on the higher philosophy that Stanton and Anthony had often spoken of and which Congress and the AASS now rejected. It would be campaigning for higher stakes. It was also raising up to a higher level what the WNLL had begun with antislavery in 1863, particularly its resolution for both black and woman suffrage in 1864. The new society took up the precedent of that formal woman's organization in an era when formal organization had become essential to conduct campaigns for specific reforms through federal and state governments. The AERA "increased [women's] ability to agitate, lobby and speak in their own voices."[25]

Paradoxically, this new organization that "buried the woman in the citizen" came when women had discovered how society's leaders interpreted that idea: if women put their own interests aside, others would quickly forget them, except to treat them as outsiders. In 1861 the women had given up their own aspirations, expecting their patriotism would bring postwar reforms for them; but at war's end, once they had been used, they were speedily discarded. Yet they were not cowed. Now, even though espousing the nobler ideal of the woman as citizen and refusing to be held back by devious and dishonest congressional behavior or Phillips' latest machinations, these women determined to work to ensure that the men would not get away again with ignoring them. By the end of May 10 the new organization with its goal for true equality was launched. The fact that it came into existence put the abolitionists and almost the whole of Congress to shame, not just for their treatment of women but also because it highlighted the much lower aims and exclusionary intentions of Radical Reconstruction politicians and the abolitionist men after abolition. The *Standard* published a supportive commentary after the AERA held a meeting in Boston on May 31.[26]

As the first organization in the United States for equal rights for all, the AERA was groundbreaking, representing a high order of determination and idealism. It meant members believed in abandoning the old oxymoron of prioritizing equality and achieving "equality" in stages and in persuading society in general and Congress in particular that women's concerns and the concerns of other groups were the concerns of citizens, to be dealt with simultaneously. The AERA was courageous, for, as politicians' behavior in Congress and that of many men were then demonstrating, anti-woman sentiment had been increasing since the end of the war; and an organization instigated by women to include woman's rights in its agenda would very likely also automatically face criticism. The AERA was courageous also, because it was a hybrid, involving not only woman's rights workers but also people focused formerly on abolition and now the rights of black men. The AERA agenda believed in an immediate shift in the paradigms of the disparate interests, to expand the focus from the now former slaves to members of society in general. This shift might not be easy. Some members—mostly women—saw equal rights for women and blacks equally; but many members—both women and men—while aiming for equal rights for all took the position that equal rights for black men were more important. This position put equal rights of the sexes lower on the totem pole. The organization was a truer reflection of society at large—not a reflection of society as the American women and other founders of the AERA wished that society to be. Even if there was a female president in Lucretia Mott, she was originally an abolitionist, one who only recently had not wanted to touch woman suffrage for the moment.

None of this describes the uneven ground on which members of the AERA stood, for the females were weaker than the males. They possessed no right of franchise at all, whereas white men and some free black men had the vote. Women had even less support among politicians—who enacted reforms—than former male slaves had. This was because in the hierarchy of priorities sex hardly rated, while in the postwar climate race was everything provided it meant men. Exacerbating the situation, Congress was now creating a new inequality for women in the proposed 14th amendment by penalizing states if they excluded southern black men from the vote, which provided an incentive to enfranchise black males. The inclusion of the word "male" created no incentive to enfranchise any women. This was a playing field that was decidedly uneven.

None of the facts of the AERA deals either with the psychological impact for women of living in a country where, even though they were citizens, they were denied participation in the polity or how it felt to face the prospect of their permanent exclusion. Freedmen could consider the prospect of suffrage with at least some anticipation because of congressional backing. Another concern was the potential change in women's status and its impact when previously excluded men were given the vote, or even what kind of behavior these men, once enfranchised, would exhibit towards the excluded women. Phillips' disparaging comments on May 10 and the insults expressed the day before by others at the AASS indicate that at least some of the men would assert their new self-importance and put women down. For many reasons such as these, the women had at least to try to have women included in the Reconstruction reforms. However, the same circumstances demonstrated clearly that the AERA, no matter its aspirations, was unequal within its structure from the start. Further, it stood on shaky ground in the country at large. The nation, despite its roots in the philosophy of natural rights from the time of the Revolution in 1776, was by now less open-minded. The AERA's position argued that the war had deconstructed the union into its constituent parts and that Reconstruction involved remaking the whole union according to its original philosophy. To state this clearly in terms that involved all in 1866 was so radical it was off the chart. Even Lincoln had not held that the union had fallen apart. Neither did President Johnson nor even the Radical Republicans. If the union had never fallen apart, there was essentially little to remake from a fundamental standpoint. It only needed tinkering with and a good adjustment here and there. This is what Congress set out to do.

Meanwhile, the women, whose visions encompassed far grander ideals, were still forced to work within the framework of the limitations of even the most "radical" position. With no say in government, they were hamstrung in effecting political change in a way that men were not. When they and their colleagues called the AERA into existence on May 10, 1866, therefore, they stood at the foot of a gigantic mountain with limited resources with which to scale it. They took this step on the very day that the House of Representatives pushed the proposed 14th Amendment with its abhorrent word "male" over the first hurdle towards ratification and incorporation in the United States Constitution. That day, debate concluded, the House passing it easily. At that point, the amendment was already halfway through the congressional part of the constitutional amendment process. That word "male" was on its way.

8. The Fourteenth Amendment and That Word "Male"

The time will surely come when the whole question will have to be reopened and an accounting made with this other subject class....
—Susan B. Anthony, 1865, *Life and Work of Susan B. Anthony II* (1899), 966.

If Congress really means to protect the negro race, they should have acknowledged woman just as much as man; not only in the South, but here in the North, the only way to protect her is by the ballot.
—Ernestine Rose, 1869, *History of Woman Suffrage II* (1887), 396.

Debate on the 14th Amendment began in the House on May 8, 1866. On May 10 it passed with modifications by a vote of 128 to 13, with 19 abstentions, the final tally well over the two-thirds majority required. That very day, the Woman's Convention dissolved itself and re-formed immediately as the AERA to campaign for true universal suffrage.[1]

The AERA represented optimism. Yet with the amendment apparently facing open passage in Congress, the cause of the organization to establish simultaneously rights to equality and the vote of all those citizens currently excluded from the white male norm was already lost, for the effects of the amendment were asymmetrical. To antislavery workers it represented some progress, for the Article 1 definition of citizenship was fashioned to include former slaves. This change also created pressure to make states fall into line with the soon-to-be amendment by removing the problem of discrimination against free black men—specifically in New York, the largest northern state, with its upcoming constitutional convention. To win equal suffrage for blacks there would be a triumph for abolitionists-turned-male-suffragists—for New York voters had long ago rejected the idea[2]—while a victory would signal a major political shift to all the other jurisdictions whose voters had already vetoed the idea in referenda since the end of the war.[3] The amendment represented, therefore, "full steam ahead" for Phillips and his cohorts.

A niggling problem for the "anti-slavery" group, however was that Stanton and Anthony had called repeatedly during the AERA's founding for a state-wide campaign in New York[4] to ensure in the Empire State suffrage for all citizens, with no race or sex distinctions, the proposal based on the notion that Reconstruction should be "broader and deeper" than simply restoring the Confederate States to the union. It should apply republican ideals to all citizens.[5] They had also declared the following: "And what we propose to do in New York, the coming eighteen months, we hope to do in every other State so soon as we can get the men, and the women, and the money, to go forward with the work."[6] This was akin to throwing down the gauntlet to the now inaptly named abolitionists, for this comprehensive plan challenged the much more limited agenda of winning black male suffrage in individual states.

The campaign represented so much of a threat that Stanton and Anthony were directly pressured to fall into line. Anthony recalled it through her biographer: "A short time [after the formation of the AERA] Miss Anthony, Mrs. Stanton, Mr. Phillips and Mr. Tilton were in the Standard office discussing the work. Mr. Phillips argued that the time was ripe for striking the word "white" out of the New York constitution, at its coming convention, but not for striking out "male." Mr. Tilton [said] the women should ... canvass the State with speeches and petitions for the enfranchisement of the negro, leaving that of the women to come afterward, presumably twenty years later, when there would be another revision of the constitution."[7] Stanton, "entirely overcome by the eloquence of these two gifted men, acquiesced in all they said," and was initially willing to go along. Anthony, "who never could be swerved from her standard by any sophistry or blandishments, was highly indignant and declared that she would sooner cut off her right hand than ask the ballot for the black man and not for woman." Dismissing the women's sense of oppression and the feeling of impending doom with that word "male" looming as a permanent fixture in their nation's constitution, Phillips and Tilton, having clearly assumed they could bend the women to their will, were taken aback at Anthony's response. Tilton's position was a shock, for he now supported Phillips "in direct contradiction to all he had so warmly advocated only a few weeks before." In other words, he was another turncoat, just the latest of many.[8] Stanton only later realized the two men wanted the women to work for black male enfranchisement and not for women.

Phillips particularly seemed to expect the women to follow his wishes quietly. This pompous, irascible man—who had addressed as "child" the then 50-year-old and mother-of-seven Stanton in a letter that January[9]—was good at deluding himself about them. Even at the worst of times for woman's rights during the Civil War, when women's only option was to work against slavery, Anthony "did not then acknowledge, nor [did] she ever admit ... that there [was] any question of more vital importance than that relating to the freedom of woman."[10] For Phillips even to consider that Anthony and her close colleague Stanton would docilely agree to put men first indicates an arrogance born of frequently making others submit. He should have known better. They had stood up to his objections to divorce law reform; they had masterminded the petition campaign that led to the 13th Amendment to end slavery, with minimal financial help from the abolition part of the Hovey Fund he managed; they had worked indefatigably to promote for others the republican creed of freedom for all; they adamantly spoke all the time of woman's rights and of true universal suffrage—not the contrived and truncated "universal suffrage" that applied to men only. They were doing so without betraying their principles or falling prey to ideas and policies expedient for the moment. Compared to their position, Phillips' perception of reality was self-serving.

The basic problem was his current—and relatively recent—objection to women's aspirations, which arose when Stanton called in the 1860 Woman's Convention in New York for marriage to be a secular contract with divorce readily available. This call represented an existential threat to men whose marriages were problematic, of whom Phillips was one. Tilton's relationship with his wife had also been unsettled and was deteriorating. The 1860 Woman's Convention debates also continued to bother Horace Greeley of the *Tribune* in New York: his marriage had long been on the rocks.[11] There was, therefore, likely much more than met the eye in the men's behavior towards Stanton and Anthony. From Phillips' perspective from 1860 on, the women needed reining in. Their defeat seems to have been his goal.

After the successful vote in the House on May 10, debate in the Senate on the amendment began on May 23, with AERA members united against Section 2. Post-abolition abolitionists and Radical Republicans objected because it did not directly enfranchise black men. Pro-women members objected because of that word "male." Their reasons had greatly different import. The proposed amendment did not expressly prohibit the enfranchisement of either freedmen or any woman, but Section 2 was pro-freedmen, while the word "male" created extensive possibilities for the deliberate exclusion and weakening of women. The now swiftly evolving events made the AERA's agenda look as if it was fighting an incoming tide: to prevent or make changes to the wording of the amendment at this point was challenging, for all the AERA could do was to protest a Congress intent on its own agenda.

After the amendment's introduction in the Senate, a new draft with a modified Section 2 was introduced for discussion on May 30. The AERA held its first meeting in Boston the next day, May 31. At this point Phillips appears to have softened a little regarding the women for, while maintaining that the "hour … is preeminently the property of the negro," he also said he was willing to "excite interest everywhere in … woman's right to vote," since the introduction of the word "male" into the Constitution was a "corruption" of that document.[12] Perhaps he felt generous when black men's rights were advancing while woman's rights were being pushed backwards. He may have feigned a change of heart simply to ensure influence in the AERA and prevent problems from the women for his own plans for black male suffrage in New York. He may have attended primarily to keep an eye on his antislavery protégée, Anna Dickinson, whom Anthony was trying to win for woman suffrage. Dickinson spoke for the first time for woman's rights at this meeting, donating $100 to the cause and giving assurances "of her services henceforth."[13] For Phillips, the AERA represented a worrisome flank that needed watching.

Abolitionists, therefore, continued to turn the screw. From December 1865, the women's only platform for publicity was the *Standard*, but now Aaron Powell, who had failed to submit the merger resolution at the AASS meeting, became its editor. "[For the AERA's work,] the executive board of the Standard offered to lease to the Equal Rights Association office-room and a certain amount of space in the paper. These, however, were put at such a price and placed under such restrictions as it was thought unwise to accept. All the matter submitted would be subject to 'editorial revision,' even though the association paid for the space ... [and] they decided they could not trust the 'editorial revision.'"[14] This "offer"—obviously intended to help fund the newspaper, which Phillips had subsidized during the war with money from the Hovey Fund—was inadequate and mean-spirited in the light of the women's work for abolition, particularly that of Anthony, who had raised many subscriptions. The AERA was now out on a limb, with the platform for airing its activities narrowed yet again. Yet they concluded they were better off without the paper, and Lucretia Mott soon recorded that Anthony, Stanton, and Parker Pillsbury favored "a separate periodical rather than take the Standd.'s [*sic*] offer of a page."[15]

The Senate debate on the proposed amendment ended with a vote of 33 to 11 in favor on June 8.[16] The House of Representatives followed with a favorable vote on the Senate's changes—120 to 32 on June 13.[17] Three days later, on June 16, 1866, the House joint resolution with the amendment in its final form was submitted to the states,[18] requiring three-quarters of them to ratify. Then the proposed amendment would become a long, curious anomaly, geared to the peculiar circumstances of the postwar era, with Section 3 imposing penalties on southerners for having supported the late insurrection and Section 4 denying any liability for Confederate debts. Sections 1 and 2 concern postwar civil rights reforms. Section 1 stated, "All persons born or naturalized in the United States, and subject to the jurisdiction thereof, are citizens of the United States and of the state wherein they reside. No state shall make or enforce any law which shall abridge the privileges or immunities of citizens of the United States; nor shall any state deprive any person of life, liberty, or property, without due process of law; nor deny to any person within its jurisdiction the equal protection of the laws." Congress designed this section to counter the Dred Scott decision of 1857, which declared that slaves, even though born in the United States, were not citizens and to provide blacks in the South with constitutional guarantees against discrimination designed to subjugate them. It gave constitutional force to the very constitutionally flawed Civil Rights Act that Congress had passed over the presidential veto early in April. Section 2 stated the following:

> Representatives shall be apportioned among the several States according to their respective numbers, counting the whole number of persons in each State, excluding Indians not taxed. But when the right to vote at any election for the choice of electors for President and Vice President of the United States, Representatives in Congress, the Executive and Judicial officers of a State, or the members of the Legislature thereof, is denied to any of the male inhabitants of such State, being twenty-one years of age, and citizens of the United States, or in any way abridged, except for participation in rebellion, or other crime, the basis of representation therein shall be reduced in the proportion which the number of such male citizens shall bear to the whole number of male citizens twenty-one years of age in such State.

This section dealt with the three-fifths clause. It also tackled state voting laws, providing a one-for-one penalty in representation when black males were not allowed to vote. It was designed to prevent the exclusion of male ex-slaves from the polls in the South—a huge consideration in a region blacks were a large percentage of the population, and in or near a majority in some places.[19] The section trod warily over the boundary between federal and into state jurisdiction, but essentially it conformed to the states' constitutional power to determine the qualifications for enfranchisement, which Republican senator Jacob M. Howard had summarized the day debate began as "merely the creature of law," not "one of the privileges or immunities … secured by the Constitution…. It has always been regarded in this country as the result of positive local law, not regarded as one of those fundamental rights lying at the basis of all society and without which a people cannot exist except as slaves, subject to a despotism."[20]

Section 2 only partially reassured abolitionists and black males, for enfranchisement of former slaves would occur only indirectly, while the section did not proscribe a variety of restrictive qualifications beyond race. The possibility of former slaves with voting rights also raised the question of equal voting laws for already-free blacks in the North, where, along with Washington, D.C., the exclusion of blacks was routine and where in 1865 white males had demonstrated several times that they were against equal enfranchisement of the races.[21] Yet there was a larger concern: that word "male." While included in the calculation of representation—and for taxation and countless other civic responsibilities—women did not count for voting and the word appeared for the first time in the Constitution, introducing, as women had feared all along, sex discrimination to fundamental law.

It did more, however, for race and sex intersected clearly in the proposed amendment. In the states, if black men were excluded from the vote white men would be excluded one-for-one, a formula heralded as ending racism while using race as the penalty for racism. Women were not counted in this calculation, but it represented no favorable treatment, for they were not included in the electorate at all. Their exclusion from the vote raised the specter of further discrimination against women after ratification. Further, the intersectionality cut several ways. Crafted to protect black ex-slaves, it was racially biased towards them and simultaneously biased against all white men. It would further discriminate, in Section 3, against white men of the South—targeted for participation in what they had seen as a declaration of independence. Black women could benefit from the equal protection of Section 1, which was designed to solve problems of blacks after the end of slavery but excluded them from the franchise for their sex. Douglass would later clearly emphasize this key distinction of the sexes.[22] The amendment, therefore, discriminated against white men and black women on one count.

Further, it discriminated against white women because they were not black and because they were not men. Very early on, Stephen Foster explained the logic: "In a Republic, there is no liberty without the ballot. We must demand that the national right of suffrage shall be conceded to the black man, and therefore to the black woman, and therefore, since we abjure distinctions on ground of color, to the white woman. We want universal suffrage."[23] The discrimination of race and sex in the 14th Amendment—using logic the opposite of Foster's—was the most discriminatory measure in the nation's history. Even though, in justice, the nation should choose no one group for preferential treatment, this is exactly what the 14th Amendment would do, with the result that white women were the most discriminated against in the nation—paradoxically the consequence of a measure purporting to end racism.

Contemporary events make this clear. "Robert Dale Owen, being at Washington and behind the scenes at the time ... related ... some of the amusing discussions. One of the Committee proposed 'persons' instead of 'males.' 'That will never do,' said another, 'it would enfranchise all the Southern wenches.'"[24] This anecdote indicates that some consideration was given to including women, but it died because the men did not want to enfranchise southern women—black or white. Charles Sumner said "years afterward, that he wrote over nineteen pages of foolscap to get rid of the word 'male' and yet keep 'negro suffrage' as a party measure intact ... [and] it could not be done." There were, apparently, other partisan considerations, for it seems the honorable gentlemen felt "suffrage for black men will be all the strain the Republican party can stand."[25] Yet, such sex discrimination need not have happened, for it occurred when the national voting population was less than half of the adult population of the United States, when free black men in the North were often denied the right to vote, either outright or through qualifications they could not meet such as literacy tests or property ownership, and when no woman counted.[26] In 1866, the most just approach to solving this nationwide problem of unequal citizenship was the equality and suffrage program of the AERA. For male legislators, however, expediency was more important. Men understood men, but woman voters were a complete unknown. Most congressmen were not ready for independent women. In debate, they regularly dismissed all women by saying that husbands represented married women, who therefore did not need the vote. The result was that all women were deemed expendable for political ends and the means to achieve those ends was sex discrimination in the Constitution for the first time. Justice was, moreover, not the politically correct solution, for it would step on too many toes. The easiest way to handle it—though dishonorable—was to ignore the women outright. This was a purely political decision, not a principled one. The result of all these considerations was that the 14th Amendment as it was eventually contrived was an importation into the Constitution of both race and sex discrimination. Specifically, it was biased most strongly against white women on account both of race and sex, which seems to be what the politicians of the time could stand, for there is no doubt from the congressional debates that the original intent of the amendment and other post–Civil War legislation related to males only, specifically black ex-slaves.

The amendment did at least attempt to right some wrongs of slavery, but the amount of time spent on such issues frustrated at least one member of the House, who proposed a resolution to the House Rules Committee that "one day in each week be set apart ... to be exclusively devoted to the public business of the country, and that during this Congress it be known as and called the 'white man's day.'"[27] Some white men, therefore, were feeling the pinch at the focus of the 39th Congress. Even then, women did not count.

The decidedly biased and unequal effects of a measure that supposedly ensured equality in the United States Constitution occurred because of the restricted focus of the 39th Congress where its leaders were Representative Thaddeus Stevens and Senator Charles Sumner. They were not alone. Outside the Congress, abolitionists-turned-male-suffragists with a narrow focus, such as Phillips, cracked the whip, setting the agenda of protecting freedmen and ensuring it happened through attempting to carry public opinion. Republicans' eyes were also intent on securing electoral control of the defeated South both to keep themselves in power and to ensure that the slave power would not rise again. As no woman had the vote in the first place, women entered virtually no calculations. Activist women such as Anthony and Stanton and the now annoying AERA, amounted to an unnecessary distraction in the eyes of all these parties. Conveniently, with electoral control of the former southern slave power the goal, the means to achieve it was through overt sex discrimination for the first time by elevating the word "male" to the Constitution.[28]

9. Censorship, Suffrage Campaigning and New York State

Of three immense classes, they proscribe two and provide for one; and that one perhaps a minority of the whole. Half our people are degraded for their sex;—one-sixth for the color of their skin.—Parker Pillsbury, 1866, *History of Woman Suffrage II* (1887), 176.

The day Washington sent the 14th Amendment to the states for ratification—June 16, 1866—the American Equal Rights Association was little more than a month old, but already half of its agenda was well on the way to defeat, the inclusion of "male" in the Constitution almost guaranteeing for women permanent political exclusion. On the other hand, the same word signaled a potential gain for the other half of the AERA's agenda, as it offered the possibility of freedmen's enfranchisement so that southern states could avoid penalties in representation. The progress of the two groups was distinctly unequal.

The woman suffrage workers had done tremendous work. Winning even minimal congressional attention was something that freedmen's suffrage never had to fight for, yet by their own efforts even before the formation of the AERA, women had forced into debate in both houses a subject that had been on few radars before 1865. If the women had caved to the AASS demands and not begun their petition campaign in late 1865, there would be little remaining to posterity to show that woman suffrage was one of the battles of Reconstruction. However, they left a significant enough paper trail to demonstrate that to ignore woman suffrage is to distort history and that a brief mention is insufficient. Yet the women's work was important not just because they campaigned for women but also because they campaigned for true equality, not for making some citizens more equal than others. Unfortunately, bringing female suffrage into the public record was unable to forestall the inclusion of "male" in the Constitution as the amendment's ratification inched closer—with all the implications, intended and not, that it might mean for women. Now, all women could do was be positive. If women had not won suffrage with the amendment, at least it did not directly ban it. Further—a plus for the AERA—restricted male suffrage in the states would be insecure under the new amendment and could prompt state constitutional amendments and conventions to remove the word "white." These, in turn, would provide opportunities for women to campaign to remove the word "male," which since the founding had been securely ensconced at state level and in federal legislation. In the meantime, abolitionists watched for the chance to win suffrage for freedmen.

President Johnson was also dissatisfied with the amendment. Even though it may even have almost reflected his position,[1] on June 22 he delivered a broadside against it. Under Article V of the Constitution the president has no authority over amendments, but as the leading individual in the nation committed under oath in Article II, Section 1, Clause 8, to "preserve, protect and defend the Constitution of the United States," he made some choice observations about the exclusion of elected southern representatives from Congress in December 1865 to ensure Republicans would get the two-thirds vote required in Congress for an amendment. He disavowed any endorsement by the executive branch because the secretary of state was executing "purely ministerial" duties required to send it to the States for ratification. As defender of the Constitution, Johnson continued: "A proper appreciation of the letter and spirit of the Constitution, as well as of the interests of national order, harmony, and union, and a due deference for an enlightened public judgment, may at this time well suggest a doubt whether any amendment to the Constitution ought to be proposed by Congress and pressed upon the legislatures of the several States for final decision until after the admission of such loyal Senators and Representatives of the now unrepresented States as have been, or may hereafter be, chosen in conformity with the Constitution and laws of the United States."[2]

Later that month Johnson announced a campaign to defeat the amendment and sent out a call for a "National Union" convention. Meanwhile, Johnson continued his opposition to congressional plans with a veto of the Freedmen's Bureau bill on July 16. Congress quickly overrode this.[3] Now, as the contentious first session of the 39th Congress drew to its close on July 28, the 14th Amendment gave both the Republican Party and the chief executive a bitter election ahead. By this time, Connecticut, New Hampshire, and Tennessee—the latter President Johnson's home state—had ratified and Tennessee was readmitted to the union. On July 30 a major riot broke out in New Orleans at the start of a convention for a new constitution in Louisiana, where many Democrats totally opposed the postwar scenario. A news article reviewing the event nine months later said that an official "report [showed] that the number known to have been killed was 38, of whom 37 were loyal, and one disloyal; 48, all loyal, were severely wounded; 98 slightly wounded, of whom 88 were loyal, and 10 policemen. Besides these there was evidence, though not fully certain, that 10 more were killed and 20 wounded. Of those known to be killed 34 were colored, of the severely wounded 40, of the slightly wounded 79."[4] Fueling the fiery arguments against President Johnson's Reconstruction policies, which derived from the plans of the late President Lincoln, this riot formed some of the background for the Philadelphia "National Union" meeting of mid–August, but the convention produced no new national party and only "called for the election of Congressmen who would support Johnson's policies."[5]

Meanwhile, eyeing these national politics, the AERA began to plan for equal suffrage in New York's constitutional convention, with Anthony casting around for a new print platform. The *Standard* had effectively stopped covering the AERA, for which Frances Dana Gage chided them. "In the report given [of the AERA meeting in May], it is said that 'Mrs. Gage presented the claims of the freedmen,' which was true; but I should regret to be thought recreant to that other and far greater interest, the claims of the sex," she wrote. Messrs. Powell, Tilton, Johnson and Stebbins "had given it unqualified support [and] No subject was brought before the meeting that had so surely the unqualified assent of the vast multitude there present as the one of 'Equal Rights.'" Only one individual had objected "to the broad platform of liberty for all," she continued, and to give the impression that "Miss Anthony and Mr. Powell alone had felt moved to speak in its behalf" distorted the truth. "I had spoken for seventeen millions of women, among them half of the 'four millions' for whom, in the 'Reconstruction Policy,' the right of suffrage is demanded," she said, correcting the record.[6] Parker Pillsbury resigned as editor of the *Standard*, partly in response to its censorship.[7] Lucretia Mott was soon writing that Anthony, Stanton, and Pillsbury were exploring how to establish an AERA newspaper, for "Wendl. P. does not satisfy them on the Woman questn."[8] In August, the censorship became obvious when the *Standard* refused a letter from Stanton, even though it had long published her work. Stanton had been arguing in print with her cousin:

> In a recent conversation Gerrit Smith told me he would accept reconstruction with negro suffrage, even if woman was left out in the cold [but] is all that we ask in this Republic that races and not persons shall stand equal before the law? With fifteen million tax-paying citizens disfranchised, is not the republican idea essentially violated? … If, my noble cousin, you demand suffrage for the black man, on the ground of his humanity, his citizenship, from the purest patriotism, because in his disfranchisement you see the death of the republican idea, by what logic or safety do you ignore the woman by his side? If you base your claim on his manhood merely, you are no better than the feudal baron who fights for his own kin.[9]

Smith replied that he held "that voting is the natural right of both men and women of all complexions," but, he exhorted, "Rob not the negro of the ballot!—of the indispensable means for protecting himself." War "will break out again if suffrage is withheld from the black man…. But, surely, it cannot be reasonably urged that putting female suffrage into the 'reconstruction' will be necessary to keep down the flames of the war."[10] In other words, because women did not resort to violence they could be ignored. Stanton's reply to this letter did not appear—the censorship yet another disturbing example of her erstwhile colleagues' attitudes. The *Standard* still published editorials and reports about the AERA and notices of its forthcoming events,[11] but editorials did not necessarily reflect the AERA's position. "The gate is shut, wholly, it would seem against any *question* of the present position of … the American Anti-Slavery Society,"[12] wrote Anthony, explaining how the *Standard* was punishing the women—and consequently the AERA—for refusing to toe the line. She was writing to Edwin A. Studwell a Boston businessman, Quaker, and abolitionist who earlier that year had launched the *Friend* newspaper. Because of the marginalization, Anthony felt their own publication was necessary— hence her communication with Studwell. "If we launch a new Equal Rights paper … might it not be well just to make it a campaign paper—for the Constitutional Convention—there will be no paper in the state through which we can urge *our* claim for *equal, impartial* suffrage—no—not one." Describing some of her proposed content, she asked Studwell if he and others could "insure advertisements enough to pay cost" so they could launch in January 1867.[13]

President Johnson began campaigning on August 28, canvassing northern support for his policies. An optimistic beginning ended in protests, with Johnson returning to D.C. on September 15[14] to try to win support through presidential patronage.[15] While the AERA prepared its campaign for the 1867 New York constitutional convention the president focused on the coming elections, and abolitionists campaigned against him. A convention opposing Johnson's policies convened in Philadelphia from September 3 to 7. The Southern Loyalists' Convention was a meeting of Unionists from southern states along with northern Republicans and abolitionists. It caused a stir because of its five female delegates including Anna Dickinson, and for the presence of Theodore Tilton beside Frederick Douglass during the delegates' parade through Philadelphia preceding the formal opening. Many at this divided convention later walked out when the president tried to terminate a contentious discussion on suffrage for freedmen and free black men. Tilton, Douglass, and Dickinson then re-formed the convention with supporters and southern Republicans, concluding with a resolution proposing yet another constitutional amendment prohibiting discrimination in voting "on account of race, color, or previous condition of servitude."[16]

The press commended Tilton, Dickinson, and Douglass for their successful takeover and results of the convention,[17] for the words of the resolution advanced the cause of black male suffrage. But this triumph rang hollow for those members of the AERA committed to true equality because the proposal reinforced yet again the inequality in the progress of the AERA's agenda, as once more men's equality was being advanced without women. The demand for another amendment also raised another potentially huge problem in a future Congress—perhaps even the next one—which women might end up having to fight alone yet again. This development engineered by Tilton, Douglass, and Dickinson—all AERA members—looked like a clear betrayal of the AERA's principles. Tilton and Douglass's part might hardly have been surprising, as men's equality was their priority. Dickinson's is less so, for only that May she had pledged her services to the AERA cause, for whom equality included women.[18] With the two segments of the AERA's agenda moving in opposite directions, to feel this treatment unjust was only natural.

In September New Jersey and Oregon ratified the 14th Amendment. Between the first and second sessions of the 39th Congress, even with ratification continuing, Phillips was rethinking it completely. By this time, he was so formidable that Charles Sumner, the leading Senate Radical, had exhorted him to keep the antislavery societies going to advocate for the Radicals' congressional agenda.[19] President Johnson, on the other hand, denounced Phillips as a traitor because he opposed presidential reconstruction and wondered whether men such as Phillips and Representative Thaddeus Stephens should be hanged."[20] Meanwhile, the Convention of Massachusetts Workingmen nominated Phillips for Congress in late September,[21] but Phillips, preferring agitating from the outside to toeing the party line, refused. He turned on southerners who now viewed the amendment as less of a disaster and more of a potentially advantageous opportunity. Phillips' definition of a win—if Congress was going to produce only half-measures like the 14th Amendment—now became to defeat it in New York and win there the equal ballot for black men in the nation's largest state, thereby leading the way for the nation.[22] He turned, therefore, to the goal of excising the word "white" from the New York constitution during the proposed 1867 convention.

As the AERA also planned to have "male" removed from the New York constitution, Phillips now coopted the goals of the AERA, which he had earlier banished from the AASS because woman suffrage muddied the issue. He now spoke out for female suffrage, writing, "We personally urge the importance of striking out the word male." It was "a question of principle," he said. "At present woman is not even shielded, as are the disfranchised colored men, from direct taxation"—yet another inequality that women had to deal with. Coopting the AERA had solid practical purposes: in Anthony, the AERA had the best organizer of statewide campaigns and Phillips wanted her for his work.[23]

In October Vermont ratified. The process might have been slow, but the word "male" was inching towards constitutional inclusion. Early that month

Stanton announced she would run for Congress "to test the constitutional right of a woman" to do so[24]—uncovering one direct way at least to demonstrate concrete opposition to male-only politics. Her candidacy would also protest the conduct of the 39th Congress. In Albany during her campaign for true equal rights, the attitude of black men to white women emerged clearly:

> The transaction of the convention's business was progressing smoothly, when Miss Susan B. Anthony, who was in company with Mrs. Elizabeth Cady Stanton, arose in the convention and after addressing the Chair … proceeded to make a speech. She had been speaking but a few moments, when … there came an objection to Miss Anthony's proceeding from … Peyton Harris, of Buffalo, N.Y., the oldest delegate in the convention. This gentleman, who had passed his eightieth year, threw the entire assembly into confusion. Miss Anthony was surprised and almost paralyzed with indignation, as was her fair companion. The Chair ruled out the objection and instructed the lady to proceed with her remarks, which she again attempted to do, but Mr. Harris appealed from the decision of the Chair and his objection was sustained. Every member of the entire convention knew the tenacious character of Father Harris, and they feared to meet the crisis. The chairman proceeded to lecture the interrupter but was interrupted himself by the interrupter, who demanded that the call for the convention be read. This was complied with by the secretary of the convention … which was for a colored man's meeting. After the reading of the call, which was written by the … Hon. Frederick Douglass, Mr. Harris again addressed the chair, and apologized for his interruption, but declared that if Miss Anthony would demonstrate to him that she was a colored man, then he would cheerfully withdraw his objection.

This incident occurred at the New York State Convention of Colored Men held October 16, 1866. This aggressive discrimination because of race and sex may have been acceptable at the time it occurred, but it was hypocritical because men, no matter their race, could always speak at women's conventions. The arrogance was yet more stunning because these two women, who were even then working for black suffrage through the AERA, had been abolitionists and were the well-known spearheads of the campaign for what became the 13th Amendment. It revealed the battle for the primacy of black men over sex equality. Further biased behavior was that some black males even saw white women campaigning as out of place, even if they also campaigned for equal black suffrage. Understanding these twisted dynamics, Anthony, initially annoyed, passed the matter off lightly, made the audience laugh, and turned the awkward situation around. Later, the irascible Mr. Harris—apparently intent on wielding whatever power he could over the women—effectively granted *his* permission to them to speak through a motion to the chair. As a result, Anthony and Stanton "were invited to address the convention which they did to the pleasure and satisfaction of all."[25]

On October 27 Texas became the first southern state to reject the 14th Amendment—perhaps unsurprisingly, for the South had reason not to trust the current Congress. When Tennessee had been readmitted to the Union in

July, the congressional resolution had recognized as prerequisites for readmission compliance with the demands of the Congress, plus ratification of both the 13th and 14th amendments.[26] With Congress increasingly adopting a hard line, there was nothing to guarantee that readmittance of any other state would not require not only these ratifications but also the fulfillment of unspecified demands.[27] That November 5 the nation went to the mid-term polls. In New York, Elizabeth Cady Stanton had campaigned on a principled platform:

> Although, by the Constitution of the State of New York woman is denied the elective franchise, yet she is eligible to office; therefore, I present myself to you as a candidate for Representative to Congress. Belonging to a disfranchised class, I have no political antecedents to recommend me to your support, but my creed is free speech, free press, free men, and free trade, the cardinal points of democracy. Viewing all questions from the stand-point of principle rather than expediency, there is a fixed uniform law, as yet unrecognized by either of the leading parties, governing alike the social and political life of men and nations. The Republican party has occasionally a clear vision of personal rights, though in its protective policy it seems wholly blind to the rights of property and interests of commerce; while it recognizes the duty of benevolence between man and man, it teaches the narrowest selfishness in trade between nations. The Democrats, on the contrary, while holding sound and liberal principles on trade and commerce, have ever in their political affiliations maintained the idea of class and caste among men an idea wholly at variance with the genius of our free institutions and fatal to high civilization. One party fails at one point and one at another. In asking your suffrages believing alike in free men and free trade I could not represent either party as now constituted. Nevertheless, as an Independent Candidate, I desire an election at this time, as a rebuke to the dominant party for its retrogressive legislation in so amending the National Constitution as to make invidious distinctions on the ground of sex. That instrument recognizes as persons all citizens who obey the laws and support the State, and if the Constitutions of the several States were brought into harmony with the broad principles of the Federal Constitution, the women of the Nation would no longer be taxed without representation, or governed without their consent. Not one word should be added to that great charter of rights to the insult or injury of the humblest of our citizens. I would gladly have a voice and vote in the Fortieth Congress to demand universal suffrage, that thus a republican form of government might be secured to every State in the Union. If the party now in the ascendency makes its demand for "Negro Suffrage" in good faith, on the ground of natural right, and because the highest good of the State demands that the republican idea be vindicated, on no principle of justice or safety can the women of the nation be ignored. In view of the fact that the Freedmen of the South and the millions of foreigners now crowding our shores, most of whom represent neither property, education, nor civilization, are all in the progress of events to be enfranchised, the best interests of the nation demand that we outweigh this incoming pauperism, ignorance, and degradation, with the wealth, education, and refinement of the women of the republic. On the high ground of safety to the Nation, and justice to citizens, I ask your support in the coming election.[28]

Stanton's manifesto enunciated republican principles and demonstrates that by late 1866 she was highly critical and acting independently of the Republican Party. Her manifesto is equally pertinent for pointing out that the proposed amendment could enfranchise not only freedmen in the South but allow for the enfranchisement of new male immigrants—even if American-born women could not vote.

The day before the election Anthony wrote to Phillips, pursuing from a new angle the search for a newspaper, which she had been exploring since June. After a meeting with Anthony, Stone had said she would run the paper, so now Anthony was fund-raising again, as they said they needed "behind them a fund of $10,000 that may be drawn upon in case the paper fails to pay cost [although] nothing for editorial or publishing services."[29] She continued:

> We *surely must have* a *paper* through which those who demand the *whole loaf* of republicanism may speak…. Mr. Powell announced to me that "henceforth all notices of our Equal Rights lectures if they went into the Standard, must be paid for, at the regular advertising prices,"—that is, if *I* was not going to give my *personal efforts to the Standard*…. I said, "I shall speak as always, that the Standard is true & uncompromising for the Negro"—but I can't say to my audiences, "subscribe for the Standard, it is the *one* & *only paper* that will bring to you from week to week *fresh installments* of the *new gospel*…." I *can't serve* the Standard efficiently, because the Standard doesn't serve the idea which to me is the pivotal one.[30]

Anthony's position was hardening against the latest turn of the screw. The next day, with only 24 votes, Stanton lost her election.[31] Although the outcome was perhaps a disappointment, her running for federal office was a precedent for American women. With the election, every northern state won a Republican majority, while both Senate and House in Washington could now assemble with rock-solid majorities against President Johnson. The balance of power had shifted.

10. Campaign Penury, Organizational Skills and Cooperation

I would not rejoice in a reconstruction that would give suffrage to woman and deny it to the black man, for I should still see the republican idea violated, and I know my rights were not secure so long as those of the humblest citizen were doubted or denied.—Elizabeth Cady Stanton, "Build a New House," *National Anti-Slavery Standard*, July 21, 1866.

With the midterm elections finished, the AERA's campaign for New York could start. If Phillips at this point saw a need for the AERA and Anthony, the AERA's financial position was precarious enough for the AERA to need Phillips, for its own fund-raising fell far short of aspirations and need. Anthony knew this better than anybody, but she also knew of the bequest money supposedly available for woman's rights work and that Phillips was trustee. Two days after her letter about a newspaper, therefore, Anthony wrote again, pitching the plan for the removal of "white male" from the constitution. "Our hands are tied," she pleaded, "unless we can get the means to start."[1] She asked for money from both 1850s bequests that included women. One of these requests, for $3,000, came from the AERA executive committee under the signature of Henry B. Blackwell, recording secretary, Stone's husband.

Phillips' own October 6, 1866, pronouncement in the *Standard* supporting woman suffrage might have bolstered Anthony's resolve to secure financing for the AERA campaign to which women were legally entitled. Yet Phillips had been less than honest in his dealings with the women in the past. A trustee since 1859 of the Hovey Bequest, which stipulated that if slavery were abolished the money freed up from abolitionism was to go to woman's rights, among other things[2] Phillips freely used the money to keep the *Standard* afloat during the war,[3] while forcing the women to beg for money to run the WNLL abolition petition campaign.[4] Now he assiduously protected the anti-

73

slavery name and title, as if still to qualify for the bequest after abolition. Francis Jackson's originally anonymous bequest of 1858, for which Anthony and Lucy Stone were joint trustees with Phillips, had early on advanced money for women's work, proving invaluable in prewar suffrage and rights campaigns. In December 1865 Anthony had received from this bequest $500 for the women's petition against the word "male" and the campaign for woman suffrage in Washington, D.C.

The differences between the AASS and the AERA essentially rested in one word—"male"—and in two contrasting philosophies. But from Phillips' latest viewpoint, Anthony's campaigning skills and the AERA's black suffrage plank were positives. Phillips, therefore, who had only recently insisted on keeping the AASS and AERA separate, granted the requests. The AERA campaign, which both paralleled and went beyond that of Phillips and the AASS, could now begin.[5] Meanwhile, former Confederate state Georgia joined Texas in rejecting the 14th Amendment on November 9, 1866, and Anthony was casting around further for an AERA newspaper, trying to involve a reluctant Lucretia Mott in discussions with businessman, Quaker, and abolitionist Edwin A. Studwell[6] and others about "enlarging *The Friend* to admit Equal Rights, seeing the *Standard* didn't."[7] But despite her presidency of the AERA, discussions of equal rights at a lunch at Stanton's house fatigued Mott, her advancing age taking its toll.

Anthony in the meantime printed brochures calling for a New York equal suffrage convention to take place on November 20 and 21, 1866, in Albany. One of these she sent to Schuyler Colfax, Speaker of the House of Representatives who hosted a reception for Stanton after the election.[8] Anthony wrote on the flyer outlining the plans for a statewide campaign asking for a letter of support to publish with others in a pamphlet.[9] In the flyer the AERA outlined its aim of having "the right of suffrage [for] all citizens, without distinction of race or sex" included in the upcoming New York State convention. "Reconstruction of this Union is a broader, deeper work than the restoration of the rebel States," it said. "It is the lifting of the entire nation into the practical realization of our Republican Idea." Anthony and the AERA received quick support from leading Radical senator Benjamin Franklin Wade of Ohio: "I am now and ever have been the advocate of equal and impartial suffrage of all citizens of the United States who have arrived at the age of twenty-one years, who are of sound mind, and who have not disqualified themselves by the commission of any offence, without any distinction on account of race, color, or sex. Every argument that ever has been or ever can be adduced to prove that males should have the right to vote, applies with equal if not greater force to prove that females should possess the same right."[10] These were encouraging words; yet offensive attitudes prevailed. A headline in a Midwest newspaper about the upcoming Albany convention was this one: "The Old Hens to Cluck!"[11] Sex-based slurs were alive and well—but at least not everywhere. Colfax, for example, wrote supporting the AERA, his letter among others being mentioned at the meeting's opening.[12] A letter from Mott "hailed" the AERA's launch of its New York program and, declared, "The negro's hour came with his Emancipation by law, from cruel bondage. He now has Advocates not a few for his right to the ballot—Intelligent as these advocates are, they must see that this right cannot be consistently withheld from women."[13]

The convention held wide-ranging discussions, from suffrage for women and black men to debate about both political parties, criticism of the conference's content, discussion of an educated franchise, recognition of protests at taxation without representation, and the challenges of working women. Anthony, Stone, Stanton, Pillsbury, Blackwell, Douglass, the Reverends Stibbens and Olympia Brown, and Charles Lenox Remond as well as others spoke.[14] Stone said Reconstruction's great failing was the refusal to include women. While women had suspended their own cause for the war and abolition, anticipating that afterwards "the ballot would be settled on a true basis and the women [would] be admitted to the long-awaited franchise," she reminded her audience that after Appomattox "even the best Republican papers came out for an extension of the franchise as being needed for negroes only." Even if newspapers declared the nation would be "a Christian republic … when blacks [were] made the political equals with whites," this was not justice. In response, women now attempted "to make common cause with the colored men for the ballot … [thinking] that as we were the only two disfranchised classes, and as we are a majority, why should we not win it? The law puts its foot alike on the colored men and the women; why should they not make common cause?"[15]

The reporting was extensive but uneven and inaccurate.[16] *Equal Rights: The Ballot for the Women of New York—Spirited Convention at Albany,* one declared.[17] This headline represented only half the story even if Douglass believed it, for when he spoke he said that the convention "was in danger of becoming merely a Woman's Rights Convention." To him, black male suffrage was more important. Citing the New Orleans and Memphis riots, New York mobs, and blacks "being driven from workshops and schools," he said that for woman, suffrage "is a desirable matter." Ignoring the same inconvenient facts about colored women, he went on: "With us it is important; a question of life and death." Douglass was entitled to prioritize his interests. His restricted approach was not new: he had presided over the National Convention of Colored Men in Syracuse, New York, in October 1864 and had written the call for the Colored Men's Convention the previous month in Albany. Yet he did not concede that the AERA was the only platform women had, that women were the main organizers, and that their status was falling behind that of black men. Charles Lenox Remond at least saw the convention as "the inauguration of a great movement for general enfranchisement" and anticipated "a kindly recognition of a large portion of our people whom no laws formerly protected."

Stanton argued that "as the proposed work of [the coming New York] Convention is to be the extension of suffrage, all disfranchised classes should be represented there," especially in the "choice of the men who are ... to act on this great question." She called on New York women to use "social opportunities" such as "balls, dinners and receptions," to promote their own interests," encouraging them to organize clubs, tracts, and petitions advocating "the ballot for her sex, not only as a question of abstract right, but as required by her own interest and the interests of the community." Woman's claims had "been suspended during and since the war," she said, but black men's enfranchisement "has become a certainty soon to be conceded. Now as women are the only parties whose status is uncertain, we demand attention on the part of the few formers and adjusters of our Constitution." She opposed educated suffrage because "the negro at the South has not the free school and cannot obtain it without first obtaining the ballot."[18] Douglass appealed for the franchise for black men "so that he may have a reason for trying to be somebody." The convention especially condemned the Republican Party, with Stanton warning it not to expect women to support them unreservedly as black men were expected to do. "She also protested against the use of the word, 'Copperhead'"[19] to denigrate Democrats, because the latter had at least in some cases supported woman suffrage. Douglass "remonstrated against such a tribute being paid to the Democratic party,"[20] but Pillsbury backed her up, if only because "we are to deal with men as men, not as a generation of vipers."[21] The "lone equal rights memorial against the [14th] amendment" was presented for the New York legislature, with the protest that it was "a gross outrage ... and on that ground alone were there no other reason we earnestly hope it will be repudiated."[22]

This Albany conference launched the only true equal suffrage campaign in the United States at the time. Other "equal rights" organizations and campaigns used "equal," but they meant black men. Their refusal to adopt truthful rhetoric—in their organizational names, for example—showed that women were not in organizers' minds. The National Equal Rights League founded at the National Convention of Colored Men in October 1864 in Syracuse, New York, aiming for suffrage and equality before the law, intended to have "auxiliaries and subordinate associations in the different States," but its "Declaration of Wrongs and Rights," spoke of ownership of "wives, homes, children."[23] This group clearly saw themselves, as a people, as male. Their rhetoric was informed by slavery when men were chattels, but it demonstrates either that they saw women as "belonging" to them in the same way as most white men had done or that the diabolical philosophy of slavery had infected them. If they were owned they then owned others, ensuring someone else was at the bottom of the heap. Women had often referred to their own status as akin to slavery because of this male-ownership philosophy. Douglass had presided at this 1864 Syracuse convention.

Men elsewhere did the same. Abolitionists of all stripes used "equal" and "universal suffrage" for men only. George Stearns, from Medford, Massachusetts, and a recruiter of blacks during the Civil War, in his "Universal and Equal Suffrage Association" aimed for black male suffrage.[24] This debasement of the prewar language of "universal" and "equal" that originally included women gathered force during the war. The Douglass-endorsed National Equal Rights League of 1864 spawned the Pennsylvania Equal Rights League—but "equal rights" in both equaled men only.[25] Fighting back, Stanton wrote anonymously in January 1866 a challenge to the Washington, D.C., formation of a so-called National Equal Suffrage Association, for the rights of black men only. "The proper title should have been 'National Male Suffrage Association'—if, indeed, the term national may be justly assumed by a society that works only for one half the nation," she objected.[26] As rhetoric determines results, women had faced hardening of the consequences of the use of "men" in the specific since 1776 through "that word 'male'" in the Constitution.

The only place where inclusive language held some sway was the AERA. Its accurate terminology reflected republican philosophy, with the AERA on solid ground, its name accurately reflecting its aims; all the other "equal" rights organizations emphasized race while excluding sex. Yet the leaders of these pro-inequality organizations, their supporters and Congressmen, pressed forward with their exclusionary agendas, filling the *Congressional Globe* for months with their contorted attempts to squeeze out of their contradictory positions something that resembled for a few more people in the nation equality with those who had enjoyed it all the time while still excluding most citizens from similar justice. This was the very opposite of equality—if only for the fact that in the AERA equality meant true equality of race and sex. Therefore, the organization holds a unique place in Reconstruction and American history.

Within days of the AERA's launch of the New York campaign in Albany,[27] Anthony and Frances Dana Gage were in Philadelphia, presenting the case at the annual meeting of the Pennsylvania Anti-Slavery Society (PASS).[28] Republican senator Edgar Cowan of Pennsylvania—who the previous April had used women's disabilities to illustrate problems with the Civil Rights Act and to limit the scope of its impact—was taking note. His later observations would prove significant. Phillips, who professed support of the AERA's goals, at the PASS meeting took the stage before a cheering crowd to goad the upcoming session of Congress to further reform for the South. "It is [the] timidity of the Republican leaders ... to imagine that they are ahead of the people, whereas they are too far behind them.... [They] are very ignorant of the desire of the people to settle this question of injustice forever."[29] Phillips envisaged putting the South under military rule so that the more civilized North would influence the former rebels and improve their treatment of freedmen, which he deemed essential for a successful conclusion to the war. He also called for impeaching the president and advised that the 40th Congress should start its first session with no break at the end of the 39th Congress the following March instead of waiting until December 1867 to ensure congressional control of this more radical Reconstruction. "We must push public opinion by demanding of Congress ... that they shall hold on to the Southern territory and thoroughly inculcate these ideas among them," he declared in this firebrand speech.[30]

He now also called for combining suffrage, education, and economic assistance to help freed slaves reach equality, but by referring repeatedly to "freedman," "black man," "black and white man," "the manhood of man," "his civil and political rights" while speaking of "impartial suffrage" and "universal suffrage" and nowhere mentioning women—although supposedly professing support of the AERA agenda—he revealed that, even if men and women had been slaves, to Phillips only men mattered. While rabidly against half-measures that failed to give freedmen the vote, Phillips had no inhibitions about measures for only half of humanity to solve the problems of the whole of post–Civil War America. Further, he seems to have had no moral scruples about expanding almost without boundaries his definition of antislavery. Anthony tackled Phillips' blinkered outlook head-on, pointing out the truth about freedom from slavery for black women. "With legal marriage established among the black race as among the white race, it subjects the black woman to all the servitude and dependence which the white woman has hitherto suffered in the North," she said. "In slavery, the black woman has known nothing of the servitude of the marriage laws of the Northern States.... Whatever money her white master would allow her to earn was her money. It did not belong to the black man who was nominally her husband. She had the entire control of her own property, so far as her husband was concerned." She had, therefore, "lived so far in [that] freedom." However, emancipation subjected her to the servitude of normal marriage, while under Phillips' prescription she was not even to have the vote. "Mr. Phillips said to us yesterday afternoon that the result we should demand as the price of this war was the equality of races. I say more than this. I say that we should demand the equality of individuals, and nothing short of it."[31]

Gage backed Anthony up. Excoriating Senator Charles Sumner for his "grand speech" the previous winter, "which the whole country applauded," she said she "heard him declare that taxation without representation was tyranny to the freedman." When she found he meant only men, she realized that "Sumner fell far short of the great idea of liberty," and she demanded "equality on behalf of the freedwoman as well as the freedman." Addressing the pressure now on freedwomen to be conventionally married and the new servitude they faced, she said that South Carolina women had declared, "We don't want to be married in the church, because when we are … our husbands treat us just as old massa used to, and whip us if they think we deserve it, but when we ain't married in the church, they knows if they tyrannize over us, we go and leffm." And so, Gage demanded, "let it be a marriage of equality."[32]

Phillips' relentless and boundless onslaught with post-abolition antislavery was raising other objectors. In October, veteran abolitionist Sarah Pugh—one of the excluded female United States delegates at the World Anti-Slavery Convention in London in 1840—resigned as treasurer of the PASS after 23 years over the continuation of antislavery societies.[33] That November 15 Lucretia Mott, having recovered from her 1865 reluctance to support woman's rights, referred to her husband's support for winding the organization up and his unwillingness to continue as president, writing, "Let's merge in Equal Rights Socy."[34] The PASS did neither, but Mott, now back in the woman's fold, seems irked with the fact that the agendas of the continuing antislavery societies countered the AERA's agenda.

Phillips' concerns about the progress of reforms were real, for by late 1866 little was resolved. Ratification was happening only slowly for the new amendment to protect former slaves. Essentially, South and North were still at war. The South was mired in economic disaster, social unrest, racial strife, and attempts by the former leaders to regain control through acceptance of the amendment and imposing discriminatory state and local codes on former slaves. Economic progress and vengeance against the South characterized the North, where reformist zeal was running rampant, as Phillips' fiery speeches demonstrated. Keeping antislavery societies going and promoting their agitation in the papers—for reasons of self-interest as much as for the interests of black men—were the drivers of the political agenda, challenging politicians to cave in and fulfill reformers' demands. The societies had cheerfully abandoned their strict Garrisonian principles of equality for all and now pressed for what was useful and expedient. Phillips declared, "The only thing we want is to press Congress in her duty of retaining her hold upon the South and not allowing them to come into power until the Northern leaven has worked longer among them." Yet, as Gage said of Anthony's words at the PASS, "the question is not whether we shall save or destroy the Republican party … but … the individual right of every human soul to govern his own thoughts and feelings and actions, subject to no law but such as have an equal bearing upon every other individual under similar circumstances, responsible at no bar but that of his own conscience and his God."[35] Such words had little clout in late 1866 when Phillips' newly defined goals satisfied men's prejudices against women and when seemingly pure evil was running rampant.

Only one small national group, along with several local organizations that had early in 1866 fed into its formation,[36] professed and attempted to work for equality for all in the republic and not just more men. The AERA's goal was much larger than that of Phillips and the antislavery societies and it was facing an uphill struggle, with fewer than 500 members.[37] Unlike others, it had few resources, little access to publicity or power, and was divided, because many of its members were already more equal than others and still promoted themselves at the cost of the rest; and many of them supported Phillips' and the antislavery societies' agenda to exclude half the population from the polity even more securely than before.

The 39th Congress reconvened on Monday, December 3, 1866, intending to lay the postwar mayhem to rest, including what many congressmen saw as a recalcitrant president. Fired up by its success in November's elections, the House immediately introduced Bill H.R. 830—"An Act to Fix the Times for the Regular Meetings of Congress." The measure would convene the 40th Congress immediately after the dissolution of the 39th on March 3, 1867, so that the president would never be without overseers. Virtually unchallenged, the bill began to move through the legislative process. Meanwhile, with the Republicans' agenda of discrimination against women being effected through the new amendment—and in compensation, it almost seems, for raising black men up to the white man's level—the nation's capital presented Congress with the opportunity to implement more sex exclusion in suffrage. That day, Senator Charles Sumner revived a bill to grant the right to vote to black men in Washington, D.C.[38]

The new push for male-only suffrage in D.C. was the last detail of the background to the second meeting of the AERA that took place in the Cooper Union in New York on December 6, 1866, where Anthony, Stanton, Emma Hardinge, and Colonel James H. Moss of Missouri argued for true universal suffrage. The meeting adopted several resolutions, one stating, "[T]he ballot, alike to the woman and the negro, means bread, education, intelligence, self-protection, self-reliance and self-respect."[39] This emphasized the benefits of true equality, which the right to vote both symbolized and facilitated, Stanton said:

> As capital has ever ground labor to the dust, is it just or generous to disfranchise the poor and ignorant because they are so? It needs but little observation to see that behind bread lies the ballot, and that disfranchised classes can never, in the race for the prizes of life, have a fair chance with their fellows. Black men, as a general thing, are cooks, waiters, boot-blacks or barbers, while those women who must labor outside the domestic circle are generally found in our workshops or factories, or they are seamstresses,

teachers, or shopkeepers in a small way. Now, why are not women and negroes as a general thing side by side with white men in the professions, the political offices, in the trades and all profitable employments, and why in the same branches of industry are they paid less for their work? If there is any philosophical reason for all this outside the ballot, I should like to hear it, as I have searched in vain for any other cause.[40]

While pointing out the benefits to women particularly, Stanton concluded, "to all it means social equality, colleges and professions open, profitable business, skilled labor, and intellectual development."[41] Countering the "age, color, sex, property, and education" arguments that politicians routinely cited to deny the vote and conceding that some of these in time might be overcome, she argued "as to color and sex, neither time, money, nor education can make black white or woman man … such insurmountable qualifications [are] not to be tolerated in a republican government."[42]

Stanton's combination of political, civil, and economic arguments consciously reached out to wider audiences to broadcast the importance of suffrage reform. By 1866, the leading women in the AERA had moved beyond the concerns of married women. Years of women's conventions discussing every minute detail of women's status and analyzing their origins had taught them the problems of inequality for all classes of women. For years, drawing the parallel between women's status and slaves, they had informed themselves of the plight of female slaves. Several important campaigns for legal, political, and constitutional reform, including the "mammoth" petition for slave emancipation of 1863–1864, equipped them uniquely for a new campaign for equal rights throughout society. They now aimed to alert all disfranchised groups to the importance and benefits of suffrage. Anthony's free tickets for poorer working women was a sign of this development,[43] but she understood this problem from experience. She had always struggled against few opportunities and discriminatory wages as a working woman, especially when trying to work for reform without any independent income. Because of their years of experience, the concern of Stanton and Anthony was women never included in the polity, along with the nation's black men who had also been excluded.

One participant at least at this Cooper Union event recognized that the women were not accepted in a similar spirit among black men. Charles Lenox Remond criticized the Albany Convention of Colored Men for its discrimination against, rude treatment of, and lack of courtesy to Anthony and Stanton in October when they had tried to speak in favor of true equal suffrage.[44]

11. Equal Suffrage
for Washington, D.C.

We must reconstruct the govt of our country on RADICAL principles—universal freedom, impartial suffrage, and equal rights.—Miles Ledford Langley, Little Rock, Arkansas, February 12, 1868, *Debates and Proceedings of the Convention* (1868), 705.

An attempt in 1865 to extend the franchise to black men in the singular jurisdiction where Congress had the power to make such legislative changes had failed, but it still represented a second front that the women had then had to face. Now the problem returned in full force. Senator Charles Sumner's relaunch of the Washington, D.C., black male suffrage bill on December 3, 1866, would mean a significant step forward. The bill to enfranchise black male residents of the District was soon successful, passing on January 8, 1867.[1] Congress, in fact, overrode the presidential veto and the measure became a triumph of Radical Reconstruction.

Besides enfranchising black men, the new law meant more.[2] It demonstrated another twist on the discriminatory use of congressional jurisdiction over D.C., for in the nation's capital, the vote was deliberately restricted to men while ostensibly establishing race equality. In fact, it reintroduced in contemporary form the federally sanctioned discriminatory enfranchisement in the United States that featured in the 1787 Northwest Ordinance[3] and further institutionalized in law and fact the exclusion of women. This D.C. suffrage bill also set a standard for state legislatures and other future franchise measures. Simultaneously, however, it brought equal suffrage into congressional debate and put on record the attitudes to women of the wholly male congress at that time. The debate clearly shows that congressmen knew exactly what they were doing in their discriminatory treatment of half of the population and that Radical Reconstruction was anything but radical.

Debate began on December 10 with an amendment proposed by the Senate Committee on the District of Columbia and an exposé of the merits of the entire measure. Senator Lot Myrick Morrill of the committee noted that while it "purported" to regulate the vote in D.C., it "not only regulates the elective franchise in this District, but it extends and enlarges it." Its "principal feature" was that it "embrace[d] the colored citizens of the District." Morrill then revealed its true nature—a sex discrimination bill. "I should say that it is impartial restricted suffrage ... to be impartial among all the male citizens of the United States resident in this District.... It is restricted in that it is confined to the male sex."[4] He added details that suffragists would castigate for years to come. Not only did the bill restrict suffrage to males, it also "confined [the vote] to persons of adult age; and in that it excludes paupers, insane persons, persons non compos mentis, and persons who have rendered themselves by crime—treason, felony, or otherwise—infamous, and so not to be trusted in public affairs." Finally, he declared, it "may be called impartial restricted suffrage, as distinguished from universal and manhood suffrage."[5]

Morrill was trying to hide the truth, but the D.C. franchise bill was replete with contradictions in a supposed republic because it deliberately excluded half of society. As Congress had introduced the word "male" into the 14th Amendment, the road was now easy to further the institutionalized exclusion of women. The bill also created another front on which the agenda of the AERA faced a stunning imbalance, with equality for black and white supposedly being solved, even though it ignored half of both. With the AERA founded on a shaky footing because of such policies, this bill heralded further stress on the fault line.

The December 10 debate ranged over the implications of the various restrictions and exclusions of the bill and the proposed amendment thereto. After several votes, Senator Edgar Cowan of Pennsylvania proposed an amendment "to strike out the word 'male' before the word 'person'" in the bill.[6] He wanted "to extend [the vote] not only to males, but to females as well; and I should like to hear even the most astute and learned Senator upon this floor give any better reason for the exclusion of females from the right of suffrage than there is for the exclusion of negroes." Cowan, reading from the proceedings of the recent PASS meeting and echoing arguments of woman's rights workers for two decades and of the recently formed AERA, he challenged his colleagues to justify excluding women. If taxation and the franchise went "hand in hand" for black males, how could the franchise not go "hand in hand" with female taxation? Why should women be tried for crimes with only male jurors and judges? Why should women be paid less than men just because they were women? He pointed out that women's subordination in society was akin to slavery. This was being ignored while the chattel slavery of blacks had been abolished. Why should manhood, as opposed to womanhood, be a special requisite of the exercise of the vote? If women were indeed the vessel of society's virtue and did indeed represent higher qualities than men, why were men reluctant to give them the vote? "If you want to widen the franchise ... to purify your ballot-box, throw the virtue of the country into it; throw the temperance of the country into it; throw the purity of the country into it; throw the angel element ... into it," he declared. "Let there be as little diabolism as possible, but as much of the divinity as you can get." Consider the women's viewpoint, he exhorted his colleagues. The "demand of fifteen million American females for this right ... can be granted and ... safely exercised in their hands as it can in the hands of negroes." How could his colleagues "go home and look in the face their sewing women, their laboring women, their single women, their taxed women, their overburdened women, their women who toil till midnight for the barest subsistence, and say to them, 'We have it not for you; we could give it to the negro, but we could not give it to you.'"[7]

The annoyance of other senators at Cowan's amendment is palpable in the record. Some called it a device to kill the whole measure; others denied that it could be an honest attempt to introduce true equality in D.C. suffrage. The accusations, which Cowan defended himself vigorously against, appear repeatedly, reflecting normal partisan politics, suspicions, possibly lies, and even the possible truth about this supporter of Andrew Johnson. After all, in April Cowan had used the preexisting discriminations against women to argue for limitations in what became the Civil Rights Act. On the other hand, while he argued then along narrow constitutional principles, here he was speaking about equality and specific legislation to enfranchise black males. In this context, his argument was logical and did not necessarily contradict the constitutional arguments he had made earlier.

Regardless of motivation, Cowan's amendment was significant. It highlighted the inconsistency of extending the vote to freedman while deliberately excluding women. It smoked out the mental gymnastics congressmen used to cement male suffrage and female exclusion in the law. His move highlighted the fact that even if the D.C. measure was controversial it was not radical. Morrill was incorrect to claim that giving black men the vote was "novel,"[8] for black men in many states had the vote, even if under discriminatory laws. The bill would only expand the male vote, albeit to more black men, not introduce something new. It was novel, however, because it represented "a policy not only strictly for the District of Columbia, but in some sense for the country at large."[9] The anomalous position of D.C. at this juncture in the nation's structure presented an opportunity for so-called radicals who grabbed whatever opportunity they could, while the measure was intended to stretch the boundaries of congressional powers when, according to the Constitution, the determination of voting qualifications belonged to the states. On the other hand, even to *propose* to open suffrage in the District to women in an actual amendment in Congress was revolutionary because it was new when women faced a solid barrier to break down.[10] The women were the ones who needed something novel, a precedent. Senator Cowan's amendment, if accepted, could have been a precedent. It would not just open the door to woman suffrage in D.C., it would also create the prospect of demolishing the barrier against women everywhere. If introducing the vote for black men in Washington, D.C., through congressional action deliberately and consciously set precedents for the nation at large, it could not avoid doing so for women.[11]

Opposition to Cowan's proposal on grounds of expediency was formidable. Apart from accusing him of insincerity, opponents said he was against any suffrage extension at all. They also claimed he wanted to extend suffrage to females because of huge differences in the background of women and freedmen. This was valid: abolitionists had consistently argued that slaves had been debased and degraded. If the vote was to be given to "debased and degraded" men, any suffrage extension should include women who, American men repeatedly argued, were the repositories of virtue. They could pull everyone in the electoral process up to a higher level and counterbalance the negatives of a new electorate debased in slavery. While Cowan used the philosophy of their inherent virtues that supported the "separate spheres" of men and women to argue for enfranchising women, many of his colleagues used the same thinking to continue excluding them. Republican senator Frederick Theodore Frelinghuysen pushed the same philosophy to its most extreme by arguing that the Bible decreed women's role was at the hearth in the home with the male at her head. He said that woman was already represented through male relatives such as husband and sons and that most women were quite satisfied with that.[12] Couverture—by which women ceased to exist upon marriage—was alive and well in such minds, even if small inroads had been made through women's reforms.

Further arguments against Cowan were that woman suffrage was coming but the timing was wrong; that linkage to freedman's suffrage muddied the issue; that woman suffrage was not the issue under discussion and it should be introduced in the correct manner; that women do not bear arms and fight for their country; that participating in politics would corrupt women; that no woman cared for the vote; that the women who did were harridans; that the vote was only a conventional and not a natural right; that representation inhered in the family, not in individuals; that there was no precedent for female suffrage; that there was one, in New Jersey, and it did not last long, and anyway was long ago and "the women of New Jersey do not desire to vote"[13]; and that reform in the election process was more important than any extension of the suffrage. Several senators said they would vote for the amendment not expecting it to pass because it was not the right time and suffrage for freedmen was a "necessity" for their protection in these turbulent times or because woman suffrage should be dealt with as a separate issue from black male suffrage. Senator Cowan asked at the start for a debate based on logic, but prejudice, discrimination, traditional views of male and female roles, and the determination to hold control of power within a limited sphere pushed logic aside.[14]

It is easy to dismiss Cowan's intentions as insincere, but his proposal was nevertheless positive. He referred to the pleadings for true universal suffrage of AERA members in the recent PASS meeting on November 21 and 22, 1866, and mentioned the AERA campaign. Advocating the AERA program, he linked female enfranchisement and the enfranchisement of black men, while the senators who attacked him for politicking through women effectively directly attacked the AERA program. Little of the debate boded well for the proponents of true universal suffrage and equal rights, for neither true equality nor a true republic seemed to matter to the nation's representatives. Their failure to recognize—or else their deliberate choice to ignore—the plight of women in the South is unmistakable evidence. Yet Cowan raised it, quoting extensively Gage's testimony from freedwomen in South Carolina demonstrating that black women needed protection from husbands who wanted total control over wives, like many men in society generally, and "behaving in many cases like tyrants."[15]

It was not only from their husbands that they needed protection, as an affidavit of the wife of a discharged Georgia black soldier demonstrated:

Myself and husband were under contract with Mrs. Amelia Childs of Henry County, and worked from Jan. 1, 1866, until the crops were laid by, or in other words until the main work of the year was done, without difficulty. Then (the fashion being prevalent among the planters) we were called upon one night, and my husband was demanded; I Said he was not there. They then asked where he was. I Said he was gone to the water mellon patch. They then Seized me and took me Some distance from the house, where they "bucked" me down across a log, Stripped my clothes over my head, one of the men Standing astride my neck, and beat me across my posterior, two men holding my legs. In this manner I was beaten until they were tired. Then they turned me parallel with the log, laying my neck on a limb which projected from the log, and one man placing his foot upon my neck, beat me again on my hip and thigh. Then I was thrown upon the ground on my back, one of the men Stood upon my breast, while two others took hold of my feet and stretched My limbs as far apart as they could, while the man Standing upon my breast applied the Strap to my private parts until fatigued into stopping, and I was more dead than alive. Then a man, Supposed to be an ex-confederate Soldier, as he was on crutches, fell upon me and ravished me. During the whipping one of the men ran his pistol into me, and Said he had a hell of a mind to pull the trigger, and Swore they ought to Shoot me, as my husband had been in the "God damned Yankee Army," and Swore they meant to kill every black Son-of-a-bitch they could find that had ever fought against them. They then went back to the house, Seized my two daughters and beat them, demanding their father's pistol, and upon failure to get that, they entered the house and took Such articles of clothing as Suited their fancy, and decamped. There were concerned in this affair eight men, none of which could be recognized for certain.[16]

This poor woman, Roda Ann Childs, could only sign "X," but she left her mark on history with testimony of abhorrent treatment of women in the United States. If, indeed, enfranchising women would give women protection from this type of horrific abuse, such a story emphasizes the arrogance of the refusal of Congress to consider the full range of the problems that tortured the country. All women in the South were facing similar horrors, but white women—rebels by definition—were hardly the focus of investigations for the record about the conditions they faced during the war and afterwards. In some minds, they likely deserved what they got.

The debate on the amendment to remove the word "male" from the D.C. suffrage bill occupied three days in the Senate, but Senator Cowan's amendment was voted down 37–39 on December 12, 1866. The debate represented a minor triumph, nevertheless: woman suffrage in the nation had been debated and voted on in the United States Congress.

12. Woman's Champion

Each and every reason, yet given, why women, as a class, should not have and exercise the right of suffrage, is equally conclusive against its possession by men.—Clarina I. H. Nichols, 1867 to the Editor, *Vermont Phoenix.*

On the very day the Senate voted down Senator Cowan's proposal to remove "male" from the District of Columbia suffrage bill, the *New York Tribune*, after attacking Cowan's motives, editorialized:

> We are not to be suspected of indifference to the question whether woman shall vote. At a proper time we mean to urge her claim, but we object to allowing a measure of urgent necessity, and on which the public has made up its mind, to be retarded and imperilled.[1]

Thus Horace Greeley's newspaper dismissed woman's concerns while promoting black men's affairs only. Simultaneously, he set apart the two wings of the AERA campaign. Whether his position, at least concerning freedmen's franchise, was consistent with the nation's outlook, at the time as he claimed it was, is questionable. Yet it was significant because he had once been a supporter of true equal rights. But now his personal battle, which began in 1860 when Stanton promoted divorce, strengthened. Pro-female AERA workers could hardly have avoided noticing this unequal treatment. Still throughout December 1866 the AERA campaign continued in New York, with meetings in such towns as Utica and Rochester.[2]

At Cooper Union before the Senate woman suffrage debate the AERA had begun to prepare a memorial to Congress protesting about discrimination in the vote in any reform. At the Rochester meeting on December 11 the proposed text was revised at the behest of Lucy Stone to render it more amenable to congressmen who favored woman suffrage.[3] The meeting, however, taking place in the middle of the senate debate, brought to the fore the gulf between women and black male supporters when Parker Pillsbury proposed several resolutions. One called for true universal suffrage and another to have women vote for the delegates to the New York constitutional convention. A third praised Cowan for his D.C. suffrage bill amendment.[4] Here trouble erupted right along the AERA's fault line. Anthony was full of praise for the proposed amendment—an indication that she perhaps had lobbied Cowan to do this in Congress. It was also further indication that the women, who had begun seeking Democrat support for their measures the year before, would look for support anywhere, for Cowan, although a Republican, supported the president.[5] In spite of Anthony's praise, however, some abolitionists felt wary, believing that Cowan's move could defeat votes for freedmen in D.C. The current bill suited their purposes. The meeting reached a compromise that "expressed satisfaction" at the measure, tiptoeing around praising the senator.[6] The compromise refused to acknowledge the inequalities between men and women that congressional policies were institutionalizing through the extension of the franchise— even though some men, white and black, supposedly were collaborating for true universal suffrage.

On December 14 North Carolina rejected the 14th Amendment, with South Carolina following on December 20, 1866. Added to the previous rejections by Texas and Georgia, they gave Radical Reconstruction congressmen the pretext to launch with impunity plans for the most extreme measures that they wanted to impose on the South. Yet this red flag about potential defeat of the 14th Amendment, its final approval requiring some of the southern states to approve it, must have raised hopes among those who opposed if for its inadequacies. Their motivations

Horace Greeley, c. February 1865, was the founder and editor of the *New-York Tribune*. Before the war he supported woman's rights, but afterwards, like Wendell Phillips and a third newspaperman, Theodore Tilton, he spoke out against women while the enfranchisement of men proceeded through several reforms to include black men. Greeley was elected a delegate of the 1867 New York Constitutional Convention. Nominated Chairman of the Suffrage Committee, in this role he denied women the vote, after a travesty of a public hearing for them the day before his committee published its report (Library of Congress).

varied. Some opposed it because it did not enfranchise black men, while
activist women opposed it not just because it enfranchised neither black men
nor women and not only excluded women but also because it enshrined
"male" in the Constitution. These two rejections of ratification in December
1866, on top of an AERA meeting requiring skillful diplomacy to maintain
a unified front, provided useful breathing room. They did not threaten the
unity of sorts that still held the AERA together, for with these two rejections,
ratification of the 14th Amendment remained up in the air.

The AERA, therefore, pressed on with its full agenda. Its memorial
protesting unequal expansion of suffrage was published just before Christmas
1866.[7] Vice presidents Mott, Tilton, Douglass, and Stanton of the AERA, plus
Anthony, signed. It stated they "respectfully but earnestly protest against any
change in the Constitution of the United States, or legislation by Congress,
which shall longer violate the principle of Republican government, by pro-
scriptive distinctions in right of suffrage and citizenship on account of color
or sex.... Neither color nor sex is ever discharged from obedience to law ...
[and] all such [discriminatory] legislation ... is essentially unrighteous and
unjust."[8] Presented in the House on January 3, 1867, the memorial was too
late to have any effect. The same day, in Ohio, state representative Henry C.
Houston submitted a woman suffrage resolution that was tabled and died,[9]
making an inauspicious start to the year's campaigning. By January 8 the D.C.
suffrage bill had passed, having been vetoed by the president and passed
again into law over his rejection. The Radicals' agenda had won a significant
victory, one that represented a step forward for some men who were black.
Yet the measure was at most a half-measure, for it gave only a tiny number
in one city in the nation the vote, while women were further cut out. From
the Radicals' point of view, black male voting rights represented a major total
victory in one location—and it was just a first victory. With the precedent
established, they could press for further changes. One followed immediately,
with passage on January 10, 1867, of the Territorial Suffrage Act, which banned
discrimination against black men in voting in the Territories. During the process of implementing these reforms,[10] the AERA saw Congress repeatedly and
deliberately ignore, write off, and further disadvantage half of its program.

Simultaneously at state level, the 14th Amendment, with its back-handed
boost for freedman's suffrage across the South, faced a setback when Kentucky
on January 8 and Virginia on January 9 became the next former Confederate
states to reject the amendment, but New York on January 10 and Ohio on
January 11 approved it and balanced these out. With all these events happening
so fast, the exclusion of women proceeded apace while the inclusion of black
men moved on. The events also demonstrated that, while the women's cause
had little backing where power resided, the future of freedmen remained
securely in the hands of a supportive Congress. Yet the progress of ratification

and the awareness the AERA was raising about true equality seems to have stirred some consciences, for in Maine on January 14 the Senate "directed the judiciary committee 'to inquire into the expedience of so amending the Constitution as to do away with the distinction between the sexes in relation to the right of suffrage.'"[11] The women, therefore, were not completely sidelined.

In Congress they were not left out completely either: there now appeared a champion who attempted to revive the rejected revolution in D.C.'s suffrage law by introducing on January 14, 1867, an amendment to abrogate the sex discrimination in D.C.'s voting rights. "No person," the amendment of Missouri representative Thomas Estes Noell stated, "shall be disfranchised from voting or ineligible to office on account of sex."[12] Noell, beginning his congressional career as a Republican, later changed to Democrat[13] and became a fiery opponent of Radical Reconstruction, with all its constitutional pretensions, contradictions, and double standards. If anyone wanted to contend that Noell was simply grandstanding, therefore, they could easily do so. If anyone, on the other hand, wanted to argue that he was attempting to undermine the D.C. suffrage law by this amendment, they would be well off the mark, for the law had already passed and black men in the District already had suffrage rights there. Noell's proposal would only ensure the inclusiveness of that law, not revoke it.[14] His amendment and any discussion of it, no matter the result, would reveal the truth of congressional and radicals' professions that once freedmen were enfranchised then women would follow. This move represented a new development in the true universal suffrage cause.

13. Stanton Speaks

Where, gentlemen, did you get the right to deny the ballot to all women and black men not worth $250? If this right of suffrage is not an individual right, from what place and body did you get it? Is this right of franchise a conventional arrangement, a privilege that society or government may grant or withhold at pleasure?—Elizabeth Cady Stanton, 1867, *History of Woman Suffrage II* (1887), 276.

While Noell was stirring Congress up about the discriminatory D.C. suffrage law, AERA member Henry B. Blackwell was trying to win the South by publishing a suffrage tract. Phillips and black men had started advocating military rule months before, and, Blackwell argued, if the South's obdurate opposition to the determined plans of the Congress led to another war, it had no chance of winning in its current economic and social condition. Its best chance of forestalling any such scenario was not just to give freedmen the vote, but to give women the vote also.[1] The suggestion is breathtaking for the time, for nationally and in the states, the AERA's agenda was not just being dismissed it was being dismembered by succeeding reforms, the D.C. suffrage bill being the latest example. Yet no one had focused on the South as a place and a means to achieve the full AERA agenda in one region at least.

"It is believed in the North," Blackwell pointed out, ["that most] of the white people of the South are at heart the enemies of the Union. The advocates of negro suffrage daily grow stronger and more numerous" He could have said this included a Congress then increasingly vengeful towards the South. "The interest of both North and South, since they must live together, is peace, harmony and real fraternity. No adjustment can fully succeed unless it is acceptable to both sections." Blackwell argued that to achieve this harmony, giving freedmen the vote was essential to satisfy the North. However, to balance white southerners' concerns about power, the South should enfranchise women, for "in the light of the history of your Confederacy, can any Southerner fear to trust the women of the South with the ballot?" They should call on "the intelligence and patriotism of the wives and daughters of the South" to attempt to resolve this "disastrous conflict between Federal and State juris-diction." With true universal suffrage in the South, "the negro [would be] pro-tected against oppression by possessing the ballot." Applying true republican principles he wrote, "If 'governments derive their just powers from the con-sent of the governed'—if 'taxation without representation is tyranny'—and 'on these two commandments hang all the (republican) law and the pro-phets'—then *these propositions are as applicable to women as to negroes.*" "If you must try the Republican experiment, try it fully and fairly," he wrote. He cited the experience of New Jersey until 1807, when both women and black men had the vote.

Henry Blackwell, the husband of woman's rights stalwart Lucy Stone, was a reformer, a self-promoter, and somewhat of a loose cannon, producing this pamphlet under his own name. His stunningly simple proposal essentially was not new. Enfranchising women in the South was implicit in the AERA's agenda of equal suffrage for all, and Stephen Foster had recognized its logic at the AASS early in 1866.[2] But to advance the idea explicitly, as Blackwell was doing, undermined the Republican agenda. It raised the problem of the safety of former slaves and the future of the South. It seemed he was "casually consigning former slaves to the tender mercies of their former masters"[3] through outright racism, the former slave power's attempts with black codes to restore slavery by other means, and the scapegoating of freed slaves for economic disruption exacerbated by a drastically increased labor force. These were legitimate concerns about Blackwell's proposals. Bearing only black males' security in mind, the idea of cancelling out the freedman's vote with woman voters was appalling, specifically for the AERA's black male suffrage advocates. The pamphlet also pointed out, however, that not all white people targeted blacks: the struggle for survival was hard enough for many southern whites who had never benefited from slavery and did not persecute former slaves. With Blackwell also proposing the enfranchisement of former female slaves, his pamphlet also highlighted the profound fallacy in Republicans' argument that enfranchisement was for protection, because they meant men only, even if freedwomen equally needed protection. Further, Republican reforms allowed white women of the South no such "protection" either. Look-ing out for women by ensuring their legal equality comported with the AERA's woman suffrage agenda.

Blackwell's ideas also highlighted problems outside the AERA. While northern radicals and reformers were resolutely demanding freedmen's votes in the South, they were slow to demand equal black male rights in the North, for it did not suit their plans to solidify their hold on power nationally through new black uneducated voters and the disenfranchisement of southern whites. Contemporary conventional wisdom argued that the unrest and lawlessness of the South required punitive and restrictive measures, including a tight control on an electorate enlarged only enough to win Republican control of the South and win the peace. Women, particularly educated women, men believed, would be uncontrollable, as would women in the South; they were excluded to avoid upending these plans. Despite its, to some, horrifying short-comings and to others its mind-boggling audacity, Blackwell's pamphlet nev-ertheless highlighted the fault lines in the whole suffrage debate. In fact, it demonstrated that whenever expediency was pressed into service throughout the suffrage argument, it was contradictory, inconsistent, and unequal. The only ground on which suffrage might stand solidly was that of justice, but as immediately after the war those in power threw aside suffrage on such grounds it never had a chance.

Whether Blackwell's proposal would have worked is unknown as it was never tried, while analyses generally emphasize the potentially appalling out-come for freed black men in the South—not the potential benefits of enfran-chisement based on equality or justice, especially for freedwomen facing new encumbrances imposed from the non-slave culture that Anthony had described in Philadelphia in November. Yet, if woman did have a civilizing influence on society, on that basis alone it might have produced some benefit. Blackwell's pamphlet may have received a little notice in the South,[4] but at this juncture it had no wider effect.[5] It did, however, whether intentionally or not, point out the central problem with the AERA agenda. From the point of view of woman suffrage, the proposal possessed some sense and logic, par-ticularly given the beating that women, along with the South, were receiving from Congress. From the point of view of freed black men and the hardline self-righteous former abolitionists and radicals it was anathema. Blackwell's proposal, in sum, therefore, was challenging, deeply disturbing, unsettling, and threatening.

His pamphlet might have partially grown out of observations of relations within the AERA. Individual members—particularly in view of the over-the-presidential-veto passage of the D.C. suffrage bill without any reference to women—could hardly have been unaware of the increasing injustice in the progress of the two sides of the organization, an unsettling development for those adversely affected. Perhaps Blackwell was hoping to repair this funda-mental weakness by advocating a way to create balance in the face of the gal-loping sex discrimination in this period. If this was his thinking he can hardly be condemned, for the cause of men was being promoted everywhere while the cause of women had difficulty edging in. Yet, overall, Blackwell's publi-cation brought out clearly the very deep crack behind the AERA's facade. His tract might have prompted the discriminatory behavior of black men against women a short time later when, during an attempt to set up an AERA group in Pennsylvania, "eight colored men gathered around us during the recess, and said they thought women were well enough represented by their husbands etc."[6] Yet this was a very old saw that always stopped the enfranchisement of women cold. As Stanton and Anthony had experienced in Albany the previous November, the attitude of this group in Pennsylvania was not unique. Robert Purvis, a wealthy black man, confirmed the impression of black prejudice against women, apparently observing that such attitudes were the norm. Most other black men, he said, "would give their influence like a dead weight against the equality of women."[7]

The AERA canvass of New York State nevertheless continued with Stone, Anthony, and Stanton sometimes traveling together and occasionally finding unexpected opportunities. Stuck on the Philadelphia-New York train because of a blizzard in January 1867, the women promoted suffrage among "gentlemen and ladies" from all over, including legislators, professional men, and people of other classes. Stone, Stanton, and Anthony separated, each to canvass a different part of the train, each of them gathering good audiences and answering questions.[8] But during the weather that brought the women on this journey to a standstill, the black male cause proceeded apace, emphasizing the increasing discrepancies emerging between women and black men. Illinois, West Virginia, Michigan, Minnesota, Kansas, Maine, and Nevada all ratified between January 15—the date of Blackwell's tract—and January 23, making 15 ratifications to that date.[9] An amendment required 27 out of 36 states: this one was now more than halfway to that number. During this time also the bill "to Fix the Times for the Regular Meetings of Congress"[10] became law on January 22, 1867. Congress was now set for an uninterrupted transition from the 39th to the 40th Congress early in March.

On the afternoon of January 23 in the New York Assembly in Albany, "an immense audience of judges, lawyers, members of the Legislature, and ladies of fashion greeted" Elizabeth Cady Stanton when the Honorable Charles J. Folger, chairman of the Senate Judiciary Committee, introduced her to a hearing before the judiciary committees of both chambers of the assembly.[11] Stanton had asked Frederick Douglass to appear also, offering to shorten her speech,[12] but he chose not to. Only she spoke for the AERA:

> I appear before you at this time, to urge on you the justice of securing to all the people of the State the right to vote for delegates to the coming Constitutional Convention. The discussion of this right involves the consideration of the whole question of suffrage; and especially those sections of your Constitution which interpose insurmountable qualifications to its exercise.
>
> As representatives of the people, your right to regulate all that pertains to the coming Constitutional Convention is absolute. It is for you to say when and where this convention shall be held; how many delegates shall be chosen, and what classes shall be represented. This is your right. It is the opinion of many of the ablest men of the country that, in a revision of a constitution, the State is, for the time being, resolved into its original elements, and that all disfranchised classes should have a voice in such revision

and be represented in such convention. To secure this to the people of the State, is clearly your duty.[13]

Stanton was in Albany attempting to push boundaries in difficult circumstances. Whereas equal voting rights for black men had been considered but rejected in New York as recently as 1860,[14] the right of women had never been contemplated. For April 23's delegate election day, only eligible voters for assembly members in regular elections were so far going to vote.[15] Yet the upcoming constitutional convention, which occurred about every 20 years, presented an opportunity to expand the state's voting criteria, which is what Stanton now aimed for pursuant to a Parker Pillsbury motion at the December 11 AERA meeting in Rochester.[16] Stanton's speech would be the AERA's first foray into state politics; a win could set a precedent for constitutional reforms during the convention, while success would also set a precedent for all states. Outlining her constitutional theory from which she proposed inclusion of black males and women in voting for delegates, she dealt systematically with arguments against expansion of the vote to the excluded classes. Noteworthy in her opening paragraphs is her choice of the words "your constitution"—clearly signaling that, to a woman, the New York State Constitution was not hers. Supporting the proposal to remove the word "white," which restricted the vote in the state largely to white men, Stanton argued in her speech for true universal suffrage that applied equally to men and women. Pointing out that there was nothing in the current state constitution "to prevent women or black men from voting for, or being elected as delegates" to the convention, she said, therefore, that there was "no reason" for the legislature not to "enact that the people elect their delegates to said Convention irrespective of sex or color." She cited precedents from 1801 and 1821 for such action, for "the Legislatures of those years passed laws setting aside all property limitations, and providing that all men black and white, rich and poor should vote for delegates to said Conventions."[17]

Aware that such precedents excluded women, she argued specifically for women:

> The proposition of the republican party to strike the word "white" from the Constitution and thus extend the right of suffrage to all classes of male citizens, placing the men of the State, black and white, foreign and native, ignorant and educated, vicious and virtuous, all alike, above woman's head, gave her a keener sense of her abasement than she had ever felt before. But having neither press nor pulpit to advocate her cause, and fully believing this amendment would pass as a party measure, she used every means within her power to arouse and strengthen the agitation, in the face of the most determined opposition of friends and foes.[18]

Repeatedly she pointed the finger at the framers of the constitution, identifying clearly those who had chosen to retain power themselves, demonstrating that they were responsible for a discriminatory franchise: "White males" are the nobility of this country; they are the privileged order, who have legislated as unjustly for women and negroes as have the nobles of England for their disfranchised classes.... If the history of England has proved that white men of different grades cannot legislate with justice for one another, how can you, Honorable Gentlemen, legislate for women and negroes, who, by your customs, creeds and codes, are placed under the ban of inferiority?"[19] Stanton attacked head-on men's flattery of women while denying them participation in the polity and producing laws disadvantageous to them: "If you dislike this view of the case, and claim that woman is your superior, and, therefore, you place her above all troublesome legislation, to shield her by your protecting care from the rough winds of life, I have simply to say, your statute books are a sad commentary on that position. Your laws degrade, rather than exalt woman; your customs cripple, rather than free; your system of taxation is alike ungenerous and unjust.[20]

She also attacked couverture—which her sources said "virtually represented" woman—as a device to restrict women. Quoting Senator Charles Sumner's "great speech on Equal Rights in the First Session of the 39th Congress," in which he argued for equality for black men in the South citing James Otis from a century before, Stanton reiterated, for women, Otis's position: "No such phrase as virtual representation was known in law or constitution. It is altogether a subtlety and illusion, wholly unfounded and absurd. We must not be cheated by any such phantom or any other fiction of law or politics, or any monkish trick of deceit or hypocrisy."[21]

Almost quoting Senator Morrill, who in December had listed those deplorables who, besides women, were excluded from the D.C. suffrage bill,[22] Stanton castigated lawmakers and laws that consigned "respectable and law-abiding women and 'men of color' to be thrust outside the pale of political consideration with those convicted of bribery, larceny, and infamous crime; and worse than all, with those who bet on elections." She suggested that the women of New York should examine carefully who comprised "the privileged classes of 'white male citizens' who may go to the polls." Potential electors, she said, included men who lived elsewhere because of their job or studies. Laws also prevented the exclusion of those "while kept at any almshouse or other asylum, at public expense ... [or] while confined in any public prison."[23] This state of affairs—the widespread protection of white men and the almost blanket exclusion of women and poorer black men—was scandalous, she held.

Despite arguments that woman suffrage faced, Stanton declared that their time had come: "The extension of suffrage is the political idea of our day, agitating alike the leading minds of both continents. The question of debate in the long past has been the rights of races. This, in our country, was settled by the war, when the black man was declared free and worthy to bear arms in defense of the republic, and the last remnants of aristocracy were scattered before our northern hosts like chaff in the whirlwind. We have now come to the broader idea of individual rights."[24] It was hypocritical, she held, "to reconstruct the South until their own State Constitutions [were] purged of all invidious distinctions among their citizens" when the North applied double standards against women at home: "[If] the North thinks it absurd for its women to vote and hold office, the South thinks the same of its negroes. [If] the North considers its women a part of the family to be represented by the 'white male citizen,' so views the South her negroes. And thus viewing them, the South has never taxed her slaves; but our chivalry never fails to send its tax-gatherers to the poorest widow that owns a homestead. Would you press impartial suffrage on the South, recognize it first at home."[25]

Stanton's speech in Albany on January 23, 1867, ranks among the best of the Reconstruction-era speeches. It was learned, well-researched, cogent, passionate, and to the point. Yet well-reasoned arguments rarely work against closed minded and prejudiced powerbrokers. After the hearing Charles Folger, the Senate Judiciary Committee chairman, submitted a resolution to allow New York's women to vote for Convention delegates. Nine members voted for it, giving the issue some official recognition in the state's record,[26] but it was not enough. Women were not allowed to vote for delegates, and only those black men who already had the vote by meeting property requirements were. No new and unsettling opinions or ideas, therefore, would have a place in the convention.[27] The day of Stanton's Albany speech, Indiana ratified the 14th Amendment. Whether or not she knew of it, she certainly knew about New York's ratification two weeks before of the inclusion of the word "male" in the federal Constitution, "whereby," she protested, "the people [had] sanctioned the disfranchisement of a majority of the loyal citizens of the nation." She added, "Happily for the cause of freedom, the organization we represent here today, the American Equal Rights Association, has registered its protest in the archives of the State against this desecration of the last will and testament of the Fathers."[28] She also rocked the AERA boat when referring to the D.C. suffrage bill by adding, "The thanks of the women of the Nation are especially due to Senator Cowan for his motion to strike out the word 'male,' and to the nine distinguished Senators who voted for his amendment." To say this seemed to ignore the upset in AERA ranks that Cowan's amendment had caused during the Rochester meeting on December 11,[29] but her words reflected closely resolutions from an AERA meeting in Syracuse three days later,[30] so she was adhering to policy. Besides, with Cowan's amendment dead, praise could not defeat black male suffrage in D.C. Stanton's statement demonstrated that she always focused on equality—particularly for women because women were being ignored. Beating this drum was important, for each time the federal amendment was ratified, it reinforced women's inequality.

By January 23, 1867, when Stanton spoke in Albany, 15 states having ratified, the halfway mark was passed and all the concomitant disabilities such constitutionally sanctioned discrimination and exclusion by sex were looming larger. Another revealing reference from Stanton that day was to the fact that the political rights of women concerned both parties. Saying that it was "pleasant to see ... the very able and exhaustive manner in which both Republicans and Democrats pressed [woman's] claims to the ballot, through two entire sessions of the Senate," she said it was "most encouraging to the advocates of the political rights of women." Such bipartisan support confirmed the decision of Anthony and Stanton in 1865 to find support for woman's cause wherever possible.

Stanton's speech was widely reported, the *Albany Evening Journal* of January 24, 1867, commenting that while she had spoken well the possibilities of winning were small. The Judiciary Committee, "Like most men of old-fashioned notions ... are slow to believe that women would be elevated, either in usefulness, or dignity, by being transferred from the drawing room and the nursery to the ballot-box and the forum."[31] However, the *NASS* apparently took umbrage at the mention of Cowan and his attempt to include women in the D.C. suffrage bill, excising references to it along with Stanton's arguments that true universal suffrage was more relevant for Reconstruction than restrictive manhood suffrage.[32] At this time also, the now shaky "friendship of Horace Greeley and the support of the *Tribune*, heretofore our most powerful and faithful allies" finally cracked—again because women refused to defer and support black suffrage only. Greeley, the women reported, argued in "an earnest conversation" with Stanton and Anthony that the times were critical "to the Republican party and the life of the Nation. The word 'white' in our [New York] Constitution at this hour has a significance which 'male' has not. It would be wise and magnanimous in you to hold your claims ... in abeyance until the negro is safe beyond peradventure, and your turn will come next. I conjure you to remember that this is 'the negro's hour,' and your first duty now is to go through the State and plead his claims."[33]

Anthony and Stanton turned this insulting and condescending suggestion down flat. "This is the hour to press woman's claims," they replied. "We have stood with the black man in the Constitution over half a century, and it is fitting now that the constitutional door is open that we should enter with him into the political kingdom of equality. Through all these years he has been the only decent compeer we have had. Enfranchise him, and we are left outside with lunatics, idiots and criminals for another twenty years." Greeley, having failed to make the women submit, quickly retaliated, cutting his coverage of the cause from the *Tribune*.[34]

14. The War
of the Politicians

It is said that woman suffrage will bring odium on negro suffrage! Have the women got so low down in the scale of humanity that their privileges would bring odium upon the enjoyment of the same privileges by the untutored African?—Representative T.E. Noell, House of Representatives, February 18, 1867.

In this fast-paced era of political developments, on January 25 Missouri ratified the 14th Amendment. Three days later Representative Noell succeeded in having his amendment to the D.C. suffrage law read twice. Defeated on a motion to send it to a select committee of the House, it landed in the Committee on the District of Columbia,[1] which traditionally buried unwanted proposals. Meanwhile, Congress's bills to admit Colorado and Nebraska to the union—both with bans on voting discrimination because of race or color, thereby expanding federal reach—sent to the president for his signature on January 16[2] ran aground. On January 28 Johnson vetoed the Colorado bill due partly to an inadequate population count and partly because the then territory had already voted down a voting discrimination ban. The Senate let this bill die and on January 29 the president vetoed the Nebraska bill for similar reasons.[3]

Federal interference by stealth in state constitutions thereby stalled, while the exclusion of women from D.C. suffrage went under assault, for Noell refused to let his amendment go. Conscious that if it were not reported and acted upon quickly it would die with the 39th Congress early in March, he introduced on February 4 three resolutions in the House, the first declaring that as "governments were made for the people … every adult citizen … has the right to vote … and representation" and that "any State which disfranchises any class of its citizens on account of sex is not republican in form and should be overturned by Congress." The second instructed the Committee for the District of Columbia to report his bill of January 28 "without delay." Female suffrage, therefore, rose again, while Noell's resolutions highlighted the high-handed behavior of the Radical Republicans running Congress. His third proposal instructed the Committee on the Judiciary to call a convention with delegates elected by every adult in Massachusetts to create a new constitution "republican in form."[4] This resolution anticipated congressional plans then circulating for the Confederacy, apparently prompted by a proposal by Massachusetts representative Nathaniel P. Banks for replicating Louisiana military rule across the South.[5] The resolution retaliated against political fanaticism born of Massachusetts Puritanism manifesting in Boston through that scourge of Reconstruction weaklings, Wendell Phillips, who on January 24 had appeared before a legislative committee in Massachusetts, objecting to its ratification of the 14th Amendment because it did not go far enough.[6] Noell's resolution, therefore, highlighted Republican postwar double standards regarding the states. The House scheduled the resolutions for debate the next Monday, February 11.[7]

That February 4 Radical Republican senators introduced "an act to provide for the more efficient government of the Rebel States," with a parallel bill introduced in the House on February 5.[8] This act proposed five military districts in the South. A military governor would be able to appoint and remove state officials; compile a register of all voters and call a convention of elected delegates of each of the former Confederate states to draft new constitutions. It applied to the ten Confederate states remaining since Tennessee's readmission to the union in July 1866. Without some of these states complying with ratification, the 14th Amendment would come up short, for 27 out of 36 states in the Union were required to ratify. The stringent measures were designed to bring the mayhem in the South under control and force ratification of the 14th Amendment. For both wings of the AERA, though for differing reasons, failure of the amendment had been a plus; but now ratification was guaranteed—a bitter pill for the combined AERA agenda.

A sweetener for the AERA's black male suffrage supporters, however, was the new Reconstruction bill's suffrage provision deeming that voters comprising all freedmen and white men who took a loyalty oath would choose the convention delegates, while the constitutions would be required to include black male suffrage. In other words, Congress would now extend the precedent of determining black voting laws established with the D.C. suffrage act beyond federal jurisdiction directly into long-established states, both in voting requirements and in new state constitutions. This meant a huge regional victory for the AERA's male suffrage agenda. Yet it was a huge blow to the female suffrage wing—another insult, even, akin to the word "male" in the 14th Amendment. It constituted still another front to fight on in the encroaching tide of sex discrimination across the nation. Once again women had little chance of being heard, for Congress and its supporters in the nation relentlessly ignored them, and the progress of the AERA's joint goals increasingly diverged.

Despite this deteriorating asymmetry, however, the AERA canvass continued,[9] with female, male, black, and white organizers sometimes in a team of two, sometimes four, all attempting to establish secure local chapters while educating the public about true universal suffrage.[10]

Meanwhile, the word "male" marched inexorably on with ratification of the 14th Amendment in Pennsylvania on February 6 and Rhode Island on February 7, 1867, making nineteen states. With only eight more states to go at this point, however, the situation changed slightly on February 8 and 9 when the Senate and the House reintroduced the Nebraska Territory admission bill to override the presidential veto, giving the green light to a new state and making the total number now 37, with 28 instead of 27 ratifications required.[11] Nebraska's admission demanded no voter discrimination against blacks,[12] allowing little likelihood that the new state would reject the 14th Amendment.[13] Meanwhile, the act represented yet another step forward for the race equality agenda, leaving AERA women behind yet again. This relentless advance of reforms ignoring one-half of the AERA's membership could hardly have failed to affect individuals in the AERA and even their thinking about its purpose.

On February 11 debate opened on the three resolutions of Representative Noell on woman suffrage and his amendment to the D.C. suffrage law. Anticipating Noell's later arrival, Democrat Charles Augustus Eldridge had the clerk read into the record the memorial of the AERA, previously presented but not read on January 3. Eldridge said he was not necessarily in favor of Noell's resolutions but declared, "My object in presenting [this memorial] was that the distinguished ladies who sent it might have a hearing in this House, as no advocate of their rights was present at the time the resolutions came up." Another representative tried to stop this.[14] By this time, Noell had appeared, to begin immediately his speech on "Equality of Suffrage." Overrunning his time, the rest was held over to the next week. On February 12, with the Military Reconstruction bill's conduct through the legislative process only a matter of time, Noell delivered a second major speech castigating the Radical Republicans for their conduct of the peace, which he characterized as "a new war—the war of the politicians,"[15] in which "the Constitution is now swept away by the unwritten constitution of the mob law."[16] He called the rule of the radicals a dictatorship, and the object of the "act to provide for the more efficient government of the Rebel States" as "not to give the people a voice, but more effectually to stifle their voice."[17]

On February 13 Wisconsin ratified the 14th Amendment, bringing the ratified total to 20. Only eight more ratifications were required to enshrine the word "male" in the Constitution, to exclude women specifically for the first time and to force states to enfranchise freedmen and avoid penalties. The dreams from the Founding Fathers of state constitutional diversity with differences reflecting each state community were dissolving with this headlong pursuit of partial and unequal justice. Supporting the unequal national agenda was the report from the Maine Joint Judiciary Committee's investigation, commissioned a month before, into the possibility of woman suffrage in that state. The committee concluded that such an amendment was "inexpedient."[18]

Back in Congress on February 18, Noell of Missouri completed his interrupted speech on woman suffrage, delivering an impassioned, comprehensive, and erudite attack on arguments against women's enfranchisement and women's roles. He posited that the responsibility for the degraded position of women in the world generally and in the United States could be laid on a society that restricted their education, opportunities, and expectations. "Are we not guarding the women to death?" he asked. "Let the women have an equal chance to take care of themselves." The typical education for women from wealthy families prepared them only for finding a husband with money. To this end, he declared, "women are sold like cattle among savage and civilized nations," while this "bartering of intelligent human beings to the highest bidder" in the marriage market was the cause of many unhappy

Wendell Phillips, c. 1853–1860, declared the "Negro's hour" in May 1865. He set the stage for the betrayal of women after the Civil War despite all their abolitionist work. His agenda led later to Jim Crow laws. Phillips had campaigned against slavery for many years, becoming second only to William Lloyd Garrison in anti-slavery. Despite the good he may have done for black men and his pre-war advocacy of woman's rights, his prejudice, discrimination, short-sightedness, and dubious record in handling woman's rights characterize his later activity, particularly beginning at the end of the Civil War (Library of Congress).

unions. Noell was saying little more than what women themselves had said for nearly a century. Judith Sargent Murray, for example, in her publication of 1790, *On the Equality of the Sexes,* stated that it was women's inadequate education and nothing inherently deficient in women that made them appear—and act—as if they were inferior to men.[19] In truth women were raised for marriage, and the wealthier their background the greater the competition in the marriage market.

Women might not want the vote, Noell conceded, but that was no reason not to enfranchise them: most slaves had never asked for emancipation, yet they got it anyway. Besides, even if women had the vote, it did not mean that female voters would flood elections, for they could choose to exercise their right or not. Without the right, however, they did not have the choice. Female voting was an imperative, he continued. "The women cannot fight and they have always lost their rights" in what he called "the game of grab," for which he excoriated extreme Republicans: "The Radicals have the power and will adopt any expedient to perpetuate it.... Talk to a Radical about justice? You had as well sing love-songs to a mantua-maker's dummy." Woman's problems permeated society. "While the upper ten need the ballot to teach them that they are mortal and are to be the helpmeets of men in politics as well as household affairs, the lower million need it to give them an equal chance with their fellow-mortals in their life struggle, their labor for bread," he said, using the same argument Radicals used to push for enfranchising freedmen. Pointing to Congress's demonstrated disparity in the treatment of women and black men he added that, while "all over the North we sing the plaintive strains of suffering negrodom," the *Song of the Shirt*—the plaint of female sweatshop workers[20]—"is not fashionable." He declared it a fallacy that women's enfranchisement would somehow contaminate black males: if women were supposed to be the embodiment of virtue, that contention did not hold water.

Like Cowan before him, Noell faced accusations of insincerity; yet anyone arguing that Noell was attempting to expunge black male voting rights in Washington, D.C., by his proposal was wrong: black male voting rights had been the law there since January. Noell did not propose to revoke it but only to expand the electorate. Challenges to Noell's motivations by such accusations, therefore, were mud-slinging attempts to destroy a measure when no reasonable arguments against it existed. The largely unspoken concern of opponents was at best the potential dilution of all male electoral decisions by female voters, at worst men's loss of control of political decisions by "strong-minded," thinking women. Like many who spoke in the D.C. bill debate in December, Noell obviously wanted women to have the vote. For many reasons—including fierce opposition to Radical Republicanism as a whole—he was passionate about it, hence his introduction of such unusual resolutions in Congress and this fiery fight for the cause. He even believed that women's enfranchisement could occur perhaps as early as the 41st Congress—just a couple of years hence. His position was the opposite of the congressmen who said in the District suffrage bill debate that they could not logically argue against female enfranchisement and that they would vote for it—some partly because it was a safe gesture, as they could not see the amendment to that bill succeeding.

Noell was a freshman Republican in the 39th Congress but a Democrat on reelection to the 40th. He served from March 4, 1865. His two speeches represented the culmination of his life's work. One of them spoke out against tyrannical government. The other represents the most impassioned fight in Congress for woman suffrage at a time when women had been forced to struggle fiercely to be heard—yet only as a whisper—by national representatives intent on a discriminatory and self-serving agenda during a period of opportunity for fundamental constitutional reform. With the life of the 39th Congress fast fading when he spoke, Noell's gesture, as was to be expected, went nowhere. Soon he was sworn into the 40th Congress, but afterwards he became ill and died in St. Louis, Missouri, on October 3, 1867, aged only 27. He remains today the youngest representative to die while still a member of Congress.

Near the end of his speech Noell noted the role women played in supporting and, specifically, raising money for "radical orators" when such men had lied to them and betrayed them repeatedly. Then he warned, "If the prominent women of the United States withdraw their support from the Radical party, it will fall to rise no more. If you provoke opposition from such women as Mrs. Mott, Mrs. Stanton, Anna Dickinson, Lucy Stone, and Fannie Gage, they will drive your radical orators from every stump in the North."

Although he was young when he died—much younger than most of the women he named—Noell had stood up for what he believed in. He again marked the trail of the history of women's long struggle with Congress for equality. With Noell, Senator Cowan and Representative Eldridge, who read out the AERA memorial, at least three non–Radicals—two Democrat representatives and one Democrat-leaning senator—had emerged since December 1866 as champions of the equality of women in the postwar United States. Although the group remained small, these names lengthened the roster of such supporters existing since December 1865. In these circumstances Noell's warning that Republicans could lose the support of women indicated that it might become a reality sooner than had ever been considered possible. If nothing else, however, Noell's stand ensured that the controversy over woman suffrage during the 39th Congress went out with all guns blazing, even as Congress moved beyond immediate issues of suffrage to the reorganization of the former Confederate states.

15. Enter Kansas

Your laws degrade, rather than exalt woman; your customs cripple, rather than free; your system of taxation is alike ungenerous and unjust.—Elizabeth Cady Stanton, 1867, *History of Woman Suffrage II* (1887), 273.

Ever since Congress had passed the 14th Amendment it had become a major issue in the states; and while Noell fought for woman suffrage in the East, politicians out west were similarly engaged. In Kansas, when the legislature convened in Constitution Hall at 429 South Kansas Avenue on January 8, 1867, the amendment finally reached center stage there. Governor Samuel Johnson Crawford issued his message to a joint meeting of the House and Senate of the legislature the next day, "exhorting members and Senators to ratify the Amendment and hoping that Kansas, in the first legislative enactment of this session, will give the unanimous vote of her Legislature in favor of this measure."[1] On January 10 the House completed the formalities and passed the ratification resolution. On January 11 the Senate passed it,[2] and on January 18 the governor approved it and forwarded it to the United States secretary of state.[3]

In his message the governor also raised "the question of impartial suffrage." Advocating enfranchisement, he said, "I know of no reason, in law or ethics, why a loyal citizen that has shouldered his musket in defense of the National flag; that pays his taxes; that is amenable to the law in every respect, should be excluded from a participation in every right and franchise that others enjoy, who are no more worthy because of their race or color."[4] By these words, under the guise of impartiality, Governor Crawford introduced into the Kansas debate the male-only agenda of the Congress in Washington, D.C. After that the House introduced an amendment to remove "white" from the Constitution. This ran into trouble when members attempted to amend it to include women. The Senate introduced two separate amendments, one for black men and one for women.[5] By January 31 the House had adopted the proposal to excise "white" from the state constitution, at the same time rejecting proposals in the same measure to strike out the word "male."[6] When the successful House resolution—without woman suffrage—proceeded to the upper chamber, Senator Samuel Newitt Wood introduced an amendment to the House's measure to reinstate the original proposal for female suffrage.[7] In the end, the two proposals passed separately, with the woman suffrage amendment proposal succeeding first, on February 14. During these legislative maneuverings in Kansas, therefore, woman's rights for once leapfrogged over civil rights for men in the contentious Reconstruction era—a first in the nation's history.

Suddenly a large expansion of the state electorate was possible, with adult women perhaps soon being eligible to vote along with men. For once, the larger part of the AERA program was in one state ahead of the black male rights program—a novel situation for the AERA. Yet under the circumstances this scenario was politically incorrect, not just in terms of national policy but also in a nation with minds still filled with ideas of distinct sex roles that went far beyond the bounds of biology, for if the word "white" was not tackled a franchise based on sex would exclude men based on race. To politicians, black women likely did not matter. The unique situation was short-lived, therefore, for on February 18 the Kansas legislature passed another proposal to amend the state constitution, this time to remove the word "white" and open the vote to blacks.

Multiple possibilities emerged from these proposed amendments. If white male voters approved both measures, all adults would qualify to vote. If the current white male voters approved only the woman suffrage amendment, all white adults—male or female—would be able to vote. If the white male voters approved only the black male suffrage proposal, all males would be eligible to vote and all women excluded.[8] In terms of justice and republican principles, the proposals were together equally important. Yet the woman suffrage amendment was the more critical, for it was the thin end of the wedge. No matter what happened that November, the 14th Amendment when ratified would still impel the state at some point to recognize black males as electors. There was nothing similar on the horizon for women. The suffrage scenario was fraught with uncertainties, however: black suffrage might benefit from linkage with woman suffrage, or vice-versa. Equally, either could bring the other down. On the other hand, with the two uncoupled, success of either or both might happen.

Politicians treated the two measures very differently. The official line promoted black male suffrage. On January 9 Governor Crawford did so when he called for ratification of the 14th Amendment in his message to the legislature.[9] Republicans supported him. Black suffrage "was a plank in the platform upon which our State ticket ran. In the canvass the subject was discussed in every county if not in every precinct," wrote one newspaper. Despite considerable opposition, "what did the people do? … elected the Republican ticket and endorsed the Republican platform, negro suffrage and all, by nearly 12,000 majority."[10] If this represented all public opinion, it reflected the facts of national policy and the implications of the 14th Amendment and any other measures Radical Reconstruction might impose on the states, plus the apparent need to prevent electoral penalties by unequal racial voting laws. One newspaper, recognizing the unpopularity of black voting rights with some, wrote that the original amendment gave opponents the chance to come out of the woodwork. Specifically, it gave one legislative member, a Mr. C.E. Parker, "an opportunity to strike a blow against 'nigger equality.'"[11] Another emphasized the political realities: "We are unquestionably going to place the ballot in the hands of our colored citizens, north and south, within the next five years. It is too late now to argue the justice or expediency of this measure; both points are universally conceded."[12] "We consider negro suffrage in Kansas a fixed fact," the same paper said only weeks later. "The amendment will unquestionably be adopted by overwhelming majorities."[13] Passing black suffrage appeared to be a matter of political necessity and resignation at the state level and benefited from Republican Party support.

Expanding suffrage to women, on the other hand, while supported by some, was viewed as unnecessary by many and was unwanted or never considered by still more. Nowhere in the governor's message to the legislature did women appear, while manhood suffrage masquerading as "impartial suffrage" obliterated women while creating the impression of inclusion and justice. Even Anthony's brother played a double game, masking his personal opposition to the measure behind his then pro-woman suffrage *Leavenworth Bulletin*.[14] Overt opposition erupted when the Senate reintroduced the proposal to strike out "male" along with "white." Castigating senators for the move, one newspaper stated "the Legislature is 'acting the fool' on the suffrage question…. If they intend to let the people decide the question of negro suffrage, why don't they finish the thing at once? … [I]t must be done, sooner or later." This writer, presuming to know what he was talking about, also declared suffrage to be an insult to women. They "will hardly thank the members of the Legislature for linking their fate with that of the negroes," he said.[15]

A competitor, however, used AERA arguments for woman suffrage, even scathingly dismissing "the talk about 'woman's sphere' [as] mere nauseating twaddle." If women know nothing about politics, this writer[16] said, it was excusable for, "of course they will not be interested in public affairs, so long as they remain lifelong aliens and minors." But, she summarized, "Every argument which can possibly be adduced in favor of granting this right to black or white men applies with equal force to black and white women." This writer underlined support for woman suffrage with a stirring call to the most general of republican principles, close to the AERA platform: "Why can't we have a really democratic social organization here in Kansas? And where, if not in Kansas?"[17] This writer conceded that some people thought that striking "male" out was "intended to throw cold water upon the movement for negro suffrage" but said, "We think that it is offered in good faith and in earnest."[18] This middle-ground view had precedent in Kansas history, for women and their supporters had actively fought for woman's rights and were partially successful during the Kansas constitutional debates in the late 1850s. This movement was not dead in 1867.[19] Black "suffragers" tended to see anyone else's measure as an "attempt to load it with amendments under which they know it must go down." Woman suffrage was "strangulation by amendments." Black male suffrage was "a pure question of justice," but "it has a hard time to stand alone and staggers terribly when anything else is put upon its back." It should be "unencumbered by less important 'side issues.'"[20] Anti-female prejudice and the old saw of "the negro's hour" continued to count for much, as during the debates "some members voted against [woman suffrage] on the grounds of expediency, not wishing to endanger the movement in behalf of manhood suffrage by less popular attachments."[21]

Despite the criticisms, the woman suffrage amendment represented a huge victory, for it had been necessary to win a two-thirds majority in both chambers to pass.[22] It was also a huge anomaly in the United States at the time, one that raised the delicious thought that perhaps women would not be reduced to nothing during Reconstruction. It might be popular and was an opportunity to win where none was ever expected. "We shall not be surprised if both questions are decided in the affirmative, by the people," stated one newspaper.[23] Anthony, writing from Albany to Amy Post in Rochester, exulted: "Don't you cry *all Hail* to *young* heroic Kansas?—How glorious if she shall now teach the nation the one & only way to rebuild our Union, as she ten years ago taught it the one & only way out of slavery[24]—Do you see she has submitted to her people the question of striking both '*white male*' from her Constitution?"[25]

16. The End of Cooperation

Yesterday [Wendell Phillips] said the ballot, in the hands of the negro, was a talisman to bring to him every weal, and ward off every woe, while today he said that it was nothing in the hand of woman, that [it] can do nothing for us, that we must go home and go to work for ourselves.—Josephine Griffing, Eleventh National Woman's Rights Convention, 1866.

By late February 1867 Representative Noell's fight for woman suffrage had slammed into the brick wall of Congress. But the 14th Amendment advanced, impelling further action: Kansas's constitutional amendment for black male suffrage for November's referendum was a result of ratification.

Black men had hardly had to fight for these victories, for others largely did the work for an official agenda. With such friends, black activists naturally gravitated to support radical reformers and the Republican Party. Conversely, all the measures that the Radicals rammed through either ignored women or affected them adversely. White politicos opposed woman suffrage as a danger to their agenda, and black men objected to it as a threat to their own equality. For Republicans and reformers, the path to political equality for men of either race was exclusion based on sex. Women were useful only if they supported and campaigned for the men's agenda. None of this was equality. With such friends, it is no wonder that Stanton and Anthony late in 1865 had begun to hunt for support outside the Republican Party. Yet they continued to work with their erstwhile reform colleagues because their equality depended on the very men who opposed them. The bright spot that the Kansas amendment represented, surprisingly, was due to Kansas Republicans, indicating perhaps that women could rely on Republicans there for support.

The potential consequences of the contrasting circumstances of women and black men for the AERA were huge. The imbalance in progress in the organization's two wings raised reasonable questions about its stability, for imbalance mocked the AERA's reason for existence. Even so, with the two amendments in Kansas for November, the AERA appeared intact, while victory for the Kansas measures would represent a victory for the AERA's founding principle of equal rights for all. Now, with the Kansas measures set for voting and Noell's congressional stand for women ended, the AERA's focus was New York, where the constitutional convention's date was set for June. During early 1867 the AERA managed at least 30 meetings, leaving where possible a formal local AERA chapter established.[1] A diverse group of campaigners—female, male, black and white—crisscrossed each other's paths racing to engagements.[2] Meanwhile, Congress largely devoted February to legislation to sidestep the contrivances of the 14th Amendment. The Military Reconstruction measure became law over the presidential veto on March 2.[3] That same day, the 39th Congress officially ended, but following the new rules[4] the 40th Congress opened on Monday, March 4, 1867.

The Military Reconstruction Act, through a requirement for the re-entry of former Confederate states to the union to guarantee freedmen's votes, fulfilled postwar demands of radical reformers and politicians, while Congress could now focus on denying southern white men the vote.[5] It also meant that abolitionists, radicals, black men, and even many AERA members no longer had any reason to oppose the 14th Amendment's shortcomings. One of the reasons for the AERA's existence—the common goal between two apparently disparate elements—was, therefore, destroyed.[6] Wendell Phillips—the "glorious, good Phillips," as Stanton had called him in December 1864[7]—now marked the occasion by pulling the plug on AERA financing.

By March 6[8] Anthony was writing to Stanton's cousin, Gerrit Smith. "To whom shall our Equal Rights work look if not to you at this hour of its great need?" she asked. "To the surprise" of the AERA committee, "the Hovey Committee refuse to do more than pay the salaries of Mr. Pillsbury" and herself for the New York campaign, she wrote. "We thought we had sure promise of at least $3,000—from the Hovey Fund,"—money earmarked to pay for several speakers, countless publications, and debts the AERA had already incurred. She begged for an advance on Smith's future contributions to the AERA to pay the salary of Charles Lenox Remond, who was in particularly difficult straits. She asked for Smith's help in finding new backing, because "if only we had the money we could carry the Convention up to equal Suffrage without a shadow of a doubt." She ended with this: "You will hear my appeals to you, Mr. Smith, I know—for your love for the principles of equal rights to all is never failing."[9]

Phillips' motivation is crystal clear. He had never wanted the AERA or the encumbrance of woman suffrage in the first place; the AERA embodied a sticky little matter of principle, specifically of equality for all Americans, essentially amounting to true republican principles—none of which had informed Phillips' actions since the end of the war. With the cry of "the Negro's hour" fulfilled in the South by congressional diktat, it was time to turn to the enfranchisement of black men in New York. Phillips needed nothing to complicate that agenda, and continuing to support the AERA's campaign for black male suffrage was a waste of resources when the Anti-Slavery Society focused on it exclusively. In early March 1867, therefore, Phillips saw it was time to ditch the AERA.

This was downright mean, if not contemptible. The Hovey Fund stipulated that if slavery were abolished the money was to be redirected to other goals, with woman's rights a major beneficiary.[10] During the war, Phillips kept the *Anti-Slavery Standard* afloat with it,[11] at the same time forcing women to beg for help to organize the WNLL abolition petition.[12] He was still using Hovey money for the *Standard* in 1867 when he pulled the plug on the AERA—despite constitutional abolition. He constantly redefined "slavery" and "anti-slavery" to justify maintaining a public platform and subsidize an otherwise financially fragile newspaper to goad politicians to extreme measures. For anyone extraneous to his own goals, he was untrustworthy, manipulative, and slippery. He acted without the integrity expected of a charitable fund trustee, while he fecklessly pushed the AERA organizers into deep financial straits when his "Negro's Hour" campaign was largely won. The loss of financing for the AERA was less problematical for the official agenda of black rights, but the women had long been marginalized and this episode was just another turn of the screw. Having excised women from Reconstruction reforms and played politics over the formation of the AERA, Phillips then ensured that the AERA's work, especially as it related to woman's rights, received ever decreasing coverage in the *Standard.* Now he left it left high and dry by misappropriating its funds. The women should perhaps have recognized that working with him was useless.

The same day Anthony frantically wrote to Gerrit Smith, the New York Senate effectively hammered another nail into the coffin containing women's aspirations by voting down a proposal to include women as electors for delegates to the constitutional convention. Also denied an opportunity to vote for the convention were poorer black men excluded by property qualifications.[13] That day, also, Stone spoke for universal suffrage before the New Jersey legislature. She excoriated the state, declaring, "In defiance of the letter of the Constitution and of the Statutes and uniform practice of a generation [in New Jersey from 1807], women and negroes were disfranchised by an arbitrary act of the Legislature, without discussion and almost without comment."[14] Targeting political hypocrisy, she demanded, "With what consistency can New Jersey continue to disfranchise her 5,000 colored men who would compose less than one twenty-fifth part of her voting population, when her Senators and a majority of her representatives have compelled South Carolina to enfranchise the colored race who form three-fifths of her entire population?"[15] She concluded: "Let no man dream that National prosperity and peace can be secured by merely giving suffrage to 800,000 freedmen, while that sacred right is denied to eight millions of American women."[16] In 1867 Stone, an original stalwart woman's rights worker, adamantly supported true equal suffrage while keeping in mind Frederick Douglass's admonition at the AERA convention in Albany the previous November that politicians—specifically Democrats—would support woman suffrage as a ploy to "split the reformers on racial lines"[17] and prevent black male suffrage. Her commitment to working with and for both groups shone through this speech in New Jersey.[18]

That March, Stone was in the AERA offices in New York when a letter arrived for Anthony from Kansas senator Samuel N. Wood asking for help with speakers for a suffrage convention he was organizing the next month in Topeka.[19] Wood, a veteran supporter of woman's rights, had spearheaded the inclusion of women in the electoral reforms that January through a separate suffrage amendment. Anthony and Stanton could not head west for several months: they were working on the AERA's New York suffrage campaign, while Anthony had started planning the AERA's first anniversary meeting for the Church of the Puritans on May 9. The New York Constitutional Convention would start in June. Lucy Stone and her husband Henry Blackwell—Stone with Blackwell's persuasion—agreed to go to Kansas. Now even more Anthony resented Phillips' withdrawal of the AERA's funding. Complaining to Anna Dickinson, she said, "Our greatest grief is that the Committee *lavish* on the *A.S. Standard* this year $3,600.00—while that paper does not *officially plead* the whole question of Suffrage as an *inherent* right of Woman as the Negro *man*—when by the reading of the Will—all the *agencies now employed* should '*believe*' in the equal Right of Woman—And now, since nearly the *whole Fund is* gone—& gone to the breaking of the chain of chattelism, it seems to me, the *spirit* of the will gives no dollar *specially to the black man*— but every dollar *equally* to all *men* & all *women*."[20]

With a second front unexpectedly opening in Kansas the 14th Amendment marched on. Abolitionists had so far successfully opposed ratification in Massachusetts because of its shortcomings in enfranchising black men, with Phillips appearing before a committee of the general court protesting the amendment on January 24.[21] But when the March 2 Military Reconstruction Act removed all obstacles, opponents in the state gave up. With ratification on March 20, Massachusetts was the twenty-first out of twenty-eight states required to ratify.[22] In such circumstances Anthony's anger and protestations about Phillips' machinations with the Hovey Fund are understandable.

Yet there was still the Jackson Fund. "Mr. Phillips was unwilling that any money from the Jackson fund should be used for [Kansas] as he did not want the question agitated at this time, but as Miss Anthony and Lucy Stone constituted a majority of the committee, they appropriated $1,500 for it."[23] Financially armed, Stone and Blackwell left for Kansas on March 26.[24]

17. Stepping Forward in Kansas

The former slave man of the South has learned his lesson of oppression and wrong of his old master ... [and] they think the wife has no right to her earnings.—Frances Dana Gage, *Proceedings of the First Anniversary of the American Equal Rights Association*, (1867), 26.

With $1,500 of the Jackson Fund money, Stone and Blackwell turned up on April 2 in the small frontier town of Topeka, the capital city of Kansas, for what opponents there derisively called "Sam Wood's Convention." Arriving early, they persuaded Governor Samuel J. Crawford and former Lieutenant Governor J.P. Root to attend. The couple's "arrival set a buzz going"[1] and the news that Anthony and Stanton would come later stirred opponents of woman suffrage.[2]

Reporting the first major victory of "Sam Wood's Convention," the two recaptured the campaign rhetoric. The governor "insisted on the term 'impartial,' which he said meant 'right,' and we must make [opponents] use it, so that there would be no occasion for any other State Association" to debase it again, wrote Stone.[3] Voting to fight for black male and woman suffrage, the convention formed the State Impartial Suffrage Association (SISA). Prominent men assumed key positions, with others from throughout Kansas put in strategic roles. "We have on our side all the shrewdest politicians and all the best class of men and women in this State," wrote Blackwell.[4] "[As a result]," he continued, "our meetings are doing much towards organizing and concentrating public sentiment in our favor, and the papers are beginning to show front in our favor."[5]

The two were obviously thrilled about the SISA, its support of the AERA agenda, and the important people falling in behind true equality. Even Anthony's brother, previously wobbly on woman's rights, reported a meeting was arranged for Leavenworth.[6] The state canvass was falling into place, with engagements planned for six days a week from April 7 to May 5,[7] later extended to May 20.[8] Stone's fee of $100 for an engagement in Lawrence would go to the campaign. "Everything has conspired to help us in this State. Gov. Robinson and Sam. Wood have quietly set a ball in motion which nobody in Kansas is now strong enough to stop," wrote Blackwell.[9]

Stone and Blackwell had already overcome significant obstacles. "We fought and won a pitched battle at Topeka," wrote Blackwell,[10] winning delegates to support both amendments. A Methodist minister and a Lawrence attorney, who was "instructed" to use the word "impartial" "as it had been used for the last two years," to mean one issue and to "drop the woman," wrote Stone, found her and "Mrs. [Clarina] Nichols ... down upon him, and the whole convention, except the Methodist, was against him."[11] By an almost unanimous vote, the amendments were accepted together. "A delegation from Lawrence came up specially to get the woman dropped," wrote Blackwell. "The good God upset a similar delegation from Leavenworth bent on the same object, and prevented them from reaching Topeka at all."[12] By late in April, he wrote confidently, "I do not believe that the Negro Suffrage men can well bolt or back out now,"[13] and enthused that "Wood has helped off more runaway slaves than any man in Kansas [and] has always been true both to the negro and the woman ... [and] while he advocates both, he fully realizes the wider scope and far greater grandeur of the battle for woman."[14]

Negative attitudes, however, dismayed them. A lawyer at the "Sam Wood" Convention had declared, "'If I was a negro, I would not want the woman hitched on to my skirts,' etc. He made a mean speech,"[15] wrote Stone. "[T]he negroes dislike and distrust [Wood] because he has never allowed the word white to be struck out, unless the word male should be struck out also," wrote Blackwell.[16] Black men found women an unwelcome burden, while sex prejudice was rampant. "One swears at women who want to wear the breeches; another wonders whether we ever heard of a fellow named Paul."[17] A woman's brother declared "'he had had a woman who was under the sod, but that if she had ever said she wanted to vote he would have pounded her to death!'"[18] Another said he was "not going to put women on an equality with niggers," said Stone.[19] Still another told Stone that "no decent woman would be running over the country talking nigger and woman."[20] Suffrage women, on the other hand, "are grand," she wrote, "and it will be a shame past all expression if they don't get the right to vote. One in Wyandotte said she carried petitions all through the town for female suffrage, and not one woman in ten refused to sign. Another in Lawrence said they sent up two large petitions from there. So they have been at the Legislature, like the heroes they really are, and it is not possible for the husbands of such women to back out, though they have sad lack of principle and a terrible desire for office."[21]

Kansas politics were complex. Too soon, Republicans were divided, while blacks were more likely to be against both women and joint campaigning. The Democrats circled, either ready to support women only or to pounce on any opportunity they could exploit. Even though Anthony's brother had earlier seemed on board, "the Republicans have decided to drop the woman, [Daniel Read] Anthony with the others," wrote Stone. On the other hand, she said, "Democrats all over the State are preparing to take us up. They are a small minority, with nothing to lose, and utterly unscrupulous, while all who will work with Sam Wood will work with anybody."[22] Blackwell confirmed this ten days later.[23]

While Stone and Blackwell provided much information on Kansas politicking at the time, they hardly understood the full extent of the infighting, mud-slinging, double-dealing, backstabbing, second-guessing, and jockeying for position in the arena where the AERA was now operating. As visitors to the state, their grasp of the import of the loyalties of convenience of Wood and of Stone's other supporter, former governor Robinson, was imperfect. The men's political dalliances with the Democrats made Republicans and black men suspicious, while Robinson's quick canvass for Democrat support for woman suffrage increased the distrust.[24] Wood's involvement was a problem rendering "the female suffrage question ... more unpopular than if taken upon its simple merits," one newspaper noted. "The people have come to regard anything with which he is connected, as a humbug or a swindle."[25] Kansas Republican intra-party strife also pitted Robinson against the establishment. Even though both referenda were Republican measures, the party had still to announce its plan of campaign, while half the party at least was against woman suffrage. Many now claimed that the SISA's founding was a ploy to hijack official Republican policy and prevent it from declaring support of black suffrage alone.[26]

Stone and Blackwell also seriously underestimated the significance of the black male position. Blackwell wrote exultantly after the Topeka meeting about a Leavenworth delegation whose train's late arrival prevented their upending the plans for forming the SISA. But the upset that made the formation of the SISA remarkably easy annoyed the Kansas State Executive Committee of Colored Men, a group that had been using "impartial" since October 1866 for black male suffrage. They opposed both woman suffrage and the formation of the SISA with its combined battle plan for women and blacks.[27] The first skirmish that Stone and Blackwell fought and apparently won in Kansas, therefore, appeared to these men as an attack on black suffrage, while the manner of the SISA creation confirmed their view that Wood supported woman suffrage to destroy black male suffrage. From the start, therefore, though Stone and Blackwell might feel enthusiastic about the welcome audiences unused to a female speaker gave them, they underestimated the opposition they encountered.[28]

Charles Langston, the pro-suffrage black male leader, apparently believed the SISA was well-funded from the East for women's benefit: news reporting of the early April Topeka meeting, which Antoinette Brown Blackwell attended, had stated that money would be "raised to prosecute a vigorous canvass in favour" of the female suffrage measure.[29] Langston told Wood he was willing to cooperate with the SISA but for black suffrage, for which he said he was attempting to raise funds. He seemed to expect the SISA to supply two separate sets of speakers at every meeting to address both issues separately.[30] Stone and Blackwell therefore, from April of 1867, faced many problems and seriously misunderstood the black men of the state.[31] Stone's national reputation as a speaker raised considerable interest when she arrived, but opposition to the campaign appeared quickly. The *Emporia News* came out against on April 12 because it said voters would not support it: "Not that we are opposed to female suffrage, but ... there are hundreds if not thousands of voters in the State who are in favor of what is commonly called 'negro suffrage,' who will not support the proposition to strike the word 'male' from our State Constitution."[32]

Another challenge was that the woman part of the AERA campaign was isolated in the West. Kansas may have become more positive with the formation of the SISA and Stone and Blackwell's tour, but Stone complained to Stanton about eastern newspapers and woman suffrage. "*The Independent* is taken in many families here [and if it] would take up this question, and every week write for it, as it does for the negro, that paper alone could save this State; and with this, all the others."[33] Stone wrote she would try to write an up-to-date report for the upcoming AERA convention, and she directed a parting shot at the eastern radical reformers and antislavery men. "I hope not a man will be asked to speak at the convention," she wrote angrily. "If they volunteer very well, but I have been for the last time on my knees to Phillips ... or any of them. If they help now, they should ask us, and not we them."[34] Stone was pledged to fight for true equality and always worked with the men, but these words signal a deep rift—almost a break—with her male reform colleagues. This is startling coming from a member of the broadly based AERA, significant coming from Stone.

Some warning lights also flashed in the otherwise positive reports of Stone and Blackwell from Kansas. "[Wood] has warmer friends and bitterer enemies than almost any man in the State," wrote Blackwell. "He is true as steel" and along with "Gov. Robinson ... a masterly tactician, cool, wary, cautious, decided, and brave as a lion," and they "would suffice to save Kansas."[35] But he later added, "If [Wood] should die next month I should consider the election lost."[36] The SISA coalition, in truth, was fragile, with one newspaper opining that Wood was an obstacle for women, the referendum being lost anyway. Women's supporters would be better to shunt him to the background if they wanted a chance of success.[37] Blackwell seemed to anticipate trouble, with some politicians readying themselves for a fight. Again, he raised Anthony's brother's wobbles, saying, "I am glad ... that our friend D.R.

Anthony is out for both propositions in the Leavenworth Bulletin. But his sympathies are so especially with the negro."[38]

More trouble was brewing behind the scenes. Early in April Charles Langston complained that the Topeka convention "ignored our movement entirely" and he now attempted to undermine the SISA program by enticing Wood into a pro-black male and anti-woman suffrage coalition.[39] With a covert attempt to split the SISA/AERA forces and the considerable amount of negativity already coming the way of their campaign, it was obvious that full-time campaigners were needed throughout the next six months. Blackwell insisted in his April 21 letter that, as Daniel Anthony was inconsistent on women, "we must have Susan out here to strengthen his hands."[40] In fact, reinforcements from the East were essential. Blackwell wrote to Stanton, saying that she, Anthony, and Douglass "must come to this State early next September ... prepared to make sixty speeches each."[41] "I fully expect we shall carry the State," Stone wrote to Stanton, "but it will be necessary to have a good force here in the fall, and you will have to come."[42]

In Kansas, Blackwell focused on the challenges, failing to realize that the repeated calls for reinforcements created a huge problem: Anthony was getting frantic about financing anything, never mind a push in Kansas. The final AERA New York rally closed in Buffalo on April 12—the campaign cut short because of Phillips' high-handed withdrawal of Hovey Funds.[43] On April 21 Anthony answered a letter from Wood in Kansas. Although by then she had received several missives, "not one of the sources ... give me the slightest light as to *financial possibilities* in Kansas—, except that Lucy Stone got $100 for her Lawrence Lecture for the Treasury of your State I.S. Association," she wrote. Stone's lectures, it seemed, failed on fund-raising—if so, perhaps because of Jackson Fund financing. But, wrote Anthony, "The fact here at the east is, that *we cannot meet expenses*."[44] While everyone is "really glad to have us work," no one, right or left of the political spectrum, nor even the religious community or newspapers was willing to help pay for it. No newspaper of significant influence or circulation had endorsed woman suffrage.[45] With no money to print anything new, Anthony arranged to send to Kansas material from their stocks of old campaign literature.[46] She asked Wood to send her a list of requirements and said "we will make the strongest possible appeal to get the *means* to help you *make Kansas* the first state to give *Universal Suffrage* ... the first [state] to redeem herself from the last vestige of Class & caste."[47] She said that she likely would leave for Kansas by September 1 and would "trust to luck" for her own expenses, but she could vouch for no one else.

On May 1 Stone wrote back expressing sympathy for Anthony, "with no one to help" in New York, and thanking her for the material she had sent. She castigated Horace Greeley and Theodore Tilton: "The *Tribune* and *Independent* alone could, if they would urge universal suffrage, as they do negro suffrage, carry this whole nation upon the only just plane of equal human rights. What a power to hold, and not use!" This calculated failure kept her awake at night. She vowed, "They MUST take it up. I shall see them the very first thing when I go home."[48] Stone challenged Phillips' thievery. "At your [AERA] meeting … I think you should insist that all of the Hovey fund used for the *Standard* and Anti-Slavery purposes … must be returned with interest to the three causes which by the express terms of the will were to receive all of the fund when slavery was abolished."[49] She also wanted an end to duplicitous anti-woman rhetoric. "[I hope]," she said, "you will not fail to rebuke the cowardly use of … 'universal,' and 'impartial' and 'equal' applied to hide a dark skin, and an unpopular client." She attacked the hypocrisy of pro-black reformers who criticized thirteen New Jersey votes against "negro suffrage." This "is unutterably contemptible from the lips or pen of those whose words, acts, and votes are not against ignorant and degraded negroes, but against every man's mother, wife, and daughter."[50] Here, Stone is seemingly ready to break with men who stonewalled on woman's rights and promoted only discriminatory "equality." Yet the AERA May meeting would not hear her impassioned criticism. Blackwell had arranged rallies for her until the "18th or 20th of May,"[51] and she could not attend. The two were nevertheless influencing Kansas. The *Emporia News* reported a survey of state newspapers showing a majority for universal suffrage—including women in this context.[52] However, the same issue fought with Wood and attacked Stone. "Her ideas of man's tyranny over woman, illy comported with the sight of a 'strong minded woman' driving over the country enlightening the Kansas heathen," wrote one observer.[53]

Meanwhile, in Ohio on April 3, "impartial suffrage" passed, "extending the right of suffrage to all male citizens except rebels, deserters and skedaddlers."[54] On April 23, mostly white men in New York elected delegates for the constitutional convention, with Republicans winning a significant majority.[55] But in neighboring Missouri women stirred. On May 8, 1867, Virginia Minor, Anna Clapp, Rebecca Hazard, Lucretia Hall, and Penelope Allen created the nation's first association for the women's cause. Named the Woman Suffrage Association of Missouri, its aim was to "secure the ballot for women upon terms of equality with men." Minor became president.[56]

18. Not Another Man

[If], being crafty, I desire to catch men with guile, and desire them to adopt suffrage for colored men, as good a trap as I know of is to claim it for women also. Bait your trap with the white woman, and I think you will catch the black man.—Henry Ward Beecher, *Proceedings of the First Anniversary of the American Equal Rights Association*, (1867), 58.

The 34th anniversary meeting of the AASS "was ample proof that the vitality of this society has departed … [sharing] in the universal human experience that men cannot be animated with dead issues," said the *New York Times*. "Only a small portion of the band of earnest unflinching spirits who gave the Anti-Slavery Society its power … now that slavery is dead and the negro armed with the ballot" were following Phillips, with the new 2,200-seat Steinway Hall only about two-thirds full. "Upon the platform there was more convincing evidence of the desuetude of the Anti-Slavery cause," the *Times* continued. "Of the old champions … the men [such as Garrison] who achieved a world-wide fame by the relentless vigor and dauntless courage with which they waged their warfare" very few were present."[1]

Yet, if the famous fire of earlier times had died, the AASS was still a symbol of resistance, for Phillips, flush with success in a legislative agenda later called "a coup d'état of the first magnitude,"[2] had still not finished. Despite the Military Reconstruction Acts, the D.C. suffrage law, control of suffrage in the territories and the 14th Amendment—all creating congressional power over the vote and elections—a resolution now presented demanded "legal guarantees of the negro's freedom and equality" as "provisions in the Federal Constitution forbidding any State to debar him from civil and political rights, and his substantial security is his actual possession and use of all those rights under the protection of the police power of the Union, as well as the recognition by the North of the same rule of impartial freedom."[3] Phillips, therefore, intended the reinforcement of all Reconstruction measures, especially the 14th Amendment, by yet another amendment to enshrine black men's rights in fundamental law. It would enfranchise all men throughout the nation and short-circuit for black male suffrage the cumbersome process of state constitutional and legal amendments and their costly and time-consuming campaigns, just as the Congress had already begun to do with its enforcement of equal suffrage for males in the territories. None of this was new. George Luther Stearns of the Universal and Equal Suffrage Association in 1866 had recognized the 14th Amendment as only a first step that required greater power, advocating "an enabling Act or a 15th Amendment."[4] The disrupted Southern Loyalists' Convention in September 1866 had also proposed an amendment prohibiting suffrage discrimination "on account of race, color, or previous condition of servitude."[5] With congressional enactment of freedman's suffrage through Military Reconstruction in March, Phillips now jumped on the bandwagon, the *Standard* raising the issue that April, which Parker Pillsbury soon criticized in a letter protesting the rush to enfranchise men and exclude women. "To rob the freed slave of citizenship to-day is as much a crime as was slavery before the war and emancipation. And to withhold that divinely conferred gift from woman is every way as oppressive, cruel and unjust.... No man is born with three ballots in his hand; one to use himself, and one to confer on, or withhold from another on account of color, and another on account of sex, at his sovereign will and pleasure."[6]

The *New York Times* also reported that Stanton, Mott, Anthony, Gage, several more well-known women, "and thirteen others of lesser fame" were on the platform at the AASS meeting.[7] Their seating may have given the impression they backed Phillips, but they had no reason to, for abolition was won and half-measures was not what they aimed for. They wanted reform more fundamental than what Phillips advocated. On the AASS platform, however, they found out what he was planning next, which was to move the goalposts yet again. In fact, the latest AASS resolution signaled yet another campaign for women to plan and work for. Equally concerning was the suggestion by Thomas Wentworth Higginson—a commander of black troops during the war—that the vote should be extended to women in the South. While speaking generally of women, the context—about the inadequacy of the vote for protecting freedmen and advocating land confiscation and redistribution—did not include white women.[8] They were not ex-slaves and besides, such women were generally regarded as traitors, unjustly or not. Nevertheless, Higginson's point raised a question as pertinent as that of votes for black women in the South: what about the women of the North? This question went to the heart of Reconstruction, for, if reformers and politicians of the time could intentionally divide society according to specific individual characteristics for their own purposes instead of establishing equality for all, it demonstrated their moral bankruptcy. They prohibited discrimination against black men but readily permitted discrimination against white women, while black women could be discriminated against or not, depending on politicians' goals. Higginson's proposal demonstrated clearly the discriminatory nature of the 14th Amendment against whites, particularly women. His idea showed why the women were fighting so hard through the AERA to establish the postwar nation on true republican principles with equality for all. Partisan, self-serving, and power-grabbing goals did not include them.

When the AERA meeting opened on May 9 in the Church of the Puritans, therefore, women knew they had already lost the Reconstruction reform-of-suffrage wars and now—on top of the New York constitutional convention and the Kansas campaign—another battle loomed with another amendment. If Anthony was already feeling extremely worried, the pressure had increased. Her financial reporting at the meeting's start was blunt: she had been so busy campaigning "no one has found time to chronicle the progress of events." Only "half a dozen live men and women" were helping to canvass "New York, to besiege the Legislature and the delegates to the Constitutional Convention with tracts and petitions, to write letters and send documents to every State Legislature that has moved on this question, to urge Congress to its highest duty in the reconstruction, by both public and private appeals." It was "a work that has taxed every energy and dollar at our command," she reported. The effectiveness of the AERA's work "has been limited only by the want of [money]," while the organization was in debt "to the tune of $617.33"—a considerable sum in 1867.[9]

Yet Anthony described the year's work and the results of the congressional agenda positively, even though it was wholly unsuccessful for the larger part of the AERA agenda. She also reported the "urgent requests from the West for articles for their papers, for lectures and tracts on the question of suffrage." There were to be "mass conventions, held throughout [Kansas] through September and October.… They urge us to send out at least a dozen able men and women, with a hundred thousand tracts, to help them educate the people into the grand idea of universal suffrage, that they may carry the State at the November election." Wisconsin, Illinois, Michigan, and New York were also asking for help. "For this vast work, as I have already shown you, we have an empty treasury. We ask you to replenish it. If you will but give your money generously," she pleaded with her audience, "this Association will gladly do the work that shall establish universal suffrage, equal rights to all, in every State in the Union."[10] During the two-day meeting, Anthony asked the audience for money several times.

As black male suffrage had advanced, even with widespread national opposition and during most of the debates women were deliberately bypassed after the restatement of the goal of true universal suffrage, the situation almost demanded that the meeting should focus on this weakness. Stanton, Pillsbury,

Samuel J. May, Ernestine Rose, and Gage that first day, therefore, largely argued for woman's inclusion in Reconstruction reforms through the right to vote. The *Proceedings* give the impression that the day was uneventful. Yet the civility of the official record and the *History of Woman Suffrage* masked significant discord, which some news coverage revealed.

Intimations of the first day's problems come on the second day when Stanton, speaking early on May 10, noted "she had heard that a few men, including Gerrit Smith and Phillips, had taken exceptions to part of the preceding day's proceedings" when the two objected to Gage's demand that Phillips and Beecher call for woman suffrage.[11] Despite the problems, "the cause, notwithstanding, would go forward," Stanton said, refusing to have the AERA back down. However, she was "sorry to observe that Henry Ward Beecher was unjustly reflected upon by a person who sat on the platform Thursday." As a friend of the AERA, she trusted his efforts.[12] Later in the day a mild protest arose when "Mr. Wright opposed an Anti-Slavery discussion," arguing that the AERA was no place for it, for antislavery was not for equal rights. "No doubt Mr. Phillips was faithful to the cause, yet he had too much to occupy his attention in his own particular field to give more of his time to the new movement."[13] These words stated the essential conflict of the AASS with the AERA and they indicate that newspaper reports and the official record of proceedings failed to convey strong undercurrents. The fact that it came up on the second day and was reported on in strong terms in the *Times* indicates its significance, even if the official record remained detached. The substance of the dispute emerged when the Rev. Samuel J. May presented a resolution: "That while we are grateful to Wendell Phillips, Theodore Tilton and Horace Greeley for the kindly mention in the respective journals through which they speak, of woman's right to the ballot, we earnestly request them, in this hour of reconstructing our State and National Governments, to demand a constitutional guarantee for woman's right as earnestly and persistently as they do demand it for the colored man's right; for until this is done we but repeat the long-tried and fatal experiment of caste and class legislation, and leave these Governments still standing upon an uneven, unsound and unsafe basis."[14]

Charles Lenox Remond, who in late December 1866 had criticized the Albany Convention of Colored Men for its discriminatory and rude treatment of Anthony and Stanton, now criticized this resolution. Notably, Anthony had begged for financial help from Gerrit Smith for Remond when Phillips pulled financing from the AERA in March.[15] Now Remond said that, while he wanted "all men" to get the ballot, "he hoped the rights of women as well as men would be considered," but "jealousy seemed to exist that the black men would get suffrage before women." Lucretia Mott, presiding, giving insight into women's feeling about the lopsided advance of the AERA's agenda, observed "that woman had a right to be a little jealous of the addition of so large a number of men to the voting class, for the colored men would naturally throw all their strength upon the side of those opposed to woman's enfranchisement."[16] Stanton denied that she was "inspired by any feeling of envy or jealousy," but that "it was not just for the black man to have suffrage while the rights of women were ignored." She said "she would strenuously oppose a measure that would increase the male vote at the expense of the women," desiring "to see both the black men and the women entitled to the same privilege."[17] Remond said he believed "that the magnanimity of the people would adjust the matter in a satisfactory manner."

George T. Downing next demanded "to know whether he had rightly understood that Mrs. Stanton and Mrs. Mott were opposed to the enfranchisement of the colored man, unless the ballot should also be accorded to woman at the same time."[18] Stanton replied, "We do not take the right step for this hour in demanding suffrage for any class; as a matter of principle I claim it for all." However, she continued, where principle was abandoned for expediency in extending the franchise, "in a narrow view of the question as a matter of feeling between classes, when Mr. Downing puts the question to me, are you willing to have the colored man enfranchised before the woman, I say, no; I would not trust him with all my rights; degraded, oppressed himself, he would be more despotic with the governing power than even our Saxon rulers are. I desire that we go into the kingdom together, for individual and national safety demand that not another man be enfranchised without the woman by his side."[19] This honest statement repeated more clearly what she had just said and was nothing new; but Downing, a politically astute black activist, had exposed for his own reasons how women felt about their exclusion, particularly since policy engineered by white men and supported by black men was deliberately excluding women in legislation.[20]

A debate involving several delegates ensued and eventually revealed that Remond was conflicted. "If he were to lose sight of expediency, he must side with Mrs. Stanton" (he said), but, while upholding the principle of equality for all, he was torn about the rights of black men, "for he could not conceive of a more unhappy position than that occupied by millions of American men bearing the name of freedmen while the rights and privileges of free men are still denied them." Stanton countered that black's men's inequality was equaled "by the condition of the women by their side." She continued: "There is a depth of degradation known to the slave women that man can never feel. To give the ballot to the black man is no security to the woman. Saxon men have the ballot, yet look at their women, crowded into a few half-paid employments. Look at the starving, degraded class in our ten thousand dens of infamy and vice if you would know how wisely and generously man legislates for woman."[21]

Remond then suggested amending May's resolution to omit the words "colored man," and insert the word "men."[22] He might have thought the change would quieten the supposed opposition of the women to black male suffrage, for the resolution was about promoting woman's rights in the future: if it did not mention race, perhaps the dissension over race and sex would disappear. The wording was convenient because it did not single black men out. However, his proposal, intentionally or not, stated the bald truth, confirming clearly that the Reconstruction suffrage agenda was driven by sex discrimination. May moved hurriedly to cover for Remond's gaffe, saying "the words were necessary to convey the meaning." Cutting them out "would take all the color out of my resolution."[23] May meant this literally, for white men had been fighting for suffrage for men who were black since 1865, which whites portrayed as solving the race problem. Yet it was equally clear in another sense: May thus confirmed that removing the words would also remove the cover of race, which disguised the true agenda of discrimination against women in Reconstruction reforms.

May underlined his bias by arguing that Phillips had also wanted nothing to cloud the issue of freedmen's suffrage—all of whom were male. "We should be much more likely to obtain the rights of the colored man" by asking for equal rights for all "than by making that a special question," he said, stating "he would rejoice at the enfranchisement of colored men." But he added that he "believed" Stanton would also support further male suffrage, "though that were all we could get at this time."[24] May presumed too much. He condescendingly spoke as if Stanton did not know or had not spoken her mind and ignored the fact that women were facing their calculated exclusion through an amendment to the Constitution. In other words, they were facing their political oblivion even before they had ever seriously known an authentic political role.[25] Stanton had been quite clear: it was the discrimination against all women that she protested—not the race of those being enfranchised—and she wanted "not another man" enfranchised before any woman. May, like other men, conveniently ignored the fact that many freedmen and other black men—in D.C. and the territories—had been enfranchised since Reconstruction began, while women had won nothing.

Downing again tried to make Stanton submit. He "offered the following resolution.... That while we regret that the right sentiment, which would secure to women the ballot, is not as general as we would have it, nevertheless we wish it distinctly understood that we rejoice at the increasing sentiment which favors the enfranchisement of the colored man." Downing "understood Mrs. Stanton to refuse to rejoice at a part of the good results to be accomplished, if she could not achieve the whole, and he wished to ask if she was unwilling the colored man should have the vote until the women could have it also? He said we had no right to refuse an act of justice upon the assumption that it would be followed by an act of injustice."[26]

Stanton reiterated that she "demanded the ballot for all ... [and] asked for reconstruction on the basis of self-government." If there was to be discrimination in voting rights, it should be based on education, even with continued sex discrimination, she said. "If we are to have further class legislation ... the wisest order of enfranchisement [is] to take the educated classes first. If women are still to be represented by men, then I say let only the highest type of manhood stand at the helm of State." But if there was to be universal manhood suffrage, "if all men are to vote, black and white, lettered and unlettered, washed and unwashed, the safety of the nation as well as the interests of woman demand that we outweigh this incoming tide of ignorance, poverty and vice, with the virtue, wealth and education of the women of the country."[27]

Stanton used against her adversaries the abolitionists' own argument that slavery debased the slaves. Aware that women would soon be under the rule of people just recently out of servitude, she wanted protection from any abuses by people with experience only of subjection. She also mirrored the position of men: if white and black men were allowed to exclude women, women could argue for the exclusion of any more men until women were enfranchised. Stephen Foster—till now clearly in favor of true equality—sat on the fence. Abby Kelley solidified her men-first position, speaking against Stanton and arguing for further black—male—suffrage before woman suffrage,[28] while Henry Ward Beecher came out for universal suffrage in a roundabout way.[29] Yet, in his long-winded speech, this man, who Stanton had defended earlier, argued that the way to win black male suffrage against opposition was to include white women; black men would win if they appeared as a compromise against something worse. The audience laughed, but Beecher realized his gaffe quickly. Hurriedly continuing, with a sincerity barely credible, he said, "I would not, certainly, have it understood that we are standing here to advocate this universal application of the principle merely to secure the enfranchisement of the colored citizen. We do it in good faith. I believe it is just as easy to carry the enfranchisement of all as the enfranchisement of any class, and easier to carry it than carry the enfranchisement of class after class."[30] Beecher might also have added state after state.

No one seconded Downing's resolution. Pillsbury protested the time spent on the discussion and Anthony tried to smooth ruffled feathers.[31] But the AERA's major subsurface fracture had broken through, with black, white, male, and female members attempting to impose agreement that equality for men was true equality and women should subordinate their interests. Downing clearly personified the men's position and Stanton personified that of the women. The dissension also emerged privately. Near the end of the meeting, Anthony had read to the assembly a telegram from Stone in Atchison, Kansas, declaring, "Impartial Suffrage without regard to color or sex will succeed by overwhelming majorities. Kansas rules the world!"[32] She unreservedly and publicly endorsed the AERA agenda. Yet, the day before, Stone had communicated a position like Stanton's. Responding to a request from Anthony for a telegram for the meeting, Stone said she could not do so, for Kansas looked ominous for women. She wrote this on May 9—the day before her AERA telegram—and Anthony would have received the letter after the end of the meeting. If read there, it would have reinforced Stanton's position publicly.[33]

The good news in Kansas, Stone reported, was the support they were garnering. The bad was black male opposition. Kansas had seen an influx of former slaves. Apparently, the ardently pro–abolition campaigner Stone was discovering that former male slaves brought into freedom attitudes incompatible with woman's equality. Obviously angry that such behavior emanated from the very men whose interest women were working for in the AERA and the SISA, she worried about their influence if they got the vote before women.[34] This stark assessment complemented with western experience Stanton's assessment in the East of women's concerns about enfranchising only more men. Because of the aggressive posture of Downing and men in the field and the failure of other key members wholeheartedly to back the AERA agenda, the AERA was now clearly cracked wide open as members tried to subordinate women, while the position expressed by one woman publicly and the other privately, if made public, could easily be used against either.

19. AERA Discord

Women want to vote, just as men do, because it is the only way in which they can be protected in their rights....—Lucy Stone, *Woman Suffrage in New Jersey.* (1867), 7.

The disruption at the AERA meeting in May 1867 was hardly surprising. If focusing on the woman's agenda was logical, disagreement was unavoidable when human beings saw things differently. Black AERA men could understandably feel that emphasis on women was unbalanced when the organization's goal was to "secure Equal Rights to all American citizens, especially the Right of Suffrage, irrespective of race, color, or sex."[1] Despite previous suffrage expansion in some northern and western states, elsewhere race restrictions still excluded some men from voting and hefty property requirements excluded others.[2] In addition, passage of the Military Reconstruction Act in March had elevated newly freed men in the South politically above free black men of the North. This reversal in the relative status of the two groups must have been particularly galling to former soldiers of a civil war ultimately transformed into a war for the slaves' freedom. The enfranchisement of uneducated freedmen ahead of the free men of the North—some educated and others both educated and wealthy—was clearly unjust. Further, northern men in 1867 still faced a long haul of state-by-state campaigns to win suffrage. Perhaps even worse in some eyes was the fact that these developments had left them on a political par with all women—white, black, educated, uneducated, poor, and wealthy. For men to be at the bottom of the totem pole with women was an insult to male sensibilities, especially the wealthy and educated among them, in a nation that was on the way to institutionalizing the word male in the Constitution. These considerations highlighted the import of Stanton's point about educated suffrage.

Essentially, black males felt sidelined in the AERA in May 1867, for their as-yet-unmet interests merited discussion and action. Phillips' resolution for a 15th Amendment at the AASS meeting just two days before—which would eradicate the inequality of northern black men—hardly mattered, for there was no guarantee it would pass, or even pass as quickly as freedmen's voting in the South. Left behind in reforms for black men, male AERA members felt their interests should be the AERA's goal. In this perspective, their protests and the controversy at the AERA meeting were understandable, and they were understandable even if the AASS was working for black male suffrage to the exclusion of female suffrage, because equal suffrage for all was the agenda of the AERA.

On the other hand, if the black men of the North were left behind in suffrage, the women of the United States were left out entirely. Unlike black men, the women had always been subjected to total exclusion, not simply the injustice of being left behind their newly enfranchised southern brethren for only the past couple of months. The women also had only the AERA to fight for them, while they now faced a larger battle front as Phillips' latest constitutional program created the prospect of more men added to the electorate before any woman. Women's interest in having woman suffrage was as important to them as male suffrage was to black men and it deserved like discussion and action.

Both groups, therefore, had understandable gripes. However, the discord at the AERA, which ostensibly was about recognizing the imbalance in suffrage law for northern men who were black, was eerily familiar to women like Stanton and Anthony, who 15 years before had encountered men in their own temperance society basically attacking its core. This was a power struggle—an attempt to sideline the greater and still potentially increasing imbalance for the women of the nation. The contentious debate pursued this unequal agenda even when several of the AERA women, all excluded from the vote, were working to enfranchise men who were black and when their work was unequally reciprocated. To be fair, the discord was nuanced. If Remond was torn for himself and his group on the emotional level, he still supported the women in logic. Stanton spelled out the problem for women in like manner.

Nevertheless, there was such disparity between aspirations and reality and the two distinct wings of the AERA were being treated so differently nationally that the huge fundamental flaw in the organization stood clearly in the spotlight. The essential differences between the two groups were that Remond's was small, male, and had the establishment promoting reforms for it, while Stanton's was female, large, and the establishment was reinforcing discrimination against it. The only way legislators could honestly call their policies a question of solving race inequality was if only men counted: segregate the women from the men, and the issue became equality of race between people of the same male sex. This is how reformers, Republicans, and the men affected conjured the means of advocating their agenda. If women had kept quiet, it would have presented no problems. When they did not, the false rhetoric was exposed and fomented conflict among members of both sexes and both races. Downing, for example, was angered when Stanton put women on a par with men. This said more about Downing's sense of justice than it did about Stanton's, for he clearly believed in male supremacy. By contrast, the positions of both Stanton and Remond were open and honorable: they each attempted to transcend sectional and personal concerns to promote justice for all. Remond even landed himself in a quagmire by proposing to remove the race terminology from the resolution, perhaps hoping that by removing "colored" or "black men" (both appear in the different reports) he would make it less incendiary and unite everyone. It might have removed the confusion, but it failed to end the controversy. His proposal exposed the truth that extension of the franchise was primarily a sex issue favoring men, which hardly helped matters among half the AERA's membership. His proposal, if accepted, would also have erased an important truth about Reconstruction, which was that the official narrative was about universal suffrage and equal enfranchisement of the races, even though it was not. Worse for Remond, however, his proposal recognized that sex discrimination was acceptable, which countered the AERA policy.

Some black men also, of whom Downing was a prime example, had their own personal agenda, which was subordinating the women to men's goals. In his complaints and proposed resolution, Downing shunted the inequalities of the distinct groups into his own hierarchy of importance. He then prioritized the eradication of those inequalities, with maleness first. Thus, he advocated institutionalizing sex discrimination. He was, therefore, intent not only on beating Stanton down, but also on trying to bend the AERA's agenda to his own will. If Stanton's vague references to Wendell Phillips and Gerrit Smith, which convention speaker Henry C. Wright put on record in a little greater detail, were indeed about an attempt to hijack the AERA's agenda, the white men were worse than some of the black men in this regard, particularly since such white men had professed support of woman's rights until they abandoned them when it seemed they might have to deliver. Some women supported this distortion of the AERA agenda. The wrangling tore the women apart. Stanton's position was clear on one side of the argument. Sojourner Truth aligned with her even if, as a black woman, her emphasis was more on economic arguments than on Stanton's fallback position of educated suffrage if justice-based suffrage failed.[3]

Abby Kelley, on the other hand, backed the male side, arguing through race.[4] Another Mrs. Foster—Harriet A.—asked "whether it was right that the freedmen of the South should enter into the kingdom of politics before the white women of the North, or the black women of the North, or the white women of the South?" A former slave, she "demanded that the freedman should be secured the right of suffrage, for that was the only way in which he could enjoy liberty to the full extent. She extolled Wendell Phillips' work and said that posterity would do him justice."[5] Mrs. Foster backed the equalities-by-sex camp, supporting men. She did not question why any choice was required. Josephine Griffing wished for the true agenda of the AERA of winning simultaneous enfranchisement, rather than prioritizing one group over the other. However, she conceded, "We must work by degrees, accepting every inch, every hair's breadth gained towards the right. I welcome the enfranchisement of the negro as a step towards the enfranchisement of woman." Recognizing in the word "negro" that black meant males only, she proposed AERA support for woman suffrage in Washington, D.C., to launch women's enfranchisement, as the issue had already been raised there and President Johnson had said he would not veto such legislation.[6] Again this meant men over women. These varied positions were a natural result of a policy that prioritized by sex using rhetoric laden with weasel words. The policy was divisive, pitting one disfranchised group against the other, responsibility for which lay with Phillips and most of the congressional Republicans. Essentially, it was a policy that pitted men against women and forced women to choose between men's interests and themselves. Men had hardly any choosing to do at all.

Further black male enfranchisement was another step in the process. The battle over votes for black males was largely won, with only free black men, essentially in the North, left without right to an equal vote. The total free black male potential voting population was 115,390, compared with a total freedman potential voting population of 875,877. Voting for free black men, therefore, represented a minor numerical add-on, when compared with the totals of white men and women and enfranchised freedmen.[7] If, for women, a major worry was uneducated new voters, enfranchisement of free black men in the north might add more educated men who were black. Yet there was no timetable for the next step—women's enfranchisement. And women had no reason to trust most men: their so-called representatives in Congress had treated them abominably since 1865. And, despite women's work against slavery and for black men, the latter were now consistently trying to exclude women as much as white men did. Stanton, Anthony. and Stone—and likely others—all had direct experience of this.

Yet all the practical arguments were only expedient, while women like Stanton and Anthony were fighting for the republican principle of equality for all. To fight for only men—whether they were black or not—and not to fight for women also, meant the AERA would have to abandon principle for what was expedient for the reformers and politicians of the time. Even expedient arguments demonstrated how the prioritization of inequalities and their rectification step-by-step, if at all, was inherently unequal—a truth demonstrated to the women daily. The anti-woman sentiment that Stanton, Anthony,

Stone, and others had experienced while campaigning for the AERA was only the tiny tip of a large iceberg, the impact of which white women were beginning to feel directly. In the South, evidence of abusive treatment of women demonstrated that sex discrimination ruled there, as freedwomen found they were no better off under the rule of freed male slaves than under the white man. "They go out washing, which is about as high as a colored woman gets, and their men go about idle, strutting up and down; and when the women come home, they ask for their money and take it all, and then scold because there is no food,"[8] Sojourner Truth said, "There is a great stir about colored men getting their rights, but not a word about the colored women; and if colored men get their rights, and not colored women theirs, you see the colored men will be masters over the women, and it will be just as bad as it was before."

Truth also understood clearly the dynamics of reform and the lessons of women's abandonment of their cause at the start of the war: it was harder to start up than simply to keep on. "I am for keeping the thing going while things are stirring," she said, "because if we wait till it is still, it will take a great while to get it going again."[9] Truth here aligned herself with women generally. Gage, mirroring to reformers and abolitionists their own terminology and concerns throughout the years of antislavery but also speaking from the experience of working for the Freedmen's Bureau to help former slaves, confirmed Truth's observations: "The slave population of the South is not yet removed a hundred years from the barbarism of Africa, where women have no rights, no privileges, but are trampled under foot in all the savageism of the past. And the slave man has looked on to see his master will everything as he willed, and he has learned the lesson from his master."[10]

It was clear that women had no reason to trust most of the men. If freedmen were dictating to black women in the South, women everywhere in the United States had little reason to believe that more male voters would guarantee any improvement in women's status. The problem was not confined to recently freed slaves. The offensive behavior of Downing at the 1867 AERA meeting towards Stanton, and that of Peyton Harris of Buffalo, New York, towards Stanton and Anthony at the New York State Convention of Colored Men in October 1866, demonstrated that black men of wealth and education were equally predisposed to look down on women and attempt to subjugate them, no matter who they were. Women such as Stanton and Anthony, therefore, had no reason to fight only for equal rights for black men. Someone had to fight for their own rights, and if not them, who? If not then, when? Not fighting for their own equal rights was simply not an option.

The May 1867 AERA meeting in effect destroyed the veneer over the original organizational cracks, despite the attempts by Anthony, Pillsbury, Truth, and others to paper over them. The discord was possibly much more charged than the proceedings and the newspapers conveyed. The *Tribune,* which provides hardly any details of the debate, had a reason not to report it if only because it was the focus of a resolution in which its owner, Horace Greeley featured, and he was adamantly opposed to woman suffrage. Fortuitously, enough contemporary material exists to see that the AERA men were dissatisfied with what they had already won. Clamoring for more, they now tried to assert their supremacy. It appears inescapable to conclude that men, both black and white, were determined to hijack the AERA's agenda for themselves, thereby destroying it.

This development is hardly surprising. The AERA was born on the very same day that the proposed 14th Amendment passed its first hurdle in the House of Representatives. From the start, therefore, a major fault line ran through it, for male equality was being promoted under the guise of race equality at the punitive cost of sex discrimination regarding women. The AERA idea had been under siege even before its launch. Phillips had resolutely opposed it, for his actions in 1866 demonstrate his lack of interest in allowing any transformation of the AASS into one based on higher principles, or in giving up his control of what he deemed to be the major issue of the day. The AERA was under siege from Congress, which tried to cut women out of any debate and aimed legislatively and constitutionally to subordinate them, seemingly permanently. It was under siege from rhetoric that passed male-only suffrage off as "Universal Suffrage." It was under siege financially, with the finger for its penury pointing directly at white men and specifically Phillips for his nefarious misappropriation of the Hovey Fund after abolition. It was under siege from black men who adamantly opposed women's equality and rights. Women had dealt with all these assaults from 1865 on. Now, in 1867 the AERA faced an attempted coup at its first annual meeting through a bid to co-opt the agenda of equality for all and make women submit to the male-supremacy agenda that dominated outside the organization. Black men and white men, emboldened by the stunning victories already won to this point, now attempted to force the women to accept male-only suffrage as the AERA's policy, to force them to become once again selfless, instead of selfish— the old saw now trotted out whenever women were not compliant as they were expected to be.

Such behavior was not unusual, for men were used to having their own way, but the men's aggression in the 1867 meeting, supported by some women, was bound to fail. Purely self-centered and ignoring women's wishes, they failed even to consider a fundamental question: why should they? Why should women cave to a hijacking of the AERA's purpose and allow their own continued subordination? The AERA was the women's organization in the first place. Lucretia Mott at the 1866 foundation meeting had astutely highlighted "that this new organization was the outgrowth of the Woman's Rights move-

ment."[11] The women did most of the planning and work at little or no pay
and provided the fundamental philosophy and major position statements.
Why should they submit to the institutionalization of their subordination
through the 14th Amendment? They argued fair and just alternatives to discrimination by sex in suffrage, specifically suffrage based on education, which
was something an individual could work towards. Why should they accept
suffrage based on something they could not change—women's sex—when at
the time male suffrage guaranteed countless illiterate voters? Why should
they agree to a male-only electorate in the first place? Women's position in
1867 was revolutionary. Perhaps few of their sex agreed, but women such as
Anthony, Stanton, Gage, Truth, and others believed in their own right—just
as white men and black men claimed the right—to the vote.

Stanton tackled this double standard later: "We should like to know why
a movement among women for the outraged and oppressed of their sex is
more 'selfish' than that of man for his sex. Is not the philanthropy of Paulina
Wright Davis pleading for the enfranchisement of the black woman of the
south as pure as that of Wendell Phillips pleading for the black man, or of Frederick Douglass for his own race?"[12] The women's position, in sum, was just
as valid for them as that of the men was for other men: hence their resolute
refusal to let the men beat them down at the 1867 meeting. A parallel to this
situation would arise in Britain 50 years later when politicians planned to
enfranchise mostly working-class men serving at the front in World War I
but previously excluded from suffrage. "The Woman's Freedom League objects
very strongly to more men being enfranchised until women are on the Parliamentary Register," the organization said. The British debate about women's
voting rights in 1916 was not encumbered by race, so the basic argument was
not muddied by racial slurs, demonstrating clearly that the issue was one of
equality of the sexes.[13] In 1867, therefore, the women fought valiantly against
the attempt at male dominance within their own organization. Equally important, at the May 1867 meeting, the women were not only standing up for themselves: they were also standing up for the true AERA agenda. The AERA had
lived under siege for the whole of its first year, with some of its male members,
white and black, and some women complicit. In 1867 the men launched this
attempted coup. It was women who defended the organization on its original
basis against the attacks on its agenda and fundamental integrity and the
external victories undermining the reason for its existence. Cut either men's
or woman's rights out, prioritize one, and the AERA's mission was void.

The women did not abandon the AERA to fight for woman's suffrage
only. They carried on despite the siege both inside and out, for they had created the AERA, it was the official agenda, and the women identified with the
vision. They refused to give up because failure for themselves was not an
option. Practically, they had to try to slip into the polity while the door was

thrown open to men who were black and before it slammed in their faces. They had to continue to try to prevent more men getting in alone, for convincing evidence suggested that the new voters would likely be anti-woman— especially as some of the proposed new voters seemed to object to sharing equality with anyone else. But they had to keep on fighting even if it was difficult because in May 1867 no one knew whether the battle was lost. At the time, they were in the thick of two major campaigns—New York and Kansas— that might finally bring a breakthrough. An official organization representing disadvantaged groups gave them more credibility than if they had been operating without one.

Unfortunately, however, the manipulation of events by the men at the 1867 AERA meeting launched a narrative that women who focused on equality for all were against equality for men who were black. This was not true. Stanton argued clearly for equality regardless of race or sex and, facing opposition, argued in the alternative: if there was to be discrimination in voting, the discrimination should be based not on sex but on education. Any argument that the women were racist does not merit discussion. However, because women refused to cave to the male attempt at domination and refused to submit to the claims of their greater importance from men who were black, it was easy to say the women were racist, even while ignoring the blatant sex discrimination that informed the whole struggle. This period may be the first time in the United States that the slur of racism, though false, was used to delegitimize an honest cause, while the people who began to smear the women were those simultaneously oppressing them. The false narrative was strengthened because it had more publicity power than the truth had, which was that the white and black men pressing their own agenda of sex discrimination created the contention. Consequently, the narrative has cast a long-lasting shadow over the real events, and this lie has assumed importance as a solid, impregnable truth that demands discussion any time this history is examined—always leaving the slur against the women hanging over the period, the slur against their character insurmountable, while the men's reputation, with all their sex bias and overt attempt at domination, escapes scotfree.

20. Anti-woman Sentiment

The present government of Kansas is "bogus" to the women and blacks of the state.—Clarina I.H. Nichols, March 21, 1867.

At the 1867 AERA meeting Stanton had said that if republican equality was not to be suffrage's guiding light, her priority would be women. At the very least, if legislation favoring any further discrimination in voting happened, she would argue for discrimination based on education, not sex. Exclusion by race was not in her reckoning. Near the end of the meeting, Anthony had read out to the assembly a telegram from Stone: "ATCHISON, Kansas, May 10, 1867. 'Impartial Suffrage without regard to color or sex will succeed by overwhelming majorities. Kansas rules the world!'"[1] With this upbeat telegram, Stone told a positive story about the upcoming votes in Kansas and overwhelmingly endorsed the AERA agenda publicly.

Yet Stone, in a letter of May 9 to Anthony,[2] who had asked for a telegram from Kansas for the AERA meeting, had already described privately a position akin to what Stanton was forced to do publicly. Stone declined the telegram idea because the political situation in Kansas was too fluid and looked ominous for women. However, obviously thinking better of it later, on May 10 she telegraphed positive tidings.[3] Her letter reveals only after the meeting that Stone was thinking along the same lines as what Stanton had said at Downing's goading. Surveying Kansas, Stone said, "Everywhere we go we have the largest and most enthusiastic meetings, and any one of our audiences would give a majority for woman suffrage." But, she continued, "the negroes are all against us." If Stone already felt concerned about woman's progress in Kansas, it was because of Kansas men. Besides Republican editors, "there has just now left us an ignorant black preacher named Twine, who is very confident that women ought not to vote," she wrote.[4] Black men in Kansas, she went on, "ought not to be allowed to vote before we do, because they will be just so much more dead weight to lift."[5] Yet Stone's views were still moderate compared with her husband's views expressed in his January 1867 pamphlet advocating female suffrage in the South to balance black votes, which he was distributing in Kansas to promote the SISA campaign.[6]

Stone's Kansas struggle reflected Anthony and Stanton's struggle within the AERA and against politicians. Not only was black opposition growing to the SISA and its AERA-aligned agenda, but white male opposition against the equal suffrage rights for women was also gathering steam. A public meeting was called for Monday, May 13, in Emporia by the "Friends of Impartial Suffrage" to take "such measures as may seem best calculated to promote this important reform." The signatories included Jacob Stotler, editor and publisher of the anti-female suffrage *Emporia News*,[7] with "impartial suffrage" clearly referring only to males, specifically blacks—and directly challenging Wood's SISA. The organizers intended to canvass for men and oppose women. There was more. The State Republican Central Committee in Kansas had already called a meeting for Topeka on May 15, which the *Emporia News* welcomed heartily.[8] The May 13 Emporia meeting was likely to prepare for Topeka.

Stone told Anthony of the Topeka meeting in her May 9 letter. It was intended "to pledge the party to the canvass on (the) single issue" of the word "white"—a development already having a negative impact on the SISA program, for a "change of tone of some of the papers" had already begun.[9] Key forces in Kansas, therefore, using race terminology, were aligning along sex discrimination lines. Attempting to counter this development, the SISA had "sent letters to all those whom we had found true to principle, urging them to be at Topeka and vote" for removing both "male" and "white." These SISA moves were occurring covertly, wrote Stone, who hoped the state Republicans' plans would be defeated. The SISA would have to wait till May 15 before deciding what to do next.[10]

In Kansas, Stone was learning much about the reality of postwar reform. One lesson was that women reformers could not trust many men—whether they were white, so-called antislavery men in whatever incarnation in 1867, freedmen, free male blacks, reformers, or radical politicians. State politics was just as prejudiced and tortuous as national politics, but state politics effectively divided and conquered within states and kept women's eyes off national politics. Yet even while in Kansas, Stone still noted federal murmurings on woman suffrage, specifically the proposal of Charles Sumner—echoing Phillips' call for yet another federal amendment at the AASS meeting—"to make negro suffrage universal." While sticking to the AERA line, she argued that women had to lobby Congress to "insist upon our claim; urged not for our sake merely, but that the government may be based upon the consent of the governed." For woman's cause, she declared, "there is safety in no other way,"[11] as it required more work than the men's. To fight for female inclusion in any federal suffrage amendment along with all black men was logical and practical, for from the vantage of a difficult campaign in the West, winning woman suffrage federally with one measure looked more enticing than state-by-state campaigns—37 in all at this point. Her last paragraph on May 9 communicated mixed fortunes in Kansas, for though she and Blackwell "had the largest meeting we have yet had in the State at Leavenworth night before last," blood ties could not be relied upon. "Dan[iel Anthony] don't want the Republicans to take us up," she wrote.

Opposition to women now became increasingly overt. At the Kansas State Republican Central Committee on May 15 in Topeka, "several negroes … expressed themselves as bitterly opposed to female suffrage, and considerable dissension ensued between the friends of the two questions."[12] Stone's concerns of her May 9 letter had come to pass, while Kansas replicated the division that had emerged in the New York AERA meeting.[13] In fact, the Kansas Republicans aligned themselves with the national party's policy and that of the New York Republican Party in favor of "Impartial Suffrage"—suffrage based on sex discrimination.[14] The committee, according to one opinion, had "wisely … refrained from any attempt to commit the party to the doctrine of Female Suffrage, but fully accepted the Congressional platform of Impartial Suffrage."[15] Further news that the party "has decided to organize a thorough and exhaustive canvass of the State, before the coming November election" was ominous.[16]

The decision was a major blow for the SISA campaign that Stone and Blackwell had helped to launch in April. The opposition from many quarters from the outset—white male, black male, and female—had already worried them if support from the East and a huge state effort did not transpire. With this decision emerging just as they were concluding their sojourn in the state and with no replacements immediately scheduled, a huge gap was developing for opponents of whatever stripe to enter the fray for their own ends. The unreassuringly realistic assessment that Blackwell had made back in April had been that they "shall probably succeed in Kansas next fall if the State is thoroughly canvassed, not else."[17] Leaving the campaign up in the air at this point, therefore, put the SISA campaign in jeopardy, particularly as the broadsides had already begun. Stone had reported even before the May 15 Republican meeting about opponents' use of the politics of personal destruction. "The papers here are coming down on us and every prominent reformer, and charging us with being Free Lovers. I have to-day written a letter to the editor, saying that it has not the shadow of a foundation."[18] This was a war against women. In fact, when the May 13 Emporia meeting formed an anti-woman suffrage organization, "not a lady was present…. We don't believe in forcing the ballot into their hands but are willing they should have it if a majority want it, which we very much doubt."[19]

In these circumstances, Kansas locals worked hard. Mrs. R.S. Bates of

Chelsea, Butler County, challenged a reader who earlier had personally attacked Stone and distorted her suffrage message.[20] Clarina I.H. Nichols regularly wrote in local and state newspapers arguing for woman. Originally from Vermont, she had moved to Kansas Territory in October 1854. A lifelong supporter of woman's rights and other reform movements, Nichols was central to the Wyandotte Constitutional Convention in July 1859, presenting a petition demanding equal political and civil rights for women at statehood and lobbying for groundbreaking equal woman suffrage. Kansas women emerged from this convention with improved rights, a very limited suffrage that was generally dismissed and a strong precedent for women's activism.[21] Late in May of 1867 Nichols was tackling the tactic of dividing sex by race to pit women against each other, arguing that attacks on "*colored*-woman suffrage" were as false as equally false arguments "against suffrage for *white* women."[22] The minds who had met up in Emporia on May 13 were clearly behind such a talking point, for it was frequently thrown against women from this time on. Simultaneously, support for the black male referendum began to appear from all quarters, with a published private letter of Representative Sidney Clarke revealing he endorsed the "proposition to strike the word 'white'" from the Kansas constitution and declaring that if Kansas Republicans "will at once inaugurate a systematic canvass of the whole State ... I shall endeavor to speak in every county."[23]

Similar divide-and-conquer tactics arose at the May 29, 1867, annual convention of the New England Anti-Slavery Society in Boston,[24] where AERA members Lucretia Mott, Parker Pillsbury, and Stephen Foster attempted, against Phillips' wishes, to have true universal suffrage endorsed. Echoing former black troop commander Colonel Thomas Wentworth Higginson's reference at the AASS meeting earlier in the month about extending the vote to freedwomen of the South,[25] they emphasized the dire straits of former female slaves. Politically, however, Phillips had to cut this discussion short. If it raised again the specter of black women's enfranchisement as a means of protecting them from postwar abuses, it also raised the wider implications for all women. Even minimal discussion revealed starkly the biases of Phillips' post-emancipation antislavery program, for when Phillips rejected the enfranchisement of former female slaves, he said "all the Anti-Slavery movement has ever undertaken to do is to put the black men of the South where the white men of the South stand, and the black women of the South where the white women of the South stand; that is all. More than that you cannot ask of us as an *Anti-Slavery* body."[26] Phillips and his followers representing post-abolition antislavery clearly saw the nation divided into two classes, and the two classes were founded on sex, not on race.

The Boston discussion of so-called true universal suffrage revealed the full extent of post-emancipation antislavery agenda discrimination. This discounted the enfranchisement of free and freed black women and discriminated against the rest of the nation's women both because they were women and because they were white. The enfranchisement of males only, who were black, was the goal, no matter what the current abolitionists might profess rhetorically. In sum, while insistently professing race equality, Phillips excluded half of the race he claimed he was advocating equality for while excluding half of the other race, to which he himself belonged, all purely because of their sex. This represents multiple levels of discrimination by which Phillips discarded all women. His unfeeling and dismissive statement about the purported equality of black women with white women revealed how determinedly he and his followers stood on the side of sex discrimination—overt hypocrisy for these purported equality-mongers, except that sex discrimination and equality rarely mattered in public discourse. Women did not have the vote and therefore, by definition, they did not count and vice-versa. His hypocrisy did not matter either. Obviously aware of the political quicksand the issue represented, Phillips ended discussion fast—once again slamming the reform door in women's faces even while he and his cohorts insistently called for full male suffrage under the guise of equality of race. They now proposed a new constitutional amendment to ensure the enfranchisement of black men, whether former slave or free. Intended to remedy the inequalities the current situation created, by focusing on black men it was still race-biased. It was also biased against women. The plan would reinforce the sex discrimination that the 14th Amendment was even then institutionalizing.

The day of the New England Anti-Slavery Society meeting in Boston, Horace Greeley's *Tribune*, surprisingly, editorialized as follows: "Womanhood suffrage is now a progressive cause beyond fear of cavil. It has won a fair field where once it was looked upon as an airy nothing, and it has gained champions and converts without number." Yet Greeley failed to advocate abolitionist support of woman suffrage, nor did he call for woman suffrage for New York, where he had recently been elected as an at-large delegate for the upcoming constitutional convention. Carefully avoiding endorsement, his editorial argued that anywhere but New York should try female suffrage: "The young State of Kansas is fitly the vanguard of this cause, and the signs of the agitation therein hardly allow a doubt that the citizenship of women will be ere long recognized in its laws. Fourteen out of twenty of its newspapers are in favor of making woman a voter.... The vitality of the Kansas movement is indisputable, and whether defeated or successful in the present contest, it will still hold strongly fortified ground."[27] Greeley the newspaperman's apparent ignorance of the latest news from Kansas is striking. Yet for him, what was happening there did not really matter. What did was that Kansas was not in his own backyard and it supplied a useful diversion from the New York campaign. His duplicitous position deliberately sidestepped the women's resolution at the AERA convention asking for support for "a constitutional guarantee" of woman suffrage; his unctuous sentiments were worthless, for he supported male enfranchisement by federal measures with states bringing their laws into line. Meanwhile, he consigned female suffrage to the much more cumbersome path of state-by-state reform. These double standards reveal once again awe-inspiring hypocrisy.

Greeley's editorial, nevertheless, might have made Stone feel better, for on her return East, despite her private concerns before she left Kansas, she publicly remained positive about the prospects there. Still, in a letter in early June, while urging true universal suffrage she lamented the greater challenges that women faced. Reciting a long, sad list of conventions, petitions, legislature appearances, fund-raising, circulation of tens of thousands of tracts, endless lecturing, and state and nationwide campaigns for woman suffrage, she asked the following question: "What more can we do? Must every individual woman demand suffrage before any of the thousands who have demanded it can be allowed to exercise it?"[28]

Her words tackled the latest argument—that few women wanted the vote and most were against it—that reformers, politicians, newspaper editorialists and legislatures were throwing at women both to justify the refusal to include them in the Reconstruction reforms and to set the bar so high that women could never comply. No politician or reformer employed this argument against men, the assumption always being that males should have the vote even if most expressed no interest in it. This blatantly subversive tactic revealed not only the sex discrimination they were espousing, but also their race bias. On the one hand, all their arguments justifying black male suffrage were designed not to prevent but to facilitate its enactment. On the other, all the conditions they demanded of women to secure their enfranchisement were designed to prevent it, and while their conditions applied to all women, most of those women were white. The men's arguments, employing race terminology that masked their true intentions of ensuring enfranchisement of black men only, starkly exposed the prejudices of the era, with race bias against white women standing as a dark shadow behind its clearly visible sex discrimination against all women.[29]

21. Fighting on Two Fronts

I want women to have their rights. In the courts women have no right, no voice; nobody speaks for them. I wish woman to have her voice there among the pettifoggers. If it is not a fit place for women, it is unfit for men to be there.—Sojourner Truth, 1867, *History of Woman Suffrage II* (1887), 193.

The day after Stone's letter, on June 4, 1867, delegates elected the previous April 23 to the constitutional convention assembled in Albany, New York. First among many proposals was the official one to reform the suffrage laws to end the $250 suffrage property qualification restricting black male votes. But buzzing annoyingly like a gnat around many of the delegates was an unofficial proposal for suffrage for women, none of whom had a vote. In January Stanton's speech had attempted to win for blacks and women the right to vote for the convention delegation. She had failed, but propertied black men already qualified for assembly elections voted for delegates. Women and men who were black, therefore, entered the proceedings on an unequal footing, but the convention brought an opportunity to equalize voting rights for all. The *Cleveland Plain Dealer* printed the following:

A Republican journal ... says it is certainly not easy to give any good and substantial reason, based on anything other than party necessities, for refusing to women what has been conceded to three millions of ignorant negroes in the Southern States, but we do not believe it will be conceded to them nevertheless ... for the same party necessities do not exist in the case of women. The radical leaders do not feel quite as sure of controlling the female vote as they do that of the negroes.... It is a pretty rich joke that the Radical leaders ... imagine they can make the ignorant Southern blacks vote as they wish [and] have forced the suffrage on three million of negroes at the South, while they will deny it to three or four times that number of intelligent white women at the North, and on the only ground that they are not sure of being able to use the female vote for securing party advantages. The joke is still heightened by the fact that the newly enfranchised negroes are bitterly opposed to women voting.[1]

This writer believed only selfishness lay behind women's campaign for true universal suffrage. "One reason for pressing female suffrage with so much earnestness just now in the North, is said to be the fear entertained" by Stone, Stanton, and others "that when the negroes are enfranchised, they will cast their votes in solid column against woman suffrage. Lucy Stone says that in her late mission to Kansas she found the negroes everywhere opposed to female suffrage." It added that "a leading Republican paper" in Kansas confirmed black men were "also opposed to women's voting."[2] Women still called for suffrage out of justice. But if some were now concerned about the effects of black male suffrage on woman's rights, it was because, while working for equal suffrage for all, they had been discovering that although some black men worked with them, woman suffrage threatened many black men, whose own selfishness was engendering woman's concerns. Women had begun to conclude that they were largely on their own in the New York campaign.

In Kansas, early in June, one newspaper belatedly criticized Kansas Republicans for abandoning female suffrage. If suffrage was to be an official issue of the Republicans, the *Kansas Chief* argued, female suffrage had as much right to party support as black male suffrage did.[3] The commentary may have pleased SISA workers, but the Kansas equal suffrage campaign still struggled against increasing opposition. Nearly two full columns of a vicious attack on women and slanders against Stone by Charles V. Eskridge[4] appeared in the *Emporia News* on June 7.[5] One of Emporia's prominent self-promoting party-line Republicans, Eskridge's anti-woman rhetoric repeated earlier lies about free love. These slanders flew around the state long before Stone, now returned East with Blackwell, could counter them. Meanwhile, the *Emporia News* sometimes would sneakily allow the impression it was evenhanded, soon publishing on its front page, for example—by request, two columns of quotes from distinguished supporters of female suffrage.[6]

That month, Senator Benjamin F. Wade, then president pro tem of the United States Senate and potential president if plans to impeach President Johnson were successful, endorsed woman suffrage during a stop in Kansas. Wade was travelling with colleagues to inspect the western forts and the fast-expanding Union Pacific Railroad.[7] The dignitaries, hunting wild game from the moving trains, were fêted along the way.[8] Arriving on June 10 in Lawrence, Wade—one of the most radical of the Republicans in Congress—gave a well-reported impromptu speech. Part of it was music to women's ears, for he said "as he had kept in advance of the people in the great strife between Freedom and Slavery, he meant to do the same thing in the contest which had just commenced for extending the right of suffrage to women." Wade, the report continued, "was unqualifiedly in favor of equal rights for all, not only without regard to nationality and color, but without regard to sex. Women were more virtuous than men … and when they gained political power they would rectify many abuses." To "laughter and applause" he added this: "If he had not believed that his own wife had sense enough to vote, he never would have married her … and if any of his hearers had wives who were unequal to the discharge of the right of suffrage, he would advise them to go and get divorced at once. (Renewed laughter.)"[9] Wade also "denounced those women who did not want to vote because it was not fashionable, and said that … female suffrage [would] be general in less than twenty years," to which an unnamed woman in the audience shouted, "That's too far off."[10]

Wade also declared that "property was not equally divided" in the United States "and a more equal distribution of capital must be wrought out." We have "disposed of the question of Slavery, and now that of labor and capital must pass through the ordeal." Phillips had raised such ideas since the war's end, along with plans to confiscate lands of former southern slaveholders for redistribution to freedmen. Just as suffrage for freedmen and equal suffrage for free black men of the North were connected, these ideas were connected, Wade said, "If you dullheads can't see this, the women will, and will act accordingly."[11]

Congressman John Covode of Pennsylvania then offered "a brief speech upon the railroad interests of the West" and George Francis Train of the Crédit Foncier, a real estate organization associated with the railroad, "succeeded in getting in a few characteristic sentences."[12] Train had earlier refused to speak, deferring to the more prominent dignitaries, but now, in Lawrence, for a brief moment woman suffrage encountered for the first time George Francis Train in the very state where concurrently a major conflict was brewing over the right to vote. Wade's ideas about the redistribution of property horrified many as the reports of the speech spread nationwide. Significantly, his linkage of woman suffrage with it raised a red flag about female voters, giving objectors to a franchise expanded to any new constituency a new argument against it.[13] Wade's words would soon bring about his downfall and led to the loss for women of a potential key supporter in the federal government in the coming years. At that moment, however, for suffrage campaigners Wade's speech appeared as an unexpected boost just three days after the horrible attack by Eskridge on Stone.

Meanwhile, Albany presented its own challenges. AERA campaigners may initially have felt hopeful about success at the constitutional convention, but on June 11 rumblings of trouble emerged with a resolution about woman suffrage—a corkscrew proposal that would give people who could not otherwise vote the right to vote on whether they should be allowed to vote or not.[14] Introduced by delegate Ezra Graves, it was either subterfuge or a troubled compromise intended to win the support of all delegates and give woman suffrage a proper airing. Yet, while it gave an impression that delegates were considering woman suffrage, it would have given women uninterested in the vote the opportunity to kill it. The process would let the men off the hook completely, while it was not a proposal that any would submit to black men only regarding their equal enfranchisement, for the outcome was not controllable.

Before much else had occurred on the extension of suffrage in New York, however, and as if to remind women that they largely were on their own, yet another step in the advancement of black men and the exclusion of women in the nation took place on June 15 when Nebraska—admitted to the Union on March 1, 1867—ratified the 14th Amendment.[15] Now 22 out of 28 required ratifications were secured.[16] Six more were still needed, but the problem of finding ratifying states would soon be overcome, for freedmen would be voting for new constitutional conventions in the ten excluded states; the new constitutions would be required to provide for black male voting; and the re-formed states would have to ratify the 14th Amendment for reentry to the Union. Full ratification had been carefully planned.

While freedmen, abolitionists, and reformers might rejoice at these developments, women such as Stanton, Anthony, Stone, Rose, Gage, and others began to feel impending doom. Across the span of 150 years, it is difficult not to feel betrayal, anger, and despair—all the negative emo-

George Francis Train, c. 1855–1865, was a well-known national and international businessman, writer, and orator, a world traveler, lauded supporter and defender of the Union in pro–South Britain when war began, latterly criticized as a Copperhead and in 1865 a tycoon busy in Nebraska expanding railroad settlement through property speculation, with ideas of a presidential run. A speaker who could hold an audience in the palm of his hand, he was invited by the Woman Suffrage Association of Missouri in early summer 1867 to speak for female suffrage in St. Louis (Library of Congress).

tions that any man would have felt in similar circumstances. The progress of the ratifications favoring former slaves must have similarly stuck in the craw of many a free black man in the North, for the amendment was institutionalizing further male inequality. The men's feelings, however, were considered understandable, indicating an injustice requiring correction, and men were so used to women's conceding that they anticipated they would continue to do so. The women were expected to have no feelings on such matters, but if they did they should suppress them for the greater good of mankind—literally.

Yet, in this instance, the men were incorrect. The leading women and their colleagues were no longer the women who before the war would mildly remonstrate and then quietly blend in with the shadows. They were women who stood up for their own rights and objected when they were bypassed. For this contumacious and still unacceptable behavior they were condemned, just as individual women had been condemned for speaking out for decades. However, though objecting to their exclusion, they upheld a key difference between their actions and men's: men would ultimately turn to violence to win what they wanted. The women did not. "Our reputed republican or democratic governments are all bogus governments to disfranchised woman. But we only arm ourselves with arguments and facts to achieve our enfranchisement.... The hour of universal freedom is coming for us without violence," wrote one presciently.[17] The discussion, argument, and disagreements, therefore, might degenerate into a war of words, vicious on the part of opponents, male and female. But if physical violence erupted, women would not have been the cause it.

In Kansas by the middle of June, despite any optimism SISA workers may have felt at Wade's pronouncement in Lawrence, turmoil was bubbling over female suffrage. A "grand mass meeting" had been scheduled for June 8 in Hiawatha, Brown County, to promote "manhood suffrage" only.[18] On June 14, James Rogers of Burlingame—one of the leaders of the pro-suffrage cause—attacked Eskridge's war on women with a letter the *Emporia News* published. Elsewhere, Nichols aimed at the "free love" dirty tricks of what she called "a certain *Hon.* (?) Mr. [Charles V.] Eskridge."[19] Attempting to douse the effects of Eskridge's slurs by presenting personal knowledge of Stone, her impeccable credentials against the debasement of marriage by slavery, and her "scorching rebuke" years before of "the free-love abomination," Nichols stated that Stone and Blackwell "were legally and publicly married some ten years ago." She added, "The ballot-box gathers around it nothing more vile and destructive to social and domestic happiness than slanders like this." She concluded with a broadside against the use of such lies to advance discriminatory suffrage.[20] Such a counterattack was essential for Stone's reputation and the cause, but its effectiveness is doubtful when it came so long after the original slanders and when each defense dug up the original accusation and revived it.

By June 17 the senatorial railroad junket was in Missouri at Pilot Knob, south of St. Louis.[21] George Francis Train had been writing and speaking ramblingly and flamboyantly on finance, business, politics, and other subjects for years.[22] Now he was a well-established nineteenth century celebrity, and newspapers jumped on his latest, for he always guaranteed good copy—though many outlets reported him with arrogant condescension. Train was unique and exceptionally successful—a well-known buccaneering national and international businessman, writer, orator, and self-promoter, world traveler, entrepreneur, lauded supporter and defender of the Union in pro–South Britain when war began, latterly criticized as a Copperhead, and now a tycoon currently busy in Nebraska expanding railroad settlement through property speculation. Train had organized the junket to view the railroad's western progress and promote land sales. At Pilot Knob he spoke extemporaneously during an impromptu gathering. In the middle of his oration—not directly about politics—one of the senators asked about woman suffrage. Train argued for it, saying he backed what Senator Wade had said in his speech of June 10 in Lawrence. He said a woman's vote would uplift the nation morally and be a firewall against difficulties associated with black suffrage. He also criticized the huge national debt caused by the war.[23] Many newspapers picked this speech up. Train wrote later that he met "Mrs. Sturgeon, Mrs. Yates and Miss Allen, of St. Louis … on the Ben Wade Senatorial Excursion [and] a correspondence was opened" between Mrs. W.T. Hazard of St. Louis, secretary of the Woman Suffrage Association, at the instigation of her three fellow members.[24] The woman suffrage group formed that May 8 was already hard at work.

With the anti-woman fight beginning to pick up out west, in Albany on June 19, delegate George William Curtis presented a petition to the constitutional convention "in favor of woman suffrage."[25] That day the convention announced the Committee on the Right of Suffrage and the Qualifications to Hold Office of the New York Constitutional Convention. Horace Greeley, delegate-at-large for Westchester, was chairman.[26] Although before the Civil War he had been in favor of equal rights for blacks and white women, Greeley had discarded the women, increasingly ignoring their cause and the AERA in his paper, the *Tribune*. In May an AERA resolution had begged for coverage like the AASS received. Greeley's negative attitude stemmed from the 1860 Woman's Convention in which Stanton had advocated divorce. In fact, as the convention approached, his wife, Mary Cheney Greeley, was returning from the latest of many extended trips to Europe. For the eight years up to 1866, she was abroad half the time and her health improved the more she was without him.[27]

The *Tribune's* censorship of women appears to have started in 1866 when Greeley told Stanton and Anthony—possibly in the presence of his wife[28]—that if they persisted "in [their] present plan, [they] need depend on no further help from me or the *Tribune*."[29] Certainly, by 1867 the women had bewailed for long that previously sympathetic newspapers refused to cover their campaign. With only occasional backtracking to praise women's work for black men, Greeley had boosted only black male suffrage from the end of the war and was adamantly against woman suffrage. Meanwhile, his wife, now interested in woman's rights, had befriended Stanton and Anthony[30] and began to support the New York campaign. With Greeley chairman of the suffrage committee, "Miss Anthony and Mrs. Stanton knew he would seize upon this occasion to repeat his hackneyed remark, 'The best women I know do not want to vote.'" They now wrote to Mrs. Greeley asking her "to roll up a big petition in Westchester. So she got out her old chaise and, with her daughter Ida, drove over the county, collecting signatures."[31]

Meanwhile, a younger woman was heading out to campaign in Kansas, a mission which Stone and Blackwell helped to organize on their return East.[32]

22. Albany Goes Down

*[Female suffrage] would be demoralising to society ... [an] exper-
iment, extremely doubtful and that at the instigation of a few dried
up old elm-peelers¹ who disgrace the petticoats they wear, and with
whom a decent man can't live, and who, therefore, think there is something wrong in society ... and that it should be revolutionized, that
upon its ruins may be established the reign of free-love when everything will be held in common.*—Charles V. Eskridge, *Emporia News*,
June 7, 1867.

The Rev. Olympia Brown, a relative newcomer to woman's rights, had
quickly become an invaluable AERA member for her speaking skills and
commitment to equal rights. She developed her oratory at Antioch College
by meeting voluntarily the memorization standards required only of men.
Overcoming more discrimination, she studied religion at the Theological
School of St. Lawrence University and upon graduation became a Universal-
ist minister, the first woman in the United States a religious denomination
ordained. In 1867 her church in Weymouth, Massachusetts, allowed her to
campaign for equal rights in Kansas. She left around June 20² to head to a
state where already campaigning was becoming tortuous. Republicans were
now abandoning the woman suffrage measure they had passed and SISA
workers increasingly had to consider winning Democrat voters for the campaign.

At that time, the *Kansas Chief* was reporting fully on the free-love slander
of Stone,³ while a further defense of her under the name of W. Price appeared
on June 21 in Emporia. There now began, however, some active Republican
canvassing featuring "notable figures such as Judge T.C. Sears, Col. John Martin, Col. Preston B. Plumb, Reverend Isaac S. Kalloch, and.... Charles V.
Eskridge."⁴ The *Weekly Free Press* reported that some of the speakers gave
"mild endorsements of women's suffrage," while Colonel Martin, editor of
Atchison's *Champion*, supported "negro suffrage, but ... did not want his
mother or sister to vote, for he felt that it would hopelessly degrade them."⁵

In Albany on June 21, delegate Ezra Graves opened discussion on his resolution about women excluded from voting being allowed to vote on a proposal to let women have the right to vote. If passed, it would likely still fail because many women were against or uninterested in suffrage—highlighting the oppressive standard reformers applied to women but not to black men, which Stone had protested in her letter to a newspaper earlier in the month.[6] Avoiding discussion of the merits, Graves argued that "four classes" had specific interests in the measure. The first was "what is opprobriously known as 'strong-minded women,'[7] who claim the right to vote upon the ground that they are interested and identified with [men] in the stability and permanency of our institutions, and that their property is made liable for the maintenance of our Government, while they have no right to choose the lawmakers or select the persons who are to assess the value of their property liable to taxation." The second group comprised men and women concerned about declining values in the nation who wished to introduce women to raise standards. The third group believed in true equality among races and sexes. The fourth group, while denying an inherent right to the vote, wanted women through the franchise to participate in the government they helped to maintain. These four classes often overlapped, but the analysis was good and even though Graves' proposal was complicated, at least he brought the issue up, giving it recognition. It was referred to the Committee on the Right of Suffrage and the Qualifications to Hold Office,[8] announced two days before.

On June 25 Greeley asked for permission for the suffrage committee to use the convention hall for a public hearing of woman suffrage advocates,[9] scheduling it for June 27. This hearing was the very least Greeley could do. Black male suffrage was an official part of the proceedings; to get it out of the convention's consideration would involve a fight. Woman suffrage, on the other hand, was not part of the official agenda and to get it included was a struggle. This simple but huge distinction was the gulf that lay between black male and woman suffrage in Albany, and when the woman question arose, it was hobbled. For example, on June 26, delegate C.C. Dwight proposed a constitutional amendment "after the adoption of this constitution" to provide for the "enumeration of all citizen females" aged 21 years or older and for an election for the females to vote on woman suffrage. If "a majority of the whole number of citizen females" voted for the vote, then female suffrage would become law.[10] This measure would set the bar even higher against women than Graves' proposal, for it is always more difficult to win a majority of an electorate as opposed to a majority of people who actually vote.

"We had to rush up [to Albany] by Wednesday night's boat, without any preparation," Anthony recorded later,[11] because of the short notice for the woman suffrage meeting that took place on Thursday, June 27. That evening, the Committee on Suffrage quizzed Stanton and Anthony before "a numerous gathering of ladies, delegates and residents of the city."[12] Stanton outlined the inconsistencies between the right to vote and the rich and poor, and the uneven and unfair distribution of taxes for the sexes. "You do not disfranchise the negro worth $250, but you tax the poor widow and give her no vote. You exempt $1,500 of a clergyman's property, but if he dies you tax his widow for it."[13] She argued for woman suffrage based on justice, restating that "taxation without Representation is tyranny, and resistance to tyrants is obedience to God. Woman here refusing to pay any more taxes would act in accordance with this healthy revolutionary sentiment."[14]

Anthony "before proceeding to her address said she would be happy to hear any objections which the committee might have to female suffrage, with a view to answering them," to which Greeley asked, "if the friends of the movement had it in contemplation that jurors should be drawn indiscriminately from men and women?" When Anthony said yes,[15] he then admonished them: "'Ladies, you will please remember that the bullet and ballot go together. If you vote, are you ready to fight?' 'Certainly.... We are ready to fight, sir, just as you fought in the late war, by sending out substitutes.'"[16] Anthony further stated that equal rights meant equal responsibility; therefore, just as women would serve on juries, women would serve if drafted. The presence of women soldiers in the late war even without a draft demonstrated they would, for "several hundred" did fight, she said, adding, "but when their sex was discovered they were dismissed in disgrace; and to the shame of the Government be it said, they were never paid for their services."[17]

These were fighting words. Anthony was clearly angry, for women still had to beg for equality when, in a Republic, it should have been theirs of right, just as it was for men. What was worse, while fighting for their rights she and other women always faced men's degrading and insulting mistreatment of them and the issues. The Albany event was the latest example of the cavalier treatment both of women and their interests. The merriment that met the questions of Greeley and others—the male audience obviously thinking that they at last had skewered these women—illustrates well the prejudices among politicians in Albany in June 1867, where woman suffrage was not taken seriously. The event showed clearly that having a hearing does not equal being listened to. This public meeting had all the appearances of a show trial of New York's "strong-minded women" for stepping out of place. Stanton and Anthony were aware of this. Years later they wrote of having heard rumors of a negative report from Greeley on suffrage for women even as he was supposed to be giving them a hearing.[18] They likely anticipated well the outcome and would have had good reason to be unhappy about it—and the inadequate meeting notice, which was obviously intended to catch the women off-guard and perhaps prevent their participation. Anthony and Stanton had known for some time of Greeley's animosity to them; they went into the fray fully aware that Greeley could intend to humiliate them publicly.

Greeley's acrimony suffused the whole event. He lectured the women on history, putting them in a bad light purely for entertainment. The *Tribune* observed, "Much merriment was caused by a question … as to why the women of New Jersey had surrendered or been deprived of the privileges of the ballot. Mr. Greeley explained that a property qualification was required, which disfranchised many of the women, but it was true that in 1800 the women of New Jersey had carried the State for John Adams against Jefferson. After that the men took the ballot away from them. (Laughter and applause.)"[19] Anthony wrote to a relative on June 28 that she had "passed the ordeal."[20]

Anthony and Stanton considered the June 27 meeting at best a public relations exercise and at worst an attempt to pillory them. In fact, early the next year Stanton wrote, "In the Constitutional Convention of New York it gave us a sham hearing, having decided in caucus, beforehand, that it would report against our rights."[21] In the convention hall on June 28, they remembered, "the galleries were crowded with ladies" when Greeley stood to present his report from the Suffrage Committee.[22] They also remembered they were poised for payback, with delegates primed with female suffrage petitions. The Democrats, eager to upset Greeley's arrogance, "entered with great zest into the presentation."[23] Republican George William Curtis, who on June 19 had presented the first female suffrage petition, had a key role. A peripatetic journalist, author, and later famed orator, Curtis had first supported woman suffrage in 1858 upon becoming active in New York politics.[24] At their special request, they recalled, Curtis held his petition for last. "When he rose to present it, he said: 'Mr. President, I hold in my hand a petition from Mrs. Horace Greeley and three hundred other women citizens of Westchester, asking that the word "male" be stricken from the Constitution.'"

It was as if a stink bomb had been dropped in the middle of the convention hall. "Mr. Greeley's chagrin was only equaled by the amusement of the other members, and of the ladies in the gallery," the women's history recalled.[25] As they had often had to face similar humiliations when arguing for woman's rights in public, it was gratifying to see their nemesis squirming—perhaps even more gratifying than they had anticipated because, while they must have imagined some reaction from their carefully orchestrated plan, they seem not to have anticipated one quite so powerful. In retrospect they certainly enjoyed the memory, for it reverberates in posterity with a sense of delicious fun. The event clearly shook Greeley: "As he arose to read his report, it being the next thing in order, he was evidently embarrassed in view of such a flood of petitions from all parts of the State; from his own wife, and most of the ladies in his immediate social circle, by seeming to antagonize the measure."[26]

It makes an entertaining story, but what the ladies related twenty years later about the day Greeley presented his report on suffrage is not what happened. On June 19, 20, and 26, the constitutional convention received more than 40 petitions for woman suffrage.[27] On June 27, two delegates presented three[28] and on June 28, nine delegates presented many.[29] That day, Curtis corrected a name previously incorrectly entered but presented nothing new and none in the name of Mrs. Horace Greeley.[30] The tale was therefore correct about the flurry of petitions before Greeley pronounced his verdict, but it was incorrect about the coup de grâce that the women laughingly remembered.[31] The significance of Stanton and Anthony's work the day of Greeley's report on woman suffrage lay not in Curtis's presentation of Mrs. Greeley's petition as the climax of the whole event, for that did not happen. Its significance lay in the fact that the two had once again managed a large sustained petition campaign and recruited Democrats once again to help their cause. The clear involvement of Democrats demonstrates how far Stanton and Anthony had already progressed in casting off what was proving to be the incubus of the Republican and reform alliance. Clearly they had endured all but enough of the prejudices and duplicity of their erstwhile colleagues and were willing to find support where they had to, if not to win woman's suffrage then at least to keep the issue alive. They succeeded in doing so with their campaign during the constitutional convention. Not only were they not beaten into submission by the delegates they could not elect, but their work also put more pressure on Greeley.

Not unexpectedly, and no matter what the women did to counter the treatment they faced or to influence the outcome, it was unsuccessful. That June 28—the day after the "hearing" of the women's case—the Suffrage Committee announced it had looked on female suffrage and found that it was not good. The report, signed Horace Greeley, Chairman; Wm H. Merrill, Leslie W. Russell, and Geo. Williams, stated, "Your committee does not recommend an extension of the elective franchise to women. However defensible in theory, we are satisfied that public sentiment does not demand and would not sustain an innovation so revolutionary and sweeping, so openly at war with a distribution of duties and functions between the sexes as venerable and pervading as government itself, and involving transformations so radical in social and domestic life."[32]

This weasel rhetoric in the long debate between universal suffrage—meaning all adults regardless of sex and race, and universal suffrage—meaning discrimination against women on grounds of sex, revealed that men's prejudices about women prevailed to exclude them from equality. All additional arguments against a female franchise applied equally against equal black male suffrage. They could also have disqualified white men[33] if they were not automatically presumed to have a God-given right to vote. Yet Greeley and three of his committee—the majority of the seven—pronounced for "universal manhood suffrage" for these very flawed reasons. They may have used terminology recognizing the existence of women, but they used it to ensure female exclusion in New York. Further, Greeley's claim that the new suffrage was to be "adult rational manhood suffrage" meant he relegated women to a netherworld of other classes excluded from the vote such as paupers, "idiots," and the mentally ill along with such reprobates as felons, deserters, rebels, election fraudsters, and the like. Greeley's report, therefore, was yet another insult to women in a long history of such insults. To add these insults to the injury of the continuing ratification of the 14th Amendment within the same month was no mean feat. Such treatment, quite simply, angered women. By June 28, however, the story had not reached its end. Greeley concluded his report as follows: "Should we prove to be in error on this head, the Convention may overrule us by changing a few words in the first section of our proposed article."[34] This statement, so obviously formulaic and hollow, still left the doors open for further attempts to have woman included in reforms. The true tale of Greeley's maneuverings on manhood suffrage and how the women tried to forestall them would take some time to play out.

Meanwhile, the AERA had already begun trying to organize a public appeal from prominent men to the people of Kansas to vote for the two referenda. By June 28 Blackwell had already drafted it and was approaching potential signatories.[35] Back in Kansas, the same day an unnamed writer continued the counter-attack against the Stone character assassination.[36] However, while Stone had categorically and publicly repudiated free love and its advocates years before, the dissemination of material about her true position trailed the original slanders and these defenses in the classic public relations conundrum and merged with the continuing controversy, helping to keep it alive.

23. Kansas Heats Up

We exclude the female [because] the best interests of society would not be promoted by allowing her to vote... —Stephen D. Hand, Albany, New York, July 24, 1867, *Proceedings and Debates of the Constitutional Convention* (1868), 520.

In Albany the constitutional convention continued work after Greeley denied woman suffrage on June 28, and so did the women. On July 1 delegate Fowler presented yet another petition, the first of many that month.[1] That day, Olympia Brown arrived in Kansas to campaign for the November referenda. Stone had told Brown that "a conveyance about the state and a traveling companion" would be available to transport and accompany her to the different towns where she would speak to "keep [suffrage] before the people during the summer."[2] Upon arrival Brown ran headlong into the opposition to women that the Republican Party had adopted the previous May 15 and the vicious anti-woman lobbying of C.V. Eskridge and his cohorts such as the Rev. Isaac Kalloch.[3] Her first encounter with the Republican Party shows how quickly circumstances in Kansas had deteriorated after the departure of Stone and Blackwell in mid–May.

"[I] went, according to Lucy Stone's direction, to Colonel Coffin, then a member of the Republican central committee. Mr. Coffin was far from cordial. He knew of no such arrangement [regarding] conveyance and companion," recalled Brown. Mr. Coffin was also downright rude: "He said in his abrupt way, 'Why did they not send Anna Dickinson? Anna Dickinson is the one we want here.'" The renowned Dickinson was known more for her support for black suffrage than for woman suffrage, even though she claimed to support the latter, and Anthony had so far failed to win her unreserved commitment to women. Republicans would have preferred Dickinson because her support of black men suited the official party agenda. A mere woman, however, even though the first woman ordained in an established religious denomination, was not. At the time, Dickinson was unwell.[4] Besides, she was always paid well, and Kansas did not pay. Brown put on her missionary hat to overcome Coffin's depressing rudeness, persuading him to arrange, "a meeting in Leavenworth and another in a small town in the vicinity." At her next stop in Lawrence, once again "nothing was known there of any arrangement for the trip"; but Mr. Brown of the Unitarian Church and Milton Reynolds,[5] a former acquaintance from Albion, Michigan, and editor of a local newspaper helped. The latter "gave good notices and continued to do so through the whole campaign, thus rendering valuable service to the cause," recalled Brown.[6]

"The next day ... began to look like business!" she remembered. In Topeka she met Wood. "'Sam' had made arrangements for meetings, two every day, including Sundays, for two months ... and he had had flyers printed to send out "all over the state to advertise the meetings." Wood also told her that "the Republican party could not furnish a conveyance or a companion, or, in fact, assist the campaign in any manner"—demonstrating clearly the impact of their repudiation of woman suffrage six weeks earlier. To compensate for the lack of official help, Wood had nevertheless "written to places all along the line where he thought there were good people who would entertain the speaker and good men who would convey me from place to place." For the whole Kansas woman suffrage campaign for July and August of 1867, "there was one lone inexperienced young woman without money or means of conveyance." Undaunted, "all that made no difference to me. 'Sam' had provided a team and a driver to take me to the first appointment where he assured me I would find a cordial reception and a conveyance for the next day, which proved true," she wrote.[7] It was true on that one occasion: Brown in the upcoming weeks often had to prevail upon a reluctant farmer for the next leg. Yet she tackled her task enthusiastically, keeping the flame of woman suffrage alive during the two hottest summer months when an older campaigner might have wilted and dropped out.

After Brown met Wood, she first spoke at "a large meeting on the Fourth of July in Topeka at which he and several others" also spoke. That day in New York a scathing letter from Stanton appeared in the *Evening Post*: "If Mr. Greeley's report is accepted by the Convention, the disfranchised classes will stand thus: 'minors, criminals, idiots, lunatics, men who bet on elections, men who sell their votes, paupers, and all women....' [O]ur last state is worse than the first. With stalwart black men, worth $250 of real estate, we could make a better fight for freedom than with sick 'white males' not worth a penny."[8] That day, too, Stanton led with Anthony an AERA meeting in Westchester County—Horace Greeley's turf. In the conspicuous absence of "Henry Ward Beecher and other prominent speakers, who it was announced would be present," Anthony read the Declaration of Sentiments adopted by the Woman's Rights Convention at Seneca Falls 19 years before when United States women first publicly called for the right to vote. Judge Culver delivered "the usual Fourth of July oration," and then Stanton spoke on "the chief principle involved in the Revolutionary struggle—that taxation without independence was tyranny." She said that "women all over the United States were being taxed without being represented ... [and] advised all women who were unmarried and had houses to refuse to pay taxes until a sense of justice should induce the American people to grant to the so-called weaker sex the right of suffrage." Stanton reminded "the men and women of Westchester" that they still needed to petition Greeley for women's enfranchisement. If he "succeeded in remodeling the foundation of the government on the basis of caste and class legislation, all the experience ... all the wisdom and philosophy that the world has uttered in the last century, was wholly lost," for his plan opposed true republicanism. She scathingly criticized the hypocritical exclusion of women from juries when women, such as "the erring girl of fifteen ... was tried for the crime of infanticide, and hung on the gallows, while he who had betrayed her trust sat on the seat as judge, or in the jury box, or perhaps even ministered at the sacred altar." She challenged the contention that the ballot and the bullet went together, for she "presumed that not a member in the Constitutional Convention had gone to the war." Concluding, she said, "The grand cause of many of our greatest social evils was the degradation of woman. Were woman granted the right of suffrage, the entire social system would be regenerated."

Charles Remond then called for equal suffrage for black men, for, although Greeley's committee had come out in favor of "manhood suffrage," many a white delegate was already maneuvering somehow to maintain the $250 property qualification. Anthony read a letter from Stone, who, calling for equal suffrage for women, compared sex and race. In New York, "the most ignorant and vicious man, the foreigner and the negro worth $250 can vote. But educated American women, the wives and mothers of the State, are ranked politically below the criminal, below the foreigner and below the negro," she wrote. The most striking comparison she could have emphasized was that foreigners could vote, but she compared the position of women and black men: "In this state there are more than three hundred thousand women and about ten thousand colored men. Are the political rights of [these] women deserving of less consideration than those of ... the colored men?" She noted that many more women than colored men had petitioned the convention for suffrage and that "thousands of women have read with unspeakable regret" the denial of woman suffrage by the Greeley committee. Stone still hoped for true "impartial suffrage," by separate measures if necessary, which she seemed to consider the right approach. "It is thus in Kansas, and I have no fear for the results. Both propositions will carry, but many think that woman suffrage will poll the larger vote." Her confident assertion about Kansas belied the concerns she and Blackwell communicated before they had left in May. The meeting concluded after passing several resolutions, including one calling for more petitions and for propertied people to withhold their taxes if women were refused the vote.[9]

Suffrage was also part of the holiday messages in Kansas, which actually included women. "I hold that suffrage is a natural right inhering in every human being, co-extensive with human life—not to be denied by any power, to be circumscribed only as the safety of the community and the intelligence of the individual may require, and not subject, so far as the mere question of right is involved, to any conditions of color, race, or sex," declared Senator Edmund G. Ross in a speech sent in response to a June invitation to speak before the Grand Army of the Republic on July 4.[10] Once again, of course, this message harbored a chill at its center, for Ross devoted long paragraphs to the importance of black male suffrage only. His lack of balance in handling the issue must have warmed the cockles of the heart of the Emporia "anti" cabal such as Preston B. Plumb, one of the signatories of a preceding letter to Ross included in the news report. The national celebrations were clearly intended largely for the male half of the population.

In Albany the women's petition campaign continued. On July 8 delegate Fowler presented the petition of Gerrit Smith and 180 other citizens.[11] On the 9th, delegates Endress, Murphy, Fullerton, Van Campen, Beadle, Hammond, and Graves all presented petitions. That day, delegate Folger requested the use of the convention chamber for the evening of July 10 for an AERA meeting. Greeley objected, as he wanted to start the debate on his committee's report with nothing to interrupt it, but the AERA won.[12] Stone, meanwhile, had been in Washington, D.C., accompanying Josephine Griffing to drum up congressional support for the cause.[13] On July 10 delegates Tucker and Graves presented more woman suffrage petitions.[14] That day, Stone and Blackwell "addressed a very large audience at the [New York State] Capitol on the subject of 'Equal Rights....' Her address was very eloquent and was well received, being in substance the same as that previously delivered in different parts of the country. Mr. Blackwell severely criticized the Report of the Suffrage Committee in offering to extend the ballot to 10,000 colored men while withholding it from 750,000 intelligent women."[15] Afterwards Stone left Albany and hurried to Hartford, Connecticut, where on July 11 she addressed that state's Joint Select Committee on Constitutional Amendments in support of women's petitions for suffrage. Once again, she faced male prejudices. Despite more than 300 signatures asking for the removal of the word "male" from Connecticut's constitution, on July 10 the committee had announced it would support the removal of only the word "white." Stone attempted to counter this by pressing for two amendments to remove both words.[16]

While Stone was busy in Hartford, delegate Curtis in Albany presented more than 500 signatures for woman suffrage in one petition.[17] In Washington, D.C., Josephine Griffing formed a local branch of the AERA,[18] following up on her proposal at the AERA meeting in May when she advocated that similar plans to those in New York and Kansas be "laid out for all the States of this Union, and especially for the District of Columbia." With the previous December's groundbreaking debate on the subject still fresh, and with black male suffrage now legal there, she had said, "The proposition [of woman suffrage] has already been made there, and the parties have discussed its merits. The question of the franchise arose from the great fact that at the South there were four millions of people unrepresented. The fact of woman's being also unrepresented is now becoming slowly understood. It is easier now to talk and act upon that subject in the District of Columbia than ever before, or than it will be again. Even the President has said that if woman in the District of Columbia shall intelligently ask for the right of franchise, he shall by no means veto it. To my mind the enfranchisement of woman is a settled fact. We cannot reconstruct this government until the franchise shall be given not merely to the four millions, but to the fifteen millions."[19]

Back in Albany on July 12, delegate Corbett presented yet another petition for woman suffrage[20] while out west, as Brown trudged on, Eskridge unleashed his second major onslaught in the *Emporia News,* which, along with the original from June 7, are examples of virulent anti-woman prejudice. Besides calling female suffrage "the most impudent, frivolous, uncalled for proposition ever crammed into the throats of the people by a *shystering* legislature" and campaigners—"Political tricksters!" who were "opposed to negro male suffrage without the manliness to make direct, open, honest opposition to it"—he denounced the women as "a few old *Sally*-manders (who) desire it; but the true, ladylike women of Kansas would as soon be invited to a 'swimming hole' with a lot of men as to be goaded into the political arena by and with such characters as are leading off in this political *she*bang."[21] This forgotten insulting rhetoric, hurled with the power, influence, and money that women did not possess, made some men retreat from supporting their own amendment.[22] Such philippics erupted with force enough also to knock men into opposition, installing antis within countless homesteads.

Yet help for Kansas was percolating behind the scenes from correspondence of "Mrs. W.T. Hazard of St. Louis, Secretary of the Woman Suffrage Association at the instigation of ... fellow-members" with George Francis Train, following his support of women at Pilot Knob on June 17. On July 15 Train wrote to Hazard: "I say yes, to the St. Louis lecture."[23] And this letter to a private individual of a small organization about a lecture on woman suffrage in St. Louis he sent to Greeley's *Tribune,* continuing "and yes to stumping Kansas."[24] The intriguing question here is where the leap came from about giving a lecture in one state to stumping in a neighbor state during a referendum campaign—without any demonstrable arrangement between the two. It was possibly from Train himself. A rich, successful entrepreneur, writer, speaker, and self-publicist for years, the senatorial junket had readied him for renewed national prominence. Dreaming of the presidency, he was alert to the promotion of his ambitions. Having been in Kansas in June, he knew of the current contentious role of woman suffrage in politics. Kansas Republicans' clear rejection made it a message to attract Democrats with, and a weapon against Republicans. Besides, it was a great cause. This could be a very useful opportunity to latch onto.

24. Another Albany Skirmish

I desire to say ... that the only objection I have to their voting is that
they are women.—Edward A. Brown, Albany, New York, July 25, 1867,
Proceedings and Debates of the Constitutional Convention (1868), 547.

As Anthony watched Albany she complained to Anna Dickinson that
so far Curtis—the woman's champion in the New York Convention—had not
"been able to get to the floor ... to move to strike *male man* out"[1] because
some delegates, arguing that blacks were inferior, had been fighting to retain
"white" and demanding the retention of property qualifications to exclude
most black men. Another attempt to stop equal black suffrage, through a
separate vote, occupied much of July. Black men submitted few petitions
throughout. Had they been women, it would have signaled lack of interest
in the vote, which—if equality were applied equally to men and women—
would otherwise have been enough to end the discussion.

Women of the AERA had to fight to have woman suffrage debated—
very different from having it already considered a fundamental principle like
black male suffrage. This was a fierce struggle, for attempting to win acceptance for something that the men in power did not want was much harder
than opposing something that the men deemed to be policy. The AERA was
still operating as before; but whether it was because of internal pressure from
men or external pressure from congressional measures and so-called postwar
abolitionists or from the exigencies of campaigning, the organization was
increasingly limping. It still held meetings to promote its whole official
agenda, witnessed by the July 4 Westchester gathering[2] and Stone's meeting
on July 10. But maintaining its integrity was becoming increasingly challenging, with both minimal resources and pressures that pitted black men against
all women.

On July 16, the convention became a place of "much amusement" when
Curtis presented "a petition from Mrs. Horace Greeley and 100 other ladies
in favor of conferring the suffrage upon women," reported the *New York Times*.[3]
The petition of Mrs. Greeley "and other citizens of Westchester County"

asked "for equal suffrage for men and women."[4] The petition "was referred to the Committee of the Whole" and immediately delegate Folger submitted a petition asking for educated suffrage for men and women.[5] In the official record Mrs. Greeley's event passed with no fanfare. It had not occurred as the final masterstroke of a grand concerted campaign at one discrete, dramatic moment in the way the women later remembered with glee. It occurred three weeks after the end of what was effectively the first act in the drama. The women's memories conflated a series of events into one thrilling incident— a small triumph in the history of woman suffrage during Reconstruction when they got their own back on one of the men who had betrayed them. They could hardly be condemned for enjoying the thought 20 years later. Some newspapers had fun with it, reporting that the petition "headed by Mrs. Horace Greeley ... raised a general laugh at the expense of Mr. Greeley, who has displayed less than his usual courage on this subject, and in fact has made strenuous efforts to prevent the discussion of it in the convention. The women say he is either afraid of them or the question. Perhaps a little of both."[6] Another headed its small notice of the event with these immortal words: "A House Divided Against Itself."[7] But all the *Standard* said was this: "George William Curtis presented to the Constitutional Convention at Albany on Tuesday last, a petition from Mrs. Horace Greeley and others for womanhood suffrage."[8]

Soon after Mrs. Greeley's petition put her husband's nose out of joint, a *Tribune* editorial sarcastically proposed that women have their own conventions and lawmaking. "A female legislature, a jury of women, we could abide," it stated. "A legislature of men and women, a jury promiscuously drawn from the sexes we do not believe in."[9] This was clear support for segregation long before the term came into use, directly from someone with prejudices against women. Greeley now became "soured" to the women's cause, leading him to withdraw "the support of the *Tribune* and [throw] his influence against the [suffrage] amendment" in Kansas.[10] Stanton wrote of the punishment in a letter that September, but she was largely unrepentant: "This may do something to retard our final triumph; but it will take more than Horace Greeley and the *Tribune* to prevent the success of the movement."[11] She understood the man: Greeley was primarily a Republican Party and reform hack already opposing women long before his wife's petition. He masked his early opposition to women with arguments of current inexpediency. Any retribution from him represented insignificant change, for his behavior was already disappointing. Another threat, to call Stanton only "Mrs. Henry B. Stanton," would have erased her completely. Purportedly levied at this time it would simply have represented another turn of the screw, but it did not in reality occur until 1869.[12]

While the women later remembered with glee Mrs. Greeley's petition, at the time nationally it became a new weapon against her husband, who then was being excoriated as a traitor because he had paid some of Jefferson Davis's bail.[13] Phillips, for example, declared, "Mr. Greeley's position is fellowship with the disgraceful."[14] A woman in Wisconsin who "had a room papered with old copies of the *Weekly Tribune* [and] … heard that H.G. had gone bail for J.D., on her wrath … set fire to the paper, and, of course to the apartment."[15] Another newspaper scathingly contrasted the pro-woman suffrage position of "Raphael Semmes, the pirate," to "Horace Greeley, the right-hand man of Jeff. Davis the murderer, [who] has reported against female suffrage."[16] Woman's rights advocate and journalist Jane Grey Swisshelm slammed him as a war profiteer: "Mr. Greeley may afford to be magnanimous [in paying Davis's bail]. He lost no husband, or father, or son in the war. He lost no limb and carries no bullets, or the scar of them, in his body. Neither he nor his [family] shivered on Belle Isle, or prayed for death at Andersonville. It is easy to forgive injuries committed against other folks. The tax the war imposed on him is a pittance to the addition it made to his business. Of the $100,000 he made by writing a record of the rebellion, he can afford to give $5,000 to the head of the rebellion, for furnishing material, and still make a profit. But every one is not so fortunate."[17]

Swisshelm's observations provided heart-wrenching details that deepen understanding of the significance of Anthony's reference to Greeley's war service during the June 27 hearing, for the man who had the vote to whom she had to answer about women having to go to war if they wanted to vote had himself avoided going to war, avoided the scars and worse consequences of fighting. Yet this man used the fact that women by convention were excluded from fighting to pontificate against woman suffrage. His position was truly rich, for the public even then was being made increasingly aware of women's war work: at that time, a new book on the subject had just been published.[18] On July 18—two days after his wife's petition—Greeley submitted a woman suffrage petition to the convention,[19] odd behavior for the man whose own committee had declared against it. Perhaps he was attempting to redeem his public image. Possibly this petition was another ploy by the women to make him look bad, for as the petitioners' representative he likely had no choice but to present it. Yet, it did not change the committee's decision. In fact, later that day, procedural skirmishing took place over ending the debate on suffrage qualifications. Delegate Tilden objected, saying that while he had "no desire to protract the discussion … beyond a reasonable limit" and pointing out that already "it has been somewhat prolonged on a single question and one question only—the question of the suffrage of colored persons," he continued that he understood "there are gentlemen here, and one of them a man of distinguished eloquence, who proposes to discuss the question of the extension of suffrage to females."[20] Mr. Tilden, therefore, fought against guillotining discussion and for allowing proper discussion to take place. That afternoon, therefore, the long-awaited moment finally arrived, and "Mr. Curtis offered the following amendment: 'In the first section, strike out the word 'male' and wherever in that section the word 'he' occurs, add 'or she,' and wherever the word 'his' occurs add 'or her.'"[21] With this move, Curtis was finally able to ensure a proper convention debate on woman suffrage.

"While the essential reason of my proposition seems to me to be clearly defined ... the opposition to the suggestion ... has been only the repetition of a traditional prejudice, or the protest of mere sentimentality," Curtis declared. "In their report, the committee omit to tell us why they politically class the women of New York with idiots and criminals," he said, pointing out that its observation that woman suffrage would be "a novelty," was odd because most political progress was "novel." They also "speak of it in a phrase which is intended to stigmatize it as unwomanly, which is simply an assumption and a prejudice. I wish to know, sir, and I ask in the name of the political justice and consistency of this State, why it is that half the adult population ... are absolutely deprived of political power and classed with lunatics and felons.... No age, no wisdom, no peculiar fitness, no public service, no effort, no desire can remove from women this enormous and extraordinary disability [of sex]. Upon what reasonable grounds does it rest? Upon none whatever. It is contrary to natural justice, to the acknowledged and traditional principles of the American government, and to the most enlightened political philosophy. The absolute exclusion of women from political power in this State is simply usurpation."[22]

Curtis continued in such a vein for some considerable time. The speech "abounded with brilliant and happy illustrations, its rhetoric was faultless, and it was delivered with all the graces of elocution for which its author is renowned, and it is the highest tribute to the ability of the orator to say that it commanded the deepest attention from a body largely opposed to the cause for which he was pleading ... [and] the speech is regarded as the most powerful presentation of the claim of woman to the suffrage ever made on this side of the Atlantic," noted the *New York Times*.[23] "We must have thousands of that admirable speech to scatter through Kansas," wrote Stanton a few days later. "Whatever may be the result in the convention or the State, you have done your duty, we have done ours & there we must rest, knowing that no true word is ever uttered in vain."[24] Stanton had reason to be philosophical about the impact of the speech, for the *Times* commentator had already concluded it was "improbable ... that it gained a single vote."[25] The convention debate on women continued but soon slid into debate on equal male suffrage. Even so, the petition campaign continued, with hope still alive that at last women would win some justice.

The next day, July 19, Congress passed the final Military Reconstruction Act, leading to a complete reconstruction of the Old South replete with black male voting in the ten unreconstructed states. While it solidified a major precedent, black males elsewhere still without the vote or facing discrimination in voting laws now found themselves in an invidious position despite having fought for the Union and ultimately for the freedom of the now enfranchised former slaves. As there was nothing as yet concrete about a 15th Amendment, removal of the word "white" in state constitutions immediately became crucial for them. For women, without suffrage, the final Military Reconstruction Act represented yet another nail in the coffin of their vision of true republicanism in the reconstructed nation. It raised the stakes for their battles—perhaps even creating a sense of desperation about diminishing opportunities for breaking down the solid wall of discrimination against them.

That same day, Curtis in New York presented yet another petition.[26] In Kansas the *Emporia News* declared that its suffrage battle "promises to grow more active and exciting as the season progresses. It is announced that Judge Bailey, Judge Thacker, C.V. Crawford, Senator Ross, Representative Clarke and President Horner of Baker University will soon make a canvass of the State in favor of negro and female suffrage." The story said that Olympia Brown was even then touring the eastern counties and added this: "She is a woman of culture, refinement and great oratorical power." The newspaper also noted that AERA help for Brown had arrived with Bessie Bisbee, for Brown was speaking up to three times every day. It anticipated Stanton's arrival after the Albany vote and was completely up-to-date with the New York events, observing that "the discussion is re-opened there, Geo. W. Curtis leading off in behalf of the movement." The article ended as follows: "We have … seen only the irregular skirmishing on this subject. The great battle is yet to come."[27]

Delegate Hutchins followed Curtis's July 19 petition with one on July 20,[28] a day also noted for complaints about "a class of members who are continually chiding the Convention for want of diligence, objecting to adjournment, &c., and who, after these public demonstrations, almost invariably slip away toward the end of the week, and leave the convention destitute of a quorum." Greeley was identified as "one of the absentees … and illustration of this remark."[29] In Kansas, a meeting of the Lyon County Impartial Suffrage League took place in Emporia.[30] On July 23 Curtis presented more petitions, one with Stanton's name on it. Delegate Fowler presented another. As debate continued, some—like those who earlier had argued about the inferiority of the black race—also put the female sex down unequivocally. Delegate Barnard righteously noted, "It appears to me that the advocates of female suffrage … have forgotten one great fact, and that is that there is a religious view of this question that, to my mind at least, is conclusive against the affirmative side."[31] He continued in this vein for some time. Delegate Lawrence stated that Barnard's argument "is the same argument that has been used by power and privilege ever since the world began to keep the masses of the world in poverty and bondage." He continued: "When I vote to extend the right of suffrage to woman, I vote to give to woman an equal chance with man in the race of life. I vote to take away all obstacles in her pathway, that the two sexes may have an equal opportunity for success."[32]

The debate went on, largely comprising reiterations of "the protest of mere sentimentality" that Curtis referenced when he introduced his amendment. On July 23 a procedural vote lost 24 to 63[33] but was very revealing. "Very much to the surprise of many who have supposed that the advocates of female suffrage were confined to the extreme men of the Radical Party, Democrats like Mr. Cassidy and Mr. Corning were found in the affirmative," the New York Times commented, wondering if they would stay the course.[34] The next day, however, delegate Opdyke began expounding more "repetitions of a traditional prejudice," self-righteously declaring that, as women were as intelligent as men and with "more purity," they would make an "elector or representative" that no one could object to. "But I would withhold from her the right to exercise either function, for her own sake. The delicacy of her nature and the fineness of her sensibilities forbid that she should enter the arena of politics, to share in its fierce and demoralizing contests. Such duties are better suited to the rougher nature of man, but even to him they are not elevating in their tendencies. The effect on woman would be more deleterious still, and, for one I am disposed to protect her from it, both for her own sake and for ours."[35]

Events on the eastern and western fronts were advancing quickly. In Kansas, where Democrats were now campaigning loudly and negatively against black male suffrage, on July 24 the Republican State Central Committee—meeting in Topeka and intent on protecting their agenda and their own prejudices about "protecting" women from involvement in the rigors of politics—decided that the black suffrage proposal needed an overt campaign effort,[36] yet no new action transpired. Supporters of expanded suffrage soldiered on, either for both referenda as in the SISA campaign or in favor of black male suffrage only. On July 25 in Albany, Curtis again tried to strike out "man" and "male," while the original proposal of delegate Graves came up for consideration, with Greeley himself objecting "because it compels women to vote in order to avoid voting." The proposal lost 9 to 33.[37] Delegate More, trying additional tricks at best to prevent or at worst to restrict woman suffrage, played the race card to exclude black women from whatever women might win.[38] Finally the vote on Curtis's amendment was called. It lost 19 to 125.[39] That afternoon delegate Wales tried to raise the question again and was laughed out of the debate.[40] In Kansas the next day the war of words continued with two strong, pro-women items published in the *Emporia News*—one from Elder C.R. Rice of Burlington, the other a letter from Lieutenant Governor Nehemiah Green to Wood.[41]

In Albany, however, the defeated campaign was winding down. Delegate Potter introduced a final, lone woman suffrage petition on July 31,[42] effectively ending the women's campaign in New York in 1867. It was a hard-fought battle—one that the women and their convention support should never have had to fight. They lost purely because of the prejudice and self-interest of male delegates. However, the women succeeded in getting the true and full history of the Reconstruction-era New York Constitutional Convention into the official record, which demonstrated that many New York women wanted the right to vote and had worked hard to win it, yet their pleadings were summarily dismissed. The further achievement, despite the campaign's failure, was the paper trail that records the sex discrimination that was being hard-wired into state constitutions alongside the same process in the United States Constitution.

Black men fared slightly better. Equal manhood suffrage was presented from the start as a basic principle and, building on the already accepted principle of black male suffrage for rich black males, the idea of their equality emerged from the convention with the possibility of acceptance. Instead of including it in the proposed new constitution, however, opponents managed to impose a separate vote at the next election and it was therefore left vulnerable, even if it was officially on the state agenda with a possibility of success. Ultimately, electors would vote the measure down. Yet, even this consideration was completely denied to women. Consequently, another wedge between the two groups of the AERA—all women and black men—emerged from Albany in the summer of 1867.

25. The Women's Money Stolen

But you see, the money ... the money... —Susan B. Anthony to Samuel N. Wood, April 21, 1867, *The Selected Papers of Elizabeth Cady Stanton and Susan B. Anthony II* (1997), 54.

In the summer of 1867 Susan B. Anthony "set forth under a blazing July sun and tramped up and down Broadway soliciting advertisements for the fly-leaves of the new literature she meant to have printed. She then visited various friends who were interested in the woman's cause, and received such sums as they could spare, but their number was not large and the demands were numerous." The problem was that the "stock of literature [was] exhausted [and there was] nothing left in the way of tracts or pamphlets" to send west.[1]

Another huge problem was scheduling nationally known speakers. Dickinson and Douglass charged substantial fees the AERA could not pay. It hardly mattered, however, for they were looking to the South, the implementation of Military Reconstruction, and the call for election of delegates to constitutional conventions where neophyte electors accustomed to the domination of former Democrat masters would require guidance to secure Republican victories. The AERA, therefore, had been able to send west only the relatively unknown Brown, later assisted by the younger and less-experienced Bessie Bisbee.[2]

In Kansas, Clarina Nichols struggled to farm and campaign for woman suffrage at the same time with no money,[3] and Brown gamely worked her way through a state with a rudimentary infrastructure, facing many of the same challenges settlers encountered, pioneering for a cause and doing so at breakneck pace. She "traveled over the greater part of Kansas, held two [and later] three meetings every day, making in all between two and three hundred speeches, averaging an hour in length." Her work demonstrated women's equality, she said, showing that women could endure talk and travel like men, "especially when we recollect how the Hon. Sidney Clark, then candidate for Congress, canvassed, in the beautiful autumn weather, a small portion of the state which I had traveled over amid the burning heat of July and August."

Brown contrasted the ease of a man's campaign with that of the women: "He spoke once a day instead of twice; he rested on Sundays; he had no anxiety about the means of travel, his conveyance being furnished at hand; he was supported by a large constituency, and expected to be rewarded by office and honors." Her work in Kansas, she said, demonstrated women's superiority, for even "with all these advantages, he broke down in health and was obliged to give up a part of his appointments, and the Republican papers said, 'It was not strange, as no human being could endure without loss of health such constant speaking with such long and tedious journeys as Mr. Clark had undertaken.'"[4] The irony of their claims compared with Brown's arduous work that summer escaped them.

Brown also encountered anti-woman agitation. Once "an organized mob ... hailed [me] with sticks and stones and shouts of derision ... determined to break up the meeting and [I had to face] the battle alone.... While I was trying to speak the rowdies kept up their noise, shouting and throwing stones until the little school-house rocked and the people inside trembled. It seemed that this mob had been organized in advance by a young lawyer who intended to prevent the meeting." When Brown invited them to speak, the thugs settled down. "All was still when the lawyer himself made an extended speech against woman's suffrage, going back to Queen Elizabeth. After annihilating her, he proceeded to denounce all later women who had attempted to do anything," she remembered. Yet some in the audience supported Brown. "A row of women in 'slat' sunbonnets who sat on one side of the school-house and were evidently not edified by his remarks kept whispering loudly, 'You had better shut up. We've got no use for you.'"[5] Brown faced male low-lifes regularly. Newspaper editors, not just in Kansas but elsewhere, joined in the bullying. A particularly nasty editor from Omaha called Brown a "weather-beaten, cross-grained, sour, snappish, fanatical, crabbed, skinny, smoked-looking old beldame,"[6] and several other newspapers picked up this mean-spirited description of the 32-year-old ordained minister. Such treatment was abuse.

In August the pro-woman Emporia-based Lyon County Impartial Suffrage League began work. Along with a news report of their July 20 meeting, the group published a petition with seventy-four signatures announcing that "The women of Emporia and vicinity, aged twenty-one years and upwards, earnestly and respectfully" request the right of suffrage. The resolutely anti-woman forces in the town took this as a threat. The same paper published a long, vituperative anti-woman article attacking the women's aspirations, their work, and their honesty.[7] Bessie Bisbee, representing the SISA, spoke there that day, becoming the target of publisher Stotler's criticism: "[She was] a not unlikely looking specimen of a girl, who thereupon delivered a school girl effort in favor of Female Suffrage, the most considerable and important portion of which was devoted to a detailed account of the mental and moral characteristics and condition of the great army of prostitutes of New York city, and which was treated in a manner indicating a thorough acquaintance with the subject, but the application of which to Kansas we fail to see the point of. Taken altogether Miss Bisbee's effort was not discreditable to her, as we are not aware that she enjoys any great reputation either as speaker or thinker. Nothing new was advanced, but the ordinary ... arguments were fairly rehearsed. The most obvious comment upon Miss Bisbee's 'effort' was well expressed by an auditor who said that 'it was barely worth [her] while coming all the way from Vermont for the purpose of delivering such speech as that.'"[8] The *Emporia News* had once again excelled in its insults, replete with innuendo designed to repel potential supporters and run off the women working publicly for suffrage. The courage of this woman in the face of such abuse, even from over 150 years away, is awe-inspiring. The same newspaper's eloquence and sarcasm extended also to Wood, who spoke at the meeting, though unannounced.[9] Two days later, on Sunday, August 4, a sermon by the Rev. Samuel E. McBurney of the Methodist Episcopal Church of Emporia added the heavy hand of the Bible to the heavy hand of the newspaper editor against woman suffrage. McBurney "spoke earnestly and eloquently against the sundering of those heaven ordained relations between the sexes which give to woman their angelic character and which bind men by the silken cord of affection, love, gentleness and piety." The paper commented, "While female suffrage received a crushing blow, its most ardent supporters could find no solid objection to the sermon."[10]

Brown struggled gamely on. With the state publishing the suffrage amendments,[11] the campaign was now official. On August 9 the *Emporia News* printed notices of upcoming meetings by Brown, including one in Emporia on August 24. In the same issue Mrs. J.H. Slocum, who had submitted the women's petition for publication the previous week, now complained about dirty tricks against the women signatories. Some names, the newspaper had claimed the day the petition had first appeared, had been withdrawn with disparaging remarks. "How came these ladies to make these remarks?" Mrs. Slocum demanded. "It looks *very much* as though somebody had taken them to task for what they had done, and that the pressure was so strong that they could not resist it. It is just this intimidating policy that we protest against."[12] Little had changed in 20 years: signatories of the resolutions of the Seneca Falls Convention of 1848 were excoriated by many media for their audacity.

Meanwhile, Anthony was struggling in New York to plan for Kansas. Producing pamphlets was paramount. "Our tracts do more than half the battle; reading matter is so very scarce that everybody clutches at a book of any kind," she wrote.[13] She was also fund-raising for the trip out west.[14] Then a bombshell hit. A Massachusetts court had decided that the Jackson Woman's

Rights Fund did not apply to women, she wrote angrily to Wood on August 9, advising him that "*every speaker who goes to Kansas* must *now pay her own* expenses *out of her own private purse*" and warning him against debts, for the AERA had nothing to pay them with.[15] Later in the month she poignantly explained the huge challenge to Martha C. Wright: "You see, our little trust fund—$1800 of Jackson money is wrenched from us. The Hovey Committee gave us our last dollar in May, to balance last year's work, and I am responsible for stereotyping and printing the tracts, for the New York office expenses, and for Mrs. Stanton and myself in Kansas, in all not less than $2,000. [No one] wants the Kansas work to go undone, and to do it, both tracts and lecturers must be sent out. We need money as never before."

The campaign would be expensive for her. "I have to take from my lean hundreds, that never dreamed of reaching thousands, to pay our travelling expenses. It takes $50 each for bare railroad tickets," she wrote. Then she and Stanton would face a grueling time. "We are advertised to speak every day—Sundays not excepted—from September 2 ... to November 6. What an awful undertaking it looks to me, for I know Kansas possibilities in fare, lodging and travelling." She was super-stressed. "I never was so nearly driven to desperation—so much waiting to be done, and not a penny but in hope and trust. Oh, if somebody else could go and I stay here, I could raise the money; but there is no one and I must go. We must not lose Kansas now, at least not from lack of work done according to our best ability."[16]

This was the second huge financial blow for women in 1867. Phillips arbitrarily stopped all Hovey funds to the AERA that March, effectively closing down the AERA's work in New York. When the call for help came from Kansas, there was no money. Worried even then, Anthony wrote to the *NASS* to publicize the AERA's need for as much as $10,000 to pay for good speakers for the upcoming campaign.[17] In May at the annual meeting, the AERA president Lucretia Mott announced "that $10,000 was needed to carry the elections in Kansas," but even several collections[18] fell far short.[19] Anthony's August 1867 letters highlighted the great weakness of the suffrage movements of Reconstruction and of woman's rights generally—lack of money due to women's subservient situation and married women's chattel status. Even the black suffrage campaigns wherever they occurred had official backing, which meant funding and other help, even if black men complained it was inadequate.

The Jackson Fund originated in 1858 when Massachusetts abolitionist and woman's rights supporter Francis Jackson established a $5,000 trust for woman's rights and made the money available immediately under the trusteeship of Phillips, Anthony, and Stone. The Hovey Fund originated in 1859 from the will of abolitionist and woman's rights supporter Charles F. Hovey of Boston. He left $50,000 for antislavery and "such as women's rights, nonresistance, free trade and temperance." Hovey stipulated that if slavery were abolished woman's rights were then to benefit from the funds freed up from antislavery work. Phillips and a committee of abolitionists were trustees. As lead trustee, Phillips used the Hovey Fund to shore up the *NASS* and after the war, having redefined antislavery as political rights for freedmen and then all black men in the United States—seemingly deliberately to keep the money flowing—he thereby kept himself in a job and financed the *NASS*. This behavior smells of a very public and brazen breach of trust, which infuriated the women. Stone railed against it early in 1867. Francis Jackson was revealed as the donor of the anonymous women's fund when he died on November 14, 1861.[20] The key difference his will made to the trust he established for women during his lifetime was that he directed more potential money to it—half of the income of the one-third of his estate left to his daughter, Eliza F. Eddy, upon her death.[21] The Jackson Fund seemed dormant between 1860 and December 1865, when $500 that Anthony extracted from Phillips for the campaign she and Stanton were launching is referred to as the "W.R. Fund."[22]

Anthony's anguish and fury when she wrote to Martha Wright highlights one of the largely unknown nefarious episodes of Reconstruction and yet another instance of the dastardly treatment of woman suffrage campaigners, not only by so-called colleagues but also by the discriminatory system in which they lived. For, while what was happening with the Hovey money took place out in the open, it appears the Jackson Fund events were handled covertly right to the point where Anthony found out about the debacle. She never knew the family had challenged the will or that the court handed down a first decision in *Jackson v. Wendell Phillips et al.* in mid–January 1867.[23] The Massachusetts court then essentially wrote women out of Jackson's will. The *Commonwealth* commented on the decision's ludicrousness: "The court has decided that money left to 'create a public sentiment that will put an end to negro slavery in this country' is a 'legal charity,' when there is not legally a negro slave in the United States! The court has also decided that a legacy made to 'give to women all other civil rights enjoyed by men' is not a 'legal charity' and therefore inoperative and void."[24] An all-male judiciary based its discrimination in the application of justice overtly on sex.

The post-abolition antislavery trustees now fought over the rich pickings the decision allowed. A second decision, in which the court attempted to dispose of the childish quarreling of the remaining trustees and beneficiaries of the so-called antislavery group, was handed down in early August 1867[25]—the first newspaper report appearing only the day after Anthony wrote to Wood of this latest debacle for the Kansas campaign. Phillips had finally come clean to Anthony then. Quite naturally she was distraught about the theft of the money. She had "never known a thing about" the law case, she wrote in fury to Dickinson,[26] even though she was a trustee. Phillips was the culprit all around. He drew up the Jackson will. His self-serving behavior was well known; and he had ample opportunities to hide the case from the women for, as a lawyer, he could have accepted service of any court documents from the Jackson lawyers without even telling women they were parties to a case they should defend. His behavior lacked professional integrity. He was also a paternalist.[27] Saving women from having to bother their pretty little heads about serious matters was second nature to him and provided him with cover. Married women's subordinate position under the law, whereby they still had to have their husband handle lawsuits, was reason enough. He might also have been thinking of an outcome beneficial to his causes at women's expense, which fits the behavior of someone who redirected money from the Hovey Fund to his own anachronistic cause of antislavery. There were good reasons how Anthony could have heard nothing about the law case that purloined the women's money. She was so busy travelling throughout New York promoting the AERA cause and busy with the forthcoming constitutional convention that news about something she didn't even know about appearing in a Massachusetts paper[28] likely did not even cross her path. From January, Phillips would still have had ample reason to hide the court's decision, because the case continued and the result was still uncertain. However, the outcome leads to one clear conclusion regarding the women, and that was that Phillips made a mess of putting his client's wishes into legal form to safeguard his beneficiaries. At the very least, his incompetence was responsible for the debacle.

Anthony quickly suspected something fishy. "Isn't it passing strange that any court should decide that heirs could take money *given by the owner during his lifetime into our hands* for the special purpose of securing the ballot for women?" she wrote irately "It does seem to me that if the money had been *in my hands,* and I a *Lawyer,* I could and would have saved it from so unrighteous a fate."[29] As a trustee, Anthony had reason for fury: obviously neither she nor Stone had been notified; therefore, effectively no one appeared at the trial to argue specifically for women or protect their especial interests, with disastrous results.[30] For Anthony this must have been especially infuriating, for unlike Stone, whose freedoms were circumscribed as a married woman, Anthony as trustee could have arranged representation in court.[31] Suspicions about Phillips' behavior and motivations are well grounded. Given his propensity for dishonesty, it appears that he wanted to keep Anthony well away so that he could engineer whatever he could devise for himself and his own causes without being hampered by the problems of mere women, especially as by 1867 to him they were only trouble by refusing to toe his line for black male suffrage only.

One reason Anthony was so shocked and angry at the news of the court's decision on the Jackson Fund was that she had obviously expected at least some of it to be available for Kansas.[32] "$1800 … taken out of our hands by the Massachusetts Court … and we *are left without a dollar*," she raged.[33] The new reality not only exacerbated the Kansas problems but seems also to have created tensions between Anthony and Stone, for there was nothing left of the $1,500 that Stone and Blackwell received from the fund in the spring. Unfortunately, "when she began to figure the expenses for her trip with Mrs. Stanton," wrote one biographer, Anthony discovered that "Stone's campaign depleted the fund."[34] An indication emerges from subsequent correspondence[35] that Anthony raised the question of remaining money with Stone but was informed nothing was left. This does not necessarily mean wrongdoing, but no accounting seems to have been required.[36] Still, Stone and Blackwell, whose financial circumstances were improving significantly, had availed themselves of every penny. The contrasting penury of Brown and Bisbee, already in Kansas, and of Anthony herself must have rankled, for so much of her time was spent fund-raising.

The political and financial challenges for Kansas in August 1867 were a huge contrast with the early stage of the campaign. Stone and Blackwell were funded, with strong support in the East when they went to Kansas in late March 1867. They began campaigning there in the cooler spring, at a time when there were objections to their presence but no organization of the caliber that they brought to support the referenda and the SISA. In March and April 1867 the Kansas Republican Party had no official plan of campaign, while Stone and Blackwell had the support and help of Wood and Robinson. The two did see the first signs of the future in political machinations and the scurrilous slanders used to discredit them, but they left for home before opposition organized.

By contrast, everyone after them—Brown, Bisbee, Anthony, and Stanton—faced both campaign penury and heated and focused opposition. None had much money or support for their work, either in Kansas or from back East. By early summer, local forces around the state—epitomized by the anti-woman publishing and organizing in Emporia—were coalescing under the banner of universal suffrage. This weasel rhetoric advocated not just male suffrage only but also characterized SISA workers as pro-woman only. When Brown arrived, the Republican Party, in line with the pro-black-male only party policy, deliberately reneged on assistance previously promised and Brown had to cobble her campaign together step-by-step. She and Bisbee had then to campaign in the height of the summer. By the time Anthony and Stanton arrived, the organization of the anti-female forces was running well, both to support black male suffrage and to fight female suffrage. By then the SISA had all but fallen apart.

In short, the character of the campaign had changed dramatically since Stone and Blackwell had left in May. Except for the initial slanders against them, they faced nothing of the firestorm that built from mid–May on. Relatively speaking, the two breezed through the state when they campaigned during the cooler season. Anthony and Stanton arrived in time for the full force of opposition to erupt. By August, neither Stone nor Blackwell had a clear idea of the situation on the ground.

26. Reinforcements

What I have had to do with is the inconsistency and hypocrisy of those who advocate negro suffrage and oppose Woman suffrage; the inconsistency and hypocrisy of those negroes who claim rights for themselves that they are not willing other human beings with equal intelligence should also enjoy.—Samuel N. Wood, 1867, *History of Woman Suffrage, II* (1887), 230–231.

On August 9—the same day Anthony wrote to Wood in Kansas about the latest financial debacle affecting the campaign—Emporia's suffrage women, at a meeting with Bisbee and Wood, found the big guns of local leaders trained on them. On August 13 there would be an anti-female suffrage assembly in the town. That day, "H.C. Cross presided, and large delegations were present. Speeches were made by C.V. Eskridge, Dr. Hewitt, Rev. Mr. McAnulty, J.C. Fraker and Jacob Stotler.... Messrs. C.V. Eskridge, C.C. Deweese and J.D. Jaquith—one from each representative district—[were appointed] to act as a central committee to organize the county against the imported and home" campaigners.[1] "Impartial" suffrage meetings were also announced for August 15 and 16 for White Cloud and Brown County,[2] while a call went out for a "Meeting of the Opponents of Female Suffrage" for Emporia for August 31. Seventy-seven names declared, "All who are opposed to Female Suffrage and believe that the best interest of the people of Kansas demand the defeat of the proposition now before them, are requested to unite with the undersigned in mass meeting."[3] The men of Emporia thus took direct aim at the "uppity" Browns, Bisbees, and Anthonys from elsewhere, while directly challenging local women who had demonstrated with their work and petition that they did not know their proper place. The August 9 meeting in Emporia with Bisbee and Wood speaking was the last sighting of Wood for several weeks. Sought out later, he said he had become disheartened and retreated home.[4] The timing of Wood's exit is close to when he likely received Anthony's letter about the Jackson Fund. His disappearance from the SISA scene in August 1867, therefore, may signal yet another impact on the Kansas campaign by Phillips and the male judicial system that resulted in the loss of the women's trust fund, for Wood had jump-started and promoted the SISA campaign and without his leadership, the campaign stumbled. Blackwell had warned about this in the spring.[5]

Meanwhile, the anti forces, in heavily sarcastic prose, increasingly complained at every opportunity of anything they disapproved of about the women. They attacked Bisbee's suffrage work and the singing troupe who provided entertainment for people living in isolated communities where entertainment was rare: "What a compliment to the people of Kansas it is to send boarding school misses and crazy singers to instruct them in their political duties. The people who can't be converted by Miss Bisbee and the Hutchinsons will, we presume, be turned over to Sam Wood, who will blackguard them into the support of Female Suffrage! Quite a dignified way of treating a delicate and important subject! What next?"[6] This mud was mild compared with that previously thrown at the women's cause. The irony and hypocrisy of presumably elite men who believed themselves civilized denigrating those who lectured and the people who were learning about enfranchising more than half of the population was probably lost on the mudslingers. The antis also attacked eastern attitudes, specifically Greeley's argument from May that the great experiment of woman suffrage should occur in a new, young state like Kansas, not a fusty, calcified, former colony: "We know of nothing more offensive to the dignity of our State, or more insulting to the intelligence of its citizens—than the howl which is borne to us from the older States, 'try the experiment in Kansas and we'll follow suit if it pays well...' If 'experiments' are to be made it seems to us better that our friends of the eastern States try them for themselves."[7] Men in Kansas had a valid complaint against New York, but the inference that woman suffrage was inherently wrong demonstrated their prejudices also.

While these anti-woman storm clouds gathered and the pro-woman forces began to crumble, Mrs. Rebecca Hazard of St. Louis, correspondence secretary of the recently formed Woman Suffrage Association of Missouri, replied to a letter from Wood "of the 17th inst."[8] Wood—out of the scene but obviously not out of the action—had enquired about Brown and Bisbee lecturing in St. Louis, perhaps an attempt to help them pay their way home after Kansas, for a communication of this date could have succeeded Anthony's missive of August 9 telling of the women's financial debacle. Hazard said the Missouri group could not currently host Brown, Bisbee, or any of several others from the east who had offered to speak because their campaign penury necessitated free lectures. She suggested "the latter part Sept. [when] we are to have a large meeting at Mercantile Library Hall," and St. Louis women would be happy to meet them. Hazard mentioned several prominent male endorsements of woman suffrage in Missouri, adding, "I propose writing with

Mrs. Stanton and Miss Anthony to see what arrangements we can make." Referring again to Wood's previous communication, she wrote she had told a colleague about "what you said about the Democrats helping you in Kansas provided it were a little stronger and I am glad to say it appears to have had a good effect." She continued: "Can we do anything to help you in Kansas? You don't know how anxious we feel for success there, everything depends on it, we feel like turning all our efforts in that direction." Then Hazard asked this question: "Do you want Geo. Francis Train in Kansas? He proposed to come here and lecture for us free of expenses and also to 'stump' Kansas. I could not tell whether you would think best or not so we merely accepted his proposal to come here."

This letter establishes that George Francis Train himself made the leap from lecturing in St. Louis to stumping for Kansas. Hazard is writing just over a month after his acceptance of the St. Louis invitation—the July 15 letter that appeared August 1 in the *Tribune*. This sequence indicates that Train's letter—revealed so publicly—may already have triggered communication from Wood to Hazard before the August 17 letter she mentions. Hazard's August 20 letter confirms that Wood was seeking Democrat support—an idea that arose in Kansas early, for Wood had a history of such cooperation, as had Robinson, while Blackwell had written enthusiastically to Anthony in the spring about Democrat votes compensating for Republican opposition. Finally, at the end of letter, upside down, in darker ink and different writing, are the words, "I wrote send Train, Wood." Here, definitively, is the origin of Train's sojourn in Kansas in 1867, which to this point has been hidden

Mrs. Rebecca Hazard, c. 1893, became correspondence secretary of the Woman Suffrage Association of Missouri on its formation on May 8, 1867. The next month, after several members met George Francis Train at an event in Pilot Knob, Missouri, where he advocated woman suffrage, Mrs. Hazard wrote asking him to speak in St. Louis. When he agreed, he also offered to "stump" in Kansas and made his letter public, which led to Mrs. Hazard's correspondence suggesting Train for Kansas. From the early 1850s Mrs. Hazard had worked to help disadvantaged women in St. Louis and would later serve as president of Lucy Stone's American Woman Suffrage Association (Wikimedia Commons).

in mystery. This letter proves that Wood is the original point of contact in Kansas with Train. It places beyond doubt information contained in an early 1870 letter regarding an interview Isabella Beecher Hooker had with Blackwell. Hooker reported from this interview that Train "went to Kansas on the invitation of one Wood ... to lecture to whomever would hear on Woman Suffrage." The 1870 document clearly shows Blackwell's input, as only two years later he revealed the broad lines of how it evolved after the initial contact. "Mr. Blackwell & Gov. Robinson & two or three others who were conducting the W.S. campaign thought it might be well for [Anthony] to accompany Train & so get democratic votes," Hooker wrote.[9]

That Train would pull the woman's cause further out of the Republican orbit was hardly a problem for Wood, for if winning was the goal and official party support was disappearing, woman suffrage had to find support somewhere. Anthony's bad financial news made the idea of a speaker who would "stump" for Kansas "free of expenses" very attractive. Blackwell likely dismissed any downside for the male suffrage measure, for arranging for Kansas such a highly visible canvasser comported with concerns that he and Stone had earlier expressed

FADED TEXT

Letter of Mrs. Rebecca Hazard of August 20, 1867, to Senator Samuel N. Wood, asking Wood if he wants George Francis Train to canvass in Kansas in 1867. This letter, cited in an earlier history as a letter to Susan B. Anthony, reveals the origin of George Francis Train's trip to Kansas in 1867. Susan B. Anthony was not involved in it until almost the last minute (Olympia Brown Papers, Schlesinger Library, Radcliffe Institute, Harvard University, Cambridge, Massachusetts).

about the negative impact of potential male black voters on women. Stone's involvement is unclear, but for her, while a win for both referenda would be the ideal, it seemed she would not be unhappy if only the women won, having clearly written on May 9 to Anthony that black male voting in Kansas should occur after female voting because they would be "more dead weight to lift."[10] A plan for Train to stump Kansas was, therefore, in the works by late August 1867. It was organized only by people in Kansas or people who had already campaigned there. Anthony—definitively—was not involved. However, the reference in the Hooker letter to Blackwell, Robinson, and others planning for Anthony to accompany Train without her knowledge, "& so get democratic votes,"[11] establish this plan as an outright conspiracy.

Meanwhile, anti-female suffrage Republicans continued their assault. On August 20 "the Rev. S.E. MacBurney [*sic*] and the Hon C.V. Eskridge addressed the citizens of Americus ... in opposition to Female Suffrage. They found the people there almost unanimously against the proposition. Every voter in the audience signed the rail for the Mass Meeting on the 31st inst. but two. It looks as if Americus will be the banner township in opposition to the 'pernicious proposition,'" it was reported.[12] Circumstances on the campaign trail continued to degenerate, with the *Kansas Chief* airing complaints about Olympia Brown that first emerged after her appearance in Fort Scott. "A condition of the question is fast approaching, which we have endeavored to avert: a bitter antagonism between negro and female suffrage," the newspaper announced. "Miss Olympia Brown, in her speech at Fort Scott, is said to have very indignantly declaimed against placing the dirty, ignorant, degraded negroes ahead of white women."[13] Brown denied this, and it may be yet another case of dirty tricks during this dirtiest of political campaigns. Others in the industry certainly believed that the *Fort Scott Press* writer was publishing lies to serve its own anti-woman agenda.[14] Yet the usually pro-woman *Kansas Chief*, commented, "The Chase County Banner, which is doubtless under the editorial supervision of Sam Wood, takes substantially the same position. [It] also copies articles from such papers as the Leavenworth Commercial, the object of which is to show the hypocrisy of the Republican party, in advocating negro suffrage. As a friend of female Suffrage, we protest against this course, as tending to ruin the cause, [for they] are doing all in their power to make suffrage a question of social equality." The article continued: "They are strengthening the Copperheads in their favorite argument against the expansion of suffrage, especially to black men, but also to women." The Republican party, on the other hand, "insists that granting political rights does not establish social equality."[15] This argument did, in fact, highlight Republican double standards. If granting black males voting rights would change nothing socially this was an equally good argument for allowing female suffrage and it was hypocrisy if enfranchising black men was acceptable but enfranchising women was not. Yet, the *Kansas Chief* warned, "if the especial champions of female suffrage intend to unite with the Copperheads and rebels of Kansas in this, they and their cause will go under with the Copperheads and rebels."[16]

A reader of the *Kansas Chief* shortly afterward stated that the Brown accusations were false. "Miss Brown has been misrepresented…. She has never spoken in opposition to negro suffrage, but has always advocated it," the letter writer with the pen-name Coeur de Lyon stated.[17] This writer conceded that a statement of Brown could be distorted. "In her speeches at Fort Scott and elsewhere," Coeur de Lyon admitted, "she did say that as we had determined to confer suffrage upon black men, however ignorant, we should be certainly as willing to bestow it upon intelligent and cultivated women."[18] Yet, all the arguments for black male suffrage applied equally to women: reverse the situation, with women being given the vote and not black males, it would equally have been true to say that if "'women, however ignorant' were being enfranchised, 'we should be certainly as willing to bestow it upon intelligent and cultivated black men.'" The same argument could apply to ignorant white men. Further, none of what Brown said tried to deny suffrage to black men or campaign against them. Opponents, however, twisted her arguments to misrepresent her, just as the Fort Scott newspaper had reported and the *Kansas Chief* had repeated—thereby slurring the character of women campaigners.

Several compelling cultural reasons motivated them to ignore her logic. Many, if not most men—black and white—saw what she said as a putdown. For reformers, the idea of black men being uneducated was a reality not to be acknowledged, even if the major fight at this time over the Francis Jackson bequest was whether to spend the money on freedmen's education before their political advancement. However, Brown's statement gave the opportunity to claim that women were against black male suffrage, which was a convenient way of saying women who advocated female suffrage were racist. Further, according to society's men-at-the-top hierarchy, for a woman to put herself on a par with men or to infer superiority meant she was stepping out of her allotted place while also demonstrating that she was anti-men. It was equally unacceptable to enfranchise "educated and cultivated" women only, for it would make some women equal with those black men who could still vote despite discriminatory high property tax voter qualifications. Besides, discrimination in voting had been standard practice in the United States since the founding of the nation, with the primary—and blanket—discrimination always "on account of sex," which men now seemed determined to reinforce. The simple fact was that Brown was not against black male suffrage: she assumed that black male suffrage was "a fixed fact" even before it happened.[19] She simply contrasted Republicans' treatment of the two issues. Yet women could not win such arguments, for opponents could twist whatever they said into the opposite meaning to discredit woman suffrage, which was acceptable behavior for male campaigners of both races.

What such a controversy indicated was that relations between women and black campaigners, if they had ever been good, had degenerated. The highly charged politics of Reconstruction and the countless public declarations on the matter since 1865 had for more than two years pitted black male suffrage against female suffrage. The two were portrayed not just as mutually exclusive but also mutually antagonistic, no matter how many well-intentioned AERA and SISA people might argue otherwise. Phillips had established this official line in 1865 and it had stuck. No matter their idealism, woman suffrage workers found this toxic calumny highly infectious, not just because of the persistent, all-pervasive official message but also because of behaviors they observed in the field. Stone, for example, from the start had spoken of "the negroes [being] all against us"[20] and had also been unable to work well with black leader Charles Langston.[21] Brown had similar trouble with Langston's personal and political touchiness and was accused of insulting blacks, which she denied. One black preacher by the name of Twine objected when he believed Wood insulted him and then claimed that female suffrage was "a club with which to beat out our brains."[22] Even so, Twine and Brown held joint meetings and publicly supported the referenda together.[23] But agitators from Republican ranks led by Eskridge would disrupt the joint proceedings and turn the ensuing mayhem into the message that female suffrage supporters were all anti-black.[24] The official campaign by midsummer was an unofficial no-holds-barred subversion operation by Republicans to destroy female suffrage, while the Democrats waited and pounced on every sign of discord in Republican ranks to advance their own interests against black suffrage. It was a juvenile and uncivilized campaign, one in which almost anyone who followed the Republican black male suffrage agenda faced little criticism. "Hon. Thaddeus H. Walker, well known as one of the most thoughtful and progressive men in the State of Kansas, recently delivered an able speech at Seneca, Nemaha County, in favor of negro suffrage and against female suffrage. A gentleman who listened to him characterized the speech as perfectly unanswerable," reported one paper, reprinting the story from elsewhere and failing to remind readers that while the Republican Party had publicly decided to support only black suffrage at the party meeting held on May 15 it had not officially decided to campaign actively against female suffrage. For the speaker to do so, therefore, represented dirty tricks.[25]

On August 23 Anthony wrote to Lydia Maria Child of her plans for this disturbing campaign. Obviously resigned to the financial fate of the women's cause, she wrote, "I have 60,000 tracts now going to press; all the old editions were gone, and we have to begin new with an empty treasury; but I tell them all, 'go ahead,' we must, and will, succeed."[26] This indomitable woman's time in the East for the moment was fast running out: she and Stanton were booked to depart New York on August 28, 1867.[27]

Brown, meanwhile, continued campaigning, visiting Emporia on the 24th, Cottonwood Falls on the 25th, Council Grove on the 26th, Americus on the afternoon of the 27th, and Emporia again that evening. Upon her arrival at Americus she found no hall arranged, "so gross, and utterly absurd had been the misrepresentations of some opponents of the cause of equal rights, concerning the personal character and appearance of the ladies engaged in this work ... that many seemed to anticipate beholding some rude, brazen-faced Amazon riding into town upon a saw log, dressed in bloomer costume with a cigar in her mouth." The simple fact in the antis' eyes was that black male suffrage would not be pitted against women if women removed themselves from the arena, which good women should do. Any attack painting the women as bad, therefore, was permissible in order to silence them. The scurrilous attackers, however, failed to consider the effect of the truth, for when Brown arrived "they saw instead, a lady-like, refined, intelligent woman, coming in a covered carriage, and becomingly attired in the neat, fashionable walking dress of the present day [and] their first emotion seemed to be that of unbounded astonishment. However, after the first shock of surprise was over and they discovered her ... a human being, most of those assembled to hear her seemed to enjoy the meeting."[28]

27. Kansas: Men v. Citizens

The Democrats say that this is a white man's government. The Republicans contend that it is a man's government. The "Equal Rights" Party affirm that this is, of right, the People's government.—Miles Ledford Langley, Little Rock, Arkansas, February 12, 1868, *Debates and Proceedings of the Convention* (1868), 707.

SISA workers expected Stanton and Anthony in Kansas on September 2. During their journey, the direction of the wind of suffrage shifted decisively. "Three or four Kansas papers that have been sitting on the Female Suffrage fence since the opening of the question, have suddenly slid off on the opposite side, and are fighting the doctrine with wonderful zeal," the *Kansas Chief* reported.[1] Meanwhile, the mass meeting launching an anti-woman campaign took place in Emporia on August 31. The gathering was large, with "all parts of the county" represented: "The enthusiasm displayed at the meeting exhibited a determination on the part of the voters to give it an overwhelming defeat."[2] Many speakers attacked the arguments for woman suffrage. The resolutions utilized Greeley's infamous words denying woman suffrage in New York: "While we would most heartily support any measure calculated to better the condition of society or government, we are satisfied that a proposition of the character of the one now before us ... 'so revolutionary and sweeping, so openly at war with a distribution of duties and functions between the sexes, so venerable and pervading as government itself, so crushing in its general effects upon domestic life and happiness,' that we pledge our active, energetic opposition to it."[3]

The new energy was undoubtedly not just because of the onset of campaign season, but because of the impending arrival of Anthony and Stanton: big guns had to be matched with bigger guns. The meeting took another swipe at people from elsewhere campaigning for what was, "in a political sense ... a question ignored by all parties, and therefore ... only a side issue ... advocated mainly by persons imported, who have no interest in common with us, nor social relations to be affected by the proposed change."[4] With this meeting, the Emporia Republicans launched a statewide, anti-female suffrage canvass by the strongest opponents of the measure and all the power of the press they could muster.[5] Such eminent men as Plumb, Kalloch, Eskridge, and Stotler now added their weight to a new, concerted effort to destroy female suffrage. These men and many of the 77 signatories of the previous call for the meeting now formed a well-financed, well-organized phalanx of antis ready to advance against the women. An anti-female rally took place during the founding meeting of the organization, with the assemblage respectfully listening to and loudly applauding Plumb and Eskridge.

This is what Anthony and Stanton faced when they finally arrived, having missed their first appointment in Atchison because of late trains, with Brown, Bisbee, and the Reverend Twine conducting the September 2 meeting there instead. The audience listened attentively to Brown, seemingly less so to Bisbee, and treated Twine abominably. The press inferred that the women, in tune with the audience, were against black male suffrage and took the opportunity to lecture readers: "*If Universal, or Impartial Suffrage means anything, it means* NEGRO SUFFRAGE, and when it means anything else to the exclusion of that, no honest Radical Republican who adheres to the *National* party upon its *National* issues, can accept it and remain true to principle."[6] At Burlingame, a committee of five formed to arrange for the canvass of Osage County against female suffrage, with a goal of electing "an entire county ticket of those opposed to the 'Pernicious Proposition.'"[7] That week also saw the announcement of a Democratic convention for Leavenworth for September 18: "The object is not announced. We do not know whether it is to unite the democracy in favor of Female Suffrage, to pay the Female Suffragers for their votes against the negro, or whether something else is to be done."[8]

Meanwhile, Republican antis again contended that the women's intentions were to defeat black males. "The Suffrageites now say that if these anti–Female Suffrage organizations are persisted in, they will go to fighting Negro Suffrage," one report said. "If they are going to vote down a party measure in revenge against somebody else who don't go for their pet scheme, the Republican party" would be on the watch for it.[9] An adjoining editorial claimed, "It is becoming more evident every day that a majority of the Female Suffrage advocates are conniving at the defeat of Negro Suffrage." It said that many observers had thought from the start that "the Female Suffrage movement was only gotten up" for that purpose and "this would seem to be true. Many good people," it continued, "are conscientiously in favor of both, but the leaders of the Female party ... are threatening the Republican Party with rupture rather than that Female Suffrage should be voted down. Let us warn Republicans against such a heresy."[10] The distortion of the truth is striking.

In New York, Stone, having spent some of the summer raising funds for Kansas, had taken over the AERA office when Anthony departed for the

West.[11] In Kansas, Anthony and Stanton found the SISA in disarray. Wood had indeed downed tools, and there was no money. A printer was holding in lieu of payment "a large bundle of suffrage tracts."[12] The two also found that "while Mr. Wood had made out a very elaborate plan for their meetings and had posters printed for each place, these still remained piled up in the printing office."[13] Notices in the newspapers stated that the meetings were on "Impartial Suffrage without regard to Sex or Color."[14] Anthony alerted Stone to the urgent need for funds, and she and Stanton began their speaking tour.

On September 4 the campaign went to Wyandotte, with Anthony speaking in the afternoon, Stanton and Brown in the evening, and the Hutchinson family entertaining the crowd. An observer wrote that the "meetings were a perfect success and gave satisfaction to all except the colored folks, who were by no means satisfied. They say the women have no right to vote and they hope they will be defeated." This stated what black men believed, not what the women believed or advocated; but commentary noted that the writer was "both bolder and more honest than ... the adherents to female suffrage in the State. He unhesitatingly declares that the interests of woman suffrage are opposed to those of Negro suffrage." This distorted the message, but the observation that black men opposed woman suffrage had given this anti-woman editor an opportunity to reiterate the narrative that woman suffrage opposed black men. The paper now tried to browbeat readers into submission to the gospel of the Republican Party: "That those who support the former mean to oppose the latter, do oppose the latter [and] consequently stand in direct conflict with the Radical Republican Party, which has adopted Negro Suffrage as the *one great reform* issue upon which all their strength is to be concentrated."[15] Yet, another paper could report of a meeting the same day in Lawrence, where "the hall was crowded to its utmost capacity by the moral, intelligent elite of the city, of both sexes. Mrs. Stanton's address was a most powerful argument in favor of equal rights limited by no race or sex."[16]

On September 5, also in Lawrence, there took place a meeting at which "a full organization was made, the object being to advance the cause of Manhood Suffrage, and oppose Female Suffrage."[17] It "comprised ... citizens from different portions of the state for consultation concerning the best method to defeat the proposition to strike the word 'male' from the Constitution of the State of Kansas and to make arrangements for a canvas of the State in opposition to the champions of 'Female Suffrage.'" Eskridge, Kalloch, Plumb, and Stotler organized it. This group resolved to "confer with the State Republican Central Committee, and to devise such measures as may be necessary to work ... in conjunction with the Republican State Central Committee." Plans were laid for a wide-ranging state canvass and publicity in every newspaper possible.[18] The campaign opened on September 7 in Lawrence.[19] About ten days later Anthony commented in a letter to the East that the anti-women forces "held a meeting here the day after ours, and the friends say, did vastly more to make us converts than we ourselves did."[20] One rare pro-female suffrage newspaper observed, "The opponents of female suffrage have evidently agreed ... to defame the women who are canvassing in favor of the proposition to blackguard them off of the track. The *Emporia News* ... intimates that Miss Bisbee possesses remarkable acquaintance with 'the bawdy houses of New York.'" The paper attributed the negativity towards the women to the fact that they squelched sexual harassment by male opponents.[21]

At the end of two weeks, with one newspaper complaining early in September of meetings advertised with speakers who would not be appearing,[22] "Anthony saw that an entirely new program was necessary." She concluded they required improved advertising and "a central distributing point for tracts, etc.," so she "stationed herself at Lawrence." Fortunately for their finances, "Senators Pomeroy and Ross gave the full use of their 'franking' privilege and the former contributed $50 besides."[23] Meanwhile, the new campaign literature was paying off. "There is a perfect greed for our tracts," Anthony reported. "All that great trunk full were sold and given away at our first fourteen meetings, and we in return received $110, which a little more than paid our railroad fare ... and hotel bills."[24] "There was scarcely a log cabin in the State that could not boast one or more of these documents, which the liberality of a few eastern friends enabled the Equal Rights Association to print and circulate," the women later remembered.[25] And while money was tight, meetings did produce contributions. "Our collections thus far fully equal those at the East. I have been delightfully disappointed, for everybody said I couldn't raise money in Kansas meetings," Anthony said.[26]

This financial information contrasts with the Stone and Blackwell reports during their campaign in the spring. In their letters they mentioned only one, albeit significant, financial success—$100 at the very start. Anthony's irony may be a stab at Stone and Blackwell, either for miserable fund-raising in the spring or for failing to try because of the availability of the Jackson money, of which they apparently had spent all $1,500. Anthony's tone indicated a new edge to the relationship between the two women. Stone, who, fund-raising and claiming she had come to the AERA offices to "relieve" Parker Pillsbury, apparently dismissed him. Anthony chided Stone about this as being "'penny wise, and pound poor.' He surely has brought us a good deal of money, and the work he does, pays richly."[27] This annoyed Stone, just as Anthony's constant concerns about money seem to have bothered her too. She obviously felt Anthony was interfering and had already told Blackwell to get Anthony off their backs by telling her they had put their own money up and they could also borrow money for Kansas, if they guaranteed it.[28] But personal contributions could hardly impress Anthony. Stone might believe that personal contributions were exceptional if she rarely if ever did it; but

Anthony used much of her own money and was accustomed to working for nothing. Stone, before marriage, had been one of the most highly paid female speakers on the circuit. Her income from public speaking attracted Blackwell, who made a calculated decision to pursue and marry her.[29]

A minor Stone success at the AERA office might have been winning a concession from East Coast men of endorsement of female suffrage in Kansas. This long-begged-for moment occurred on September 14 in the *NASS*, which endorsed both black male suffrage and woman suffrage on grounds of justice. For women it threw in expediency as well, for it argued that a female electorate would tip the balance for temperance measures while strengthening support for the Republican party in many electorates.[30] The *Standard* was finally recognizing for Kansas—and by extension the nation at large—the potential political value for Republicans of women voters, even though advocates of black male suffrage in the South from 1865 studiously ignored its potential there. This grudging endorsement of the woman referendum in Kansas was a potential double-edged sword, for while it might encourage some Kansas men finally to support the woman suffrage measure it could equally as well turn others off for fear that enfranchised women would vote to ban alcohol. This might have been the intention.

In mid–September, Stanton wrote to Theodore Tilton of the *Independent* reporting on the AERA/SISA's meeting held the day before in the new courthouse of Louisville, Kansas: "The people came in from miles round & seemed deeply interested in the question. I spoke yesterday on the political advantages of the enfranchisement of woman; today being Sunday I am to give the Bible argument for the equality of the sexes."[31] Locals received Stanton's political arguments positively. "[N]one who listened, without prejudice, could fail to be convinced of the justice of her case," one reporter wrote.[32] Her now regular Sunday speech on the Bible, which she gave from her first Sunday on in Kansas, demonstrated "that the whole spirit and tone of the Bible was favorable to absolute equality, and the utter annihilation of all class and caste distinctions."[33] Such a talk was a necessary antidote to the diatribes of church ministers beating the women down with the Bible. Their fulminations regularly occupied long newspaper columns and if Stanton had difficulty convincing hearers about woman suffrage through political and social arguments, religious arguments were more difficult, for the Bible was the word of God, God was a He, and His word was the ultimate authority. To counter this mental straitjacket was a tall order for a mere woman.

As Stanton campaigned, Anthony "directed affairs from ... Lawrence," making "herculean efforts to raise money for the campaign, which ... was dependent on the collections at the meetings."[34] Although an essential role, it largely confined her. But with no escort—which both propriety and practicality demanded of a woman for the kind of journeys the campaign required over prairies and unmarked roads and through miles of emptiness[35]—her movements were circumscribed. Men never faced such problems. Surveying the overall prospects of the campaign, Anthony wrote, "The 'Anti-Female Suffragists,' are making a bold push now; but all prophesy a short run for them…. The fact is nearly every man [is] notoriously wanting in right action toward woman. Their opposition is low and scurrilous, as it used to be fifteen and twenty years ago at the East."[36]

Anthony expressed her optimism two days before Charles Langston appeared with the Republican "Manhood Suffrage" group in Leavenworth,[37] where he "virtually committed himself to the plans of those beastly mischief-makers [Kalloch and Eskridge]."[38] The wealthy black activist and orator had won fame for his antislavery work before the Civil War, participating in the daring Oberlin-Wellington rescue and ultimate escape to freedom in Canada from U.S. marshall custody of the escaped slave John Price, who was being transported south under the Fugitive Slave Law. Langston was fêted for his 1858 role. By contrast, leading antislavery stalwart Garrison and others in 1860 excoriated Anthony when she tried to help Mrs. Phelps and her child escape from her abusive U.S. senator husband, who, the law said, owned both wife and child.[39] At the start of the SISA campaign, Langston had attempted to win Wood's support for black male suffrage only. Failing, he thereafter complained that female suffrage was undermining black men, which earned him the wrath of Stone and Blackwell. By appearing on the antis' campaign trail, Langston, whose "brother John M. had met with much kindness from Miss Anthony and her family before the war,"[40] attracted both bigger audiences than he normally could and vast statewide coverage for the black male cause. He was particularly treacherous because all the SISA lectures called for both female and black male suffrage. The statewide coverage blacks won from the spurious complaints in the Republicans' anti-woman campaign about the pro-women workers being against black men showed up Langston's move as cold political calculation, for with the misrepresentations gaining strength the anti-woman Republican movement likely looked like a bandwagon worth hitching himself to.

The even-handed *Kansas Chief* criticized Langston: "A persistent effort has been made by the enemies of female suffrage to get up a fight between that and negro suffrage, [the contention circulating that] female suffrage was sprung for … defeating the other proposition." With "the negroes … very anxious to vote … their pretended champions have poured such stuff as this into their ears, until they have begun to think that the female suffrage people are their worst enemies, and some of them have been led into public demonstrations against the woman movement." The article continued: "Mr. Langston is a man of intelligence, and ought to know that all their random assertions are the fabrications of demagogues."[41]

When this editorial appeared, Langston was already trying to modify the anti-woman message from his appearance alongside Kalloch, whom one newspaper called ironically "sweet-scented."[42] By this time, Langston had already "vowed he would never be caught in such company again for it did the negro far more harm than good."[43] Now Langston told the *Chief* that appearing at that meeting did not mean he was anti-woman. "His position on woman suffrage ha[d] been misunderstood and misrepresented.... The woman suffrage question is one in which the negroes have no voice but is to be settled by the whites alone." His intention was "to secure the enfranchisement of his own race, not to pull any one else back," and he was "determined to take no part either for or against the woman proposition, and [would] resist all the attempts ... to draw him into the fight on the question." Still, he expected forbearance if it seemed he was "departing from this rule if unavoidable circumstances should occasionally place him in positions having that appearance."[44] This hedged his bets. However, no woman was allowed any such latitude, as Brown had just recently discovered.

In all, Langston never clearly stated that he supported the women, even though female suffrage would have included black women. A more positive statement was obviously too much to ask of him, both as a man and as a campaigner. Besides, after he tried to stop the criticism by calling on the editor of the *Kansas Chief*, it emerged that he had already spoken to "an opponent of woman suffrage," saying "he thought the conferring of the right of suffrage upon women would be very bad policy; that decent women would have nothing to do with it, while bad women would vote; and the result would be that pimps and prostitutes would rule the day, especially in cities like Leavenworth."[45] This truth emerged only a week after Langston's excuses to the *Kansas Chief*, showing his untrustworthiness. Meanwhile, he had damaged the women.

The day after Langston's appearance in Leavenworth, the Republican Party officially endorsed the anti-woman campaign begun with such great fanfare in Emporia on August 31, with efforts redoubled in Lawrence on September 5. After the resolution there that officials should "confer with the State Republican Central Committee" to come up with ways to establish cooperation between their efforts, on September 18 the committee proclaimed in a declaration "To the Republicans of Kansas" its support only for removal of the word "white" from the constitution. "A thorough canvass is demanded. Let no other issues distract the party," it proclaimed. The statement signed by the chairman and secretary of the Republican State Central Committee at Leavenworth said that individuals could address their own interests but emphasized that "upon the great question of 'manhood suffrage' they and the whole party may and ought to stand as a unit." Woman suffrage was left out in the cold. Some of the names on the declaration belonged to the anti-woman campaign.[46]

As if to add insult to injury, the Democrats that same day held their state convention, also at Leavenworth, and opposed suffrage expansion in a resolution stating that they were "opposed to all the proposed amendments to our State Constitution."[47] The Democrats' move completed a trio of sudden new blows to the women within three days. Langston's appearance with the Republican anti-woman campaign had turned a harsh spotlight on the black male position against women. The Republican Central Committee's endorsement of the anti-woman campaign meant that the party that had voted for the female suffrage amendment had jettisoned it for more restricted and discriminatory goals. Finally, the Democratic convention had made the women's isolation complete.

This campaign, therefore, was shaping up as historic for reasons beyond the central issue of suffrage. The referenda brought out clearly the virulent sex prejudice of male reformers, voters, and men in power, no matter their race. These events also clearly highlighted the two-way race bias operating in Kansas, just as it had operated at the national level, against both white women and black women. White women enfranchised by the female suffrage amendment would outnumber any blacks. Blackwell's pamphlet arguing that enfranchising white women would more than cancel out the black male vote emphasized this. Concerned black males, therefore, had an interest in ensuring failure of suffrage for this large bloc of whites. Campaigners against this amendment, therefore, no matter their color, were primarily anti-white women. In addition, with black women also being potential beneficiaries, the white male antis were against black women. For most white men, their support of "manhood suffrage" arose less from what they believed and more from the congressional reform impetus, which was forcing them to change. Most of the black men wanted equality with white men, regardless. Not one of these positions was honorable. Nothing of these positions accorded with true republican principles. And just as what had previously happened in Congress had not reflected well on the men of the era who wielded all the political power in the United States, none of them reflected well on the beliefs, convictions, or behavior of so many of the men of Kansas of that time.

Just at this point, the *Emporia News* baldly reported the following: "We see it stated that George Francis Train will stump this state in favor of Female Suffrage.[48]

28. Desperate Measures

Negro suffrage is an issue of the great Republican Party. Female Suffrage is a mere side issue.—*Emporia News*, September 6, 1867.

On September 21 Highland "colored people" held a great "Suffrage Celebration." This event to commemorate the announcement of the Emancipation Proclamation of exactly five years before featured Brown "by request."[1]

> [Brown] explained that she and the other friends of female suffrage, were not enemies to negro suffrage, but that they had been among the most earnest workers to secure freedom and civil rights to the negro and that reports to the effect that she had spoken against negro suffrage were false.… [T]he negroes were highly pleased with her remarks; and at their close, the following resolution was offered: "That the colored People of Kansas recognize in the advocates of Female Suffrage, many old and tried friends of the colored man; and that we deprecate any conflict between the friends of the two propositions, preferring rather to plant ourselves upon the broad platform of Impartial Suffrage, without regard to sex or color."[2]

This declaration from a black suffrage meeting was almost unique. When voted on, it was said to be "adopted without a dissenting voice,"[3] which, however, excepted Langston, who declared "that many had not voted their true sentiments, but been led away with enthusiasm, and proposed another vote. Before voting, he addressed them, requesting every one to vote his true sentiment, regardless of everything else. Again, the vote was unanimous in favor of the Resolution,"[4] while Langston's true colors were clear.

On September 23 Anthony reported on the Kansas front.[5] There had been a convention of Germans that day in Topeka who declared "en masse" against female suffrage because women might vote for restrictive alcohol laws—just ten days after Phillips encouraged[6] support of woman suffrage in Kansas to help temperance. His argument had come to haunt women. Despite this latest setback, Anthony still seemed optimistic that the antis helped the cause rather than hindered women. Stanton would soon head off with ex–Governor Robinson,[7] Anthony wrote, saying she would "not return to port again until Nov. 4th—when all our Canvassers are to meet at Leavenworth."[8] Brown was continuing to work the state, with "a Capt. Geo. A. Martin," an Atchison realtor and SISA member accompanying her.[9] "A Mrs. Brinkerhoff & husband are making tour of state with their own team," and Anthony was scheduled to go out the next week. "And beside these four sets 'streaming' through all the principal *cities* of the state—*home talent* is canvassing every school district of every county," she reported. Anthony was also awaiting Senator Pomeroy's statement the next day on woman suffrage, saying, "If we can harness [Senator] Pomeroy into our forces we feel we shall surely win."[10]

Anthony was writing to Dickinson, whose help she still wanted in Kansas, but Dickinson was again ill. Also inhibiting any appearance by her in the West—apart from the penury of the AERA/SISA campaign—was the prospect of campaigning for freedmen's votes in the South. The ten former Confederate states, now under military rule, were registering freedmen as voters for constitutional conventions and then legislative elections. Already by the summer of 1867 fulfillment of the first step was in train. Elections were fast approaching. This prospect was much more appealing for people whose primary passion was antislavery in its postwar permutations—apart from the attraction of fees to speak paid by a campaign supported by the well-financed Republican Party. Antislavery in a post-slavery world ensured that, when it came to geography and prioritizing equalities, Kansas and women were far down the list.

Anthony then wrote to Dickinson, seemingly as an afterthought: "But, how funny; that Geo. Francis Train is coming into the state for a month—to talk for woman—What sort of furor he will make."[11] Anthony had obviously heard the news recently reported in the state.[12] Her words demonstrate she was no part of the Wood/Blackwell conspiracy. Train seemed to be another independent canvasser, like Mrs. Brinkerhoff from neighboring Missouri.[13] Anthony is puzzled, however—by the personality. She clearly knows of Train. His reputation of risk-taking, flamboyant speechmaking, colorful writing, a gigantic ego, international business acumen and success, huge earned fortune, and a link to a consortium building the railroad from the Missouri River at Council Bluffs, Iowa, to the far west quickly while nurturing ambitions to win the presidency traveled ahead of him. "Curiously combining keen sagacity with wild enthusiasm, a man who might have built the Pyramids, or been confined to a strait-jacket for his eccentricities, according to the age he lived in, he observed dryly that since he began to make money, people no longer pronounced him crazy! ... He drinks no spirits, uses no tobacco, talks on the stump like an embodied Niagara, composes songs to order by the hour as fast as he can sing them, remembers every droll story ... is a born actor, intensely in earnest, and has the most outspoken faith in himself and his future," a contemporary said.[14]

Train began to impinge upon the suffrage campaign in Kansas as a rail-road and real estate mogul. Under the Pacific Railway Act of 1862, which authorized the building of the railroad beyond the frontier, the first of either the Union Pacific or the Central Pacific to reach the 100th West meridian won the rights to continue building farther. If the Union Pacific Railroad reached the 100th meridian first, it would continue building to the West to link with the Central Pacific Line heading east from San Francisco. The result was no foregone conclusion, but the conglomerate that Train and his asso-ciates put together went full steam ahead; and on October 6, 1866, more than a year ahead of schedule, the Union Pacific won the railroad challenge. Man-agement decided to celebrate with a grand tour to the 100th meridian. With Train handling PR, acting as a lobbyist and marketing real estate ahead of the anticipated immigrant flood that would soon follow the tracks to the new lands in the West, what became known as the "Elkhorn Club" was quickly formed from responses to invitations sent to the movers and shakers of the nation. The "Club" involved about 200 well-known personages,[15] including Senator Benjamin F. Wade, then president pro tem of the United States Senate, a strong contender for the presidency whose prospects were then strength-ening because of the gestating plans to impeach President Johnson. This was the Wade who, on June 10 in Lawrence, Kansas, spoke out for woman suffrage. That speech linked the senatorial junket directly with suffrage and at a side trip to Pilot Knob catapulted George Francis Train into the issue when, answer-ing a question during an impromptu speech of his own, he argued that the nation would be morally uplifted if women had the vote. He also contended, as Blackwell had done, that female suffrage would more than balance out concerns associated with black suffrage, essentially advocating enfranchise-ment of women not to cut black men out but to soften that controversy. This might have been about all of Anthony's understanding of Train—three months after Train's convoluted entry into the issue.

Train's pronouncements on female suffrage bothered antis, but he was even more troubling for Republicans, radical or otherwise. Having taken a very public and active part in the Democratic Convention of 1864, the Boston-born Train was branded a Copperhead, a term originally applied to North-erners who were pro–Confederacy and one of the worst insults to throw at the time. Train later said that the *NASS* "was the paper that first called [him] names."[16] Yet Train was hardly a Copperhead, for he was a very public Union defender in pro–South England during the Civil War, honored in Philadel-phia in December 1861 when prominent citizens signed a resolution prais-ing "The Eloquent Champion of the American Union."[17] In the U.S. later, a Kansas newspaper would remind readers "he electrified the whole North into wild patriotism by his English Speeches which were read in every family."[18] As the Civil War ended, Train took stock of the contentious social, economic, and political upheavals that sudden emancipation and enfranchisement brought, even as the reality in 1867 was that freedmen were already being enfranchised despite white men's concerns and prejudices. Train's broader perspective on this was not pro–Democrat, for he espoused female suffrage. Like Blackwell, he viewed the situation partly from expediency, advocating for women's leavening influence in the new social and political reality. He also argued partly from logic: if black men were given the vote despite white men's concerns and prejudices, why not women? Train also saw value in an educated suffrage to alleviate the strains of the postwar social upheaval. Therefore, if the originally pro–Union Train was now a Democrat, he was no hard-liner. Besides, the Copperhead slur by 1867 had become more of a catch-all for discrediting and destroying an opponent, no matter the truth,[19] while the sad fact is that when a lie is repeated enough it becomes the "truth." One newspaper, summarizing the process of the destruction of nonadherents to official Republican creed, said that ultimately "every man who did not want a negro to vote, or desired that his wife, mother, sister or daughter should have that privilege, would be a Copperhead."[20] This distortion gave Anthony good reason to ruminate about the "sort of furor" Train would make. Unavoidably piquing her interest, however, were Train's advocacy of woman suffrage and the news that he was "coming into the state for a month—to talk for woman."[21]

The next day, September 24, at a meeting of the Lawrence Women's Impartial Suffrage Association,[22] Senator Pomeroy endorsed woman suffrage. He argued that it was "safe for a Republican to take deliberate and earnest action" for women[23] despite the Kansas and National Republican Parties' avowed opposition and given the Democrats' own avowed opposition. Because of Pomeroy's endorsement, many women signed an "Address" of the Women's Impartial Suffrage Association, refuting men's well-peddled argument that women did not want to vote.[24] On the succeeding day, the state temperance association met,[25] where Stanton spoke, as did Pomeroy: "The meeting took one turn which was hardly expected. A strong address in favor of negro and female suffrage, which had been previously prepared, was introduced, and created quite a storm. It was at first laid upon the table, from whence it was afterwards taken and passed."[26]

This address "To the Voters of Kansas" advocated support of all the suffrage amendments on November 5 and was signed by Senator Pomeroy and more than 40 other politicians, editors, and other prominent men.[27] The support of the address for each amendment was for different reasons. For women it said, "We believe the word 'male' should be stricken from the Constitution, because its presence there is in violation of the great principles that underlie all just civil governments, because it is subversive of the highest political and social interests of society."[28] In other words, the address used republican principles to support woman suffrage, the same powerful reasoning that Stanton and Anthony had used since 1865 to call for just Reconstruction.

Anthony had told Dickinson that she herself was scheduled "to go with some *honorable*" out on the campaign trail the last week in September, yet somehow it didn't work out and she remained in Lawrence.[29] At this point, finally, Blackwell's public statement from prominent men regarding female suffrage appeared in the *Tribune* on October 1, 1867. Headlined "Kansas," it was addressed to the voters of the United States: "In this hour of National Reconstruction, we appeal to good men of all parties, to Conventions for amending State Constitutions, to the Legislature of every State, and to the Congress of the United States, to apply the principles of the Declaration of Independence to Women." Thirty-one distinguished names were appended from many different states including Governor Crawford and Senators Pomeroy and Ross of Kansas. Antislavery names such as Gerrit Smith and Theodore Tilton also appeared and for the second time within a week a large group of prominent men publicly endorsed the political philosophy of Reconstruction that Stanton, Anthony, and Stone had propounded since the end of the war after Phillips' betrayal of women with his "negro's hour" proclamation. Phillips even signed it. This boost for the female half of the population after the Temperance Address "To the Voters of Kansas" meant that at long last some of the establishment had combined to exhort legislators to include women in Reconstruction. The appeal concluded with these words: "The problem of American statesmanship is how to incorporate in our institutions a guarantee of the rights of every individual. The solution is easy. Base government on the consent of the governed, and each class will protect itself."[30] Whether this would lead to action was an open question. Greeley did not sign it, while the value of Phillips' signature is debatable given his anti-woman behavior and his theft of the women's money. The least and cheapest thing he could do was append his name to something not affecting him.

Meanwhile, however, the grassroots situation was concerning. A considerable amount of behind-the-scenes discussion must have been taking place among principals of the campaign in Kansas about what to do. These included Stanton, Anthony, Robinson, Wood, the newspaper editor Milton W. Reynolds, and Mrs. J.H. (Elizabeth Mary Baldridge) Lane, widow of the late senator of the state and a member of the Lawrence Impartial Suffrage Association. The SISA was desperate for whatever help it could get. It was already public knowledge that Train had announced he planned to stump for the women of Kansas. In the background of this meeting—not known to Susan B. Anthony or many others—there was the Wood/Blackwell conspiracy. The subject of Train either arose or was deliberately raised.

Already some of these participants were behind Train. For others, however, Train presented problems. On the one hand, he was called a Democrat and Democrats were anathema to Republicans. On the other hand, the women had welcomed since 1865 any help—Democrat or Republican—for the cause. Then again, to enlist the help of such a prominent and controversial purported Democrat to win votes in the election would be a significant break from the women's alignment with Republicans to date. Yet the truth was that most Republicans had already rejected women, abjectly failing them. Republicans' work for manhood suffrage while rejecting female suffrage and women campaigning for their own rights was a major double standard. Conversely, to welcome a reinforcement that could win votes for female suffrage specifically as opposed to true impartial suffrage was a major departure. The difficulty was obvious: the proposal meant discarding the rules and expectations of everyone they had ever worked with. It was, perhaps, downright scary. Yet, despite the recent support expressed for women, prospects in late September for the women were so desperate, with press, politicians, pulpit, Republicans, and black males overtly attacking them and only about six weeks of campaigning left, drastic measures were needed. On October 2, therefore, Stanton, Anthony, Robinson, Wood, newspaper editor Reynolds, and Mrs. Lane dispatched a telegram from Lawrence to George Francis Train in Omaha: "Come to Kansas and stump the State for Equal rights and female suffrage. The people want you. The women want you."[31]

29. Waiting for Train

I am going [to Kansas] to hunt the white male citizen out of that region.—Elizabeth Cady Stanton, *Kansas Chief*, September 26, 1867.

When Isabella Beecher Hooker interviewed Blackwell in 1869 about the split between Stone and Anthony following the Kansas campaign, Blackwell revealed that Train went to Kansas at Wood's invitation "to lecture to whomever would hear on Woman Suffrage." Blackwell said that he, Robinson, and several others involved in the Kansas campaign "thought it might be well for [Anthony] to accompany Train & so get democratic votes."[1] The names of at least two of these conspirators were on the invitation telegraphed to Train on October 2, 1867. It is impossible to know who the others were, but Mrs. Lane and Reynolds, or either of them, may have been part of it. With the telegram, Anthony and Stanton were roped in to this long-developing plan.

The decision to send the telegram was understandable because the women's circumstances were dire. Apart from campaign penury, the day before they sent the telegram a half-hearted, mean-spirited, back-handed statement in favor of the Kansas amendment had appeared in the *Tribune*— months after the women had begged Greeley and other editors of major newspapers with many readers in Kansas for their endorsement. "The experiment of Female Suffrage is to be tried; and, while we regard it with distrust, we are quite willing to see it pioneered by Kansas," the *Tribune* opined. "If the great body of the women of Kansas wish to vote, we counsel the men to accord them the opportunity. Should the experiment work as we apprehend, they will soon be glad to give it up."[2] This grudging "backing" could have raised little support for female suffrage or hardly erase the negativity of the September 14 "endorsement" by the *NASS*, which supported women in Kansas using the expedient argument that it would help the temperance cause.[3]

It might even have caused damage, for the Kansas campaigners were like pioneers on a wagon train trapped by a band of outlaws attacking from every direction. This was true much more for female suffrage than for black male suffrage. The Republican Party was two-faced. It had initially promoted women then reneged in favor of black male suffrage only. A strong, well-organized group of hardline, negative, backward-looking Republicans who had received a strong nod from the official Kansas party was conducting an all-out anti-woman campaign. Further, the national Republican Party policy was against woman suffrage, while their hints that women would get the vote "later" was the kind of commitment that the women had been learning not to trust. Other states, meanwhile, were setting a negative example. Referring to the Kansas campaign, the women made the following observation 20 years later: "The action of the Michigan Commission, in refusing to submit a similar amendment to her people, and the adverse report of Mr. Greeley in the Constitutional Convention of New York, had also their depressing influence."[4] In addition, while temperance in Kansas endorsed woman suffrage, the linkage launched a battle between anti-liquor and pro-liquor forces, specifically the German community, whose almost libertarian outlook contradicted itself. It was libertarian for itself but not for women, while the Germans annoyed average male Kansans because they were different.[5] Further, the Democratic Party was openly against the women, but it discriminated equally, for it was also against black males. Add to that an assortment of ministers preaching anti-women diatribes each Sunday and reinforcing their fulminations later in newspapers that gladly published the screeds of anti-female rhetoric. These long-winded men overwhelmed anything the women could do, because either the women lacked the time or newspaper editors locked them out.[6]

Finally, while women should have been able to count on black men because they campaigned for them from the start, they believed the women were a threat. Any work they did together was largely only in parallel, such as Twine's appearances with Brown. The black male movement did not combine with the SISA equality campaign, fearing it would pull them down, though it might have strengthened them both. Anti-woman papers played on the black men's fears, operated a dirty campaign to whip up latent anti-woman sentiment and create further complications for women. Langston, probably the most prominent of the black men, openly worked with the anti-woman Republican forces and tap danced around the controversy about his appearances with Kalloch. This was as bad as the betrayals of the women by the antislavery men back East.

Apart from a male world that fought against cracking open its collective closed mind to allow female equality in, women's biggest problem was resources—specifically people and money. They were outnumbered in support and campaigners. Anthony stayed in Lawrence busy trying to solve organizational problems. One newspaper complained "that the cause has a sufficiently doubtful fight on its hands, without making it still bluer by bungling management of the work."[7] The women were also outrun in the news, publicity, and promotion. And the establishment out-financed them, partly because men controlled most finances of the nation and because eastern men had stolen the women's money. All these factors, along with campaigning in an undeveloped state, rendered progress difficult. Even so, women did not abandon the AERA platform.

Awareness of the forces against them, plus Langston's behavior and Greeley's mean-spirited editorial, seemed to have added up to the breaking point. The signatories to the Train telegram, it appears, had therefore considered everything, agreed a change was necessary and with no other options chose to approach Train. Even if he was reputed to be a Democrat with all the baggage of a "D" after his name, they likely wondered what they had to lose, for there was nothing to say that some Democrat electors could not be won for female suffrage. While hardline and radical Republicans had ignored, abandoned, and worked against it, some Democrats—admittedly often with mixed motives—had supported women in Congress and New York. By now, working with individual Democrats was nothing new for Stanton and Anthony, who had sought Democrat support since their first postwar campaign in December 1865. Robinson and Wood had already worked with Democrats in Kansas and, in fact, the *New York Times* argued that they had passed the woman suffrage referendum in January "by the persistence of the Democrats," who had "argued and speechified [with them] until their colleagues were prone to yield from sheer exhaustion."[8] Stone had toyed with Democrat support, having written to Anthony from Kansas: "[T]he Democrats all over the State are preparing to take us up. They are a small minority, with nothing to lose, and utterly unscrupulous, while all who will work with Sam Wood will work with anybody."[9] Blackwell wrote, "If the Republicans come out against us the Democrats will take us up."[10] In Kansas, therefore, long before the presence of Stanton and Anthony, Democrat support had been on the radar. To bring Train in was simply a more conspicuous evolution of this tactic. Now, on October 5, P.L. Hubbard,[11] chairman of the Woman Suffrage Association in Atchison, telegraphed Train asking him to participate in a debate on October 13. Train replied that he was just heading off to Omaha with newspaper editors and could not make it. All these documents demonstrate that many people worked to bring in Train after Mrs. Hazard had initiated the plan with Wood that August.[12]

Mrs. Hazard's letter to Senator Samuel N. Wood of Kansas, asking him if he wants George Francis Train for the 1867 campaign, in full, said:

Woman Suffrage Association of Missouri
St. Louis, August 20, 1867
Hon. S.N. Wood
Dear Sir
  Your letter of the 17th inst is before me in reply would say that we would be glad to have Miss Brown and Miss Bisbee lecture for us if we could secure an audience but at

present we are not sufficiently strong to hazard the attempt. That is if we had to charge an admission fee … all the lectures we have now must be free. Some have offered to come from the east and lecture for us this fall[.] If our treasury was a little more plethoric we would say to all these ladies come and we would bear the expense.

We hope by the time these ladies return from Kansas to be in funds and to secure them then. In the latter part of Sept. we are to have a large meeting at Mercantile Library Hall and shall have speeches by Gen [William A.] Pile, Gov. Fletcher (I think) and many others. Could you not come down then? Gov. Fletcher came out for us the other evening at a public dinner, he had promised me he would do so on the first available occasion and was true to his promise. I told Mrs. McKee what you said about the Democrats helping you in Kansas provided it were a little stronger and I am glad to say it appears to have had a good effect. Can we do anything to help you in Kansas? You don't know how anxious we feel for success there, everything depends on it, we feel like turning all our efforts in that direction.

Do you want Geo. Francis Train in Kansas? He proposed to come here and lecture for us free of expenses and also to "stump" Kansas. I could not tell whether you would think best or not so we merely accepted his proposal to come here. If Miss Brown or Miss Bisbee should come to this city we should like to see and talk with them. My address is 1119 Pleasant St and I can refer them to the other ladies. I propose writing Mrs. Stanton and Miss Anthony to see what arrangements we can make.

Yours truly

Mrs. R. L Hazard[13]

It is to be wondered what Olympia Brown knew, for at the top of the signature page, in different writing, upside down, appeared words ending, "I wrote send Train, Wood," preceded by, "Replied (?) to Olympia Brown (?)." If Anthony and Stanton were told of all this maneuvering, it seems they said nothing.

In the middle of these developments, on October 3, the *Independent* came out for women.[14] The *Emporia News* would soon write, sarcastically, "The New York *Independent* thinks it looks as if the female suffrage proposition would be carried in Kansas. We have heard of folks who thought the moon looked like green cheese." Then it attacked Stone for keeping the *Independent* informed of the situation in the West.[15] Still, something must finally have begun to prick the consciences of the wise men from the East. Because of their insistent obduracy in excluding women and abandoning them to their own fate, Kansas had erupted in a virulent anti-woman campaign shocking even to some hard hearts. Yet the half-hearted, uninformed, and belated endorsements from men who expected women's full support for black male suffrage ahead of their own equality was insulting. The grudging support may have made the SISA campaign happier about the Train initiative. After several days, Train telegraphed that he would be in Kansas to stump for female suffrage as soon as his trip west was over.[16] Now, several months of brief appearances on the fringes of the woman suffrage cause were ending: Train was coming on board. With only Anthony in town, her solo signature was the fastest way to reply and so, while six names were on the telegram from

Lawrence only Anthony's was on the reply. "God bless you…. Yes, with your help we shall triumph," she wrote.[17] As a result, Train's Kansas sojourn is associated only with Anthony, rather than six people—and possibly more—in all, some of whom had been conspiring for this moment for several months.

The news of Train's coming spread fast. He was an interesting character. His career began in Boston shipping, in which, to turn a loss into a profit, he encouraged Irish men to promote immigration from post-famine Ireland in the early 1850s and fill ships deadheading back from Britain to the U.S. after delivering passengers and cargo.[18] Train had also been known for years for his newspaper writing and what were considered his increasingly outlandish opinions. In 1867, with a presidential run on his mind, his speechmaking had been prodigious, tackling varied subjects such as the national debt and even the medical profession.[19] His oratory was controversial, both stylistically and in substance. Allied with his flamboyant personal appearance, commentators tended to deal with him flippantly or critically. "His disgusting egotism and obtrusive nonsense is said to have created a general nausea," it was reported about newspapermen on their October 1867 railroad junket.[20] "On announcing his coming departure for Kansas, he recalled his earlier influence with the Irish and claimed that Irish women would later help the Presidential vote."[21] The *Kansas Chief* laughed outright. Train "has been blowing again…. He says he is coming to Kansas, to carry the State for female suffrage, that it must prevail in every State," it wrote, adding they were "afraid Train wants to defeat the proposition."[22]

Meanwhile, Stanton, writing to Henry from Council Grove, said she could no longer "endure the thoughts of living again that contracted eastern existence" and was imagining a future in the West, where land was cheap: "You would feel like a new being here … be a leader … as there is not a man in the state that can make a really good speech."[23] She said, "Everybody says the woman proposition will be carried, but the negro one will not. The Democrats here go for us strong." Anthony at the same time, in Lawrence, was reporting to Wood her arrangements for Train. With Milton Reynolds accompanying him,[24] he would begin at Atchison on Saturday, October 19. She talked about notices, tickets, distributing tracts, and getting information into papers. She spoke of a canvass by Senator Pomeroy, herself, and her brother, Colonel D.R. Anthony, beginning on October 22 at Ellsworth, where she dreamed of winning support from among a thousand voters.[25] This was a woman who knew the business of politics well and who could have been much more successful had she had more resources. Yet someone with such ability was denied the vote.

In this same letter Anthony, who said she had approached several male speakers whose expenses she would pay "if they would take the field at once,"[26] noted that "Stone has been quite successful in getting money."[27] Yet, almost simultaneously, Stone was writing to Blackwell about campaign financing, for Anthony had obviously been pressing them. Blackwell was heading back to Kansas on a land speculation trip for investors.[28] "If SBA pushes to know about funds, tell her we paid a good deal from our private money," Stone wrote.[29] Her wording and verb tense point to the past rather than a more recent time. Yet either way they did nothing exceptional: most reform workers ended up contributing money, even if they were paid. Stone added that Phillips was "willing" for them to draw from the Jackson fund if they personally guaranteed it.[30] This statement is curious: borrowing could deal with the current crisis, but not with repayment. More startling is the reference to the Jackson fund. Anthony's response or even if Blackwell relayed the information is unknown. Whether Stone borrowed from it or how much of their own funds they spent is also unknown.[31]

Stone's annoyance in this first letter to her husband after his departure clearly demonstrates that Anthony and Stone were rubbing each other the wrong way. Why is unclear. Perhaps Anthony had asked for a full accounting of the Kansas expenditures from Blackwell and Stone, to which, as a trustee of the Jackson Fund, she was entitled. The words indicate such a possibility. The letter, therefore, stands out not just for the obvious discord but also for the unanswered questions it raises. Stone's reference to the Jackson Fund is also strange, because for women the Jackson Fund had been dead since early August. Phillips might have been willing to let the Kansas campaign borrow from the antislavery portion of the Jackson fund; but this is also curious, because the interested parties were then still warring about the ultimate use for the money. Even if Anthony was unaware of this, the Jackson Fund statement was odd. The Hovey Fund might have been more likely, yet Stone does not mention Hovey. For several reasons, therefore—and despite Anthony's comment about Stone's success at fund-raising—this letter signals both something odd about the Stone and Blackwell Kansas financing and the strained relationship between Stone and Anthony. Stone was further annoyed because of her early return from Martha's Vineyard to manage the AERA office and Anthony's second-guessing her dismissal of Pillsbury.[32]

Brown, meanwhile, ploughed on. On October 10 in Oskaloosa, because of double-booking, she came face-to-face with Judge T.C. Sears, who was anti-woman, and in the ensuing unique debate between the two Brown won handily.[33] The double-booking might have been an attempt to derail Brown, for around this time she was "refused the use of the Church at Highland to deliver a lecture in favor of female suffrage. But it was opened to Mr. Kalloch … to speak against" it.[34] The newspapers now carried notices daily of meetings by several speakers on both sides, while Train announcements were appearing regularly. Much of what Anthony was organizing at this time never came to pass, however. Train would not be ready to start until October 21.[35] Daniel

Anthony would speak only twice with him—on October 22 in Lawrence and in Leavenworth on November 4. Senator Pomeroy left for Boston late in October and returned only just before the election. Reynolds, an old friend of Train, never turned up.[36]

Before Train arrived, a survey of state newspapers concluded that support was split 21 for and 19 against woman suffrage.[37] The newspapers, ignoring reporting of substance, demonstrated their differences clearly. A pro-woman newspaper noted, "Mrs. Stanton ... delivered the most able, scholarly, and eloquent address which we have listened to during the canvass."[38] An anti newspaper on the other hand, sarcastically commented, "Mrs. Stanton's speech was really a fine specimen of oratory. It contained many finely rounded periods. With her, female suffrage is the great panacea for all the world's ills. It is to bring women down to a level with the men and at the same time raise them up to a level with them. She made many assertions without attempting to prove them. She is a splendid talker, but altogether her speech was more pleasing than convincing."[39] These reports demonstrate that the women made substantial presentations, but they say more about the reporters than the women. If Brown "made a most eloquent appeal to the voters to support woman's suffrage" and "Anthony spoke very briefly and well," none of this says much.[40] Neither does criticism of Mrs. Brinkerhoff, whose speech "was a rehash of what we have heard from all the advocates. She is a new hand at the business, as is clearly shown by her awkwardness on the stage, and her occasional use of such words as inalienably, etc. Her 'piece' is written down and spoken with some force. She has more fight in her than any other of the female speakers."[41] Again, content remains elusive. The reference to her use of the word "inalienably," however, indicates a speech more intellectual than emotive—even if the word "inalienable"[42] was recognizable if only because of the Declaration of Independence. Performance, rather than substance, seemed to matter more to these observers.

At the time, meetings and speechmaking were central to community life—considered recreation and even entertainment. If speeches given in favor of woman suffrage were intellectual, they would have appealed more to the cerebral. They may not have touched people who needed to be moved rather than convinced. Although listeners would have come away informed, they might not necessarily have been inspired. This situation, however, was fixing to change.

30. Unprecedented Audiences

The Republican Party is too rotten to be trusted.—Susan B. Anthony, *The Great Epigram Campaign of Kansas* (1867), 16.

When Blackwell arrived in Kansas on business in mid–October he began assessing the situation as it stood just before Train first appeared, writing to Stone around the time the first news of Train's speeches was appearing. Wood had all but abandoned the women's campaign early in August, Blackwell reported. He said he fell ill and was incommunicado "for six weeks" because of a mail robbery. Without Wood's direction the campaign "ran into the ground." Woman suffrage was already lost, and the only unknown was the vote tally—perhaps 5,000; 10,000 would be a triumph. He believed that black male suffrage would win, even though most locals anticipated defeat. He had supreme confidence in his personal influence, possibly doubling the vote because of the "tickets" he was printing, the flyers he was distributing, and letters he was writing to every county. Earlier in the month Stone had complained about money. Blackwell did now also, for he seems to have expected a payment from Wood, but received none; Wood had spent everything, plus $150 of his own. The man who took Blackwell to Wood's home in Cottonwood Falls was not paid either, though Wood promised to fix that. This individual, named Baker, said that Wood had expected "strong backing & large pecuniary aid from the AERA" and felt let down. Blackwell added that Wood was as disappointed because Kansas electors had shown they were unready for female suffrage and one campaign could not turn them around.[1]

Blackwell's letter confirms that Wood had misread the AERA's circumstances back in March. It established that Blackwell understood well how challenging the Kansas situation was in October 1867, two weeks before the election. Stone quickly knew it all from this letter. Blackwell also recognized the sterling roles then of Brown, Stanton, and Anthony, whose work had prevented the campaign being "a *complete fizzle*."[2] These campaigners had all arrived long after the initial surge in favor of women that Blackwell and Stone claimed had occurred in April and May. Neither had any solid understanding of events since, for they left Kansas just as the forces against women were coalescing. They had opened the campaign in an atmosphere of optimism, complete with financing and solid support back East in the form of Anthony. By the time the others arrived, the campaign had become like an uphill climb in an ice storm rather than one simply against prevailing winds.

When Train finally arrived in Kansas a few days before Blackwell wrote his letter to Stone, he and Anthony began campaigning in Leavenworth. "George Francis Train is to ... [appear here. He] speaks in favor of woman suffrage, and everybody will want to hear him," wrote one paper. "There is no other such talking man in the world as Train.... On that subject his head is level, and he will give more good reasons for his position in one evening than [antis] can give against it in a month; and he will tell more good stories, be more impudent, saucy, funny, and keep an audience in better humor than any other two men that ever undertook to talk in public. Whoever fails to come out and hear Train will make a very great mistake."[3]

With such fanfare, Train headed out in Kansas. He did so without Milton Reynolds, whom Anthony had scheduled as his co-canvasser, for Reynolds had gone with the Indian Peace Commissioners "to investigate the Indian question."[4] Such a venture was highly appropriate for a newspaper editor. But his sudden departure for this project may actually have been a convenient cover to carry out the wish of Wood, Robinson, Blackwell, and others involved in the Train conspiracy to have Anthony "accompany Train & so get democratic votes."[5] With no one else available, Anthony went in Reynolds' stead— heading into the most interesting campaign she ever experienced. The prospect of an evening's entertainment by Train drew unprecedented crowds.

"GEO. FRANCIS TRAIN'S FIRST GREAT SPEECH," trumpeted a local newspaper afterwards. "Our town has not been so stirred up for a generation as it has been by Geo. Francis Train in his recent display of fireworks. He talked at least twelve columns of our journal, but we have only space for some of the striking points of the speech. He swung all around the circle of knowledge, and trod on everybody's toes with impunity. Yet all applauded and cheered sentiments which would have sent another speaker off the stage."[6] Although the paper dismissed some of his solutions to such very much to-the-point concerns as the dangers of a runaway national Civil War debt and though he was controversial, the fact was that Train apparently gave voice to what many listeners thought but were afraid to say, made them laugh, and charged through and mowed down the shibboleths of conventional political wisdom. Aware that the Republicans for several months had been organizing and running a no-holds-barred campaign against women, Train, who always supported the underdog, gave as good as the women had been facing and more. Cynical about most politics in the United States at the time, he had earlier coined a slogan—"Down with Politicians, Up with the People"—and said that his modus operandi was to "act on instinct, impulse, intuition—seldom on reason."[7] His iconoclasm shone through his speeches in Kansas. Drawing crowds from everywhere, he was a barnstormer of the first magnitude, a verbal tornado that flattened everything in its path, a rhetorical hurricane that stirred up everything in its way, rendering it forever changed. Afraid of no criticism, he attacked his critics, turned their slurs, their facile pronouncements, and their lies against them and drove through Kansas for the last two weeks of the campaign a political juggernaut that, in terms of the issues, had the insider political forces scrambling. For many listeners it would have been the event of a lifetime—much more fun than the hell they had lived through in the 1850s in the fight in Kansas against slavery. It is difficult not to imagine that when the crowd dispersed there was a buzz, a hum, grins all around, hoots of laughter at remembered one-liners, and a sense of buoyancy imparted by Train's unique approach in a hotly debated contest.

The anti-woman suffrage press immediately went hysterical. Obviously threatened by a virtuoso and unforgettable performance, the *Leavenworth Bulletin* in a short editorial snootily denigrated all of Train's "at least twelve columns" that the *Leavenworth Commercial* had referred to and ultimately had to admit that "his audience was delighted."[8] Yet this commentary was the least of it. The *Atchison Champion*, announcing that "this ridiculous blowhard" was apparently scheduled to speak in the town, compounded the negativity by quoting the *Leavenworth Conservative*, which, calling Train "the low comedy clown of female suffrage," said he spoke "in favor of the woman, and either argues against the negro or else says nothing about his claims." The editorial sneeringly continued: "Last evening, to a large audience in Laing's Hall he was produced, to the infinite amusement of such as are pleased with the performances of clowns and harlequins ... [and] he boldly announced himself against the negro."[9]

On this key issue the *Atchison Champion* was wrong. Nowhere in his speech, as reported in the *Leavenworth Commercial* and republished by Train himself—along with many critical items and much written by himself in his ego-inflationary style—did he say anything of that nature. He positioned his own views in the light of Republican politicians, specifically against Mr. Pinckney, the editor of the *Leavenworth Bulletin,* who was "for woman suffrage and negro suffrage, but he wishes to make sure of the latter first." Train, in contrast, declared, "This is where we disagree. Woman first, and negro afterward."[10] Reversing priorities, he positioned sex against race instead of race against sex. He thereby highlighted the hypocrisies of Republicans, for none of this debate could have arisen if they had promoted equality for all. Republicans, virulent reformers, and the black men who were anti-woman had created this situation. The reversal of priorities such as Train unabashedly

advanced clearly threatened the establishment, for its members equated support for women with opposition to black male suffrage. Yet, to reduce to a
slogan what Train said conveniently ignored the fact that his ideas were much
more complex and that his point highlighted the hypocrisy and sex bias of
the politicians, reformers, and black advocates of male suffrage only.

What Train obviously understood—just like Anthony and Stanton had
when they talked about a reconstruction based on true republicanism with
equality of all, and unlike Republicans who promoted partisan politics on
steroids once the war was over—was that the Civil War had been a watershed
in the history of the nation wherein institutionalized inequality as manifested
in slavery was over. "Slavery, Secession, State Sovereignty and civil war went
out with Old America," Train declared, painting a picture of the victory of
the Revolution of 1776—finally. The end of this blatant inequality in a nation
founded upon equality should mean the end of all inequalities, including
that of women. "Woman's suffrage … come[s] in with New America," he proclaimed. In addition to the end of revolution, Train was also describing a
huge shift in the nation, which already was radically different from before
1861 for reasons even other than abolition. "Instead of "hugg[ing] the Atlantic
shore idols … [America] has a soul that reaches the Pacific," Train declared.
The old social, political, and economic system had effectively died with the
Civil War, as had the evil that had brought it about. "Instead of a country
of little States, America has become a great nation. When Democracy lost
its independence, the Democratic Party died. When the Republican Party
accomplished its mission … that party also died." He looked at society in
total, rather than in competing interest groups. "The days of Old America
are gone when woman is emancipated," he declared. Contrasting the "Old
America" with the "New America" based on people of America attuned to
American culture and innovation—not people who still looked to Britain
and old ideas—he outlined a future for a renewed country, with a vision even
grander than that of Stanton and Anthony, who relied on constitutionalism
to press their point. Train, in fact, gave no simple stump speech for a state
referendum: this was a speech with a clear focus on the presidency, one which
presented a vision for the future, engendered optimism, stirred national pride,
aroused the imagination, and challenged narrow thinking, prejudices, and
pettiness.

Yet this was not what his critics heard. Republicans heard that Train
opposed the official Republican Party line promoting black men and excluding women. When he showed the multiple conflicting standards of that policy
by turning it upside down and putting women before black men, they trans-
lated his position into pure political and racial animosity. The *Atchison Champion*, for example, quoting the *Leavenworth Conservative,* proclaimed several
pointed "truths." Train was "a negro hater by sympathy; a Copperhead by

most notorious and shameful practice; a brilliant, sharp, inconsistent, voluble and incomprehensible advocate of humbugs and shams."[11] This writer took great liberties with the truth, concluding with false ideas. The editor of the *Leavenworth Commercial,* which attempted to capture Train's words for its readers, facilitated a look beyond the slogans by its extensive coverage of both the style and substance of Train's first speech in Kansas. The newspaper also published a report-cum-editorial of the meeting, commenting briefly on the speeches of four other speakers, plus Anthony. "This meeting was a magnificent success, and a scene of rich and racy enjoyment, such as is not witnessed once in a century in a political gathering," it said.[12]

There was at least one other fact that opponents distorted. If Train himself did not speak in favor of black male suffrage, the meetings did not ignore it. At Leavenworth, Train spoke in the context of a campaign for equal suffrage by sex and race. Even antis recognized this. About the Olathe meeting on October 23, one newspaper said this in a report-cum-commentary critical of Train: "Col. Moonlight also spoke earnestly in favor of Negro Suffrage, and was followed by ... Anthony, who ably advocated the cause of all disfranchised classes."[13] The first excitement in Leavenworth was just the start. Train continued to "Lawrence, Olathe, Paola, Ottawa, Mound City, Fort Scott, LeRoy, Humboldt, Burlington, Emporia, Junction City, Topeka, Atchison, Wyandotte," and perhaps even elsewhere."[14]

After each succeeding meeting, the papers constantly criticized Train and put their own slant on his effect. "The general belief here is that Train is a sympathizer and a Copperhead, and will add largely to the vote in favor of negro suffrage," said one.[15] "The great unwashed Copperhead spoke here," another said of this fastidious man. "We could gain but one idea from Train's speech ... that his mission to Kansas is to defeat Negro suffrage.... He is trying to get the Democrats to go for female suffrage ... to aid in creating a split [among Republicans]. He says he is succeeding in some places. Will the Republicans of Kansas permit this bloviating, senseless, Copperhead dandy to influence them to go against negro suffrage?"[16]

Such coverage demonstrated clearly that many Republicans refused to accept that male and female suffrage were not mutually exclusive; for them, anyone who promoted the latter was automatically against the former because of race. This was their position, and they stuck to it.

31. Against Men's Arguments Against Women

This great Kansas Reformation dissolves the Divine right of men over women. (Loud cheers.)—George Francis Train, *The Great Epigram Campaign of Kansas*, (1867), 72.

"On the Kansas Stump for Woman Suffrage—He Commits the Democratic Party to the Cause—The Largest Audience ever seen in Leavenworth—He fires a Bombshell into Old Fogydom—Old America Dead, New America Born—Discord Departed, Concord Assumed—Woman the True Reformer—Greenback Idea, Train's Copyright—Magnificent Future of America—The next President of America—Sunshine in the Sky." The *Leavenworth Commercial* summarized Train's long speech in its extensive subhead, capturing its essence in breathless words.[1]

Leavenworth was Train's first appearance with Anthony, whose brother was a pillar of the town's Republican establishment. Yet he soon took a direct swipe at Republicans. "I think it is time the honest democrat and republican voters should rise up in their might and wipe off all those corrupt Republican leaders from the Kansas state," he declared.[2] The powerful were facing a formidable opponent. Worse, however, in Republicans' view, though the SISA had asked him "to come to Kansas and stump the State for Equal rights and female suffrage,"[3] Train focused on women, threatening in Republicans' minds their all-male suffrage agenda. Commentators believed Train intended to destroy the party using woman suffrage. "It has become clear that the advocacy of woman suffrage embarrasses and endangers the Republican party. For that reason and no other Train takes hold of it. Copperheads know that the Republicans can carry Kansas unless they are divided. Therefore, they try to divide the Republican strength," a Missouri newspaper explained.[4]

Train said as much. At Paola he praised Democrats for "having split the Radical party here ... carrying off all honors by going solid for woman suffrage."[5] Writing of Olathe on October 23, he described a meeting of "half

Democrats and half Republicans and all for woman suffrage and against negro suffrage," and said that Democrats there "intend to carry woman suffrage as a democratic measure—Democrats having voted for it in the legislature."[6] Train also pointed out that Democrats were simply taking advantage of a situation the Republicans had created. "Democrats all see that the Republicans, by going back on woman suffrage are killing their party."[7] In Junction City, he crowed, "The Democratic party never had such an opportunity."[8] Yet Train was doing nothing new. To try to split a dominant party's support is a time-honored political tradition. The main problem for Republicans in Kansas in 1867 was that they were not the ones doing the splitting. In 1867 it was Train, by giving a clear, strong alternative. Worse in their view was that Train declared, "Democrats are jumping in *for* women and out for our colored brother."[9] Yet, this was subterfuge. The Democrats had never supported black men. Rubbing salt into the wound, he said, "Kalloch, Blunt, Sears, and Liggett have killed the Republican Party," inferring they were doing so "in the interest of the Democrats."[10]

Yet, to dismiss Train's words as demonstrating political tactics only is too simplistic. He was an outsider, not a politician. His approach to politics was not as a politician and his message was broader than using woman suffrage to split Republicans in Kansas. In 1867 he promoted the revolutionary idea of "We the people instead of We the Politicians."[11] He spoke out for those whom the powerful ignored and despised, presenting a plan the forgotten people might agree with. He did so as a brilliant, entertaining orator who knew how to stir his audiences and left his opponents reeling, for he made them spin like a top and they had no idea how to counter him. "He has swept [through Kansas]… like a prairie fire scattering the on-the-fence politicians … carrying the entire democratic party almost solid for woman suffrage," wrote an observer.[12] He outclassed them and changed the dynamic in Kansas during an unforgettable once-in-a-lifetime, not-to-be-missed political campaign.

Train had not descended on Kansas with no context: if he was politically cynical as Republican editors claimed, the Republicans were equally so by enfranchising black men to hold onto power. They were also cynical to dismiss Train's sympathies as opportunism. Train always supported the underdog, which in 1867 in Kansas was women and female suffrage. Train made much of campaigning for women. "Mankind means womanhood too,"[13] he declared, stating the obvious for anyone except Republicans during Reconstruction and the males of any party and ethnic group who believed in the "divine right of men over women."[14] Praising Anthony's campaigning skills, he pointed out the irony that she was a "perfect steam engine" who "has kept all the advertised engagements … and yet she has no vote."[15] In fact, he said, the injustice was that "white men have three votes—one for themselves, one for the woman, the other for the negroes." He proposed "that woman take some of this work off their hands."[16] He challenged the further injustice that "woman is not allowed to be tried by her Peers," for juries came from male-only electoral lists.[17] He also argued for equal pay and opportunity for women, if only so that women could afford to live.[18] He argued that women's influence in politics would lead to general reforms[19] and temperance specifically.[20] Train himself did not drink or smoke. He dismissed claims that "women had no interest in the government," for in Kansas, with a voting population of 26,000 men, "6,000 women a year or two ago signed a petition for [suffrage and] now there are over 15,000 who demand it," he said.[21] In one of his impromptu rhymes lampooning Republicans for political opportunism in promoting black male suffrage to maintain power, he said his "mission to Kansas" would break "woman's chains."[22] Train, therefore, was as overtly pro-woman as he may have been deliberately intent on splitting Republican Party support in 1867.

He also presented facts: Republicans were cynical to dismiss female suffrage as unworthy and insignificant, even at that time. Republicans were the unworthy ones: they supported continuing a republic "based on caste and class,"[23] while women wanted a true republic based on equality for all. Women were the ones being excluded and restricted more than before. The men were not. In fact, the manhood suffrage measure in Kansas was less crucial than female suffrage: within then-current politics, manhood suffrage across race lines was in the works, guaranteed through the 14th Amendment at least through penalties on states without black male suffrage. Ratification was only a matter of time. For black males, if the Kansas referendum failed it would not be the end; it would only be a delay in one state. More male suffrage in Kansas represented no precedent, for Congress had already hammered all-male suffrage into the governance of Washington, D.C., and several new states. For women, the situation was radically different. Ratification meant the hard-wiring of that word "male" into the federal Constitution, excluding all females. The women's campaign there was a fight to have female suffrage accepted as a legitimate proposition in the first place. With the 14th Amendment clock ticking against them, the referendum represented a push by women to get a foot in the door before that sex-biased, race-clad barrier clanged shut and all women's exclusion became fundamental law. Woman suffrage was the much more critical issue.

Yet the truth hardly mattered. Train's critics believed he was successfully driving a political wedge through Republicans' support and agenda by speaking out for women. Attempting to counter this apparent juggernaut, Republicans, therefore, attacked him for being against black men. Conveniently, they had a ready-made weapon in some of Train's words. In Humboldt, for example, Train proclaimed that "Democrats [at Fort Scott] going solid for the cause; but nigger suffrage is nowhere."[24] "Sambo must wait awhile for Sarah," he declared in Ottawa. In Mound City he wrote a report of his campaign where he called black men "the nig."[25] In Topeka he wrote a letter to a Democrat bigwig saying, "White Women before niggers."[26]

These words are painful to read, for the "N-word" today is unacceptable. It means racism. Yet, such words come from the past. They appear in documents from the past, and history deals with the past. The past is not the same as the present. In other disciplines, such as movie retrospectives, understanding their use requires making allowances for the context and instead of being judgmental recognizing them as a measure of how far society has evolved. So it should be with history: in those days, people used regularly some of today's taboo words, such as the N-word, or "Sambo," or, for that matter, "Paddy" or "Mick" for Irishmen, "doughfaces,"[27] and countless other terms for almost every group ethnic or otherwise, sometimes insultingly, sometimes not.[28] Newspapers employed them. Individuals found them a convenient collective noun or as an adjective at one end of the spectrum or a means of expressing disgust and hatred on the other. Today's taboo words were often, in fact, the vernacular of the time. The drastic change in usage must be remembered when considering the past. Train's use of today's forbidden word, therefore, while possibly indicating racism, does not automatically mean he was racist. The *Kansas Chief*—a reasonable newspaper—unhesitatingly used it in assessing opposition to female suffrage.

Train's arguments, however, could describe black men negatively. "Give [the negroes] votes before the women and the women will never get the franchise. Ignorance never votes for intelligence," he said.[29] Train here was, however, noting that "the negroes to a man are against white woman suffrage" and echoing what women had worried about for at least two years, with Stone's observations in Kansas being the latest.[30] But Train also criticized clear facts, such as Langston's anti-female suffrage appearances with Republicans[31] and his specific anti-woman actions—which may have been a trigger behind SISA's call for Train's help in the first place. Uproar ensued when in Topeka, he proclaimed, "Every man in Kansas who throws a vote for the Negro on Tuesday, and not for a woman, has insulted his mother, his daughter, his sister, and his wife."[32] The truth at the heart of this question was that if possession of the franchise did not somehow personally and socially elevate the enfranchised it is difficult to imagine why there was such a huge battle over it. If it would facilitate only the Republican attempt to consolidate its voter base, enfranchising women could have done the same thing. The simple fact was that the male-only elective franchise did put all men above all women in the nation, which was particularly reprehensible for white men to finagle and black men to insist on when women had so assiduously worked for the freedom of slaves and the rights of black men.[33] It made a mockery of the philosophy of equality that they had trumpeted as lying behind the whole antislavery movement. The changes were more than straightforward legal reforms. They were constitutional reforms that reinforced long-held prejudices and norms. This was a fact even as imposed male race equality shocked to the core people's long-established internalized sense of propriety, which was equally based on long-held norms and attitudes replete with acceptance of social stratification according to race and sex. When Train described the effect of all-male suffrage so shockingly, he rocked the boat and provoked stunned agreement,[34] as if the men in his audience awoke for the first time to the implications of a sex-discrimination franchise. Train's methods were so effective "his anecdotes … sounded [the] death-knell" of the black suffrage measure, one newspaper commented. It also added that Train did it "without opposing negro suffrage"[35]—a telling observation from someone who was there.

Train also argued that the equality based on all-male suffrage did not solve the old inequalities. If all *men* were created equal, where did that leave women? If women were on a pedestal, how could they be inferior to men who, until only recently, were considered subordinate? These were perfectly *logical*—not racist—questions, but the presence of race allows the argument to degenerate easily into slurs of racism while ignoring the real issue of equality for all. Proponents of male-only suffrage would brook no opposition to their agenda and many would do whatever it took to undermine it. When voting was to be based on one sex with only black males added as electors, racism too readily becomes the easy argument to use against opponents. The clearly hysterical hatred by opponents of female suffrage ramped up the racism mud-slinging. Directed at Train and women with great force and volume, it remained resolutely stuck. With sex-based suffrage rammed through during Reconstruction, and racism the slur cast at those who objected, nowadays racism is the lens for analyzing the period. Yet, the emphasis on race masked the inherent, deliberate, discrimination in sex of the 1860s franchise reform, so that even some men of Kansas did not appreciate what was happening until Train pointed it out when he contrasted the solidly race-based rhetoric of the pro-male side with strong pro-female rhetoric. He also highlighted another parallel with similar effects, where race was not the issue, declaring that Republicans proposed to "disfranchise the Rebel and kill Woman Suffrage; thus putting the Women of Kansas on the back seats with the rebels. (Laughter and shame.)"[36]

With women the marginalized group, and the largest marginalized group in the nation, Train had good reason to want to highlight the truth, for political leaders pushed race and promoted the political equality of black men with white men as the primary inequality to tackle, airily dismissing for their own agenda their own philosophy of inequality and sex bias while characterizing opponents as racist. In fact, anyone opposed was automatically characterized as racist, no matter the reason for the protest—even though the Rebel analogy demonstrates the issue was equality. To brand opponents as racist ensured control of the narrative and covered up the truth. Defining the issue in narrow black-and-white terms, it excluded from the debate the wide range of intermediate potential ways of examining the issues at stake, while creating the means to slur and dismiss opponents. This happened with Train. Yet, his advocacy of female suffrage did make a dent in a debate that was apparently locked up. He pointed out the absurdity and hypocrisy of the white men's rigging of the electorate and the Kansas men's rigging of their campaign against the women. And within the narrow confines of the further discriminatory suffrage those men created, it brought up educated suffrage as an alternative for those who both found the rigged proposals unacceptable and who tried to offer a compromise between the hard-line Radical Republican agenda and true equality such as Stanton proposed.

Essentially the purported "impartial"—though in truth male-only suffrage—created a conundrum for white men that went to the heart of taboos touching their own sense of self, their own image, and their image of their own society. It was a conundrum that could be used against them to win votes, which Train proceeded to do, making the antis spin. This thinking lay behind Train's most explicitly reported racial statement, which occurred at Junction City, where he declared, "The most remarkable fact in our century is the attempt in Kansas to enfranchise the African, and disenfranchise the American (shame), or in other words to exalt the Ethiopian, and enslave the Christian race." Again, however, appearances were deceptive. A member of the audience had questioned the effects on religion if women were excluded. The broader context was the social implications of the expansion of the vote based on discrimination by sex. Bringing the issue back to the "aristocracy by sex" and mixing sex up with race like the Republicans did, he declared, "All those in favor of making black men the guides and political protectors of white women say aye. (Dead silence and considerable thinking.)"[37] Within the political and social climate associated with the referenda, these considerations were valid. None of these problems would arise if Republicans were promoting true equality. Yet, anything threatening white men's concerns for black men, whatever the reasoning, was fast becoming taboo in postwar America. During Reconstruction, white men created a hierarchy of victims where black men were at the top and women at the bottom. For anyone to challenge their hierarchy was to be against black men. By extension, they were racist.

Yet Train was fearless. If discrimination was going to be further institutionalized, base suffrage on education, not on an inborn human characteristic, he argued, advocating a restricted franchise in a nation where discrimination in voting had been the norm from the start. He took slurs and turned them back on the perpetrator. "The Negro Press as usual attacks me with the stock epithets, Copperhead, Rebel, Traitor," he said. "Yes, I am a Copperhead who dared to be an American in Europe when Americans were scarce (applause). I am a Rebel who dared ... to be an American in America, when Americans were scarce. (Loud applause.) I am a Traitor whose patriotism does not consist in cheating the Government, but who had maintained his Manhood by cheering for the Constitution—the Union and people of his country. (Loud cheers.)"[38] Yet, opponents capitalized on this again in reporting, converting his words into anti-black male tirades because he dared to challenge the prevailing policies and men in power.

In fact, countless Train statements could be and were used to cast him as a racist. His opponents hated the fact that Train's audiences generally loved his irreverence and fearlessness, which the response to his own defense demonstrated. In fact, listeners enjoyed his speechmaking so much that commentators said that the campaign for Democrat votes made these deplorable people's congenital racism worse. He disgusted Republicans. Anthony's second cousin publicly castigated him for asserting that black men were the spies of the Rebels and traitors. George T. Anthony told Train personally that "there was intelligence and loyalty enough in any ordinary black man to manufacture a brigade of men like him."[39] Train's apparent success using what they considered the meanest of tactics to split Republicans while employing the insignificant issue of the rights of women, thereby threatening the much more important question of manhood suffrage, infuriated them. They believed he was a blackguard. His Kansas audiences ignored these characterizations. Yet this is the picture of Train that spoke most loudly at the time elsewhere in the nation, and the slur of racism was hurled so forcefully then that it stuck.

This racist view of Train, however, is one-dimensional. Even if it were justice to dispatch him by character assassination, the substance of his message deserves consideration, for he presented a comprehensive contrast to the establishment's approach to political justice in the postwar nation. The official position was manhood suffrage across race lines, resulting in benefits for black men and the retention of power by Republican white men. Republicans were not bothered by further implications. Its impact on women did not matter because women did not count; they just had their place, like all blacks in slavery before abolition. Any attention the manhood suffrage crowd paid to women was to keep them in their place with a picture of social mayhem if women won the vote. Train's approach was to present the extreme opposite of this warped picture. His poem lampooning his Republican opponents specified not just "woman's chains" but "white woman's chains."[40] In his speeches he explained the effects of enfranchising men only, outlining three main points—race, class, and age—while he added that male-only suffrage created fertile grounds for demeaning women further and creating insulting language. These points appear throughout his rambling speeches, each argument rarely proceeding immediately and tidily upon the previous one, while everything he said rocked the debate.

"The Rads want to place our wives and mothers below the negro. Shame on the cowards," he declared.[41] "Your mother, your wife, your sisters, your daughters" would not become "the equals *politically* of the negro—by giving him a vote and refusing it to woman." Consequently, he claimed, "you … place your family politically still lower in the scale of citizenship and humanity. (Sensation and cries of shame.)"[42] Exploring the implications of the voting proposals further, Train called, "All those in favor of making the servant the master say aye. (Loud laughter and a confusion of ideas on negro suffrage.)"[43] "Give negroes votes, and when the woman suffrage idea is more advanced, the fair women of Fifth Avenue," Train went on, "will have to petition their Boot-Blacks, Barbers, Porters, Waiters and Coachmen for the high-toned privilege of casting a ballot. (Sensation)"[44] Train was clearly against black men—apparently. Yet, that last point was, in fact, a class argument, for not all such workers were or would be black men. Before the end of the century, suffrage women complained about this socially topsy-turvy situation.[45] More important, Train also argued that if Republicans abandoned their anti-woman bias and other distinctions were removed society would benefit. "Give the sex votes and men will have more respect for women than to treat them as children or as dolls," he said. Without the vote, women would be denigrated across age lines. "The ten-year-old boy will say to his woman relatives, 'Oh you don't know anything, you are only a woman.'"[46] The creation of a class or caste based on sex and encompassing 50 percent of the population also created widespread opportunities to demean that class wholesale. "When man wishes to insult his fellow man, he calls him a woman," Train said.[47] Nothing in this was an improvement on how black people were treated because of race, but it could mean a transfer from one group to another of the national propensity at the time to insult, demean, and marginalize anyone who was not a white man and even pointed to a deterioration of sex relations. Manhood suffrage, Train was arguing, created something worse out of a purported solution to a national problem.

Once again, statements like these allowed Republicans to paint Train as a racist for failing to include black women. Yet to do so dismisses his method. "Mr. Train is probably the best living example of our old style of stump speakers. Dashing, defiant, rapid, full of power, full of spread-eagleism, and of a kind of eloquence always popular in this young country, he cares little what he says so that it [may] reach and stir up the hearts of his hearers," one commentator wrote.[48] By doing what he did, he was awakening Democrats to the implications of their anti-woman position. He did so by presenting the extreme opposite of the Republicans' agenda to enfranchise men only. His statements mirrored to Republicans their own biases and prejudices. If Republicans focused on black males under the rubric of "manhood suffrage," and Train spoke of breaking "white woman's chains," Republicans equally failed to include black women. If posterity absolutely requires that the position of either side be characterized as some sort of "ism," both were racist and sexist, for each seemed to discriminate against individuals of the opposite race and sex. The whole so-called equality controversy, therefore, was rotten to the core. Yet it was the Republican postwar agenda that determined the controversy and Republicans were the ones intent on excluding women. Train's speeches did not set the agenda or advocate exclusion. Despite these crucial differences, he became a highly visible and easy scapegoat for anything that went wrong with Kansas Republicans' plans to enfranchise males only and keep themselves in power, while the men in power considered any conduct of their own to derail him acceptable.

In the details, Train's message contrasted with the official line of all-male suffrage only. He was not against black suffrage per se for he did not oppose it. He promoted suffrage for white women first, black suffrage after, with education the standard, and argued for ultimate equality through enfranchising both sexes eventually across race lines. If there was to be discrimination in suffrage, "woman first, and negro last, is my programme, yet I am willing that intelligence should be the test."[49] In Junction City answering the question "how about the negro?" he spoke of education first and then enfranchisement.[50] He said many times that if there was to be voting discrimination, it should be based on education. In fact, he endorsed a proposal from the previous year's legislative session that would demand literacy of voters.[51] After July 4, 1870, "all of age who cannot read the American Constitution, the State Constitution and the Bible in the language in which he was educated" would be disfranchised. While setting the standard high and while such literacy laws would ultimately gain a bad name as a footing for Jim Crow laws later in the century, there was nothing to say that a voter qualification based on literacy was inherently discriminatory on racial lines. In fact, literacy was essential for informed voters. Train's support of educated suffrage, therefore, is not an anti-black position. His position, in fact, seems shot through with a large dose of the realism that many Republicans, such as Garrison, the now retired antislavery advocate, who called for black education, also held.

The fact is, in 1867 neither the Republicans nor Train advocated "equality." Putting either race or sex first is prioritizing equality—an oxymoron. In their overarching arguments, they each advocated an extreme, presenting contrasting ways of remaking the nation in a manner that was, if not equal, at least more just. The starting point of the debate was the Republican agenda. Yet it is still always easy to advance as the full picture the race positions Train presented. The rest of his argument has largely been lost. While anything to do with race purporting to be against black men caused a sensation, alternative viewpoints attracted less interest even though they were well represented in his speeches. Even the headlines did not shout racism.

Other factors also played a role. Race discrimination has always trumped sex discrimination in the United States. Yet, Train's position contrasts starkly with that of the Republicans. Put simply, the position of Republicans and the anti-female suffrage groups discriminated against 50 percent of the population. Train's pro-woman position, however, excluded a much smaller number of people and only temporarily. The measure with a wider impact was woman suffrage. If, as Republicans deemed, race was important, then, Train argued, white women should come first. He audaciously brought the problem full circle: only true equality for all was just. Despite thereby making the injustices of the Republicans clear, Train has come down through history as a "notorious racist,"[52] for Republican white men and some black leaders, both of whom were overtly against women, established the rhetoric and threw massive volumes of mud at him. That mud makes the truth difficult to uncover. But if Train was racist it was a racism that favored—for a change—a significantly large and until now excluded part of the population, namely white women. If Train was racist, his bias was partly to counter the race and sex bias of those in power. If Train was "racist" it was because he espoused "equality" prioritized by sex first, combined with race. This was the opposite of Phillips' policy of prioritizing "equality" by one idea for a generation, putting women last after black men, temperance, and the eight-hour day.[53] Train's rhetoric did confuse matters, but he custom-designed it for a debate with predetermined biases that Kansas and national Republicans created. These were men who had not only failed to unify the nation after the Civil War but also had further divided it in a fashion as pernicious as before 1861 but employing different criteria. The men who did this deserved to be held accountable for the unjust implications of their policies and actions. Train was the individual with the presence, the guts, and the political opportunity to highlight the situation, while the Republicans and black male leaders had brought his criticism upon themselves.

32. Campaigning for the Forgotten Woman

Success to Train in everything but Female Suffrage!—"Kalloch's Home Journal," Kansas, 1867, no specific date.

Train was a must-see. "It is worth more to hear him than to see the best theatrical performance that was ever put on the boards," said one newspaper.[1] "Mr. Train … always appears in Lavender kids, black pants, closely buttoned blue coat with brass buttons and patent leather boots," said another, adding, "he was received with loud cheers."[2] "He talks with his eyes, his hands, his legs as well as his mouth," said a third.[3] The most contentious campaigner on the last two weeks of the Kansas campaign was "a tall handsome man with curly brown hair and keen gray eyes" who "gave his audiences the best entertainment they had had in many a day."[4] Train's unconventional appearance was a feast for the eyes of hard-working pioneers on the frontier where the fine things of life were rare. Some of them travelled twenty or thirty miles for the experience.[5]

Train presented his unconventional views with inborn showmanship. Many skeptics, it was said, caved on hearing him. His Leavenworth presentation, "packed with Irishmen who were building the railroad to the West," rapidly turned this anti-woman suffrage audience around.[6] In his multifaceted, wide-ranging speeches calling for reform—particularly more just suffrage than the ossified establishment's current proposal—Train was an antidote to the restraint of the norm. "His anecdotes, his analysis, his bitter sarcastic comments on the milk and water style of some of the Kansas politicians cannot be transferred to paper," said one commentator.[7] Specifically, he thundered against double standards and prejudices of men who had formerly hurled verbal lightning against plantation owners and politicians who refused to do anything about slavery. He had the full measure of Republicans, "abolitionists," and "anti" black men. Their victory in the dismantling of one huge injustice had been through a devastating, nation-destroying war, Train held. This crew's quest now was for power through black male suffrage and the control of the vote by sex discrimination. Their biases had contrived the postwar debacle, including the current twisted, tortured, and inherently unjust political controversy and corruption over female suffrage. Now, in Kansas, their surrogates tried to impose their wishes with unrelenting agitation and dictatorial direction from bullying church pulpits and through press propaganda.

"Where is Wendell Phillips today?" demanded Train. "Inconsistent in all things and cowardly in this. He proves Congress a swindling concern, and the President a traitor. Yet asks a *swindling* Congress to impeach a *traitor* President," he answered to laughter and applause. Train was in his element hurling such barbs at the women's opponents. *"Where is Horace Greeley in this Kansas war for liberty?* Pitching the woman suffrage idea out of the [New York] Convention and bailing Jeff. Davis. (Hiss and laughter.) Where is *William Lloyd Garrison?* Being patted on the shoulder by his employers, our enemies abroad, for his faithful work in trying to destroy our Nation. (Applause and hisses against Garrison.) Where is *Henry Ward Beecher?*... All these fair-weather champions fled at the first approach of danger (shame)."[8] Train, who clearly loved America, nailed the villainy of the wise men of the East. "When principle went over for expediency, old Thad [Stevens] thanked God the Republican party had departed. (Loud applause.) [Greeley] set the example at Albany, throwing over women for negroes.... Phillips says, one idea for one generation, and the negro is our generation, temperance the next, eight hour labor the next and women last. What hypocrisy! ... postponing woman's emancipation four generations. (Shame and sensation.)."[9]

Every one of these accusations was true. Train also hammered Phillips for his theft of the women's money. "When my old friend Hovey ... told me that he had given fifty thousand dollars to Wendell Phillips and the Trustees for the enfranchisement of Women and emancipation of the Negro, he little thought that the Women would get but seven thousand and the Negro forty-three thousand. (Sensation.)"[10] He lambasted Kansas commentators for complaining about the women of the east. The editors objected to these "foreign emissaries,"[11] but, Train retorted, they "are no foreign emissaries. They came expecting support. They thought the Republicans honest. They forgot that the Democrats alone were their friends. (Applause). They forgot that it was the Republican party that publicly insulted them in Congress. That it was Charles Sumner who wished to insert the word Male in the amendment of the Federal Constitution two years ago, when the old Constitution by neither inserting male nor female had left it an open question.... Mrs. Cady Stanton, Miss Susan B. Anthony, Mrs. Lucy Stone and Miss Olympia Brown are the foreign emissaries that will alone have the credit of emancipating women in Kansas. Your trimming politicians left them in the lurch. Not one of you were honest. (Applause)"[12]

Train essentially nailed government and reformer corruption. He also nailed the shocking sex bias of the nation's men. Train was the most fearless man of the era to support woman's rights, to criticize the anti-woman agenda and to challenge the inequalities and inconsistencies that male leaders promoted and dismissed in their push for a purported impartial franchise. Only by viewing Train's speeches in this perspective can justice be accorded him, for the attacks that the women faced from their opponents were worse than anything that Train said about black men. It may be that the campaign record excludes the worst of what Train said about black men, for he published his own speeches.[13] Yet, the same can be said about the newspapers' anti-woman bias, for men controlled the press and many were overtly anti-woman. If it is assumed, therefore, that Train was more racist than the documents record, it must equally be assumed that men were worse in their negativity to women than history records.

The male pillars of society first attacked the women campaigners' morals, for "strong-minded" individuals fighting for justice were automatically immoral in society's eyes. Earlier, Stone and Blackwell saw this with the lies about their marriage and the accusations of "free love."[14] These men besmirched Brown and Bisbee as prostitutes simply because they argued that equality for women would raise women's status and that equal pay would ease the destitution that drove women to prostitution. One nasty anti, Samuel E. McBurney, castigated Brown for having "come out to [Kansas] for fifty dollars a month, expenses paid, and the privilege of wearing short dresses and riding about the country with fast young men."[15] Many such people even disparaged Brown's profession as an ordained minister, increasing the scandal associated with these lies. McBurney knew the ministry and scandals well, for he was implicated in some reprobate behavior along with one named J.D. Liggett[16] and Isaac S. Kalloch—all reverends and ferocious antis. These upstanding men of society then attacked the campaigners for allying with temperance, which women advocated to eradicate female penury resulting from men's alcoholism and the family's subsequent collapse. They also insulted women through race, with one speaker excoriating his audiences for "'preferring every old thing that had a white face' to the negro."[17] The attacks on the women were mean-spirited in the extreme. One newspaper attacked criticism of Kalloch's position—he had scarpered from Boston after sexual indiscretions[18]—with offensive anti-woman comments. "They have been 'screeching' Kalloch's name in every school-house," the paper said, "but Kalloch still lives, and gives them home thrusts that disturb their digestion, and their dreams." This editorial exulted in the effect of Kalloch's scurrilous behavior on some women. "A few of the female suffragers were taken suddenly ill and left, and the rest couldn't see any point in either of the speeches," it crowed.[19] Such treatment should be excoriated like the purported racism of Train, who was defending women.

The men, naturally, were proud of their highbrow achievements, next turning their superiority and verbosity to lecturing women. If women would just attend to procuring the passage of laws to give women property rights, one newspaper argued—clearly ignorant of what happened when voteless women tried to do so—they would be doing some good for their sex. The point was outdated; but continuing the assault in terms the most degrading that these scribes could conjure up, one argued as follows: "If all the female monstrosities [who] go perambulating about the country, talking of 'Women's rights,'" did what this newspaper advised, they would be better employed.[20] This editor apparently never ventured to investigate how women—treated in this depraved manner by so-called educated male editors in charge of informing the public—could ever convince politicians to make legal changes when many politicians came out of the same kind of sewer. The men went further, calling female suffrage "the infamous and disgraceful doctrine"[21] or "the pernicious dogma,"[22] marginalizing it outside acceptable belief and dismissing it as "the crazy craft," inferring it was occult or even witchcraft.[23] Religious worthies fulminated against the very sex that society was supposed to hold in high regard. Ignoring their own hypocrisy, they slighted women at every opportunity—for in this sex war, the means justified the end.

The women who braved this storm were courageous indeed. Brown, for example, noted that one anti speaker asked his audiences "if they wanted every old maid to vote."[24] General Blunt, one of the most virulent antis, at one point attacked Anthony and other unmarried women like her who devoted their lives to woman's rights and other causes such as antislavery, telling them "every woman ought to be married." Anthony gave Blunt as good as she got, retorting, Train scathingly told an audience in Blunt's presence, that "to marry it was essential to find some decent man, [who] could not be found among the Kansas politicians who had so gallantly forsaken the woman's cause at the least approaching danger. (Loud laughter.) She said, as society was organized, there was not one man in a thousand worthy of marriage—marrying a man and marrying a whisky barrel were two distinct ideas. (Laughter and applause.)"[25]

Attacks on the women constituted a nonstop, brutal assault, much of it certainly unreported. A correspondent complaining to one paper that it was "always saying … that females, commonly called women, should vote," illustrated this.[26] He described Highland, where locals had previously "shut the doors of the church on Olymp. Brown because she is such a man of a woman … [but] the boys who go to hear Miss Olymp. would stamp their feet, and whittle up the benches, and the men would spit on the floor, and other bad things would be done." Kalloch spoke at the meeting this correspondent attended and though Kalloch said he would not attack personalities, he "gave Dr. Blackwell fits, calling him a miserable, hen-pecked husband"—but at least admitting that Stone and Blackwell were married. This correspondent reported that Kalloch said "these women … come like a pestilence from the East, to cause disturbance in our domestic circles, are a set of miserable, demented traducers.… [I]t gave our womanly women an insight into the kind of manly women they were being led astray by." He "triumphantly said the true women of Kansas did not want to vote." He ridiculed the women's campaign literature and cynically dismissed the value of woman suffrage because increasing voting rolls would devalue votes on the market at elections, and he lectured long on women being women and men being men. "We want," said the correspondent, "to be saved the mortification of having our wives and daughters go to the polls and vote; thus degrading themselves by saying through the ballot, what their future destiny shall be. We are their lords and masters, and will attend to that ourselves."

This statement revealed the true male agenda: deny women all freedom. Continue dominating them. The meeting over, the correspondent said his wife had felt "like slapping her hands" but refrained because the meeting was in a church, "whereupon one of these women's rights women, of whom we have entirely too many here, saucily said she felt like slapping his ears." When Kalloch recited some poetry, "our women," the correspondent said, "were delighted with the high-sounding words … [but] I heard one of those tormented strong-minded women say, 'That fellow [would be] better [to] borrow his whole speech from old sayings.'" This letter seems so demented that it sounds almost tongue-in-cheek, but it communicated well the real nature of the battle that the women canvassers were continuously facing against their cause and integrity. Train helped to push back against this sexual hatred in a way that could not be dismissed as women were dismissed. Train's secret weapon was that he was a man.

The meeting at Ottawa at the end of October that pitted Train against Blunt highlighted another dirty trick. Train's speech in Lawrence "attacking Kalloch, Blunt and others, had made a terrible outcry in Ottawa," where the antis—also known as "the idols of Ottawa"—had their base. "[T]he mob spirit was a little imminent [and] Blunt had taken the hall to keep Train from speaking." His attempt failed, for during a lull in Blunt's talk, the call went out for Train. Blunt ceded the hall to him. When the general "abruptly closed his speech … Mr. Train took up the point, and for an hour the General was under the most scathing fire of ridicule and sarcasm that was ever fired at mortal man. The audience roaring and cheering over the General's discomfiture. [Blunt] was really to be pitied. Every shot told, and this remarkable debate will long be remembered in Ottawa, and probably never be forgotten."[27] Blunt was angry with this coverage. Within a few days he wrote the editor criticizing the news report, including Train's claim that he had attempted to stop the Train meeting. He also castigated Train as a Copperhead.[28]

The great differences between the two sides about the relative importance of true equality versus inequality defined by sex—used to restrict and control the vote—led to the vicious anti-woman campaign in Kansas during 1867. Republicans entered this with disgusting zeal. Black men joined in to protect their perceived threatened interests. In late October, after six months of increasing anti-woman mud-slinging from well-funded politicians, press, pulpits, and men of every stripe who shouted suffrage down and slandered the few penurious female canvassers, the appearance of Train made the women's cause take on new life like a launched rocket. This development infuriated Republicans, especially Train's handling of black male suffrage. Their fury increased because Train, unlike the official SISA campaign, had plenty of money to cover expenses. The Train canvass may also have caused discomfiture for women who had always supported blacks in everything. The *Atchison Champion*, for example, commented on what it considered at one Train meeting to be "the intense disgust of the Female Suffrage Committee, who seemed to be more eager to take up a contribution than to add elements of strength to their movement."[29] This newspaper was a rabidly Republican newspaper that referred to Train's speeches as "harangues" and utilized the *Leavenworth Conservative*'s "clown" put-down. The full truth of this story is unknown, for, although it said the "committee" was disgusted it failed to confirm this but inferred the problem was Train. The disgust could have equally been directed at manhood suffrage Republicans and other antis.

No one really knows how the women who campaigned in Kansas truly felt about Train, but it is easy to assume his speeches disgusted Anthony, that his arguments shook her; that she must have bitten her tongue and forged stoically ahead, feeling completely out of place in the apparent charade. Besides Train's comments about black men, two specific incidents might have set her on edge. One was Train's references to the difficulties on the road from Paola to Ottawa.[30] The other was when Train declared, "The first woman I had to convert to woman suffrage was…. Miss Anthony (Laughter and applause.) She commenced the campaign four-fifths negro and one-fifth woman (laughter); now she is four-fifths woman and only one-fifth negro."[31] Yet, like everything to do with Train, to assume Anthony's abhorrence may be incorrect. Through all the dirt of the Kansas campaign, she maintained her position on equal rights for all and opened meetings with a speech in favor of true impartial suffrage, still doing her bit for black men. She had nevertheless seen and experienced too much since 1865 and was too astute not to understand the forces she was facing. If in April 1865 she was still idealistic about achieving true equality for all, by late in 1867 she could not have been anything but realistic, all the males with whom she had worked having made her aware that men, both black and white, could not only be racist but anti-woman as well. Even if she found Train's comments about black men offensive, instead of rejecting him wholesale she seemed to see his good points and in the thick of campaigning could rejoice that such a prominent, if contentious, man was not only advocating female suffrage but also appearing to win support for it. Train, besides, was helping financially.

The "one-fifth" and "four-fifths comment," was, indeed, a land mine. Social opprobrium weighed down any degree of blackness back then and Anthony may have had to turn a blind eye to it. Yet there was also a metaphoric meaning to it: that of abandoning full support for manhood suffrage and converting fully to woman suffrage. She may have taken this as an off-color joke by Train—which it was when applied to Anthony, with her years of work for slaves, freed blacks, and women. Beyond that, it is difficult to see her objecting to the intention behind such statements as these: "All those in favor of lifting women to an equality with the negroes, say aye!"[32] and "The fact of the negroes being opposed to woman suffrage is injuring their cause and helping the women."[33] Both were truths that Anthony could hardly have denied, while black men had made choices even if she wished they had not. Comments like these, in fact, were offensive largely to anyone who put women last. Besides, any assumed disgust imputed to Anthony assumes she had no sense of humor, which is a huge leap to take when Train's speeches were full of irreverent humor and his relationship with his audience sparked and sparkled. Further, as she spent hours travelling with him, she had the opportunity to find out what he really believed and acquire understanding of his methods when he went out to speak. Also, hearing Train talk night after night, her views of his purported racism must have been significantly different from anyone who heard just one speech or read only Republican or anti commentary. Hearing him repeatedly, she could hardly have failed ultimately to appreciate that beyond the delivery and the contentious comments he dealt in the substance of the important national question of true political equality. Using highly entertaining and unconventional means and connecting with the people, Train zeroed in on the implications of manhood suffrage in a society already riven with the divisiveness of unequal, corrupt politics and contrived inequalities. His oratory stunningly contrasted with conventional politicians' pablum of lies masquerading as common sense. For Anthony, having for so long experienced derogatory comments, insults, and put-downs by men both black and white, to see anti-female suffrage canvassers now squealing about receiving a little of what they had meted out to women for years must have been somewhat satisfying, especially as they had brought it on themselves.

Anthony herself could be pointed in her observations, denouncing the "mean, low sneaking editors" of the Republican press of Leavenworth, upbraiding them and the Republican party for being "recreant to their professed principles and unworthy of the confidence of the advocates of human rights."[34]

She could easily have also criticized their "professional" standards. Anthony, said Train, also demanded of "General Moonlight who was arguing stronger for the negro than for the woman … 'why does he not set an example to the milk and water politicians and talk as enthusiastically for woman suffrage as negro suffrage?'"[35] She spiritedly pushed back against the anti-woman prejudice, even as Train directed his scathing barbs at the same misogynist men, needling them by pointing out they "have helped the woman's cause by opposing it."[36] A factor unquantified about the campaign is how much new fire Train's refreshing, irreverent, entertaining, humorous, substantial, and honest approach rekindled in Anthony and woman suffrage canvassers.

33. "One of the best misunderstood statesmen"

[George Francis Train is] one of the best misunderstood Statesmen in our country.—*Fort Scott Monitor*, October 26, 1867.

"With her heart in her throat," Anthony left from Olathe at 4:00 a.m. "She took her seat beside him. The situation was entirely unforeseen and decidedly embarrassing."[1] This unplanned development occurred when Milton Reynolds, whom Anthony had scheduled to accompany Train, suddenly headed out of state with the Indian Peace Commissioners.[2] "But she never turned back, never allowed any earthly obstacle to stand in her way."[3] She took Reynolds' place. And so, on October 24, 1867, Anthony and Train started for Paola "in a pouring rain, stopping at a little wayside inn for breakfast at six. The meeting was at eleven, in the Methodist church."[4] They addressed people not just from Paola but from afar, for Anthony had distributed flyers to post offices even 50 miles distant. As Train reported it, "Miami county is here in a body. Farmers and their wives are here from all the surrounding towns. Some have come twenty miles. Everybody is wide awake. The Methodist church is fairly jammed. Shops all closed. Business suspended. All full of enthusiasm. People most intelligent. Splendid country."[5]

From Paola, Anthony related years later, "the county superintendent of schools … took them to Ottawa in a lumber wagon. The steady rain had put the roads in a fearful condition and by the time they reached the river bottoms it was very dark and pouring in torrents. The driver lost his way and brought them up against a brush fence." Train "jumped out of the vehicle, took off his coat so that his white shirtsleeves would show and thus guided the team back to the road; then he and the county superintendent took turns walking in front of the horses. The river finally was crossed and they reached Ottawa" two hours late for their meeting, at 9 o'clock.[6] Train's telling was that he and Anthony "got lost in the woods at six o'clock, and remained there in the mud, water, and the dismal swamp of darkness for two hours, amid the chirping of the insects and the hooting of the owls—no lantern. No one for miles around in hearing distance, and Mr. Bannister [the coachman] as completely bewildered as ourselves. Miss Anthony and self made up our minds to remain all night in the carriage in these dark woods, when Mr. B. found the track, and after a night of horrors got into town at nine o'clock."[7]

Train had turned this tale of difficult travel into an incident with additional meaning: the inference was that he and Anthony might have spent the night together in an era when such behavior, considered immoral by society, reflected badly especially on women. Anthony may have pursed her lips at it. Then again she might not have. To assume she did is to believe she was a prude, for Train did it more humorously than salaciously, more in passing than otherwise. If she did not find it completely objectionable she had a sense of humor. The racy telling won the hearts of audiences round to Train and Anthony personally, which seemed to sway them towards woman suffrage. Anthony's comfort with mild suggestiveness emerged in December, when, with Train in Buffalo, New York, she asked him publicly "if he had ever counted the miles traveled on the tour." "We were together, Miss Anthony," he replied. "It did not seem long to me." The audience loved it.[8] Anthony appeared to relate well to him. Train was the most gentlemanly man she had ever met.

He was used to luxury and speedy railroad travel. A few years later he would take a rapid round-the-world trip, inspiring Jules Verne's novel. In Kansas in late 1867, however, he tried to back out on discovering the campaign's punishing schedule through storm, rain, and shine to dusty pioneer towns in wagons, mule-drawn carts, and whatever other form of scroungeable transportation could be found to speak every day, sometimes several times, and then to rest overnight in a rude cabin on the frontier with sickening food locals offered generously. When Train balked, Anthony told him she had organized and advertised the campaign and that she would go regardless. She had not envisaged touring with him when she signed the telegram asking for his help, but the work was waiting and she would do it if no one else did. If he wanted to drop out, so be it. Train, ashamed, arrived in the carriage to pick her up for Olathe. Anthony had saved the whole mission.

For a woman to head off alone with a man she hardly knew was taboo at the time, but after the wet stretch to Olathe the two never looked back[9] and developed a good working relationship. Train was fastidious, but Anthony had too much to do to allow for dressing up. Besides, she was used to Stanton, and Train was like her friend. And so on this occasion, too, at Ottawa, while Train "went to the hotel, Miss Anthony, wet, hungry and exhausted, made her way straight to the hall to see what had become of their audience."[10] This event led to an altercation with Blunt and to Train's first spin of the great yarn. "You know I was lost two hours in the forest primeval, where I expected

I would have to remain with Miss Anthony till daylight (laughter) amid the company of the lizards and the hooting of the owls," he said. The delay in the forest occurred early in the evening. As time went on, however, Train displaced the story to a night-long adventure that acquired racy overtones audiences gobbled up with relish and opponents pounced on.[11]

Train conveyed in his colorful style a powerful, pro-woman message, part of which argued that woman suffrage would improve the whole of American society. "Woman suffrage will correct abuses—purify elections and compel reforms," Train declared to applause.[12] He referred to a recent change in the law regarding liquor licenses whereby "no rum seller [could] get a license without one-half of the citizens of his district, black and white—male and female, alike sign[ing] the petition.... Already this concession to the rights of women" had brought benefits. "Another step and we will have fewer jails, fewer penitentiaries, fewer pauper institutions and more schools, colleges and churches." The audience applauded approvingly and loudly.[13]

Train always spoke of winning, for he was a master at optimism. Women, he concluded early on to raucous cheers, would "soon settle this liquor question when they have votes, as they are going to have on the 5th of November, in Kansas."[14] Upbeat from the start, he said on October 23 soon after his first major speech, "You can bet your bottom dollar on Johnson County for the women."[15] His reports to the newspapers were mainly for the *Leavenworth Commercial,* but a letter to the editor signed "Franklin" sounds like him. Referring to the Ottawa meeting, it said, "We had a meeting of the friends of Female Suffrage last night ... [and] on the whole [it] was a perfect success, and the cause ... was greatly advanced."[16] He polled his audiences at every meeting. "On a vote for woman suffrage there was not one dissenting voice," the *Topeka Leader* reported.[17] "I finally carried my motion without a dissenting voice," he wrote of the Emporia meeting when anti-woman McBurney tried to upend it.[18] In Topeka, shouts of "aye" met his call for "all those for woman suffrage," with "no dissenting voice."[19] He spoke of winning with the anti audiences in Ottawa, where he had his altercation with Blunt. "Suffice it to say that I carried the vote as unanimously as at Leavenworth, Lawrence, Olathe and Paola, for woman suffrage."[20] He demolished objections, speaking "under great excitement and [carrying] the whole audience, to a man, for woman's suffrage, just after Blunt and Kalloch had made them vote the other way,"[21] ending with "a vote for women, with one dissenting voice—old Tipton—and I converted him."[22]

An old-timer from the area recorded the 1867 canvass there as his father remembered it: "In 1867 the interest in the political canvass was upon the ... proposed amendments. One of them for ... women suffrage. The suffragists secured the aid of Miss Susan B. Anthony, Mrs. Elizabeth C. Stanton and others. Father was a very strong woman suffragist. It was during this campaign that my parents entertained Miss Anthony and her officers, there were more than fifty at the banquet." This man also gave insight into the conduct of elections at the time, referring to the "county seat struggle," which his father often referred to. "We were living not far from Ottumwa, but he was in favor of Burlington. When it came to voting, votes were bought with corn, flour, money and whisky—more whisky used than anything else. Men even voted their dogs, and men who had died years before."[23] Referring to this event, Train wrote, "A good dinner at Prouty's. A full house. A fine speech from the woman suffrage leader."[24]

He claimed he turned not just voters around but also political hacks. "Local politicians are turning their vote, and Republicans are getting into the Democratic cars," he wrote. "Leroy Band serenading Miss Anthony at Mr. Coffin's—Torch Light Procession—Great enthusiasm."[25] "Junction City all on fire for the cause. Democrats are for women. Fenians for women, and Republicans are trying to get on the cars as the Train is leaving."[26] "We met the enemy and they are ours.... Women victorious everywhere. Politicians played out."[27]

Train said nothing negative about the campaign. "The revolution has commenced," he declared at Olathe. "Sunday last [before the start of the canvass] woman suffrage looked blue in Kansas, today there is sunshine in the sky."[28] "We are sure to carry Kalloch's town against him, and this is the stronghold of our enemies. What a grand thing for Kansas—carry woman suffrage."[29] Train always said woman suffrage would win. He became more effusive by the day for he was "carrying the entire democratic party almost solid."[30] His relentlessly upbeat outlook was unique on the stump. His appearance, his sense of humor, his showmanship, and his innate skills to sweep an audience into the palm of his hand were outstanding and he used these abilities masterfully to awaken minds to the demeaned if not actually censored idea of woman suffrage and many other issues into the bargain. He had an instinctive sense that people need to enjoy themselves, to hear something positive or something serious presented in a new way, to see opponents opposed and flattened, to be flattered themselves, to feel good, and to laugh. Audiences loved him.

It left the powerful scratching their heads. Even cynical newspapermen commented on Train's attraction. "The hall was crowded, although the notice was so short," reported the *Leavenworth Commercial* of his first speech, "and the way the hits were received indicate an appreciative audience.... [T]here is little doubt that Mr. Train's lightning will sweep through the State like a prairie fire, sweeping down all opponents of woman suffrage."[31] The *Lawrence State Journal* said he was "a sensation. He came! He saw! He conquered! Never before did such an audience crowd the hall—everybody before the time, and as many [who] could not get in."[32] Train was different. Puzzling to opponents was his exemplary personal behavior. He did not smoke or drink and his private life was impeccable. None of this passed reporters by. "[H]e has certainly got a wonderful power in the West. His extraordinary life, his great wealth ... his magnetism on the masses, and his singular moral record is opening the eyes of the people," said the *Fort Scott Monitor*, while quibbling about the number of zeroes in his wealth, "which may be exaggerated."[33] The *Lawrence State Journal* referred to the encyclopedic range of his speeches: "He will give you feed for a two-week's intellectual feast, and you come out in the end, strong in your faith in Train and Female Suffrage. You had better hold your meetings out of doors, if you wish to be accommodated."[34] "There is no mistake about this man's popularity," said the *Topeka State Journal*.[35]

The influence of this larger-than-life standout personality was sometimes solidly practical. "The woman suffrage Republicans and the Democrats of this county meet in mass convention on Monday, to nominate a county ticket in opposition to the regular Republican ticket,"[36] reported one newspaper of the Train effect. Train became so positive as the canvass progressed—his natural optimism responding to audience enthusiasm despite the difficulties and the punishing campaign schedule—that he soon spoke of female suffrage as "a foregone conclusion."[37] Quickly he employed the present tense while talking about the future. "The tide has turned; all now wish to be in with the victors," he reported a couple of days into the campaign.[38] At the contentious meeting in Ottawa, where he targeted the antis' accusation that reprehensible women from the East had invaded Kansas to impose their radical views on the state, he countered: "To them and them alone is due the credit for carrying Kansas for woman's suffrage."[39] He referred to Mound City, "where Democrats jumped into the woman suffrage boat and will steer it into port on the 5th,"[40] and Humboldt, where Democrats were going "solid for the cause."[41] To cheers from another assembled multitude he proclaimed it the time "to commence New America on Tuesday by emancipating one half of the human race."[42]

Some hard-liners attacked for the sake of it. "We are glad ... this distinguished gentleman has commenced a campaign in Kansas, and that Ottawa is announced among the list of his engagements. We say we are glad, not of course because he comes in behalf of Female Suffrage, but because ... mainly it will do our people good to have their blood stirred as Train knows how to do it," commented *Kalloch's Home Journal*.[43] "Language has never served so despicable a purpose as when it conveys to a disgusted auditory the ridiculous conceits and jabbering fancies of this mountebank."[44]

Despite the naysayers, Train predicted a clear win. Faced with Blunt's skepticism, he declared, "If I were a betting man, I would wager ten thousand dollars that Kansas will give a 5,000 majority for women."[45] "Many think that woman suffrage will carry by ten thousand. I say five thousand, sure," he declared after the Humbolt meeting on October 28.[46] Yet, if he was effusive about female suffrage, he was negative about the prospects for black men, which he said just a few days into the campaign were "nowhere."[47] "The Negro must wait…. The Rads want to place our wives and mothers below the Negro. Shame on the cowards," he told Manhattan on November 1, turning the normal political priorities upside down.[48] He also spoke of suffrage not based on sex or race distinctions. The audience at Junction City greeted with cheers and passed unanimously a resolution "that education be the test of the franchise." When at the same meeting he called for enfranchising "half the human race" and was challenged about black suffrage, he clearly included black Americans. It was a question of timing. "Educate him, send him to school, teach him the meaning of a vote; and when he is equal to self-government, give him the franchise," he answered unhesitatingly."[49] Whether he meant the masculine in its broad or narrow sense here is unclear.

While effusive and always positive, Train was also practical, realistic, idealistic, and challenged all types of oppression. He prioritized the solution of national inequalities—just as the Republicans had done—but in an order they disagreed with. Speaking at Leavenworth the day before the election of an upcoming speaking tour in major cities, he said, "The burden of my thought will be the future of America; my mission, with the aid of women, to reconstruct the country and save the nation. (Cheers.) Tomorrow our amendment will pass with a startling majority. The other … will be lost. (Applause.) The negro can wait and go to school. And as all are now loyal, the war over, and no rebels exist, no American in this land must be marked by the stain of attainder or impeachment. (Cheers.) No so-called rebel must be disfranchised. I represent the people, and they speak to-morrow in Kansas, emancipating woman (loud cheers)."[50]

Train always included black suffrage under the rubric of educated suffrage. Categorizing broadly, he included all black men in the "uneducated" category who would have to wait to qualify, even though there were educated free black men who should immediately be eligible to vote under this system. The anti-female suffrage forces' priorities were the opposite of Train's. Categorizing even more broadly than Train, they defined suffrage by sex, a proposal fundamentally different from an educated franchise because basing the vote on a sex qualification was to establish it upon an "accident of the body," as Brown put it[51]; whereas education was something that could be acquired by all, with the class caveat that more money equaled a greater likelihood of education. The antis' categorization by sex was also significantly different for another reason. If the black suffrage amendment failed, the prospect of black suffrage was still in the offing, because it would become a reality when the 14th Amendment was ratified, even if only through penalties for noncompliance on states under the new fundamental law. More than that: already by

1867, Phillips had begun promoting a new amendment enfranchising black males. For women there was no such measure to fall back on, while the antis' pronouncements demonstrated it was unlikely they would ever seriously consider enfranchising women. At the very best, according to Phillips' estimations, their enfranchisement was decades down the road and meanwhile ratification of the 14th Amendment guaranteed women's exclusion. The relative political positions of black male and female suffrage were vastly different and unequal.

Yet in terms of the 1867 Kansas vote, the antis' view regarding the woman suffrage amendment paralleled the realism that Train showed towards the black suffrage amendment. "We have no idea that his visit can effect any reversion of the doom" of female suffrage," commented one newspaper.[52] "Of course, Mr. Train is too sensible to suppose that he or anybody else can save [it] from the rocks."[53] "It won't carry," said General Blunt during the contentious meeting in Ottawa.[54] Even though Train was a great attraction for the "female sufferers," the measure "hadn't a chance."[55] This summary of the Train juggernaut appeared in a scathing commentary on Train's report of the Ottawa meeting with Blunt. The writer ironically called him "Truthful Train" because Train exaggerated.[56] Another argued that Train's influence on any vote for female suffrage was negative: "Had there been a spark of vitality left in the Female Suffrage cause, the advent of George Francis must have smothered it entirely."[57]

Whatever Anthony's reservations might have been about some of Train's statements or of the whole venture, an intense trip in the company of such a contrasting character could hardly have failed to affect them both. Both of them adjusting to strange circumstances—flamboyance on the one hand and earnestness on the other—the record gives only tiny glimpses of the result. It remains largely a mystery open only to conjecture and imagination how Anthony adapted to being in close quarters for two weeks with a man whose personality seemed the opposite of her own. There is no record of how such an outgoing individual as Train might have challenged her self-image, revealing and bringing to the surface traits that had never had the opportunity of expression and enabling her to open up to new possibilities. The same mystery applies to Train, but he praised Anthony, who, he said, "during our exhausting campaigning trip never faltered while I gave out before I got half way over Kansas (applause)."[58] The campaign certainly opened for him a window into the world of reform for women. In a practical sense, Anthony made the fastidious Train meet a commitment in circumstances he would never otherwise have tolerated, and he began to appreciate the value of this determined woman who pursued an unpopular cause with no resources. Increasingly during his speeches, he praised her for her personal traits and organizational abilities. Anthony, for her part, at the very least found out what a real man could be like, for Train was courteous, mannerly, and not only supportive of women by words but also by deeds. Besides, a man with such an outgoing personality must have been fun to be around and his varied enterprises during his well-traveled life provided a huge stock of tales to regale Anthony with during the arduous hours of travel through Kansas, just as Anthony's own dedicated work for temperance, antislavery, and woman's rights gave him deep insight into the era's life of women in America and the challenges of reform work.

For Train, Anthony's world was a stark contrast to global enterprise, railroad-building and land promotion. For Anthony, Train was a stark contrast to the boorish men who appeared without fail on the anti-woman campaign or the duplicitous, self-serving, pompous, antislavery men in the post-slavery world of the East that Anthony had dealt with. The congenitally unconventional Anthony, who pursued unpopular causes long before they percolated to the surface in the minds of the average citizen, would intuitively understand the equally unconventional Train, relate well to him, and respond naturally to and appreciate his unusual personality. The alienation of both, being different, allowed mutual understanding. The campaign, once Anthony's initial discomfort at the unusual circumstances subsided, opened to her a different world in which a woman was treated as she had always known they could be. Although the canvass with Train lasted just over two weeks at most, the experience likely confirmed that in the right circumstances and with the right support woman suffrage and woman's rights were not just a pipe dream but a vision eminently winnable and worth pursuing. As he came to know more clearly Anthony and the challenges she faced, particularly the financial hardship, his mind opened up to her world. He himself raised the direct impact on the Kansas canvass of the theft of the Hovey Fund by Phillips for the *Anti-Slavery Standard*, which Train called "a bad investment for the trust fund."[59] But this trip gave Train an idea that would make a considerable difference to the women's cause. He announced it during the Junction City meeting: "Miss Anthony's new paper … [with] … a significant and startling name and a comprehensive motto. It is called *The Revolution* (applause). MOTTO— *Equal Justice to All, Favors to Friends Alone.* (Loud applause.)"[60]

Out of the blue, Train was handing Anthony the opportunity to turn a dream into reality.

34. *"Women at the polls"*

We would prefer to see women vote, at once, to bestowing the right of suffrage upon the colored people, and we should look on either as the accomplishment of one of those absurd notions that haunt only effete and morbid imaginations.—*Murfreesboro Monitor*, October 7, 1865.

Earlier in the year, while the women, awaiting Train, continued campaigning in Kansas, national events pointed a way for Kansas voters. On October 8 Ohio voted a black suffrage amendment down and later the *Chief* noted that since then some "in Kansas who were in favor … have turned square around; and many who were about persuaded to do right, have gone back, and are among the hardest opponents of the measure."[1] This event occurred long before Train arrived. His work, therefore, was not the originator of any apparent downturn in the fortunes of male suffrage. Kansans still had the right to go their way on November 5, as could voters in Minnesota. In these states decisive change was at least in electors' hands.

By contrast, white male politicians had repeatedly excluded female suffrage since 1865 even from mere consideration on the ballot. Since then, with ratification of the 14th Amendment proceeding in the background, New Jersey, Connecticut, Massachusetts, Missouri, Maine, Ohio, Wisconsin, Michigan, and New York had denied women the vote,[2] while Congress denied women suffrage in Washington, D.C. In 1867 Michigan women did win the right to vote for school trustees,[3] but this was the kind of meager, partial, unequal suffrage like the victory—soon ignored—that women won in Kansas in 1859 before statehood. It could perhaps be looked on as "a first step." Yet to acknowledge "a first step" is also to accept the continuing inequality of women by ignoring the fact that with abolition, reformers and many legislators assumed that freedmen should have full and equal suffrage immediately without any first steps and they worked directly, deliberately, and ruthlessly for that end. Even the process of winning suffrage was unequal. Michigan was a rare case. Female suffrage in this period was dismissed nationally, both in the nation's capital and in one-quarter of the states. Only in Kansas—the tenth state—did woman suffrage make it to the ballot. Participants, writing later, mentioned the negative effect of the Michigan Commission's refusal "to submit a similar amendment to her people, and the adverse report of Mr. Greeley in the Constitutional Convention of New York."[4] But throughout 1867 and earlier, there was a sustained push by women for the vote, against which the constant anti-woman barrage pushed back. Only Kansas took up the challenge. It is remarkable the measure went so far, for during 1867 it became clear that the primary qualification for the vote was not race or citizenship. It was maleness. This fact became clear when the Minnesota amendment for manhood suffrage included "all males over the age of twenty-one who were citizens of the United States, *persons of foreign birth who declared their intentions to become citizens*" and some Indians.[5] "Persons" clearly meant "male" when it is considered in its full context. Again, the politicians' weasel rhetoric and biases were specified and expanded. If American-born or already naturalized women were angry, such overt and blatant sex discrimination gave them good reason to be.

Yet the discomfiture of mere women was generally too trifling for men to bother about, while in Kansas by late October 1867 what other states did hardly registered with campaigners, for the Train canvass was the big concern for antis. It bothered pro-female politicians also. Governor Crawford was annoyed because his name appeared, apparently without his authorization, on the notices for the meetings. He quickly attempted to disown the connection, but adverts were distributed widely, with the link established very publicly.[6] Crawford was a supporter of female suffrage and he was reacting against Train. Wariness about such reactions may have delayed the SISA decision to call Train until the end of September, for whether the Copperhead slur was accurate or not, Train was controversial, leading women campaigners far outside their previous boundaries and the expectations of colleagues. Some of these colleagues, such as the antislavery men in the East, merited jettisoning. Yet some honorable supporters found this departure disturbing. Governor Crawford was an example. Concern about his impartiality as governor may have influenced him.

Meanwhile, as the Train canvass started attracting publicity for the women's cause from October 21 on, black leaders including Langston on October 25 started a counterattack, calling a public meeting in Leavenworth to rectify "certain misrepresentations made by some speakers engaged in the present canvass, with reference to the position of colored men in the present momentous political struggle."[7] This was apparently a response to Train's comment early on quoting Anthony, saying that "a colored orator had spoken against woman suffrage, and that the negroes generally were against the measure." This was true: Langston had indeed campaigned against female suffrage since

August, even when he was saying he was for women. Black male opposition to woman suffrage had been evident from the start, for, reflecting attitudes elsewhere, they considered it a threat. These facts inspired one of Train's poems, pointing out how most Republicans and black men had marginalized women.[8] Even if equal suffrage, with speakers embracing true impartiality, was the original intention of Langston's meeting, by October 31 General Blunt—fresh from his defeat at the hands of Train—and George Hoyt, also a fierce anti, had joined in.[9]

Blackwell was still in Kansas the week before the election on November 5, but he wrote to Stone on Tuesday, October 29, saying he would go to Leavenworth on Wednesday and head home that day—if, that is, he was "not detained there by negotiations with the Democrats."[10] This is intriguing. On arriving in Kansas earlier in the month, he had said woman suffrage was already beaten, that it would be lucky to get a vote of 5,000 and if double that it would be a triumph. He also predicted that black male suffrage would carry by a slight but decreasing margin though most locals said it would be lost. So the question arises: what was Blackwell doing in "negotiations with the Democrats" a week before the election? Blackwell and Stone had considered working with Democrats since the spring and later he told a relative of his role in the conspiracy to bring Train to Kansas to counter Republican black opposition to women. Blackwell's words now show he was cooking up something with the Democrats at this last minute. It speaks volumes about him, Stone, and politicking in late 1867. From the start, Blackwell and Stone, far from being little innocents from the East dutifully and faithfully toeing the Radical Republican and antislavery line, seem to have tried whatever they could to win victory over all the forces against the women. In fact, it appears that Blackwell and Stone were close to Anthony and Stanton in their views. It does not mean that all four were acting in concert or that Stanton and Anthony knew what the other two were up to. It indicates their own little scheme, which Blackwell was hoping to tie up before he left for the East in advance of the election.

The Sunday before the vote, Colonel Anthony entertained Anthony and Train "in his inimitable manner till midnight," the colonel declaring later that Train "knew more about more things than any man living." When Robinson and Stanton were held up and an Atchison meeting fell apart because of a derailment, some scheduling changes had to be made. Meanwhile, Train told Anthony he was serious about the proposed newspaper for women and now wanted Anthony and Stanton to join him in an all-expenses-paid, pro-female suffrage tour. On November 4 the campaigners all met up in Leavenworth and on election day voters saw something novel and startling: "Mrs. Elizabeth Cady Stanton and Susan B. Anthony … visited the polls in each ward of Leavenworth … in carriages and addressed the voters," reported the

Tribune of Lawrence, "probably the first [time] in this country."[11] This was new because without the vote women never went near rowdy, drunken men–crowded polling places.

Early in the Train and Anthony canvass at the contentious Ottawa meeting General Blunt declared of woman suffrage, "It won't carry. No doubt Train is a great card for the female sufferers. But they did not get him on the track in time. He found it dead as Chelsea. He has breathed a little life into it. But he hasn't time to resurrect it. The fault isn't his. Not that the Train, but the time is too short." Blunt was right: woman suffrage failed. But so did the black male suffrage measure. When the votes were tallied, black male suffrage received 10,843 for and 19,421 against. Female suffrage received 9,070 votes for and 19,857 against. The pro-black vote represented 36.25 percent of a total 29,904 votes. The pro-woman vote represented 31.35 percent of a total vote of 28,927.[12] With a higher percentage of the vote and 1,773 more votes than female suffrage, the manhood suffrage results look better. Yet, failure of black male suffrage after all the forces had combined in its favor represented a huge defeat, especially as Republicans were a majority in the state. Conversely, female suffrage had almost doubled the 5,000 votes that just three weeks before Blackwell had estimated might be the meager result. The support for women meant that if not victorious they were—to use Blackwell's own word— "triumphant" in the first-ever vote on woman suffrage in the United States. Train's conservative estimate of victory for female suffrage by 5,000 votes was likely always unrealistic. When he made the prediction, he might have been using positive thinking to stir up support. The actual vote for the two suffrage propositions was close, in spite of "all the enginery of the controlling party" for manhood suffrage.[13] "[W]ithout press or party, friends or politicians … this vote for woman's enfranchisement represented the best elements in the State, men of character and conscience, who believed in social order and good government," wrote the women many years later.[14] "How many of [these 9,070 votes] were Republican and how many Democratic, and how much influence Mr. Train may have had one way or another, never can be known," wrote Anthony's biographer later."[15] Antis were clear on their narrow escape, however. "It is appalling to think what would have been the result if [Train] had only been here in season. The Republican Party would have been 'busted'; the Democrats and female suffragers would have given the ballot to women," said the highly critical *Western Home Journal*.[16]

Some believed that Train had helped the black suffrage vote. The result reported on November 8 for Emporia Township for female suffrage was 338, with 97 against and 202 for; for black male suffrage it was 96 against and 208 for. About 100 voters declined to vote on either amendment. One anti newspaper wrote, "The visit of [Train], together with the extra exertions put forth by the friends of the measure for the week previous, saved negro suffrage by a tolerably respectable majority." The vote "should have been larger, but under the circumstances, Republicans of Lyon County can feel tolerably well over the result." This editorial also observed, "Female suffrage made a better run in the country precincts than we had expected it would." It also complained, "We were surprised to find many of the warmest advocates of female, impartial suffrage, 'without respect to sex or color,' voting straight against the proposition to strike out the word, 'white.' Their professions and their votes were not very consistent."[17] This was another double standard, for it was acceptable for voters to support the male referendum without supporting the female one. In Lyon County the final tally for all-male suffrage was 503 votes for and 273 against—and 209 votes for and 565 votes against female suffrage.[18]

Despite this editor's complaints about the pro-female vote in the referenda, modern studies have shown that largely "the same people" voted for both, which would indicate that the Train campaign had little effect.[19] However, Train was able to cover only eastern counties in Kansas during his short tour, and Leavenworth County—the strongest Democratic county—where Train began his campaign, produced a respectable showing in spite of the many months of opposition, with 1,588 in favor of woman suffrage and 1,775 against.[20] The Leavenworth result has sometimes been considered "anomalous" because of ballot improprieties.[21] With local Democrats very active, untoward influence is a possibility and it is worth considering if such planning was part of the "negotiations" Blackwell had referred to in his letter to Stone the previous week.[22] Governor Robinson himself indicated he believed there was election fraud, denying any Train effect in Leavenworth County and laying the strong showing of female suffrage at the door of "a few men in L. [not influenced] by [Train], who for party ends had all their tickets printed for female Suffrage & the mass of the voters did not know how they voted, but took it for granted that they were all right as they were the regular democratic tickets."[23] In this light, Blackwell's mention to Stone soon after his October arrival in Kansas about the possibility of doubling the vote and "tickets" he was having printed assumes great importance.[24] This may have been his business with the Democrats before he left for the East. Yet Stanton and Anthony's innovative electioneering that day must also have had an impact. Accompanied by the Hutchinson family cheering reform on with campaign songs, "all were received at every precinct with hearty cheers for woman's rights and female suffrage.... The proposition to strike the word 'male' from the Constitution will probably receive a larger vote" than otherwise, said one report.[25] The election-day advocacy of the two major players in the campaign likely influenced the "anomalous" result in Leavenworth—a town where Anthony herself was well known.

Afterwards in Kansas, Train was fiercely criticized. Robinson backhandedly felt "it was fortunate that Train's caravan did not canvass the state thoroughly for I am told that they made the question a party issue in some places so offensively to Republicans that large numbers voted against us who would otherwise have voted for us."[26] Yet Republicans had set the bar so low for political rhetoric about female suffrage that long before Train's appearance they lost all rights to complain. Besides, even when the referenda were debated in the legislative assembly the previous January, they constituted an issue that virulently divided voters, with not only Democrats but also many Republicans against women. Republicans simply ramped up their opposition so quickly that soon women had little prospect of succeeding. To blame Train is Republican finger-pointing of the first order. The finger really pointed back at themselves. They were bad losers, blaming a despised opposition with a broader campaign attempting more justice and with much more appealing workers. Any Democrats voting for woman suffrage, whatever the reason, made it even more annoying. The truth, as the women wrote later, was that "Kansas being Republican by a large majority, there was no chance of victory. For although the women were supported by some of the best men in the State, such as Gov. Crawford, Ex-Gov. Robinson, United States Senators Pomeroy and Ross, and a few of the ablest editors, the opposition was too strong to conquer. With both parties, the press, the pulpit and faithless liberals as opponents, the hopes of the advocates of woman suffrage began to falter before the election."[27] In other words, if Congress was against women so were the voters, and women had little chance. The call to Train was to salvage something from an impending debacle and he provided a contentious, entertaining, and powerful ending to a vicious six-month campaign.

Train was not the whole campaign, however. If the Democrats had been up to dirty tricks, so had the Republicans, with, in some polling places, Republican tickets printed with "No" beside the woman suffrage amendment.[28] The dirty tricks by both sides may have balanced the impact: voters in either party could have voted or not voted the way they had planned, whether Train influenced them or not. Yet, if nothing else, Train brought both suffrage measures massive publicity. He energized his audiences with controversial, challenging questions, raising issues no one else would uncover. Manhood suffrage did better because Republicans were a majority in the state; with a preponderance of Republican voters, it may very well be that Republican dirty tricks depressed the pro-female vote. Yet none of these considerations explain the victories in Cherokee County, with 249 votes for and 239 against, and Ottawa County, with 34 votes for and 32 against. These might reasonably be attributed to the solid work of Brown, who traveled the whole state during her four-month sojourn in Kansas, with Bessie Bisbee's help. Or possibly it was due to local and independent female suffrage campaigners in small counties with a small population and, perhaps, little evidence of party machines. Republicans' objections to Train were intended to destroy his credibility. One complaint was that he wrote his reports before the event. This was true in one case: a derailment prevented his appearance in Atchison, but a report still appeared in the *Leavenworth Commercial.* The *Atchison Champion* took the "Great American Gas-Bag" to task for it. The city voted "four to one against the infamous and disgraceful doctrine of 'female suffrage,'" it reported, while Train's report about something that literally was derailed sounds jingoistic and overblown and demonstrates the practice and perils of writing a news story before the event.[29] The incident raises pertinent questions about all his writing.

Yet, whatever Train did and the effects of partisanship on the Kansas vote in 1867, the fact remains that the record of both Republicans and Democrats is dismal in the history of woman suffrage. Train at least promoted suffrage for women. The political parties require equal scrutiny, with both Republicans and Democrats under the microscope for "anomalous" results in Republican counties where dirty tricks are known to have occurred and Democrats examined for "anomalous" results in Democratic counties.[30] No matter where the mud might stick, the simple fact is that not enough voters of either persuasion voted for either measure. Not to be forgotten either in assessing the Kansas vote were outside influences—that of Ohio, which depressed the all-male suffrage vote before Train arrived, and that of the refusal of nine states to consider female suffrage. Stunningly important and internal to Kansas was the overt anti–woman suffrage campaign begun in Kansas in late August, which black male antis joined.

Afterwards, Brown "felt … crushed and humiliated,"[31] but this was only natural after the arduous work and the new vitality Train's presence on the trail had brought. One eastern newspaper gleefully wrote about the post-election depression of women: "The result of the Kansas election, piling up an immense majority against woman's rights, has profoundly astonished, amazed and utterly crazed all the woman's rights people. The mission of Mrs. Cady Stanton, Susan B. Anthony and Lucy Stone has brought forth no fruit, and the long-haired and short-petticoated folks are bewildered, if not altogether demoralized, by the result."[32] This writer then insultingly wrote about sending the women back to their homes, housework, and husbands and besmirched Train as a pansy-man, the limp advocate and supporter of "rampant women" who had tried to usurp the proper male and masculine power of Kansas.[33]

These highly offensive comments employed false facts. While it must have been disappointing for the women not to win, they had faced so many setbacks for so long, had encountered so many betrayals and so much skullduggery, that they were adepts at turning negatives into positives. Anthony did so immediately. "Never was so grand a success—never was *defeat* so glorious a victory," she wrote to Brown two days after the election when the count was continuing[34] and before the defeat of women seriously reinforced overt sex bias in politics and throughout the nation.[35] Anthony attributed the success in Leavenworth City and County to Train's influence. "If only Geo. F. Train could have lighted the fires you had prepared all over the State—we should have carried it overwhelmingly," she wrote to Brown, whose time in Kansas, partly with young, courageous Bisbee's support, formed the solid backbone of the campaign of the women from the East—the bridge between the early optimistic and the late frantic stages.[36] Anthony fully believed in a positive Train effect on the female suffrage referendum and her only regret was he came so late.[37]

The *Leavenworth Commercial* said, "When we consider the many obstacles thrown in the way of the advocates of this measure, the indifference with which the masses look upon anything new in government and their indisposition to change ... the success of these advocates is not only remarkable, but one of which they have a just right to feel proud. To these two ladies, Susan B. Anthony and Elizabeth Cady Stanton, to their indomitable will and courage, to their eloquence and energy, is due much of the merit of the work performed in the State."[38] It added the following: "While in the recent election these ladies were not successful to the full extent of their wishes, they have the consciousness of knowing that their work has [equaled] ... the combined efforts of party organization, congressmen, senators, press and ministers to enfranchise the negro, and that the people of Kansas are not more averse to giving the franchise to woman than to the black man."[39] In other words, they achieved, despite the odds, a result almost equal with all-male suffrage, with a lot less help and significantly fewer resources. This says much about the justice and of the women's cause and effectiveness of the campaign.

Yet the fact remained that the loss of woman suffrage in Kansas was of much more critical significance than the failure of manhood suffrage. The black male suffrage vote and defeat was only one of several in the nation, but this attempt to establish equal suffrage for women by vote in the United States was the only one. Anthony saw this campaign as the first positive step, but despite the work, women had not yet hammered in the thin end of a wedge against prejudice and legalized discrimination against women, specifically in the right to vote. They could reflect with satisfaction at having run a campaign despite the fiercest opposition, with all their money stolen from them and amid the greatest of controversy. Unlike black male suffrage, however, they had no ratification of the 14th Amendment to fall back on. Meanwhile, that ratification would mean a huge step back for women—and there was increasing talk of a positive black voting amendment. In the immediate aftermath of the Kansas vote, while it was psychologically beneficial to identify positives, the reality was dicey. For women's history at least, the women had created a record for posterity demonstrating the fact that men lied when they said women did not want the vote; a record that showcased their work and commitment, showed clearly what they were up against, and shone a spotlight on the hypocrisy of the men of the time. Their spotlight from 1867 still shines on that duplicity and dishonesty of Reconstruction—the time when white men betrayed women after the Civil War under the guise of civil rights for blacks, demonstrating that in their world, while "equality" meant everyone, some people were more equal than others—and that the "some people" were men.

35. "No press, pulpit or politicians"

It is no use to tell us to wait until something else is done. Now is the accepted time for the enfranchisement of woman.—Olympia Brown, 1868, *History of Woman Suffrage II* (1887), 310.

After the referenda Anthony moved on fast to reignite the campaign for women elsewhere. After all, there was the 14th Amendment and that word "male" that would soon carve in stone women's subordinate status in the nation. Uplifted by the last two weeks of the campaign that transformed defeat into an excellent showing, Anthony was also elated at her wider prospects, for at Junction City Train had announced that he would put up the money for her to publish a newspaper, to be called *The Revolution*.[1]

Before the end of the campaign Train also proposed a speaking tour for Anthony and Stanton in major cities to drum up support for woman suffrage and raise funds. He would also speak and pay all expenses. Before agreeing, Anthony had to take an adventurous nighttime river trip in a skiff to confer with Stanton, which she did with as much guts and determination as she had shown during the previous weeks.[2] The publicity she afterwards launched for the tour elicited vinegary observations about pursuing equal civil rights after the defeat in "radical" Kansas. "[W]e fancy that none of those who now advocate female suffrage will live to see the full fruition of their hopes.[3] It opposes the inate [*sic*] delicacy of feeling which nature has given the gentler sex, for ninety-nine ladies in a hundred object to this reform," said a New York newspaper,[4] disregarding the more apt statistic of so many men with the vote who objected to female suffrage. Ignoring such nastiness, the women began the tour at Omaha on November 19. St. Louis reported Stanton's speech before "a very large audience," many of whose members "were ladies, who sympathized heartily with the speaker, and showed very positive evidence of a deep and growing interest in this question." Kansas had obviously sparked women's interest in voting elsewhere. The Female Suffrage Association in

St. Louis was to hold a meeting the next day, while "a grand rally for the advancement of [female suffrage was] announced for the 26th instant, at which George Francis Train will speak."[5] The tour ended in New York on December 14, having included 18 towns in all.[6]

Train's newspaper for woman's rights for Anthony was also to provide a vehicle for himself and his presidential ambitions. By now he knew Anthony's managerial abilities, which he had praised publicly. He knew that the wise men of the East had stolen the women's money and the women had no paper of their own. He had been a newspaper publisher in Britain, producing the *London American* to support the Union cause, which he helped with news on blockade-runner movements from Britain to the Confederacy.[7] Train's expansive interests, therefore, meant that *The Revolution* would deal not only with woman's rights but would also cover broader issues, some of which he would write about.

Colleagues abhorred what they called the betrayal of antislavery and equal rights by Anthony and Stanton by the Train connection. The two had been Republicans since the party's beginning; to go with that man was traitorous. More important to these colleagues, however, was the refusal of Anthony, Stanton, and some of their other colleagues to give up their commitment to woman's rights, particularly female suffrage. Yet they continued to advocate the republican philosophy that equality inhered in human beings, not in any one race and not in only one sex, refusing to accept that civil rights applied to men only. They had espoused these ideas for years and had not abandoned reform or the Republican Party. The Republican Party had abandoned the women. The establishment, whose hypocrisy Stanton and Anthony's position highlighted, was furious at the women for its own failure to control them, for they had to cover for themselves as the women's position revealed the great fraud at the heart of the postwar era. This fraud was that Reconstruction was not about establishing equality of suffrage across race lines. It was about establishing inequality of suffrage across sex lines and carving that inequality in stone. Now, therefore, Stanton and Anthony, thus betrayed, were cast adrift and Republicans accused them of betraying their principles, of self-interest and of racism. Yet only Stanton and Anthony and a few like-minded people had seen clearly the game the war victors and establishment were playing and did their best to stop it, battling for a reconstructed nation founded on true republican principles of equality of all.

It can only be imagined how the postwar United States could have evolved had they won. Unfortunately, prejudiced males held the levers of power, almost all economic resources and the means of publicizing their own selfish agendas; women operated within a straitjacket imposed by that very establishment and had few resources to call upon. While men diligently chiseled out their own sex interests from the bedrock of a time-honored all-encompassing philosophy of equal rights they pitched women like extraneous shards, forcing them to adjust. By May of 1867 in the AERA meeting, Stanton argued that if discriminatory suffrage was to continue in the United States, it should be on grounds of education and not of sex, which she had originally dismissed.[8] However, this was not a change in beliefs; this was a change in emphasis to salvage something nearer to equality than the proposals of sex-discriminatory suffrage that the powers-that-be were assiduously promoting and establishing. If there was going to be discrimination, she argued, establish it on grounds that individuals can overcome, like education; do not base it on something they cannot, like race or sex. This was a compromise in the face of continued advancement of male sex bias. The women still adhered to and campaigned for equality for all. The more excluded they were, however, the more they were left with fighting to win equality only for themselves as the only remaining part of their agenda.

In the process, the women had to cast around for alternative support to replace the treacherous Republicans and reformers. They did so to try to forestall the imminent disaster facing the nation, for even if only half of the population had to submit to this institutionalized sex discrimination, the special privileges would still contaminate through its repercussions the half of the population that had established this monumental inequality, just as slave ownership had contaminated the free population. The women's only option was to turn to Democrats—not an ideal solution for Republican women. With new Republican suffrage laws at the federal level, however, the continued failure of state campaigns, and the pressure from Republicans, reformers, and black men to silence them, they had few options. When the vicious Kansas campaign combined all these pressures publicly in one venue directing them against their interests, they sought help from anywhere they could find it. Ironically for women, in a male society if only for credibility, it had to come from a man. Ironically for Republican women, it had to be someone who could stir up Democratic support among the electorate to counteract Republican obduracy and meanness. And to Republicans' horror, the women's knight in shining armor happened to be the most colorful, brash, outspoken, incisive, wealthy, charismatic, dazzling, entertaining, newsworthy, controversial, egotistical, and mercurial orator and operator in the American firmament at the time.

This contradictory man's heart was in the right place, but his feet were always in his mouth, at least in his opponents' eyes. His ideas appeared both reasonable and outrageous. On the one hand, he was for the underdog whether it was a group like women or despised immigrants like the Irish. As a nondrinker and witness of the disastrous effects of alcoholism on women and children by husbands and fathers, he supported temperance.[9] Some groups agreed with these ideas, while others saw that supporting the underdog and temperance had merit. But others thought Train's ideas oddball, like the campaign to move the national capital to St. Louis, which Greeley also backed.[10] This proposal was to accommodate the transforming nation, which by 1860 had states on both coasts and a center of population now far from the East.[11] Female suffrage was just his latest crazy pet project. Train advanced a fascinating jumble of ideas, some interesting, some questionable, triggering incomprehension in the minds of narrow thinkers and those who held on to the past. His rhetoric made some observers flinch while the commentariat and men in power could not make head nor tail of this infuriating, constantly moving, quixotic, and changeable character that audiences loved. In the view of eastern elitists Train was bamboozling the electorate and threatening their own hold on power. Rather than give him a proper hearing, therefore, they dismissed and denigrated him. These self-serving politicians and do-gooders had dismissed Train before Kansas; when he arrived there for female suffrage their howls of protest echoed across the vastness of the prairies.

If Train was confusing overall, his one position the élites understood clearly was his support for female suffrage. The postwar discourse, therefore, degenerated further. To the combined establishment, the easiest way to deal with such as Train was to use the official, though false, agenda employing lies about race equality, which was already masking the imposition of sex discrimination. With this race card the official narrative became that anyone who opposed sex discrimination was racist. The political bullies' slur stuck. Kansas may have been its first overt and concerted use to destroy an opponent, because for the first time, in post–Civil War America, men whose agenda could be characterized in such a direct and duplicitous manner were in charge. With no other choices, women either had to cave or to welcome Train in. Anthony and Stanton were not going to cave on woman's rights. They had to accept Train, warts and all.

Advantageously by this time, Stanton, Anthony, and Train already agreed on educated suffrage as a preference to Radical Reconstruction's exclusion policies. The argument failed, for suffrage during Reconstruction, despite the official line, was less about enfranchising blacks than about enfranchising men and excluding women. The arguments employed from the start to promote the most biased measure ever passed and operated in the United States, affecting half the population and both major races, claimed current measures were to promote equality of race. These arguments incorporated the assumption that men were more important than and superior to women. Because Reconstruction suffrage reforms were said to promote racial equality, anyone objecting to the reforms was racist. This twisted argument would have remained unnoticed had it not been for such as Stanton and Anthony. And while they still supported true equal political rights, with educated suffrage as their fallback, they and those in their camp were blackened with accusations of racism. This slur tarnished Anthony particularly. Only she traveled with Train during the final two weeks of the Kansas campaign—an apparent last-minute arrangement because a man had failed to turn up. Even though this failure may have been part of the conspiracy, the narrative that she—and Stanton—turned racist in 1867 has traveled down through history.

Kansas became the center of the maelstrom because of the unintended consequences of abolition. With slavery existing before the war, such voteless noncitizens included partially in population counts for representation meant a bias against the Republican power base. After the war, counted whole and not two-thirds of a person, they now increased congressional representation in a region dominated by Democrats. As such they wholly threatened Republicans. Abolition triggered transformation of the United States and quickly Phillips threw his one-sex "negro's hour" slogan into the ring, bringing sex discrimination to the fore under cover of so-called race equality for black males. Stanton later castigated him for his achievement,[12] for Phillips' baleful influence would take countless costly campaigns and the tortures of Democratic President Wilson's administration for women finally to overcome it. Yet, the Women's Rights National Park at Seneca Falls, New York, while relating Phillips' early support for women, ignores his later critical betrayal.[13]

Phillips' key role in promoting sex as the primary means of discrimination in postwar America also debased the work of Stanton and Anthony and other abolitionist and woman's rights workers. His agenda did not just pass over the work the women had done for abolition before and during the war, but it also ignored, forgot, and dismissed it, relegating it to oblivion. The false narrative used against women made uncovering the truth difficult, so that a perception arose from the contorted history that the women forged alliances with former opponents with little soul-searching. This was patently untrue, given the course of events. A further criticism is that advocating and working for woman's rights meant they operated on a faulty philosophy: for example, collaborating with previous opponents was "not objectionable" to Anthony as she and Stanton were willing to "sell out" abolitionist principles to advance their own rights. Their end justified their means, their actions demonstrating their failure to develop "a broader philosophy of human rights by which to govern their actions."[14] The truth is, however, that Anthony and Stanton and their colleagues were the only ones who advocated a broad philosophy of equal rights for all humans. Everyone else advocated rights for men only. Besides, they had no road to victory other than courting Democrats supposed and real because of the mass betrayal by reformers, Republicans, and black men of half of humanity. "It was the utter desertion of our cause by those to whom we had a right to look for aid that forced us to our present affiliations," Stanton wrote.[15] To accusations of selfishness, Stanton retorted, "We should like to know why a movement among women for the outraged and oppressed of their sex is more 'selfish' than that of man for his sex. Is not the philanthropy of Paulina Wright Davis pleading for the enfranchisement of the black woman of the south as pure as that of Wendell Phillips pleading for the black man, or of Frederick Douglass for his own race?"[16] Evidencing the double standard, reformers unceremoniously shoved the women out of reform even as they demanded that they support the measures that excluded them. Yet when men denied the women the right to promote their own goals, restricting their choices along with their freedom, the thrust of the women's work was still not to fight for themselves alone but for a true republic based on equal rights for all—including sex and race—even though no law denied women the right to campaign for themselves, just as men could do. Only culture imposed that standard. Ultimately, it was not the women's fault that the only part of their aspirations that required a separate struggle after they were marginalized was female inequality with men. It was not the women's fault they had to fight with what was available. The decision of men in power establishing an unacceptable double standard for women forced this upon them. There was little option to do otherwise. Consequently, they countered vigorously unjust criticisms. As they wrote later in response to slights from antislavery advocates in the post-slavery world, "So long as opposition to slavery is the only test for a free pass to your platform and membership of your association, and you do not shut out all persons opposed to woman suffrage, why should we not accept all in favor of woman suffrage to our platform and association, even though they be rabid pro-slavery Democrats? Your test of faithfulness is the negro, ours is the woman."[17]

This second statement, written twenty years after the Kansas events,[18] reveals anger, protest and pain—very understandable feelings—and to criticize such feelings is to dictate to women what they had to feel, believe, and act. There is little to distinguish between this statement and that of Frederick Douglass years before when he said "the battle of Woman's Rights should be fought on its own ground,"[19] as he jettisoned equality and shoved women down the totem pole. Yet, the two positions were, and still are, received remarkably differently. Douglass was hardly then and is rarely if ever now criticized for what he said and how he acted. Posterity is still critical of the women. In their own defense and tackling criticism of their 1867 campaign, the women jabbed at these critics for their narrow, exclusionary, and discriminatory interests. "The broadest platform, to which no party has as yet risen, is humanity," they wrote.[20]

A further effect of Phillips' grand declaration of the "negro's hour" was that he effectively instigated and promoted in U.S. thought, in its Constitution, and in individual and social relations the acceptability of discrimination both official and personal. It was not discrimination because of race—that was being addressed. It was sex discrimination. And this fundamental discrimination was pernicious. Its reach was enormous, affecting half the population and entering every home. Official sex discrimination established

within a supposedly free society a clear and powerful precedent for the positive acceptance of discrimination per se, which the women and their colleagues in the 1860s fought to avoid. As Anthony warned later, "If we once
establish the false principle that United States citizenship does not carry with
it the right to vote in every state in this Union, there is no end to the petty
freaks and the cunning devices that will be resorted to, to exclude one and
another class of citizens from the right of suffrage."[21] She said this when Jim
Crow attitudes and laws were sending up shoots in the South on the ending
of Reconstruction. All these factors add up to the simple fact that, at the most
propitious moment in United States history for the establishment of true
equality, Phillips, his cronies, beneficiaries of his proposals, other reformers,
Republicans, and those in the game merely for their own benefit had deliberately turned their backs on republican principles, raised the cover from the
sewers of rhetoric, and let loose on society political discourse in which debate
degenerated into slanderous slogans with which to destroy opponents and
create conflict among all groups. Those validly and valiantly trying to secure
their rights as citizens were set against each other under the guise of honorable ends, while the door was left wide open for the rapid defeat of true equality in the nation despite all race reforms because it was founded on a notion
of equality with an inherent contradiction embodying discrimination in
itself—that of excluding the female sex.

　　The two women who had fought most against this debacle could be satisfied that they, and quite a few of their colleagues, had at least honestly tried
to prevent this disaster. They had no need to disavow their work. Instead,
they spoke in terms appropriate for the Kansas circumstances. "In reviewing
the situation," they wrote, "[they] had no reason to regret their course, feeling
that their determination to push their cause and accept help from whatever
quarter it was proffered aroused lukewarm friends to action; who, though
hostile at first to the help of Democrats, soon came to appreciate the difficulty
of carrying on a movement with the press, pulpit, politicians, and philan-
thropists all in the opposition."[22] Even later, Stanton wrote to a friend: "Susan
& I were so desperate we said to each other when considering Train's proposition Yes we would work with the Devil if he would advocate our cause."[23]
This statement shows either incredible generosity of spirit towards their erstwhile colleagues or a remarkable naivety, as if they were unwilling to admit
or were unaware that they had no need to start working with the Devil. They
had been doing so all along in the shape of untrustworthies such as Phillips,
Douglass, Greeley, Tilton, and the other reformers and politicians who finally
showed in all their garishness their true colors as far as women were concerned when Reconstruction began. Train was an improvement for women
over the traitorous, sex-biased abolitionists who tried to force woman's rights
advocates to bend to their demands and betray their own principles. In fact,

Stanton fearlessly challenged head-on the conventional wisdom about their famous Kansas campaign colleague: "All this hue and cry about Train is a *mere cover*, a *sham*. The real trouble is, he has made it possible for us to utter the thoughts that radicals wish to hold in abeyance until the black man is safe beyond a peradventure, and Grant is enthroned in the White House."[24] To break free from the incubus of such traitorous former colleagues was imperative if women were to win rights for themselves.

If, therefore, Anthony and Stanton brought Train on board for woman suffrage in Kansas and then joined him on a female suffrage campaign on their way back East it was the most significant step they had ever taken. In doing so, they did not betray their principles: they found their voice. And when they did, all hell broke loose.

36. Finding Their Voice

The removal of the political disabilities of race is my first desire—of sex, my second.—Gerrit Smith, 1868, *History of Woman Suffrage II* (1887), 317.

... not another man...—Elizabeth Cady Stanton, American Equal Rights Association, 1867, *History of Woman Suffrage II* (1887), 214.

When Stanton and Anthony arrived back East with Train a hurricane of bitter criticism hit them. Already blamed for defeating black male suffrage, the post-election tour brought condemnation on their heads. Stone was furious that the tour had associated her with the "Democrat and racist" Train.[1] Her moral outrage ignored her early interest in Democrats, her husband's pamphlet promoting female suffrage for whites over black men in the South, his role in the conspiracy that contrived to have Anthony campaign with Train in Kansas, and his planned meeting with Democrats for some undisclosed purpose in October, possibly about printing election tickets.

By late 1867, the two were closely allied with eastern men who also excoriated Anthony especially for her "betrayal of republican values" and "betrayal" of black men. Apparently, while Stone oversaw the AERA offices when Anthony was away, she and Phillips revved up their old friendship from the late 1840s—when Stone's priority was woman's rights and when Phillips helped her with woman suffrage petitions in Massachusetts. Now, instead of supporting Anthony, Stone's emphasis changed, widening the rift over money between her and Anthony. Stone and Blackwell—who seem to have provided no record of what they received from the Jackson Fund for their time in Kansas—soon challenged Anthony on her accounting for Kansas. This development appears suspiciously like a smear campaign to destroy Anthony's reputation. "The Anti-Train party was headed by Mr. and Mrs. Lucy Stone Blackwell, who formed their attack [on Anthony] in the guise of a call for the Treasurer's report, to various items of which they objected," said one report.[2] Interestingly, at this point, Stone received $88 from Phillips,[3] while leaving Anthony stuck with Kansas bills.

Bearing in mind Blackwell's role in the Train conspiracy, it is not unreasonable to infer that the virulence of the Stone-Blackwell attack on Anthony reflected guilt and that it was a cover-up because they were aghast that the chicanery might have led to the defeat of black male suffrage. It was easier to frame Anthony than to accept any involvement. Isabella Beecher Hooker, whose research of Blackwell's complicity and knowledge in 1869 and record of it in 1870 originally revealed that Wood, Robinson, "and two or three others" brought Train to Kansas, wrote as follows: "I cannot think they were honorable in throwing the whole blame on Mrs. Stanton & Susan, when they themselves initiated the enterprise." Members of this group, she recorded from her conversation with Blackwell, "advised and promoted [Anthony's] Kansas trips with Train and she went as General Agent of the Equal Rights Association & with their full approval on that whole Kansas Campaign."[4] Blackwell's complicity is clear from "a nervous letter" he wrote to Hooker emphasizing confidentiality of his statements.[5] The virulence of Stone's attacks also indicates guilt, for it created distance from Anthony and Stanton while aligning them with the Phillips faction. Their behavior may have represented some sort of atonement: to cement that alliance, the two clearly had to establish their own integrity. Blaming an innocent party to cover one's tracks is a time-honored political technique for such goals.

Anthony fought back with her history of meticulous record-keeping and all her fund-raising for Kansas. In the May 1868 AERA business meeting, when trying to get payment for her legitimate expenses there, the debate degenerated into a fight between the pro–Train group and the anti–Train factions, during which the attempt to destroy Anthony continued, with Stone and Blackwell leading. Anthony gave as good as she got:

> [She told] them pretty plainly that [the AERA] never had any treasury; that she had always been obliged to spend the money first and collect it afterwards; that [the AERA] had always been willing to let her do all the work of collection almost; that she had been subjected to ridicule as the beggar of the concern; that her expenditures had never before been questioned or censured; that she had got up the posters for Mr. Train … [that] he was in favor of enfranchisement of women, and drew crowds to the polls in Kansas, and finally [that] if they did not choose to pay the bill she would pay it herself.[6]

The hoax worked. The association with Train merged with these unfounded accusations of financial wrongdoing and mixed with slurs of selfishness and racism to damn Anthony. This is unjust. If Anthony had worked with Train, Blackwell and others had set the whole episode up without her knowledge. Besides, Stone had no claim to any moral high ground: she had now allied with Phillips. From women's perspective, Train had supported the women. In fact, he was granted permission to use the hall of the New York Constitutional Convention at 4:00 p.m. on December 4, 1867, to advocate woman suffrage there.[7] Phillips, on the other hand—the man Stone had chosen to align herself with—had openly betrayed women.

Charges of selfishness and racism arose at the AERA's public meeting, over which Stanton presided on May 14, 1868. That day, the gulf between the true-equality advocates and the supporters of the constitutionally sanctioned class-based society with sex discrimination at its heart, split the proceedings. One group, mostly women, still demanded simultaneous establishment of equality for all; the other—men and women and represented by Douglass— deemed black male enfranchisement the priority. Douglass was particularly offensive.[8] When Brown demanded an explanation of "the difference *in principle* between the position of the Democratic party opposing the enfranchisement of 2,000,000 negro men, and the Republican party opposing the emancipation of 17,000,000 white women"[9] he could only give lame answers based on expediency. Race-based rhetoric, however, backed the women's adversaries. Stanton's own cousin, formerly a stalwart supporter of woman's rights, essentially backed Phillips' warped definition of equality, writing in December 1868 that politically equalizing the races was his priority.[10] He put "sex" second, however, so he meant men only, and if solving the race problem was the priority, to ignore freedwomen was reprehensible and should have been impossible, for even if Douglass officiously downgraded their plight, it was as dire as the men's. Brown pointed to these inherent conflicts in sex-based exclusion when she compared the positions of Democrats and Republicans. Men like Douglass and Smith assumed that all women were secondary, subordinate, and could be subjugated. The women's fight against them forced them to spell their philosophy out during Reconstruction debates.

Stanton early in 1867 had proposed the antidote to this travesty. Enfranchising even some women would recognize the principle of women's equality, but "not another man" should be enfranchised without women because of the negative effects on the nation. She objected not because men who were black were being enfranchised but because only men were being enfranchised. To enfranchise men while refusing to enfranchise women was to render an already existing injustice worse. Anthony challenged the lie that Stanton opposed black male enfranchisement because of race. "It is the establishment of an aristocracy of sex" that Stanton protested, "not race," wrote Anthony to the *New York Times* in 1869, while restating her friend's advocacy of educated suffrage. "It isn't that Mrs. Stanton objects to the voting of ignorant men per se, but that she most strenuously protests against the principle and the practice that gives them civil and political superiority over [not only] the women by their side ... but [also] over the educated and cultivated as well."[11] This was not a race argument but a class argument used only when presenting as an alternative to blanket discrimination on the grounds of femaleness a distinction that existed between classes that was not insurmountable.

Stanton similarly opposed the enfranchisement of male immigrants, many of whom could not speak English—especially when in some states they could vote simply by declaring their intention to become a citizen. In Missouri, men "of foreign birth, who have declared their intention to become citizens of the United States" might vote under certain circumstances. Similar laws applied in Alabama, Arkansas, Florida, Georgia, Indiana, Kansas, Minnesota, and Texas.[12] Although clearly unjust to female American citizens, especially American-born women, promoters of sex-discriminatory legislation expediently found slurs of racism easier to hurl than facing the women's objections to the men's prejudiced reforms. Following the principle that a lie often repeated soon becomes the "truth," the smears of racism against arguments for women's enfranchisement based on solid republican principles stuck, muddying understanding of the issue.

Stanton used "not another man" again in *The Revolution* and during the 1869 AERA meeting.[13] Her words placed her against Phillips' sex-based philosophy, demonstrating her opposition to the hard-wiring of the already existing "aristocracy of sex"[14] in the laws and Constitution of the United States and in the laws and constitutions of the several states. It made "all men nobles, all women serfs"[15] by substituting the slavery of sex for the slavery of black people. She protested the cascade of further civil rights injustices that would result against women: their exclusion from juries, for example, or denying all women trial by their peers or the prohibition in states of a right to run for office. She protested the Phillips philosophy of discrimination against all women by castigating its effect in many areas of life, from education to entry to the professions to equal pay—all of which rendered them guaranteed victims of unequal "justice" such as capital punishment. This same sex discrimination also rendered them almost powerless to change the discriminatory laws and customs, because they were cut out from representation by exclusion from the franchise.

Stanton incessantly challenged this scandal at the heart of Reconstruction, criticizing northern men who found it easier to denounce discrimination against black men in the South than to recognize their discrimination against the women at their own hearthside.[16] Yet posterity has little noticed the overriding sex prejudice and discrimination of the period, little noticed that the men of the time did not care about women except to make their situation worse. Measured by results, sex discrimination for them was clearly the more important discrimination to defend and uphold—more than race—hence the vicious battle against women in Kansas. After Kansas, men elsewhere continued to reject women's aspirations. In late January 1868 the constitutional convention in Arkansas laughed out of debate a proposal for female suffrage, making it the eleventh such state failure during Reconstruction.[17] In February delegate Ezra Graves failed to revive female suffrage at the continuing New

York Constitutional Convention.[18] The same month, Stone and Antoinette Blackwell's latest proposal in New Jersey failed again, with the legislature rejecting it in early April.[19] That July the Texas Constitutional Convention under the Military Reconstruction Act also failed to enact a voting qualification with no discrimination by sex, though a majority of the examining committee recommended it.[20] A total of 13 jurisdictions up to the middle of 1868 had rejected woman suffrage.[21] It must have been very painful for women to reflect on the expanded civil rights that might have been had justice prevailed.

Meanwhile, women's civil debasement had moved forward at the federal level, with Charles Sumner bringing up in the Senate on December 5, 1867, a bill to remove the word "white" from the laws, ordinances, and charter of Washington, D.C., and Georgetown, with no mention of sex discrimination.[22] Reintroduced the day before Anthony's paper, *The Revolution,* which first appeared on January 8, 1868,[23] by the end of May D.C.'s new charter removed the offending word, while ignoring women.[24] Then on July 9, 1868, the 14th Amendment reached the required number of ratifications by forcing southern states to ratify it as a prerequisite of reentry to the union. On July 28 the amendment was formally adopted, by which time 30 states out of 37 had ratified.[25]

The word "male" was now part of the United States Constitution, establishing through sex discrimination in fundamental law a bulwark against equality throughout the nation. Yet, against this background of exclusion of women, that August one Catherine J. Hudnall Balfour stood up to the Ku Klux Klan with only a small dagger as a weapon when the marauders, armed with guns, appeared at her home north of Rayville in Northeast Louisiana intent on dragging away and killing her brother for being a known Republican. Because of her fury and courage, the KKK gave up their plans for immediate execution, ordering her brother out of the area. He took a steamer to New Orleans, giving testimony to the military on September 4, 1868.[26] This story demonstrates that if black men needed the vote for their protection in the post–Civil War South, so did women—no matter their race.

Yet, General Grant's 1868 narrow popular vote win and the Republicans' loss of 4 seats to Democrat's win of 20 in the House of Representatives despite freedmen's votes, demanded action.[27] That December, therefore, Congress, began reinforcing the nation's sex discrimination bulwark against equality by introducing the 15th Amendment to secure black men's voting rights across the nation. This strengthening of sex discrimination against women advanced even though the mixed election results prompting the new amendment had proved that the exclusion of black women in the South had resulted in only uncertain success for the Republicans' goal of holding onto power. Nevertheless, the party for once stuck to principle—exclusion—and ignored the injustice of sex discrimination in voting. *The Revolution* called this "manhood suffrage" amendment "an open, deliberate insult to the women of the nation" and questioned men's ability to govern.[28] The Republicans could have done much better, for on December 7 Senator Pomeroy of Kansas presented an amendment resolution with citizenship as the basis of voting rights,[29] while the next day George W. Julian introduced his version in the House.[30] The exclusionary 15th Amendment passed out of Congress on February 26, 1869, Congress having deliberately refused to include one word—"sex"—thereby excluding all women from full citizenship.[31] Now all men—including, through state laws, many men only intending to be citizens—had the vote, the amendment's passage aiming to ensure Republican political hegemony as far as the eye could see.

Stanton, incensed about the immediate implications for women, wrote that the 15th Amendment and its precursor allowed open and legalized discrimination against women. She could have, however, also pointed out that the institutionalization of sex inequality in the nation created a dangerous precedent of unequal and separate treatment that could easily be extended and applied to other groups. She could also have argued that Congress was clearly establishing a sex-based double standard for the actual process of enfranchising different classes of citizenry. If the disfranchised were males, Congress would promote reform through federal statute and even by the extremely difficult and rare process of a constitutional amendment, likely ensuring individual states would fall in line. This "top down" process imposed the standard of the right to the franchise for males relatively quickly across the nation. If the citizens were female, however, Congress excluded them, forcing them to work from the bottom up for their own enfranchisement. Yet, winning a constitutional amendment from the grass roots up was exceedingly difficult. Equally challenging was Congress's cavalier decision to cast women to the mercies of the several states to win woman suffrage through constitutional amendments state by state. This was an impossible task, with 37 states in 1870 and the number regularly increasing. Women's equality would be a never-ending struggle. The process imposed on a group economically disadvantaged throughout the nation, gargantuan demands of time and money. These discriminatory options demonstrated the full extent of the inequality to which Congress was consigning all women of the nation during Reconstruction and why women like Anthony and Stanton fought so frantically for inclusion when the door to constitutional change was open.

State-by-state enfranchisement of women would also create more inequalities as some states enfranchised women while others lagged and still others would refuse. The process for women was unequal through and through. The 14th and 15th amendments set the bar against women so high that it was almost insurmountable, whichever way they chose to proceed. Besides, there was no telling how far such a precedent of double standards in reform for women might later be extended. It is no wonder that such injustices should infuriate women for whom the rights of citizenship mattered. "No oppressed class ever yet emancipated itself," Stanton wrote. "We did not wait for the negro to plead his own cause. The mass of the freedmen do not appreciate the ballot, yet the Republicans and abolitionists keep up the cry of 'negro suffrage.' Why not 'Woman's Suffrage?' Why should women be expected to do more for themselves than stalwart Africans have done?"[32] This was a logical question to ask—one that applied to any man, no matter the race.

Stanton also castigated several times another effect of the new amendment in *The Revolution*: by playing the race card to advance a national agenda of male suffrage, Republicans and reformers fomented national division when establishing unity should have been the priority. It turned white men against black men, black men against women, and some women—who could supposedly influence their husbands—against black men. Observing how black men were campaigning against women, the latter now believed that their enfranchisement would lift "the negro above the [white] woman, and make him her Ruler, Legislator, Judge and Juror."[33] However individuals thought about it, the deliberate exclusion of women created a problem across the nation, argued Stanton. "If even northern women rebel, what can you expect at the south? The 'negro element' at the south, of which we hear so much, may make voters for the Republican party, but it does not give us what we need in government. The people are concerned about deeper principles than such as serve the shifting purposes of politicians."[34] Principled action, not expediency, was statesmanlike. Only true equality proponents were statesmanlike in this situation—and they were women.

A further crucial consideration now benefited the Republicans. The female constituency, despite its varied contributions to the war effort and abolition, was already weak because it had no voting rights and politicians did not have to answer to it. Playing the race card further weakened the nuisance of protesting women by dividing the nonvoting female constituency further. Not only were white women divided, now black women were too, for race concerns sucked them into the male political machinations. Many black women saw the Reconstruction amendments as a choice between votes for black men only and no votes for black people at all. Aware of the legal fiction that women received protection through their men who voted—even if in practice the device often meant that women were totally unprotected— some black women concluded that white women already had half a loaf. Black women, therefore, went for the half-loaf for themselves, for black male enfranchisement still represented progress for them. Frances Harper in this way adopted a stronger position than the older Sojourner Truth. A Maryland free black from an orphaned but comfortable background exiled from Maryland when a law was passed in 1853 preventing free blacks from reentering, before the Civil War Harper committed to abolition, often appearing alongside such luminaries as Garrison, Douglass, and Stone. After the war the honored poet, writer, and public speaker, having visited the South and seen the appalling conditions black women suffered there, promoted black advancement and lectured on equal rights for black women.[35] Harper had come to support woman's rights through becoming a widow in Ohio, finding her husband had been deeply in debt, and losing everything, including her own personal possessions, as lawyers settled his estate.[36] Yet she sided with Douglass for black male suffrage. "When it was a question of race, I let the lesser question of sex go," she said.[37] White male legislators partially forced this on her, but it was also due to a dislike of white women, whom she abrasively condemned. "If there is any class of people who need to be lifted out of their airy nothings and selfishness, it is the white women of America," she said.[38] She thus dismissed the white women who had worked for the emancipation of all black people. If dislike equaled racism, Harper's position demonstrated that racism could work both ways. What was worse, many white women supporting black male enfranchisement also pushed woman's rights to the back burner.

The pressure on Stanton and Anthony continued throughout 1868 and into 1869. In November Stone upset the recently formed New England Woman Suffrage Association convention by proposing a resolution supporting true universal suffrage for black males and all women simultaneously rather than sequentially with no timetable.[39] But at the turn of the year she wrote to Brown: "We are now in the midst of a serious quarrel with Miss Anthony and Mrs. Stanton and the Train admixture."[40] A huge part of the problem was Train, yet by January 1 he had written to Anthony as follows: "You no longer need my services. *The Revolution* is a power. Would it not be more so without Train? … Would it not bring you more subscribers, and better assist the noble cause of reform?" Train's situation had changed, for when travelling to Ireland early in 1868 with a copy of *The Revolution* in his pocket and known as a Fenian sympathizer, he was arrested and spent a year in jail.[41]

Then, on January 14, 1869, Stone relegated her lifelong primary interest in women, declaring in Washington, D.C., "women must wait for the Negro."[42] Now in line with the New England women, Stone was selling out on true equality. She may have been bending to what she saw as the inevitable, but it seems that in doing so she wrecked what might have been possible. The AERA and D.C. women were working hard for congressional support for a D.C. woman suffrage bill and a constitutional amendment to remove the sex discrimination of the 14th and 15th amendments, but Stone was "silencing" that work "with her cry of the 'Negro's hour,'" commented *The Revolution.* A member of Congress wrote that Stone had undermined that year's action "by declaring 'Women must wait for the negro.'" This correspondent added that the "proposition is both wrong and insulting to the intelligence of the age. While I am for the negro, I am and many more members of Congress, for woman *equally—and for all.*"[43] Parker Pillsbury, coeditor of *The Revolution*, the next week rebutted criticism of this criticism. "I will never ask the colored man to postpone his claims for woman, nor woman to postpone hers for the colored man, or any man. Both are alike needy, alike worthy. In the name of their equal humanity, in the name of eternal justice, I demand the right for both."[44] As it seems that in February Stone received $500 from the Francis Jackson Fund,[45] Phillips' influence haunts these events.

The most momentous event after this January realignment was the passage on February 16 of the 15th Amendment, which brought new urgency to the women's concerns. In response, George W. Julian of Indiana introduced on March 16 a joint resolution for a 16th Amendment: "The Right of Suffrage in the United States shall be based on citizenship, and shall be regulated by Congress; and all citizens of the United States, whether native or naturalized, shall enjoy this right equally without any distinction or discrimination whatever founded on sex." The resolution was revolutionary not just because of the sex discrimination ban but also because it clearly based the vote on citizenship and placed suffrage's regulation in the hands of the federal government. With the proposed ban on sex discrimination, Stanton said, "I feel an added dignity!"[46]

The next month, recent woman's rights adherent Mary A. Livermore of Chicago, famous for medical work in the war, told Anthony, "I have written to the New England friends to let bygones be bygones and come to the May meeting. It seems personal feelings should be laid aside and women should all pull together."[47] Unity among women was important for Anthony and Stanton, but for others Train represented a problem that required settling. Having already written to Anthony about severing his ties with *The Revolution*, his leaving was only a matter of time. It happened on May 1, when Train left, writing, "Omit my name from your journal—and let me work out my destiny alone."[48] His financing went too.

Train's departure seriously weakened the paper, but it suited opponents of Anthony and Stanton to have him out of the way, for they could now plan their next step. The moment arrived at the AERA anniversary meeting of May 12–14, 1869, in New York. On the first day Stephen Foster attempted to oust Stanton and Anthony from office for having abandoned the AERA's philosophy, specifically through her support of Train and advocacy of educated suffrage as an alternative to male-first suffrage. They had not repudiated Train, Foster complained. Train had only departed, and Massachusetts members found unacceptable the prospect of continuing work with AERA leaders aligned with him.[49] Foster's arrogance in blaming the women when antislavery supporters had promoted only male suffrage is awe-inspiring. His long-winded speech about antislavery elicited protests, and further uproar ensued when he accused Anthony of "falsehood"[50]—journalese for the contention over Anthony's accounting for the Kansas campaign. It related to a check for $1,000 that Anthony said the Boston auditors had issued after approving the accounts. Despite the uproar, the meeting voted Foster's proposal down.[51]

However, Douglass was poised to strike. With the 15th Amendment now proceeding to ratification, Douglass shamelessly promoted the all-male "race" agenda, with no regard for women, dismissing sex discrimination out of hand and declaring that oppression of black women in the South was "not because she is a woman, but because she is black."[52] He left unanswered a question. Why, if the oppression of freedwomen was due to race, did he not argue for their enfranchisement along with freedmen? Excluding such women also instituted yet another inequality in a society supposedly based on equality, rendering them legal nonentities and, under family laws newly applied to them,[53] putting women below men in the home. Sojourner Truth saw this: "[C]olored women do not know scarcely anything. They go out washing, which is about as high as a colored woman gets, and their men go about idle, strutting up and down; and when the women come home, they ask for their money and take it all, and then scold because there is no food. I want you to consider on that…. I want women to have their rights. In the courts women have no right, no voice; nobody speaks for them. I wish woman to have her voice there."[54]

Douglass stuck rigidly to his doctrine of the primacy of men, dismissing black women and contradicting his own position on race equality, as did others. The audience protested loudly when Blackwell said he "was willing that the negro should have the suffrage, but not under such conditions that he should rule the South."[55] Douglass excluded all women from Reconstruction while welcoming men in. Anthony nailed this hypocrisy: "Mr. Douglass talks about the wrongs of the negro; but with all the outrages that he to-day suffers, he would not exchange his sex and take the place of Elizabeth Cady Stanton."[56] The same argument would apply to Douglass's changing his sex with Sojourner Truth or Frances Harper. No matter—men were asserting power over women and women were fighting back, refusing to be silenced. The meeting was so disrupted that Mary Livermore observed, "Throughout the day the men who have attended our Convention have been turbulent. I say it frankly, that the behavior of the majority of men has not been respectful."[57] And as women were being sidelined, Ernestine Rose suggested that "the name of this society be changed from Equal Rights Association to Woman's Suffrage Association."[58]

This male attempt to impose an unequal philosophy on the AERA marked its collapse. Even without this 1869 power grab, there was no future for an organization founded to establish true equality when it ignored the majority and with the 15th Amendment late in February heading to ratification. Though antislavery supporters were exultant, so-called equality by increments was not the AERA's mission. Simultaneous equality—each wing of the AERA supporting the other—was. When legislators and members abandoned the women, the AERA was dead. This was not the women's fault, though only a few individuals such as Anthony and Stanton by this time argued for true equality and most others argued for male primacy. Adding insult to injury, reform men and women—the AERA generally—tried to make the founders of the organization submit, for they needed to legitimize what they had done to women. Naturally, the women did not submit. They refused to take it silently. Their anger, frustration, and pain at these injustices is understandable. Their antagonists, nevertheless, roundly criticized them for failing to conform; and they did so through race, for the pain of race discrimination has always trumped the pain of sex discrimination.

The question remains as to why women who were so betrayed submit? Why should women who were so abandoned and mistreated by the organization they founded to create equality across the nation still support it? Stanton and Anthony had both played this scene before. Back in 1852 in Albany, in protest at men's silencing of women in temperance, Anthony had created the Woman's State Temperance Society for New York, called a convention in Rochester, had Stanton appointed president, excluded men from the vote, and advocated radical reform. At the anniversary meeting in 1853, however, men were allowed the vote; they ousted Stanton from the presidency and got rid of the radical agenda. The two forthwith left behind the now warped organization that Anthony had created in 1852.[59] In 1869, therefore, they already knew the script. The AERA had become a travesty of its name and its mission. For a long time, members had been trying to impose the unequal, male-first agenda. Perhaps antislavery individuals had deviously joined up just to ensure control of the women. Perhaps, even, Tilton had supported the AERA idea in December 1865 to bring the women under men's watchful eyes. Perhaps for many members the AERA idea was just a sham at the outset. Now, in 1869 with the male agenda all but imposed nationally, the AERA could banish the women.

Anthony and Stanton had no need to hang around for that or for the ignominious, deserved death of the organization with its now-empty name and mission. They knew what to do: replaying 1853 they went out and created the National Woman Suffrage Association (NWSA), on May 15, 1869. And if Stanton, the leading woman's writer of the time, should sometimes express bitterness towards all those of both races—especially men—for their great betrayal, it is understandable. The AERA had been the women's dream and those people had worked against it and destroyed it. Besides, women, just like the slaves for whose freedom and political equality these women worked

indefatigably, are human beings. They have feelings. If they had strong feelings about what happened, it was natural. If they expressed anger about this
monumental betrayal towards the very men for whose freedom and political
equality they had promoted for decades, the women's response should have
been expected. To deny all this is to impose on women standards much higher
than those demanded of men. It is to deny their humanity. Such denial of
humanity is remarkably akin to the underlying philosophy of slavery.

Inequalities against women, solidly and deliberately reinforced, and
opposition to the advocates of true equality led to the demise of the AERA.
Participants blamed Stanton and Anthony, but it was inevitable, perhaps even
intentional. In the NWSA, therefore, formed at the end of the 1869 AERA
anniversary meeting, only women could become officers: "There had been so
much trouble with men in the Equal Rights Society, that it was thought best
to keep the absolute control henceforth in the hands of women. Sad experience had taught … that in trying emergencies they would be left to fight
their own battles, and therefore it was best to fit themselves for their responsibilities by filling the positions of trust exclusively with women."[60] By this
time, the women had tried forbearance long enough. Now it was time to act
for themselves alone. Uplift after Kansas and the Train tour and the launch
of *The Revolution* triggered initial considerations in 1868 of national organizing, while a key next step occurred in 1869 with the first National Woman
Suffrage Convention being held that January 19 and 20 in Washington, D.C.

Ignorance did not produce Reconstruction's institutionalization of sex
discrimination, for men had many opportunities to open their minds. Most
refused. Some tried to silence women. Some believed they could make women
back down. Some simply dismissed them. Yet, because Anthony, Stanton, and
others continued to fight for women, the result was an increase in women's
awareness of and interest in suffrage. From the end of 1867 American women,
at least in the West and the North, inspired by the results of the Kansas campaign, the Train tour afterwards, and the other state campaigns—and buoyed
up beginning in 1868 by a national weekly newspaper devoted to promoting
their own interests—began to organize for suffrage. And if Congress had set
the bar so high against them by refusing to facilitate their enfranchisement
as they had helped American men and if they had abandoned women to their
own devices to work either through the complicated constitutional amendment process or to win enfranchisement state by state, Congress had failed
to consider that the women were creative and might find another way to try
to win what should have been theirs by right. This is exactly what they now
did.

37. The Aftermath

I do not see why it should be called magnanimous for a woman to say, I yield to man just what he has always asserted as his, the right to rule.—Paulina Wright Davis, 1869, *History of Woman Suffrage II* (1887), 336.

… the women of the country … must not look to these men as their champions at this hour.—Elizabeth Cady Stanton, *The Revolution*, January 14, 1869, 24.

Vineland, New Jersey, had hosted Stone, Anthony, Stanton, and other suffrage speakers for several years.[1] Now, against the background of the latest attempt at woman suffrage by Stone in the state legislature and before final ratification of the 14th Amendment, women there began to revolt. On March 10, 1868, Portia Gage tried to vote in a local election to demonstrate that the Constitution already gave women the right to vote. She was turned away because she had not registered.[2] Her initiative would ultimately spawn a national attempt to have women's right to vote declared constitutional by judicial decision.[3] After Gage, many women voted or attempted to vote in many local, state, federal, school, and temperance elections throughout 1868.[4] In "a large and enthusiastic meeting of the women of Vineland held in Union Hall," on October 15, 1868, they "resolved almost unanimously to go to the polls on election day and offer their votes."[5] That November 3, one hundred seventy-two women, including three black women, voted[6] to protest the sex discrimination that the 14th Amendment enshrined in the Constitution. "Among the incidents of the election was the appearance of several ladies, soon after the polls were opened in Union Hall, who offered their ballots which were refused. The ladies then provided a table and ballot box, appointed the necessary officers and received their votes."[7] The Vineland women argued they had possessed the right to vote in New Jersey throughout the nineteenth century and still had it, even if they had not known it, for the 1807 disfranchisement of women and black men was unconstitutional because it was passed only by statute and not a constitutional amendment.[8]

The protests would continue throughout 1869, which also saw more conventional developments. That February the Woman Suffrage Association of Missouri petitioned the legislature for the vote[9] following an 1867 rejection. Yet again they failed. In March, attempting to prevent a worse debacle with the 15th Amendment, Representative George W. Julian introduced a resolution reviving and modifying the discarded and ignored "citizenship" proposals of December 1867. Passage would have nullified suffrage sex discrimination in the Constitution, federal law, state statutes, and constitutions. It became known as the proposed 16th Amendment,[10] the first amendment for women ever.[11] The women quickly printed up petitions. Stanton and Anthony called for the formation of woman suffrage associations and newspapers in every state for signatures and for submission to Congress.[12] The women also continued pressure against the sex discrimination of the 15th Amendment, now being ratified.[13] Summarizing the women's opposition to it and publishing in response to criticisms, Stanton wrote that *The Revolution* "criticises, 'opposes,' the fifteenth amendment, not for what it is, but for what it is not. Not because it enfranchises black men, but because it does not enfranchise all women, black and white." This insult hit Stanton hard. "I have seen and felt, with a vividness and intensity … the far-reaching consequences of this degradation of one-half the citizens of the republic…. It is sufficiently humiliating to a proud woman to be reminded ever and anon in the polite world that she's a political nonentity; to have the fact gracefully mourned over, or wittily laughed at, in classic words and cultured voice by one's superiors in knowledge, wisdom and power."

Stanton also highlighted the fact that, with all men their superiors, burgeoning immigration could badly affect American women. American-born men hardly supported women's equality and their miserable example to immigrants set a low standard for the treatment of women, she said. Many new immigrants brought philosophical differences, behavioral expectations, and religions based on the old regimes of Europe and she wondered how women would fare "when the millions educated in despotism, ignorant of the philosophy of true government, religion and social life, shall be our judges and rulers?"[14] This was a pertinent question, but critics jumped on her. To ask it, however, did not mean she was wrong, for American-born men routinely insulted women. A Baltimore correspondent, observing a celebration of men, heard a toast: "Our wives and daughters—May the women of our race never unsex themselves by becoming strong-minded."[15] This was mild compared with what happened in Kansas, yet it was still an insult emanating from the reinforcement of men's sense of superiority through enfranchisement, demonstrating contempt despite the women's work for the end of slavery, for this was a black man attacking mostly white women.

Nevertheless, Stanton and Anthony plodded on. The creation of the

NWSA in May 1869 was logical when only women were now excluded from equality and with American women's deteriorating circumstances as citizens. Yet, besides the nastiness of the behavior of newly elevated men to depress Stanton, there were more problems—the main difficulty being the struggling finances of *The Revolution* due to Train's departure. Then the great divide among women worsened. That November 24 and 25, 1869, in Cleveland, Ohio, Stone convened with Julia Ward Howe the American Woman Suffrage Association (AWSA) to rival the NWSA of Stanton and Anthony.[16] Having received Phillips' imprimatur the previous November for "a woman's hour"[17] some women now felt it was legitimate to work for themselves. By officially accepting the existing reality, this new organization philosophically deferred to men's rights. It did so in more ways than one. It allowed male members, and in promoting the state-by-state suffrage route gave a female imprimatur to the more difficult enfranchisement process that Congress had deemed appropriate for women.

The AWSA's challenge was huge, but progress did seem quickly to follow, with the enfranchisement of women in two territories—first Wyoming in late 1869 then Utah in 1870. Stone and AWSA members must have felt that women were finally making progress. Stunningly, when women in Utah territory were enfranchised, it was for the same reason that freedmen were enfranchised—protection. The measure for Utah, first introduced in Congress in 1869 to discourage polygamy there,[18] demonstrated that the men in Congress, could, if they chose, use federal power to enfranchise women. Yet even if these two measures indicated a little progress it was nothing compared with the speedy nationwide enfranchisement of black men. The two advances for women also reinforced the idea that women, unlike men, had to crawl up the ladder one rung at a time and simultaneously gave the impression that constitutional amendments were for men only. These measures also created a new inequality for women in the nation, with women in new territories enfranchised and women in old states excluded.

As Stone's work continued from 1869, it would become clear what lay behind her betrayal of her previous principles. In January 1870 she launched her own newspaper, *The Woman's Journal,* to rival Anthony's paper. Again, as with her "Negro's hour," against woman suffrage, she demonstrated clearly a lack of solidarity with women and sounded a death knell for *The Revolution.* She obviously felt comfortable doing so, for she and the AWSA headquarters were now based in Boston, where she also published *The Woman's Journal.* Well financed, the new newspaper may have garnered substantial backing from the Jackson Fund, for Stone received at least a total of $3,660 from that source between September 20, 1869, and November 13, 1871. Another entry for February 11, 1869, might make the actual amount $4,160.[19] These substantial moneys add another layer to the mystery of Phillips, the Jackson Fund, and his betrayal of women. By this measure, Phillips, it appears, was directly implicated in the split of the woman suffrage cause—presumably the achievement of a long-held goal. This points to a supreme historic irony. Many writers have denigrated Train down the decades, but he worked for the women. Yet few have criticized Phillips for leading the cause of the great betrayal of women during Reconstruction. Stanton wrote the following in the middle of these events, hammering the truth home: "Mr. Phillips, with his cry, 'this is the negro's hour,' has done more to *delay* justice, for women, and to paralyze her efforts for her own enfranchisement, than any man in the nation."[20]

These Jackson Fund payments also point to the real possibility, if not the likelihood, that Stone was essentially bought by Phillips—a truly bitter pill for Anthony and Stanton. Realization of this could explain the years-long rift between the former colleagues as would any discovery of Blackwell and the Train conspiracy. The price Stone paid for her victory over her abandoned colleagues was betraying her own principles—a sad rejoinder to her claims for the higher moral ground over Anthony and Stanton. It was yet another part of the moral upheaval engendered by Reconstruction and reform policies after the Civil War. Subsequently, Anthony was forced to close *The Revolution*. Without backing, she had no other choice. She and Stanton went on the lecture circuit—Stanton making money for her family, Anthony earning to pay off the debts of the venture.

Meanwhile, the Vineland women's 1868 vote protest had expanded to a constitutional challenge nationally through what became known as the New Departure—a movement to encourage women throughout the nation to vote based on the 14th Amendment's equal protection clause of Section 1, despite the use of the word "male" in Section 2. This development occurred at the Missouri Woman Suffrage Association convention on October 6, 1869, when Virginia Minor—one of the founders—declared, with Anthony in her audience, "I believe the Constitution of the United States gives me every right and privilege to which every other citizen is entitled; for while the Constitution gives the States the right to regulate suffrage, it nowhere gives them power to prevent it."[21] Minor soon afterwards published pamphlets encouraging women to register and vote on this basis. The NWSA endorsed and promoted the initiative nationally and in Congress, sending 10,000 copies of *The Revolution* everywhere.[22] Many women tried to register. Some did so, some tried to vote, and some in several states succeeded.[23]

The 15th Amendment creating male suffrage by enfranchising black males became part of the Constitution on March 30, 1870. Women's 16th Amendment was now crucial. By 1871, however, the proposal had made no headway and Stanton reiterated her concerns about women's degradation. Republicans, "with their shameful record on our question," had sold women out. "I have seen it coming for the last three years & warned one & all, &

have been denounced as a democratic for laying" the Republican hypocrisy bare. While the Democratic Party had the better record on the rights of woman, the women had fooled themselves about the Republicans, who had squandered a "glorious opportunity," the "result of the false idea among women, that because the Republicans were forced by a military and political necessity to do justice to the negro, [the same] moral power would induce them to do the same thing for the women."

"Be not deceived," she warned. The 15th Amendment was "a new stab at womanhood to result in deeper degradations to her than she has ever known before. I felt the humiliation. I knew it would tell somewhere somehow. When that was pending my soul travailed in anguish. No mortal but Susan knows, what vague apprehensions, of coming evil I felt. At times I felt desperate, at times desponding. My worst fears were realized. Swift on the heels of the 15th Amendment came the propositions in several of our legislatures to license prostitution."[24] Stanton mentioned judicial victimization of women, referring to the trial in 1870 of Daniel McFarland, the former husband of Abby, whom he abused, for his murder of Albert Richardson, whom she had known before the divorce. Crafty lawyers turned this into a crime of passion, destroying Abby's character and successfully defending the deliberate killing.[25] This was "our Dred Scott decision," said Stanton. She also criticized New York's new guardianship law of April 25, 1871, which ensured once again that only the father had rights over the children. "Had woman held the ballot—that weapon of protection—in her hand to punish legislators, by withholding her vote from those thus derelict to duty, no repeal of the law of 1860 could have possibly taken place," Stanton wrote later.[26] Recording her anguish at all these developments, she noted it had all occurred under Republican rule. "Sometimes I exclaim in agony to myself can nothing rouse the self-respect of woman. I despise the Republican party for the political serfdom we suffer today, under the heel of every foreign Lord & Lackey that treads our soil."[27]

Meanwhile, 1872 became pivotal for the New Departure,[28] when on October 15, Virginia Minor tried to register to vote in St. Louis and the registrar, Reese Happersett, refused to allow it. As a married woman, Minor could not sue, so her husband filed a petition on January 2, 1873. The court first heard and denied the case on February 3.[29] Meanwhile, the federal government was trying Anthony. On November 1, 1872, a notice in the Rochester newspaper exhorted electors to register. Anthony went with three of her sisters to the registrar in the local barber shop. Citing the 14th Amendment, Anthony demanded that they be registered. The registrar caved and the next day many other women in Rochester also registered.[30] On election day—November 3— she and the others voted in Rochester's eighth ward,[31] Anthony voting for President Grant—"the Republican ticket—strait."[32] On November 18, a United

States deputy arrived at her house, asking her to accompany him to the commissioner's office for him to arrest her. Anthony insisted that he arrest her then and there, as he did with men. Examination started on November 29 and continued until December 23 to determine the indictment. She was charged with the crime of being female, voting without "the legal right to vote" because she was "a person of the female sex."[33] Fourteen other women were also charged.

On December 26 the commissioner set bail and signed an order to send Anthony to the Albany County jail. By December 30 only Anthony had refused to pay, but the court left her free. During January 1873 Anthony's lawyers tried to force her case to the Supreme Court through a writ of habeas corpus. Ultimately, however, a grand jury on January 24 in Albany indicted Anthony and the other female voters. Anthony pled not guilty and refused to pay bail of $1,000, hoping to reach the Supreme Court, but her lawyer paid, killing the opportunity.[34] Before the trial during March and April 1873 Anthony travelled throughout Monroe County educating the public about the upcoming trial. She castigated the idea of limiting the citizen's right to vote, pointing out that to do so with one class of individuals would make it easy to extend the ban.[35] Native-born men could combine, she said, "to abridge the rights of all naturalized citizens, as in Rhode Island," while "the poor, hardworking, uncultivated day laborers, foreign and native born, learning the power of the ballot and their vast majority of numbers" could combine to exclude the rich—just as men had combined to exclude women: "Establish this precedent, admit [to the states] the right to deny suffrage ... and there is no power to foresee the confusion, discord and disruption that may await us. There is, and can be, but one safe principle of government—equal rights to all. And any and every discrimination against any class, whether on account of color, race, nativity, sex, property, culture, can but embitter and disaffect that class, and thereby endanger the safety of the whole people."[36]

While Anthony was thus arguing for equal rights for all, the Supreme Court was interpreting narrowly the rights of citizens of the United States as opposed to the rights of citizens of a state. In the Slaughterhouse Cases and *Bradwell v. Illinois* the decisions went against the plaintiffs. Delivered on April 14 and 15, 1873, they left the powers of the states virtually intact and interpreted narrowly the rights of United States citizens under Section 1 of the 14th Amendment.[37] Justice Joseph P. Bradley's opinions demonstrated the uneven terrain women were having to fight on. Disagreeing with the decision in the Slaughterhouse Cases, he argued that "the right of any [male] citizen to follow whatever lawful employment he chooses to adopt (submitting himself to all lawful regulations) is one of his most valuable rights, and one which the legislature of a State cannot invade, whether restrained by its own constitution or not."[38] With Bradwell—whose exclusion from the bar in Illinois was based on her sex—he argued the opposite. Although the majority decided the case on other grounds, Bradley, along with two other justices, found Bradwell's sex to be key, arguing that, unlike men, women had no right to a career, citing "the law of the Creator"[39]—demonstrating that sex prejudice and discrimination were alive and well and featuring in the decision-making process of the Supreme Court of the United States. This was injustice to one-half of the nation.

Virginia Minor's case proceeded to the Missouri Supreme Court on May 7, 1873, where the court based its judgment on the congressional debates for the 14th Amendment, which showed the clear intention to give voting rights only to newly freed slaves to "protect themselves against oppression."[40] Before the 14th and 15th amendments, the states had the right and power to determine who had and who did not have the right to vote. The congressional debates demonstrated that, except in regard to freedmen, there was "no intention [in the amendment] to *abridge the power of the States to limit*" the states' powers to determine electoral qualifications.[41] Save for the protections that all black males derived from the 14th and 15th amendments, states retained their almost all-encompassing right to determine the right of any of their own citizens to the vote. Thus, by specifying men or male persons they could exclude women legally from the vote. Minor's exclusion from voter registration was legal, while citizenship rights and equal protection under the law under the 14th Amendment's guarantee for women born or naturalized in the United States looked useless. The Minors appealed to the Supreme Court of the United States.

In New York, on May 22, 1873, all the women charged with Anthony for the crime of voting pled not guilty and were released pending Anthony's trial, now the test case. That day United States attorney Richard Crowley requested the transfer of Anthony's case to the circuit court in Ontario County. This maneuver would remove the case from the county where the defendant had informed every possible potential juror—all male—of the issues, speaking in 29 towns and villages. This move also allowed U.S. attorneys time to incorporate the two Supreme Court decisions of April and further allowed Ward Hunt, a justice of the Supreme Court, then also a circuit judge in New York and a President Grant appointee, to hear the case. Despite Anthony's Republican vote, this was no political favor, for the judge was avowedly against woman suffrage. Anthony immediately began speaking throughout Ontario County to educate potential jury members there.

The trial began on June 17 in Canandaigua Courthouse, New York, before a jury of twelve men. Yet on June 18, at the end of evidence and arguments from both sides, Justice Hunt read out a prepared decision. Hunt defined the 14th Amendment's privileges and immunities narrowly, deeming that states had lost virtually nothing of their rights to determine who should and should not vote within their jurisdiction. If they wished, they could discriminate among citizens in voting, except for all black men because of the 15th Amendment. Hunt declared that Anthony knew that New York enfranchised only males, that she had no right to vote, and that she acted knowingly to violate the law. Hunt concluded there was nothing to consider, directing the jury to return a guilty verdict.[42]

When Hunt asked Anthony if she had anything to say, she protested the "ordered verdict of guilty [which] trampled under foot every vital principle of our government. My natural rights, my civil rights, my political rights, my judicial rights, are all alike ignored. Robbed of the fundamental privilege of citizenship, I am degraded from the status of a citizen to that of a subject; and not only myself individually, but all of my sex, are, by your honor's verdict, doomed to political subjection under this, so-called, form of government." Then, when Hunt fined her $100 and costs for the female crime of voting in the United States, she declared:

> I shall never pay a dollar of your unjust penalty. All the stock in trade I possess is a $10,000 debt, incurred by publishing my paper ... four years ago, the sole object of which was to educate all women to do precisely as I have done, rebel against your man-made, unjust, unconstitutional forms of law, that tax, fine, imprison and hang women, while they deny them the right of representation ... and I shall work on with might and main to pay every dollar of that honest debt, but not a penny shall go to this unjust claim. And I shall earnestly and persistently continue to urge all women to the practical recognition of the old revolutionary maxim, that "Resistance to tyranny is obedience to God."[43]

Anthony never paid the fine and never served time for not doing so. Congress rejected a petition from her in 1874 to overturn the verdict.[44] Her trial was one of the most celebrated in the nineteenth century and her published history and documents of this travesty shook many Americans.[45] Anthony's brave protest and forbearance during this tyrannical treatment of a woman who was attempting only to exercise a fundamental principle of United States citizenship of consenting to government highlighted the import of the fundamental arguments that she and Stanton had advocated throughout Reconstruction. It redeemed her reputation from the bigoted calumnies of that era, when to oppose the Republicans' exclusionary policies and to attempt to have justice established throughout the nation meant that she was treated as a reprobate. Anthony's voting challenge was a failure, but it marked a turnaround for the era in the public's perception of this brave and determined woman.

Virginia Minor's case in the Supreme Court was quietly plodding on. It was equally important, as the Supreme Court, with a broad reading, might still overturn the discriminations against women built into the Reconstruction amendments. Francis Minor argued for his wife in *Minor v. Happersett* before the Supreme Court on February 9, 1875. In their opinion of March 29, 1875, the justices affirmed the Missouri Supreme Court decision.[46] Minor was, indeed, a citizen of the United States not only under the 14th Amendment but always. The Constitution, they held, however, "does not confer the right of suffrage upon any one." This unanimous decision was a strict interpretation of the Constitution.[47] With the decision putting the final nail in the coffin of the New Departure's attempt to secure female suffrage, the NWSA revived its other strategy and began to work again for a constitutional amendment to win women the right to vote. The stage was now set for the long, unequal struggle for women to win their civil rights with little or no help from men in power.

Meanwhile, in *Bradwell* and *Minor*, the Supreme Court had reinforced sex prejudice and discrimination. Further, through the criminal law the courts had conducted a vendetta against a woman whose civil disobedience had highlighted the legal and civil rights injustices for women in the postwar United States. Anthony's trial demonstrated how far the courts would pursue the judicial victimization of women and the kind of treatment that authorities would mete out to women who challenged such discrimination. This was strong stuff. While this travesty of justice would deter such civil disobedience, it also taught authorities so inclined how much governmental power could back anything they might do if they prejudicially employed discrimination against any other group to support their own interests. If a state could not discriminate on grounds of "race, color or previous condition of servitude" but discrimination because of sex was excepted, who was to say other grounds on which to discriminate did not exist? Within a year of *Minor v. Happersett*, the Supreme Court pointed the way in its first decision on the 15th Amendment, *United States v. Reese*,[48] confirming that the 15th Amendment did not confer suffrage on black men but only prevented the states from discriminating against them "on account of race, color, or previous condition of servitude." The doors were thus flung wide open for any state to devise the variety of "petty freaks or cunning devices" that Anthony had warned about, to target any group on other grounds—such as illiteracy, failure to pay a poll tax, or fulfill residence regulations—to restrict the right to vote. It was only a matter of time until creative individuals who were intent on further restricting the now clearly narrow remit of the Reconstruction amendments would press their advantage. The stage, therefore, was set for widespread postbellum discrimination—not just the fundamental and statute laws already discriminating against women but new ones both against them and against black men. Thus the dawning era of Jim Crow stood on a solid foundation of legalized discrimination sanctioned by the Constitution, statute law, and judicial decision, which began with institutionalized discrimination against women after the Civil War.

Anthony and Stanton and their close colleagues had been laughed at, scorned, demeaned, besmirched, and vilified for arguing that more discrimination would result from the refusal of the male legislators to listen to women from 1865 on. Summarily dismissed when they begged legislators not to create legalized discrimination against them, the women forecast the truth, while more than half the nation was left with a long struggle ahead. This situation pertained after full manhood suffrage was introduced through the enfranchisement of black men, after Reconstruction, after abolition, after Emancipation, after the Civil War, which was supposed to make the nation whole. After all this, more than half the nation still had to face the same struggle again to win true equal rights. It was a sad legacy of a noble cause. And the saddest part was that so much of it could have been avoided—if only the men had listened to the women and acted upon their wisdom.

Epigraphs

Although those who demand "woman's suffrage" on principle are few, those who would oppose "negro suffrage" from prejudice are many, hence the only way to secure the latter is to end all this talk of class legislation, bury the negro in the citizen, and claim the suffrage for all men and women, as a natural, inalienable right.—Elizabeth Cady Stanton[1]

When one considers how these women had spent the best part of their lives in working for the freedom of the negro, their humiliation can be imagined at seeing educated colored men laboring with might and main to prevent white women from obtaining the same privileges which they were asking for themselves. It was a bitter dose and one which women have been compelled to take in every State where a campaign for woman suffrage has been made.—Ida Husted Harper[2]

But from this opposition on all sides true woman suffragists learned their power to stand alone and to maintain the right against large and honorable majorities.—History of Woman Suffrage[3]

It is almost impossible for the most liberal of men to understand what liberty means for woman.—History of Woman Suffrage[4]

To think I have had more than sixty years of hard struggle for a little liberty, and then to die without, it seems so cruel.—Susan B. Anthony[5]

Abbreviations

AASS—American Anti-Slavery Society
AED—Anna Dickinson
AERA—American Equal Rights Association
AK—Abby Kelley
CG—Congressional Globe
ECS—Elizabeth Cady Stanton
EPNY—Evening Post, New York
FD—Frederick Douglass
FDG—Frances Dana Gage
FSM—Fort Scott Monitor
GFT—George Francis Train
GS—Gerrit Smith
HBB—Henry Brown Blackwell
LS—Lucy Stone
NASS—National Anti-Slavery Standard
NYT—New York Times
PASS—Pennsylvania Anti-Slavery Society
SBA—Susan B. Anthony
WAC—Women Writers Project, Emory University
WP—Wendell Phillips

Appendix A: States Where Woman Suffrage Failed During Reconstruction

1867

1. New Jersey
2. Connecticut
3. Massachusetts
4. Missouri
5. Maine
6. Ohio
7. Wisconsin
8. Michigan
9. New York
10. Kansas (only state to poll the electorate) (1867)

1868

11. Arkansas
12. Texas
13. Washington, D.C.[1]

Appendix B: Milestones of the 14th Amendment State by State[1]

1866

Congress

May 10: Passed in House of Representatives
June 8: Modified and passed in Senate
June 13: Passed again in House of Representatives
June 16: Sent to the states for ratification

Ratifications

1866

1. Connecticut	June 25		4. New Jersey	September 11
2. New Hampshire	July 6		5. Oregon	September 19
3. Tennessee	July 19 (readmitted to the Union)		6. Vermont	October 30

1867

7. Ohio	January 4		15. Nevada	January 22
8. New York	January 10		16. Indiana	January 25
9. Kansas	January 11		17. Missouri	January 25
10. Illinois	January 15		18. Rhode Island	February 7
11. West Virginia	January 16		19. Wisconsin	February 7
12. Michigan	January 16		20. Pennsylvania	February 12
13. Minnesota	January 16		21. Massachusetts	March 20
14. Maine	January 19		22. Nebraska	June 15[2]

1868

23. Iowa	March 16		26. North Carolina	July 4
24. Arkansas	April 6		27. Louisiana	July 9
25. Florida	June 9		28. South Carolina	July 9

Ratification by Three-Quarters of the States Requirement Met

29. Alabama	July 13
30. Georgia	July 21

14th Amendment Certified by the Secretary of State, July 28, 1868[3] Ratified in 757 days

Rejections

Texas	October 27, 1866		Virginia	January 9, 1867
Georgia	November 6, 1866		Louisiana	February 6, 1867
North Carolina	December 14, 1866		Delaware	February 8, 1867
South Carolina	December 20, 1866		Maryland	March 23, 1867

Rescissions

New Jersey	March 24, 1868
Ohio	January 15, 1868

Appendix C: 1860 Census
Data Related to Slaves

	Total Number of Slaves	Percentage of State Populations[1]	Males	Females[2]
1. Alabama	435,080	45%	217,766	217,314
2. Arkansas	111,115	26%	56,174	54,941
3. Delaware*	1,798	2%	860	938
4. Florida	61,745	44%	31,348	30,397
5. Georgia	462,198	44%	229,193	233,005
6. Kansas*	2	0%	0	2
7. Kentucky*	225,483	20%	113,009	112,474
8. Louisiana	331,726	47%	171,977	159,749
9. Nebraska	18	0%	6	12
10. Maryland*	87,189	13%	44,313	42,876
11. Mississippi	436,631	55%	219,301	217,330
12. Missouri*	114,931	10%	57,360	57,571
13. North Carolina	331,059	33%	166,469	164,590
14. South Carolina	402,406	57%	196,571	205,835
15. Tennessee	275,719	25%	136,370	139,349
16. Texas	182,566	30%	91,189	91,377
17. Virginia	490,865	31%	249,483	241,382

*Did not secede.

Appendix D: 1860 Census Data
Showing Potential Voting
Population Totals[1]

	Male	Female
Free Blacks	115,390	131,778
Slaves	875,877	858,674
Subtotal	991,267	990,452
Whites	7,061,106	6,371,734
Total	8,052,373	7,362,186[2]

Chapter Notes

Chapter 1

1. Unless otherwise stated, all descriptions and quotations in this section relating to Wendell Phillips are from "The Anniversaries: Important Session of the Anti-Slavery Society. Speeches of Wendell Phillips et al." *New York Times*, May 10, 1865, hereinafter cited as *NYT*; and "The Anti-Slavery Society; Exciting Debate and Final Action on Mr. Garrison's Resolution of Dissolution. The Society Votes to Live," *NYT*, May 11, 1865.

2. Diary of Susan B. Anthony, April 26, 27, 1865, quoted in Alma Lutz, *Susan B. Anthony: Rebel, Crusader, Humanitarian* (Washington, D.C: Zenger, 1959), 112, hereinafter cited as Lutz, *Rebel Crusader*, retrieved from Project Gutenberg April 9, 2018, at http://www.gutenberg.org/ebooks/20439.

3. Elizabeth Cady Stanton, "Pronunciamento," *The Revolution*, July 15, 1869. Phillips witnessed the attempted lynching of William Lloyd Garrison in October 1835 and by 1836 had given up law to join Garrison's movement.

4. Elizabeth Cady Stanton, *Eighty Years and More: Reminiscences, 1815–1897* (New York: European, 1898), 89.

5. Wendell Phillips, "Speech at the Convention Held at Worcester, October 15 and 16, 1851," in Wendell Phillips, Theodore Parker, Mrs. Mill (of England), T.W. Higginson and Mrs. C.I.J. Nichols, *Woman's Rights Tracts* (Boston: Robert F. Wallcut, 1854).

6. Elizabeth Cady Stanton, Susan B. Anthony and Matilda Jocelyn Gage, ed., *History of Woman Suffrage*, vol. 1 (New York: Fowler & Wells, 1882), 667, hereinafter cited as *HWS* I; Faye E. Dudden, *Fighting Chance: The Struggle Over Woman Suffrage and Black Suffrage in Reconstruction America* (New York: Oxford University Press, 2011), 22–23, hereinafter cited as Dudden, *Fighting Chance.*

7. *HWS* I, 667–668.

8. Ibid., 53–61, at 60.

Chapter 2

1. *HWS* I, 686, 743.

2. Wendell Phillips, "Suffrage for Women," from *Addresses Made at the Tenth Woman's Rights Convention at Cooper Institute, New York, May 10 and 11, 1860*, Wendell Phillips and Theodore C. Pease, *Speeches, Lectures and Letters of Wendell Phillips*, vol. 2 (Boston: Lee and Shepard, 1891), retrieved December 7, 2015, http://www.perseus.tufts.edu/hopper/text?doc=Perseus%3Atext%3A2001.05.0189%3Achapter%3D11.

3. See House Joint Resolution proposing the 13th amendment to the Constitution, January 31, 1865, *Enrolled Acts and Resolutions of Congress, 1789–1999*, General Records of the United States Government, Record Group 11, National Archives.

4. See, for example, Serena Covkin, "The American Civil War and Women's Citizenship: Susan B. Anthony, Elizabeth Cady Stanton, and the Women's Loyal National League," *Ezra's Archives*, a Journal of the Cornell Historical Society (2014), accessed May 7, 2017, at http://creativecommons.org/licenses/by-nc-nd/4.0/.

5. See "An Ordinance for the Government of the Territory of the United States Northwest of the River Ohio, Northwest Ordinance; July 13, 1787," *The Avalon Project: Documents in Law, History and Diplomacy*, Yale Law School, Lillian Goldman Law Library, Newhaven, Connecticut, retrieved April 30, 2018 from http://avalon.law.yale.edu/18th_century/nworder.asp, known as the *Northwest Ordinance, 1787*. See also Alexander Keyssar, *The Right to Vote: The Contested History of Democracy in the United States* (New York: Basic Books, 2000) for details on state constitutions and laws.

6. WP to ECS, May 10, 1865, Elizabeth Frost and Kathryn Cullen-DuPont, *Women's Suffrage in America: An Eyewitness History* (New York, Facts on File, 1992), 179, hereinafter cited as Frost and Cullen-DuPont, *Eyewitness History.*

7. See Kathleen Barry, *Susan B. Anthony: A Biography of a Singular Feminist* (New York: Ballantine Books, 1988), 51, hereinafter cited as Barry, *Singular Feminist*.

8. Frederick Douglass, *The Anti-slavery Movement: A Lecture by Frederick Douglass before the Rochester Ladies' Anti-Slavery Society* (Rochester, NY: Press of Lee, Mann, 1855), hereinafter referred to as Douglass, *The Anti-Slavery Movement*.

9. The timing of the women's cancellation and the sequence of events, with references to cancellation by AASS men beforehand, points to this conclusion.

10. Bernadette Cahill, *Where There's a Will, There's a Crowd of Greedy Relatives,* presentation for the Women's History Network Conference, Women's Material Cultures/Women's Material Environments, Leeds Trinity University, England, September 16, 2016.

11. Frederick Douglass, "The Mission of War," speech before the Women's Loyal League at the Cooper Institute in New York City, January 13, 1864, blackpast.org, An Online Reference Guide to African American History, accessed at http://www.blackpast.org/1864-frederick-douglass-mission-war, April 17, 2018.

12. See Philip S. Foner, *Frederick Douglass on Women's Rights* (New York: Da Capo, 1992).

13. Andrea Moore Kerr, *Lucy Stone: Speaking Out for Equality* (New Brunswick, NJ: Rutgers University Press, 1992), 73–74, hereinafter referred to as Kerr, *Stone: Speaking Out*.

14. Ibid., 73–76.

15. Dorothy Sterling, *Ahead of Her Time: Abby Kelley and the Politics of Antislavery* (New York: Norton, 1994), 275, hereinafter cited as Sterling, *Kelley*.

16. Douglass, *The Anti-Slavery Movement*, 29.

17. Kerr, *Stone: Speaking Out*, 110–111.

18. "Reconstruction: Wendell Phillip's Views on the Question. No State to be Re-admitted except on the Basis of Negro Suffrage; The Pressure of Public Sentiment Invoked upon the President; Gen. Banks' Policy in Louisiana Reviewed and Denounced; ADDRESS OF MR. PHILLIPS," *NYT*, December 28, 1864.

19. ECS to SBA, Theodore Stanton and Harriot Stanton Blatch, *Elizabeth Cady Stanton as Revealed in Her Letters, Diaries and Reminiscences*, vol. II (London, New York: Harper & Brothers, 1922), 103–104, hereinafter referred to as Stanton and Blatch, *Letters, Diaries and Reminiscences*, II.

20. "Negro Suffrage: The New Agitation of the Anti-Slavery Society; The Platform Announced, the Principles Discussed, and the Campaign Opened," *NYT,* May 13, 1865.

21. *HWS* I, 462.

22. WP to ECS, May 10, 1865, Frost and Cullen-DuPont, *Eyewitness History*, 175.

23. ECS to WP, May 25, 1865, Frost and Cullen-DuPont, *Eyewitness History*, 175.

Chapter 3

1. See *House Joint Resolution proposing the 13th amendment to the Constitution, January 31, 1865*, National Archives, America's Historical Documents retrieved June 11, 2018, from https://www.archives.gov/historical-docs/13th-amendment.

2. The most recent—1860—Census population was 31,443,321, made up of 16,085,190 men and 15,358,105 women. See Joseph C.G. Kennedy, Superintendent of the Census, *Population of the United States in 1860; Compiled from the Original Returns of the Eighth Census* (Secretary of the Interior: Government Printing Office, Washington, D.C., 1864), 597, hereinafter referred to as Kennedy, *1860 Census*. Note that the total of males and females should be 31,443,295.

3. "Obituary: Susan B. Anthony," *NYT*, March 13, 1906.

4. "Trains' Speech at Ottawa," *Fort Scott Monitor*, Kansas, October 30, 1867.

5. Ida Husted Harper, *The Life and Work of Susan B. Anthony* (Indianapolis & Kansas City: Bowen-Merrill Company, 1899), I, 243, hereinafter cited as Harper, *Life and Work* I; Katharine Anthony, *Susan B. Anthony: Her Personal History and her Era* (New York: Doubleday, 1954), 187, hereinafter cited as Anthony, *Anthony Era*.

6. "Speech of Wendell Phillips at Cooper Union," May 21, 1863, *The Liberator*, May 29, 1863; also cited in James M. McPherson, *The Struggle for Equality: Abolitionists and the Negro in the Civil War and Reconstruction,* 2nd ed. (Princeton, NJ: Princeton University Press, 1995), 240, n. 6, hereinafter cited as McPherson, *Struggle for Equality*.

7. Quoted from *Douglass' Monthly*, cited in McPherson, *Struggle for Equality*, 240, n. 6.

8. "Proceedings of the Colored Convention of the State of Kansas Held at Leavenworth, October 13, 14, 15 and 16, 1863," at *Colored Conventions,* accessed November 28, 2016, at http://coloredconventions.org/items/show/270.

9. Alexander Keyssar, *The Right to Vote: The Contested History of Democracy in the United States* (New York: Basic Books, 2000).

10. Letter, "President Lincoln to Hon. Michael Hahn, March 13, 1864," reprinted from the *Washington Chronicle*, in *NYT*, June 23, 1865.

11. Frederick Douglass, "Speech before the Massachusetts Anti-Slavery Society, Jan. 26, 1864 and May 9, 1865," *Frederick Douglass Papers*, Library of Congress retrieved June 12, 2018, from http://hdl.loc.gov/loc.mss/mfd. 22010. Quote at image 4. This speech, usually called "What the Black Man Wants," is regularly undated in the sources where it is available or dated to April 1865. This work references the Library of Congress manuscript and follows the Library of Congress dating.

12. "Wendell Phillips on Reconstruction," *NYT*, December 29, 1864.

13. "Negro Suffrage in the South," *NYT*, June 3, 1865.

14. Ibid.

15. Derived from Kennedy, *1860 Census*, 597. For a modern summary of the trends this census showed, see Adam Goodheart, "The Census of Doom," *NYT*, April 1, 2011, accessed March 18, 2018, at https://opinionator.blogs.nytimes.com/2011/04/01/the-census-of-doom/.

16. Harper, *Life and Work*, I, 243.

17. Harper, *Life and Work*, II, 966–967.

18. Ibid., 960–967.

19. Ibid., 967.

20. Harper, *Life and Work*, I, 247.

21. Rheta Childe Dorr, *Susan B. Anthony: The Woman Who Changed the Mind of a Nation* (New York: Frederick A. Stokes, 1928), 174, hereinafter cited as Dorr, *Anthony*.

22. Ibid., 174–177.

23. On July 18, 1865, Susan wrote in her diary: "Got a letter from Mrs. Stanton from Johnstown. Sent one from Phillips to her. He says, 'Tell Susan to come East; there is work for her to do'" (Katharine Anthony, *Anthony Era*, 185–206); see also Bernadette Cahill, "Silencing Women: Susan B. Anthony and Suffrage in 1865 Leavenworth," *About Leavenworth Blog*, accessed at http://www.visitleavenworthks.com/blog-page October 20, 2017.

24. Anthony, *Anthony Era*, 190.

25. Harper, *Life and Work*, I, 220–221.

26. Ibid.

27. ECS to SBA, New York, August 11, 1863, Stanton and Blatch, *Elizabeth Cady Stanton as Revealed in Her Letters, Diaries and Reminiscences*, II, 105.

28. Anthony, *Anthony Era*, 191.

29. Benjamin Gratz Brown, "Universal Suffrage: An Address by Hon. B. Gratz Brown Delivered at Turner Hall, St. Louis, Mo," *Democrat*, St. Louis, September 22, 1865.

30. *Chicago Daily Inter Ocean*, Tuesday, August 29, 1865.

31. Anthony, *Anthony Era*, 191; Harper, *Life and Work*, I, 221.

Chapter 4

1. Ernestine Rose had gathered and presented to the assembly of New York in Albany in 1836 the first petition asking for equal property rights for married women. See Carol A. Kolmerten, *The American Life of Ernestine L. Rose* (Syracuse, NY: Syracuse University Press, 1999), 33, citing *HWS* I, 99. In 1846 she spoke twice in the legislative hall in Detroit, Michigan, in favor of female suffrage. See Octavia Williams Bates, "Municipal Suffrage for Women in Michigan," Mary Kavanaugh Oldham Eagle, ed., *The Congress of Women: Held in the Woman's Building, World's Columbian Exposition, Chicago, U.S.A., 1893* (Chicago: Monarch Books, 1894), 664–667, transcript in Mary Mark Ockerbloom, "A Celebration of Women Writers," retrieved from http://digital.library.upenn.edu/women/eagle/congress/bates.html April 9, 2018, hereinafter referred to as Eagle, *Congress of Women*.

2. *HWS* II, 92; Harper, *Life and Work*, I, 220–221.

3. "Pausing only for a brief visit, she went on to New York to fulfill the purpose which brought her eastward. She stopped at Auburn to confer with Mrs. Wright and Mrs. Worden, but found both very dubious about reviving interest in woman's rights at this critical moment" (Harper, *Life and Work*, I, 220–221).

4. Lucretia Mott to Martha Coffin Wright, November 2, 1865, Beverly Wilson Palmer, ed., *Selected Letters of Lucretia Coffin Mott* (Champaign: University of Illinois Press, 2002), 365, hereinafter cited as Palmer, *Mott Selected Letters*.

5. "Letter from Frances Gage," *NASS*, November 25, 1865, 3.

6. Kerr, *Stone: Speaking Out*, 119–120.

7. Diary of SBA, December 4 and 11, 1865, in Patricia D. Holland and Ann D. Gordon, *Papers of Elizabeth Cady Stanton and Susan B. Anthony*, 45 Reels (Wilmington, DE: Scholarly Resources, 1991), reel 11, frames 90, 97, cited in Dudden *Fighting Chance*, 225, n. 39, hereinafter referred to as Holland and Gordon, *ECS and SBA Papers*.

8. Though Harper (*Life and Work*, I, 251) says this $500 came from the Hovey fund, it seems an unlikely source, as for years Phillips had allowed women nothing from Hovey. In fact, the money advanced for the WNLL emancipation and abolition petition was extracted from him only with pressure from the Hovey Committee. Dudden (*Fighting Chance*, 68 and 225, n. 39) states the disbursement was from the Francis Jackson bequest—the "only dedicated" Women's Rights fund.

9. *13th Amendment to the U.S. Constitution*,

Library of Congress, Primary Documents in American History, retrieved June 11, 2018 from http://www.loc.gov/rr/program/bib/ourdocs/13thamendment.html.

10. Senator Charles Sumner, S.R. 1, "A Joint Resolution Proposing an Amendment to the Constitution to the United States," *U.S. Congressional Documents and Debates, 1774–1875, Bills and Resolutions, Senate, 39th Congress,* December 4, 1865, retrieved from https://memory.loc.gov/cgi-bin/ampage?collId=llsr&fileName=039/llsr039.db&recNum=0 June 11, 2018; *Congressional Globe,* 39th Congress, December 4, 1865, 2, hereinafter cited as *CG.*

11. *HWS* II, 92, note; Harper, *Life and Work* I, 220–221, 253; Anthony, *Anthony Era,* chapter 13, 191.

12. Their covering letter is held at the Records of the U.S. House of Representatives, National Archives and Records Administration, Washington, D.C., ARC Identifier 306684; image available at https://en.wikipedia.org/wiki/American_Equal_Rights_Association, accessed October 5, 2015.

13. Laura R. Jolley, "Benjamin Gratz Brown," in *Historic Missourians,* the State Historical Society of Missouri, accessed October 20, 2015 at http://shs.umsystem.edu/historicmissourians/name/b/brownb/index.html.

14. SBA to Caroline Healey Dall, December 26, 1865, Gordon, *Selected Papers,* I, 562–563.

15. Diary of SBA, 27 December 1865, Gordon, *Selected Papers,* I, 567. See also *The Liberator,* April 1, 1865.

16. *The Liberator,* May 19, 1865.

17. Stuart Galloway, "The American Equal Rights Association, 1866–1870: Gender, Race and Universal Suffrage" (PhD diss., School of Historical Studies, Leicester, University of Leicester, 2014), 33–37, hereinafter cited as Galloway, *AERA, 1866–70.*

18. Galloway, *AERA, 1866–70,* 35.

19. On December 4, 1865, Charles Sumner introduced several bills on republican government and suffrage in Washington, D.C., while Thaddeus Stevens in the House proposed the joint Committee of Fifteen, which was to examine, among other things, whether and how the former Confederate states were to be allowed representation in Congress; voting in Washington, D.C; and the proposed 14th Amendment. Another contentious proposal was to use the number of voters—as opposed to total population—in individual states to determine congressional representation. (see *CG,* 39th Congress, 1st Session, 2, 6, 10).

20. Diary of SBA, Wednesday, December 27, 1865, Gordon, *Selected Papers,* I, 567–568, n. 1.

21. "A Law Against Women," *The Independent,* January 18, 1866; *HWS* II, 93.

22. ECS to Martha C. Wright, December 30, 1865, Stanton and Blatch, *Letters, Diaries and Reminiscences,* II, 108.

23. Gordon, *Selected Papers, I,* 564–566.

24. ECS to Martha C. Wright, January 6, 1866, Frost and Cullen-DuPont, *Eyewitness History,* 180.

25. Harper, *Life and Work* I, 253.

26. ECS to GS, January 1, 1866, Gordon, *Selected Papers,* I, 568–570; Ellen Carol DuBois, *Feminism and Suffrage: The Emergence of an Independent Women's Movement in America, 1848–1869* (Ithaca and London: Cornell University Press, 1978), 61, hereinafter cited as DuBois, *Feminism and Suffrage.*

Chapter 5

1. ECS to GS, January 1, 1866, Gordon, *Selected Papers,* I, 568, 569, n. 4.

2. ECS letter dated January 2, 1866, to the editor of the *NASS,* reproduced in *HWS* II, 92. The text or a summary of only the Broomall and Stevens measures appear in the *Congressional Globe.* Several other proposals likely never made it into the record. Representative William Darrah Kelley (R), also introduced a measure to remove race discrimination in voting in Washington, D.C., with no mention of sex. Postponed to January 1866, it became H.R. 1, dated February 6, 1866. For a summary of this bill's early history, see "A Bill Extending the Right of Suffrage in the District of Columbia," Library of Congress, *U.S. Congressional Documents and Debates, 1774–1875, Bills and Resolutions, House.* For its first mention, see *CG,* 39th Congress, December 5, 1865, 10.

3. ECS to Martha C. Wright, January 20, 1866, Stanton and Blatch, *Letters, Diaries and Reminiscences,* II, 112–113.

4. ECS letter dated January 2, 1866, to the editor of the *NASS,* reproduced in *HWS* II, 92.

5. ECS to Martha C. Wright, January 20, 1866, Stanton and Blatch, *Letters, Diaries and Reminiscences,* II, 112–113.

6. Terminology from the January 1866 Senate Bill No. 60 to enlarge the Freedmen's Bureau.

7. Senator Lyman Trumbull, *CG,* 39th Congress, January 5, 1866, 129; Senate Bill No. 60, Library of Congress, *U.S. Congressional Documents and Debates, 1774–1875, Bills and Resolutions, Senate.*

8. *HWS* II, 91; Gordon, *Selected Papers,* I, 566–567.

9. See *HWS* II, 3–6, for Anna Ella Carroll's influence in the strategy of the Tennessee and

Mississippi River campaigns in the Civil War. This chapter includes references to much varied work done by women for the Union during the Civil War. The work of Clara Barton is well known.

10. *HWS* II, 93–94.

11. Ibid.

12. *The Liberator*, December 29, 1865.

13. From the woman suffrage petition, *HWS* II, 91; Gordon, *Selected Papers*, I, 566–567.

14. The 13th Amendment became the fundamental law of the United States after certification on December 18, 1865.

15. SBA to Sidney Clarke, Gordon, *Selected Papers*, I, 573.

16. *CG*, 39th Congress, January 23, 1866, 379–380; SBA to James Brooks, January 20, 1866, Gordon, *Selected Papers*, I, 572.

17. *Journal of the House of Representatives*, 39th Congress, January 29, 1866, 194.

18. Brown changed affiliations several times during his career. Laura R. Jolley, "Benjamin Gratz Brown," *Historic Missourians*, the State Historical Society of Missouri, accessed October 20, 2015 at http://shs.umsystem.edu/historic missourians/name/b/brownb/index.html.

19. *CG*, 39th Congress, January 24, 1866, 390.

20. Ibid., 403.

21. Ibid.

22. Harper, *Life and Work* I, 256; Dorr, *Anthony*, 180.

23. "Special Meeting of the American Anti-Slavery Society," *NASS*, February 3, 1866.

24. Ibid.

25. Harper, *Life and Work* I, 256.

26. Powell would replace Parker Pillsbury as editor of the *Standard* in May 1866, the latter removed because he advocated original Garrisonian policies of reform of all injustices, instead of supporting only rights for black males. See Stacey M. Robertson, *Parker Pillsbury: Radical Abolitionist, Male Feminist* (Ithaca: Cornell University Press, 2007), 138–142.

27. Harper, *Life and Work* I, 256.

28. SBA to Phillips, January 28, 1866, Gordon, *Selected Papers*, I, 574–576, at 575.

29. Ibid., at 574.

30. *CG*, 39th Congress, January 24, 1866, 380.

31. Lawrence Jacob Friedman, *Gregarious Saints: Self and Community in Antebellum American Abolitionism, 1830–1870* (Cambridge: Cambridge University Press, 1982), 271; "The Massachusetts Anti-Slavery Society—The Resolution to Disband the Society Defeated," *NYT*, January 26, 1866.

32. The Boston meeting occurred the day before the meeting of the Massachusetts Anti-Slavery Society. Anthony attended both. SBA

to WP, January 28, 1866, Gordon, *Selected Papers*, I, 575, n.1, 576 n. 6.

33. SBA to WP, January 12, 1866, Gordon, *Selected Papers*, I, 570–571, including notes.

34. Harper, *Life and Work* I, 256.

Chapter 6

1. *Journal of the House of Representatives*, 39th Congress, January 29, 1866, 194.

2. *HWS* II, 96–97.

3. Despite the story, research has found no petition from Child presented by Sumner. See Milton Meltzer, Patricia G. Holland, Francine Krasno, *Lydia Maria Child: Selected Letters, 1817–1880* (Amherst: University of Massachusetts Press, 1983), 467.

4. *CG*, 39th Congress, February 14, 1866, 829.

5. "Colored men themselves opposed us, saying, do not block our chance by lumbering the Republican party with Woman Suffrage" (*HWS* II, 97).

6. Representative James Hammond of South Carolina proposed the gag rule in December 1835. It tied up debate for weeks and Speaker James Polk of Tennessee referred this to a special committee to resolve the problem. See "The House 'Gag Rule,' May 26, 1836," *History, Art & Archives*, United States House of Representatives, retrieved June 29, 2018, from http://history.house.gov/Historical-Highlights/1800–1850/The-House-of-Representatives-instituted-the-%E2%80%9Cgag-rule%E2%80%9D/. Polk was a Democrat. Hammond was originally elected as a member of the Nullifier Party, which held that states could nullify federal laws within their borders. He later became a Democrat.

7. SBA to Caroline Healey Dall, January 30, 1866, DuBois, *Feminism and Suffrage*, 62.

8. SBA to WP, January 28, 1866, Gordon, *Selected Papers*, I, 574–576, at 575, n. 1.

9. Deborah Pickman Clifford, *Crusader for Freedom: A Life of Lydia Maria Child* (Boston: Beacon Press, 1992), 277; 278, n. 17. The dating of the Clifford sources is unclear.

10. Lucretia Mott to WP, April 17, 1866, Palmer, *Mott Selected Letters*, 371–372.

11. ECS to GS, January 1, 1866, Gordon, *Selected Papers*, I, 568; quoted also in DuBois, *Feminism and Suffrage*, 61.

12. Laura E. Free, in "Gendering the Constitution: Manhood, Race, and Woman Suffrage, 1865–1866" (PhD diss., Ithaca, Cornell University, 2009), focuses exclusively on the overt inclusion of sex discrimination in the Constitution. See 58–84, quotation from 59, hereinafter referred to as Free, *Gendering*

the Constitution. See also, Laura E. Free, *Suffrage Reconstructed: Gender, Race and Voting Rights in the Civil War Era* (Ithaca: Cornell University Press, 2015), hereinafter referred to as Free, *Suffrage Reconstructed*.

13. Senate Bill S. 1, December 4, 1865.

14. Benjamin Burks Kendrick, *The Journal of the Joint Committee of Fifteen on Reconstruction* (New York: University of Columbia, 1914), 140–141, accessed at https://archive.org/details/journaljointcom00recogoog March 23, 2018.

15. See Alice Stone Blackwell, *Lucy Stone: Pioneer of Woman's Rights* (Boston: Little, Brown, 1930); James M. McPherson, "Abolitionism, Woman Suffrage and the Negro," *Mid-America* 47 (1965), 40–47, cited in Kerr, *Stone—Speaking Out*, 120.

16. *HWS* II, 95.

17. *San Mateo County v. Southern Pacific Railroad*, launched in U.S. 9th Circuit Court, San Francisco, September 6, 1882, and determined in the U.S. Supreme Court in 1885. During the case "Senator Roscoe Conkling waved an unknown document in the air and then read from it in an attempt to prove that the intent of the Joint Committee was for corporate personhood." See Jan Edwards, *Timeline of Personhood Rights and Powers,* 2002, Women's International League for Peace and Freedom, accessed at http://www.ratical.org/corporations/ToPRaP.html April 3, 2018. This website and others with the same information give no source for the Conkling anecdote. The specific ruling that a corporation is a person for the purposes of the law occurred in 1889 with the Supreme Court case of the *Minneapolis & St. Louis Ry. Co. v. Beckwith*. See also Benjamin Burks Kendrick, *The Journal of the Joint Committee of Fifteen on Reconstruction* (New York: University of Columbia, 1914), 28, retrieved March 23, 2018, from https://archive.org/details/journaljointcom00recogoog.

18. *CG*, 39th Congress, February 21, 1866, 951.

19. Free, *Gendering the Constitution*, 219.

20. *HWS* II, 92. Lutz, *Rebel Crusader*, 118, says "by the end of January."

21. *CG*, 39th Congress, January 6, 1867, 129.

22. Barbara Goldsmith, *Other Powers: The Age of Suffrage, Spiritualism and the Scandalous Victoria Woodhull* (New York: Harper Perennial, 1999), 110, hereinafter cited as Goldsmith, *Other Powers*.

23. *CG*, 39th Congress, February 27, 1866, 1064.

24. Ibid.

25. S. 61, *CG*, 39th Congress, January 6, 1867, 129. This bill passed over the presidential veto on April 9, 1866.

26. *CG*, 39th Congress, March 9, 1866, 1293.

27. Ibid.

28. *CG*, 39th Congress, April 5, 1866, 1784.

29. Ibid., 1781–1782.

30. Ibid., 1782.

31. Ibid.

32. Direct elections of senators began only in 1914 after the 1913 ratification of the Seventeenth Amendment. This emasculated the role of the states in the United States.

33. See also Amy Dru Stanley, *From Bondage to Contract: Wage Labor, Marriage and the Market in the Age of Slave Emancipation* (New York: Cambridge University Press, 1998), 55–59.

34. Legislative history, "Civil Rights Act of 1866," Wikipedia, retrieved April 10, 2018 from https://en.wikipedia.org/wiki/Civil_Rights_Act_of_1866.

35. See "Proceedings of the National Convention of Colored Men, Held in the City of Syracuse, N.Y., October 4, 6, 5 and 7, 1864, with the Bill of Wrongs and Rights, and Address to the American People" (Boston: J.S. Rock and Geo. L. Ruffin, 1864), in *Colored Conventions*, http://coloredconventions.org/items/show/282, retrieved March 14, 2018; hereinafter referred to as *Colored Men Proceedings*. This document includes the constitution of the National Equal Rights League. Miss Edmonia Highgate of Syracuse, presented as the colored men's counterpart to Anna Dickinson, addressed the meeting. The language throughout, including the documents, focused on men. The discrimination against women remained contentious. In the 1869 *Proceedings*, at 11–12, retrieved March 14, 2018, from this website at http://coloredconventions.org/items/show/452, for example, admission of a Miss Johnson of Alleghany was fiercely contested.

36. *Colored Men Proceedings*, 41.

37. This later bill was sometimes referred to as S. 1; Eric Foner (*Reconstruction: America's Unfinished Revolution, 1863–1877* [New York: Harper & Row, 1988], 240, hereinafter cited as Foner, *Reconstruction*) notes that this was the "only Radical proposal to meet with even partial success." In December 1865, a Washington, D.C., referendum resulted in 35 in favor of black suffrage and 6,951 against it.

38. S. No. 292 and H.R. 544.

Chapter 7

1. T.W. Gilbreth, Memphis, Tennessee, to Major General O.O. Howard and Commissioner B.R.F. and A.L., Washington, D.C., May 22, 1866, "The Freedmen's Bureau Report on the Memphis Race Riots of 1866," *Records of the Assistant Commissioner for the State of Ten-*

nessee, Bureau of Refugees, Freedmen, and Abandoned Lands, 1865–1869, National Archives Microfilm Publication M999, roll 34, in "Reports of Outrages, Riots and Murders, Jan. 15, 1866–Aug. 12, 1868"; hereinafter cited as Gilbreth, *Memphis Race Riots Report.*

2. See "Memphis Massacre," *Independent,* May 17, 1866; see also, "The Horror of Memphis," dated May 14, 1866, *Independent,* May 31, 1866.

3. "The Anniversaries," *New York Tribune,* May 9, 1866.

4. Ibid.

5. Harper, *Life and Work* I, 258–259.

6. "The Anniversaries," *New York Tribune,* May 10, 1866.

7. Ibid. See also, "Bursting of a Woman's Rights Bomb" in "A Woman's Rights Diversion in the 'Anti-Slavery' Society Meeting; Talk from Women Declared 'Out of Order,'" *New York World,* May 10, 1866.

8. *HWS* II, 95.

9. Free, *Gendering the Constitution,* 58–84.

10. *HWS* II, 153.

11. Ibid., 152–153.

12. Ibid., 153–154.

13. Ibid., 168–171.

14. Ibid., 154.

15. Goldsmith, *Other Powers,* 112–116.

16. *HWS* II, 155.

17. Ibid., 159, 160.

18. "Mr. Phillips throws a Pail of Cold Water on the Audience," *New York World,* May 11, 1866, cited in Dudden, *Fighting Chance,* 84, 230, n. 140.

19. Carol A. Kolmerten, *The American Life of Ernestine L. Rose* (Syracuse, NY: Syracuse University Press, 1999), 244.

20. Gilbreth, *Memphis Race Riots Report;* "The Horrors of Memphis," *Independent,* May 31, 1866.

21. *HWS* II, 171.

22. "Appendix: The Membership of the American Equal Rights Association," Galloway, *AERA, 1866–70,* 198–209.

23. *HWS* II, 173.

24. Ibid.

25. DuBois, *Feminism and Suffrage,* 64. See also Galloway, *AERA, 1866–70,* 39–41.

26. "Our Boston Correspondence, June 4th, 1866," in *NASS,* June 9, 1866, quoted in *HWS* II, 178.

Chapter 8

1. Garrett Epps, *Democracy Reborn: The Fourteenth Amendment and the Fight for Equal Rights in Post Civil War America* (New York: Henry Holt, 2006), 225–239, at 228–229, hereinafter cited as Epps, *Democracy Reborn.*

2. Several proposals were made before the war to remove voting discrimination against black men, but all failed. See Charles Z. Lincoln, *Constitutional History of New York,* 1822–1894 (Rochester, New York: Lawyers' Cooperative, 1905), II, 294–317.

3. Connecticut, Wisconsin, Minnesota, Colorado Territory and the District of Columbia in 1865. See Foner, Reconstruction, 223, 240; Newsum, Dani, Lincoln Hills and Civil Rights in Colorado, 8, retrieved August 28, 2019 from https://www.google.com/search?q=https%3A%2F%2Fwww.historycolorado.org+%E2%80%BA+files+%E2%80%BA+lincoln_hills_primary_resource_set&rlz=1C1CHBF_enUS719US719&oq=https%3A%2F%2Fwww.historycolorado.org+%E2%80%BA+files+%E2%80%BA+lincoln_hills_primary_resource_set&aqs=chrome..69i57.1975j0j7&sourceid=chrome&ie=UTF-8.

4. *HWS* II, 154; *HWS* II at 172: "We want to make a thorough canvass of the entire State, with lectures, tracts, and petitions, and, if possible, create a public sentiment that shall send genuine Democrats and Republicans to that Convention who shall strike out from our Constitution the two adjectives, 'white male'.… giving to every citizen, over twenty-one, the right to vote, and thus make the Empire State the first example of a true republican form of government."

5. See "Susan B. Anthony Boldly Writes the Speaker of the House Asking for a Public Endorsement of Women's Suffrage," in *Equal Rights Convention for New York State,* Raab Collection, accessed March 23, 2018, at http://www.raabcollection.com/american-history-autographs/anthony-susan-1866#sthash.uBtelNst.dpuf.

6. *HWS* II, 172.

7. Harper, *Life and Work* I, 262. This event's timing is disputed. Anthony's biographer places it soon after the founding of the AERA in mid–May 1866. Dudden puts it in the middle of that February. See Dudden, *Fighting Chance,* 76, 227, n. 85. It is assumed here that this event occurred after the May 10, 1866 Woman's Convention and formation of the AERA. See also Barry, *Singular Feminist,* 171–172.

8. Harper, *Life and Work* I, 262.

9. WP to EC, January 14, 1866, Stanton and Blatch, *Letters, Diaries and Reminiscences,* II, 112, n. 1.

10. Harper, *Life and Work* I, 218.

11. Barbara A. White, in *The Beecher Sisters* (New Haven, CT: Yale University Press, 2003), 201, hereinafter cited as White, *The Beecher Sisters,* reports on the Victoria Woodhull 1872 revelation of the affair of Wendell Phillips and Anna Dickinson, citing the publication late in 1872 of the claims in *Woodhull & Claflin's Weekly.* See also Goldsmith, *Other*

Powers, 115–117. For Goldsmith's observations on the Greeley marriage, see 56–62. Goldsmith, *Other Powers*, is a history of the Tilton marriage, leading to the Henry Ward Beecher scandal of 1875.

12. Charles K. Whipple, *NASS*, June 9, 1866, quoted in *HWS* II, 178.

13. Harper, *Life and Work* I, 262.

14. Ibid., 262.

15. Lucretia Mott to Martha Coffin Wright, June 10, 1866 Palmer, *Mott Selected Letters*, 374.

16. Epps, *Democracy Reborn*, 232–238.

17. Ibid., 238–239.

18. Just over two years later, on July 9, 1868, it would be fully ratified and become the 14th Amendment, even though Congress passed it in a dubiously constitutional manner.

19. See Appendix C.

20. Jacob M. Howard (R), May 23, 1866, "Congress Debates the Fourteenth Amendment (1866)," *Dictionary of American History*, 2003, retrieved from Encyclopedia.com March 23, 2018, at http://www.encyclopMedia.com/doc/1G2-3401804785.html.

21. In 1865 equal black male suffrage referenda were defeated in Connecticut, Wisconsin, Minnesota, and Colorado Territory; that December, voters of Washington, D.C., almost unanimously turned down equal black voting rights in the nation's capital, where Congress had jurisdiction. This last referendum was an attempt to stave off Radical Republican attempts to open the door to equal black suffrage through federal power.

22. The Third AERA Annual Convention, May 12–14, 1869, New York; *HWS* II, 383.

23. Stephen Foster in "Special Meeting of the American Anti-Slavery Society," *NASS*, February 3, 1866.

24. *HWS* II, 91.

25. Ibid.; Kerr, *Stone—Speaking Out*, 120.

26. See Appendix D.

27. Mr. Lewis W. Ross (D), Illinois, *CG*, 39th Congress, February 5, 1866, 646. This first session of the 39th Congress also passed the Civil Rights Act, 14 Stat. 27 (1866), tackled black male voting rights in Washington, D.C., and expanded the work of the Freedmen's Bureau. The First Reconstruction Act passed on March 2, 1867. In April 1866 war began between Congress and President Johnson because of his veto of the Civil Rights Act, leading to the president's impeachment in early 1868. The 1866 Civil Rights Act, enacted April 9, 1866—in a period when Congress was debating the various proposals for the 14th Amendment while the women battled against the inclusion of the word "male"—defined citizenship in federal statute for the first time and declared equal protection under the law, the intention being to protect the rights of blacks, particularly freed slaves. Its wording anticipated the 14th Amendment's wording, and the key fact for women was the deliberate lack of reference to sex equality.

28. Dorr, *Anthony*, 185, attributes the 39th Congress leaders' dismissal of woman suffrage to their focus on extending their power in the South, which they believed would be among "negroes and yeoman whites."

Chapter 9

1. Eric L. McKitrick, *Andrew Johnson and Reconstruction* (Oxford: Oxford University Press, 1960), 355, hereinafter referred to as McKitrick, *Johnson and Reconstruction*.

2. *CG*, 39th Congress, 1st Session at 3349, quoted in McKitrick, *Johnson and Reconstruction*, 357.

3. Ibid.

4. "The New Orleans Massacre," *Harper's Weekly*, March 30, 1867, 202. See also, United States Congress Select Committee, *Report of the Select Committee on the New Orleans Riots* (Washington, D.C.: Government Printing Office, 1867), 12.

5. Foner, *Reconstruction*, 264.

6. "Letter from Mrs. Frances D. Gage," *NASS*, July 21, 1866.

7. DuBois, *Feminism and Suffrage*, 73–74; Stacey M. Robertson, *Parker Pillsbury: Radical Abolitionist, Male Feminist* (Ithaca: Cornell University Press, 2007), 139–143.

8. Lucretia Mott to Martha Coffin Wright, June 10, 1866 Palmer, *Mott Selected Letters*, 373–374. Meetings of other organizations did speak of equal rights for women. See for example, "The Longwood Meeting," *NASS*, 23 June 1866.

9. ECS, "Build a New House," *NASS*, July 21, 1866.

10. "Letter From Hon. Gerrit Smith," *NASS*, August 4, 1866.

11. Galloway, *AERA, 1866–70*, 191, 99–103.

12. SBA to Edwin A. Studwell, August 20, 1866, Gordon, *Selected Papers* I, 590–592.

13. Ibid., at 591.

14. Beverly Palmer, ed., *The Selected Papers of Thaddeus Stevens*, vol. 2: *April 1865–August 1868* (Pittsburgh: University of Pittsburgh Press, 1998), 201, n. 2.

15. Foner, *Reconstruction*, 264.

16. *The Southern Loyalists' Convention: Call for a Convention of Southern Unionists, to Meet at Independence Hall, Philadelphia, on Monday, the Third Day of September, 1866* (Tribune

Tracts No. 2, Philadelphia [?], 1866), retrieved March 23, 2018 from Hathi Trust Digital Library, at https://babel.hathitrust.org/cgi/pt?id=loc.ark:/13960/t3417359p;view=1up;seq=3; Goldsmith, *Other Powers*, 122–125; McPherson, *Struggle for Equality*, 360–363.

17. McPherson, *Struggle for Equality*, 363, n. 47.

18. Harper, *Life and Work* I, 262.

19. Charles Sumner to WP, March 17, 1866, quoted and cited by McPherson, *Struggle for Equality*, 350, n. 20.

20. McPherson, *Struggle for Equality*, 363.

21. Dudden, *Fighting Chance*, 88 and 231 n. 1.

22. Ibid., 89.

23. "State Constitutional Convention," *NASS*, October 6, 1866.

24. *HWS* II, 180–181.

25. William Henry Johnson, *Autobiography of Dr. William Henry Johnson* (Albany, NY: Argus, 1900), 211–212, retrieved from archive.org March 14, 2018, at https://archive.org/stream/tohisadoptedhome00johnrich/tohisadoptedhome00johnrich_djvu.txt.

26. For the Resolution, see Frederick E. Hosen, *Federal Laws of the Reconstruction: Principal Congressional Acts and Resolutions, Presidential Proclamations, Speeches and Orders, and Other Legislative and Military Documents, 1862–1875* (McFarland: Jefferson, NC, 2010), 132.

27. One early Civil War historian noted that even if the ten remaining Confederate states ratified they might have to wait for full ratification of the amendment for readmission. He stated that they "were justified" in being suspicious about the future. See Ellis Paxson Oberholtzer, *A History of the United States Since the Civil War* (New York: MacMillan, 1917), I (1865–8), 187–188.

28. "Elizabeth Cady Stanton to the Electors of the Eighth Congressional District, October 10, 1866," *HWS* II, 180–181.

29. SBA to WP, November 4, 1866, Gordon, *Selected Papers*, I, 597–599, at 597.

30. Ibid., at 598.

31. *HWS* II, 1.

Chapter 10

1. SBA to WP, November 6, 1867, Dudden, *Fighting Chance*, 90, 231, n.6.

2. *HWS* I, 667; Dudden, *Fighting Chance*, 22–23.

3. *HWS* I, 667. Phillips refused a request in 1864 from Garrison for aid for freedmen. See James Brewer Stewart, *Wendell Phillips: Liberty's Hero* (Baton Rouge: Louisiana State University Press, 1986), 253.

4. Sterling, *Kelley*, 337.

5. Dudden, *Fighting Chance*, 89–90.

6. Studwell started the *Friend* in 1866.

7. Lucretia Mott to her Philadelphia Family, November 15, 1866 Palmer, *Mott Selected Letters*, at 377.

8. *HWS* II, 181.

9. "Susan B. Anthony Boldly Writes the Speaker of the House Asking for a Public Endorsement of Women's Suffrage," *Equal Rights Convention for New York State,* Raab Collection, accessed March 23, 2018, at http://www.raabcollection.com/american-history-autographs/anthony-susan-1866#sthash.uBtelNst.dpuf.

10. Senator B.F. Wade to SBA, secretary American Equal Rights Association, Jefferson, Ohio, November 14, 1866, *HWS* II, 117.

11. *Plain Dealer*, Friday, November 9, 1866.

12. "Equal Rights: The Ballot for the Women of New York—Spirited Convention at Albany," *Sacramento Daily Union*, 15 December 1866, section "Afternoon Session," retrieved from California Digital Newspaper Collection, May 13, 2018, at http://cdnc.ucr.edu/cgi-bin/cdnc?a=d&d=SDU18661215.2.19&e=-------en--20--1--txt-txIN--------1, hereinafter cited as *Daily Union*, "Equal Rights."

13. Lucretia Mott to the AERA Convention, Albany, November 18, 1866 Palmer, *Mott Selected Letters*, 2002), 379.

14. For the speeches see *Daily Union*, "Equal Rights."

15. Ibid.

16. "Editorial Note, New York Equal Rights Convention," Gordon, *Selected Papers* I, 599.

17. See *Daily Union*, "Equal Rights."

18. *Daily Union*, "Equal Rights"; Gordon, *Selected Papers* I, 601.

19. Originally applied to Confederacy sympathizers who worked for the South in the North, it was one of the worst insults of the time, often used without justification.

20. Gordon, *Selected Papers* I, 600.

21. *Daily Union*, "Equal Rights."

22. *New York World*, November 22, 1866, DuBois, *Feminism and Suffrage*, 65.

23. *Colored Men Proceedings*, 41.

24. McPherson, *Struggle for Equality*, 323.

25. See *A Great Thing for Our People: The Institute for Colored Youth in the Civil War Era, Classes of 1856 to 1864; The Equal Rights League and Voting Suffrage* (Villanova, PA: Falvey Memorial Library, Villanova University, 1919–2015), retrieved April 3, 2018, from https://exhibits.library.villanova.edu/institute-colored-youth/community-moments/equal-rights-league-and-suffrage/.

26. "National Equal Suffrage Association," *NASS*, 6 January 1866. The letter is signed "A."

27. "Equal Rights Convention at Albany, New York, *Philadelphia Press*, November 21 and 22, 1866.

28. Ira Brown, *Mary Grew: Abolitionist and Feminist, 1813–1896* (Selinsgrove, PA: Susquehanna University Press, 1991), 112.

29. All quotations from, "Pennsylvania Anti-Slavery Society: Impeachment of the President Demanded—Speech of Wendell Phillips," *NYT*, November 25, 1866. Phillips gave a similar speech at Cooper Union in New York on October 25, 1866. McPherson, *Struggle for Equality*, 369, n. 5.

30. "Pennsylvania Anti-Slavery Society: Impeachment of the President Demanded—Speech of Wendell Phillips," *NYT*, November 25, 1866.

31. "Remarks of Miss Anthony, Meeting of the Pennsylvania Anti-Slavery Society, November 22, 1866," *NASS*, December 1, 1866.

32. "Remarks of Mrs. Gage, Meeting of the Pennsylvania Anti-Slavery Society, November 22, 1866," *NASS*, December 8, 1866.

33. See Ira Brown, *Mary Grew: Abolitionist and Feminist, 1813–1896* (Selinsgrove, PA: Susquehanna University Press, 1991), 111. She was soon helping to organize for the AERA in Pennsylvania. See also Galloway, *AERA, 1866–70*, 54–58 for the AERA's widespread local organizing.

34. Lucretia Mott to Philadelphia family, November 15, 1866, Palmer, *Mott Selected Letters*, at 378.

35. "Remarks of Mrs. Gage, Meeting of the Pennsylvania Anti-Slavery Society, November 22, 1866," *NASS*, December 1, 1866.

36. New York formed the first equal rights organization (Galloway, *AERA, 1866–70*, 36). Attempts to either reorient the PASS to Equal Rights or to disband it had failed at the annual meeting in November 1865 ("Pennsylvania Anti-Slavery Society," *NASS*, November 4, 1865).

37. Galloway, *AERA, 1866–70* (198–209) lists "252 individually-identified AERA members."

38. *CG*, 39th Congress, December 3, 1866, 2.

39. Elizabeth Cady Stanton, "Bread and Ballots," in "Shall Woman Vote? City Convention at Cooper Institute," *New York Tribune*, December 7, 1866, retrieved April 11, 2018 from *WAC Emory* at http://womenwriters.library.emory.edu/advocacy/content.php?level=div&id=suffragist_009&document=suffragist.

40. Ibid.

41. Ibid.

42. Ibid.

43. Ann D. Gordon, ed., *The Selected Papers of Elizabeth Cady Stanton and Susan B. Anthony, II: Against an Aristocracy of Sex 1866–1873* (New Brunswick, NJ: Rutgers University Press, 1997), 1, hereinafter cited as Gordon, *Selected Papers*, II..

44. Galloway, *AERA, 1866–70*, 90, citing 'Shall Women Vote,' *NY Tribune*, December 8, 1866.

Chapter 11

1. *CG*, 39th Congress, January 8, 1867, 328.

2. See Robert Harrison, *Washington During Civil War and Reconstruction: Race and Radicalism* (New York: Cambridge University Press, 2011), 120–133.

3. Section 9 of the *Northwest Ordinance, 1787* based voting on sex, citizenship, whether slave or free; residence and property ownership and organized new states politically primarily on sex.

4. *CG*, 39th Congress, December 10, 1866, 38.

5. Ibid.

6. Ibid., 46.

7. Ibid., 55.

8. Ibid., 38.

9. Ibid.

10. Women had won the right to vote in school elections in Kentucky in 1838. See Reinette Jones, "Women's Right to Vote in Kentucky," in *Notable Kentucky African Americans Database*, University of Kentucky Libraries, 2016), accessed April 30, 2018, at http://nkaa.uky.edu/record.php?note_id=1621. This database reveals how the men in power combined sex and race to discriminate against all women. While propertied single women and widows won school district voting rights, only some women could vote due to additional voting requirements. But when African American women began to outnumber white women voters in 1902 over the appointment of an unpopular African American as head of schools for blacks the men revoked all the women's limited voting rights.

11. *CG*, 39th Congress, December 10, 1866, 46.

12. Senator Frederick Theodore Frelinghuysen, *HWS* II, 134–135.

13. Senator Reverdy Johnson, Democrat, *HWS* II, 130–134; Senator Frederick Theodore Frelinghuysen, *HWS* II, 134–135.

14. For an edited version of the debate, see *HWS* II, 102–151.

15. Speech of Senator Edgar Cowan, *HWS* II, 110–118.

16. "Affidavit of Roda Ann Childs, 25 Sept. 1866," Freedmen & Southern Society Project, History Department, University of Maryland, accessed April 30, 2018, at http://www.freedmen.umd.edu/Childs.html.

Chapter 12

1. *HWS* II, 103; *New York Tribune*, December 12, 1866.

2. Galloway, *AERA, 1866–70*, 88.

3. Ibid., 88–89. Dudden (*Fighting Chance*, 231, n. 25, 26) lists many of the meetings.

4. Galloway, *AERA, 1866–70*, 88–89.

5. Dudden, *Fighting Chance*, 90–91.

6. Galloway, *AERA, 1866–70*, 89–90.

7. "Memorial of the American Equal Rights Association to the Congress of the United States," *NASS*, 22 December 1866, cited in Galloway, *AERA, 1866–70*, 88, n. 34.

8. "Memorial of American Equal Rights Association to the Congress of the United States, 1/3/1867," Record Group 233, Petitions and Memorials, 1813–1968, National Archives Catalogue, Records of the U.S. House of Representatives, 1789–2015, accessed at https://research.archives.gov/id/7452160 June 11, 2018.

9. Gordon, *Selected Papers*, II, 22, n. 9.

10. Affecting Nevada, Colorado, Dakota, Montana, Washington, Idaho, Arizona, Utah and New Mexico, the legislation was "An Act to Regulate the Elective Franchise in the Territories of the United States," H. R. 508, *Journal of the Senate*, 87 and *House Journal*, 147-148, January 10, 1867.

11. Gordon, *Selected Papers*, II, 22, n. 8. Ohio was the first state to rescind its ratification of the 14th Amendment, doing so on January 13, 1868.

12. H.R. 987.

13. Noell ran for reelection as a Democrat to the 40th Congress, which began March 4, 1867. He served from March 4, 1865, until his death in St. Louis, Missouri, on October 3, 1867. See "Thomas Estes Noell (1839–1867)," *Biographical Directory of the United States Congress*, retrieved June 11, 2018 from http://bioguide.congress.gov/scripts/biodisplay.pl?index=N000123. See FindAGrave at http://www.findagrave.com/cgi-bin/fg.cgi?page=gr&GRid=6908141 accessed June 11, 2018.

14. The first D.C. election to include black men took place in February 1867. See Eric Foner, *Reconstruction: America's Unfinished Revolution 1863–1877* (New York: Harper & Row, 1988), 272.

Chapter 13

1. Henry B. Blackwell, *What the South Can Do: How the Southern States Can Make Themselves Masters of the Situation* (New York: Robert J. Johnston, January 15, 1867).

2. Stephen Foster in, "Special Meeting of the American Anti-Slavery Society," *NASS*, February 3, 1866.

3. Dudden, *Fighting Chance*, 93.

4. "Henry W. [*sic*] Blackwell of New York: Southern States," *Dallas Herald*, February 23, 1867, also mentioning the *Galveston News*.

5. Dudden, *Fighting Chance*, 93.

6. LS to AK, January 24, 1867, Leslie Wheeler, *Loving Warriors: Selected Letters of Lucy Stone and Henry B. Blackwell, 1853–1893* (New York: Dial, 1981), 215–216, hereinafter cited as Wheeler, *Loving Warriors*.

7. Ibid.

8. Ann Smith to Gerrit Smith, January 20, 1867, Ralph Volney Harlow, *Gerrit Smith, Philanthropist and Reformer* (New York: Henry Holt, 1939), 471.

9. See Appendix B.

10. H.R. 830.

11. *HWS* II, 270, 271.

12. ECS to FD, January 8, 1867, Gordon, *Selected Papers*, II, 11–12.

13. *HWS* II, 271.

14. Charles Z. Lincoln, *Constitutional History of New York, 1822–1894* (Rochester, NY: Lawyers' Co-operative, 1905), II, 241.

15. Ibid., 243.

16. Galloway, *AERA, 1866–70*, 89.

17. *HWS* II, 271.

18. Ibid., 269.

19. Ibid., 273.

20. Ibid.

21. Ibid., 274.

22. *CG*, 39th Congress, December 10, 1866, 38.

23. *HWS* II, 275.

24. Ibid., 276.

25. Ibid., 278–279.

26. Ibid., 271.

27. See "New York Legislature," *NYT*, March 7, 1867. Gordon (*Selected Papers*, II, 12, n. 2) draws the contrast between support for female voting rights and equal black voting rights for delegates to the constitutional convention at this time. Women were excluded very early, while ultimately no change was made to the property qualification for black men to vote for delegates. See Homer Adolph Stebbins, *A Political History of the State of New York, 1865–1869* (New York: Columbia, 1913), 212, n. 2: "All persons entitled to vote for a member of the assembly might vote for the delegates."

28. *HWS* II, 280. Lucy Stone, Henry Blackwell, Stanton, and Anthony had apparently signed the petition. See Lutz, *Rebel Crusader*, 125 and 316, n. 185. Kerr, *Stone—Speaking Out*, indicates that Stone, Stanton, and Anthony presented this petition earlier in January 1867, but DuBois, *Feminism and Suffrage*, 65, quotes from "the lone equal rights memorial against the amendment" reported in the *New York World*, November 22, 1866, 2.

29. Galloway, *AERA, 1866–70*, 89–90.

30. "Resolution of the Equal Rights Convention in Syracuse, New York, December 14, 1866," Gordon, *Selected Papers*, II, 8–9.

31. *HWS* II, 282. For more details about anti–14th Amendment activity by such as Wendell Phillips and the AASS. See McPherson, *The Struggle for Equality*," 372–374.

32. Gordon, *Selected Papers*, II, at 14–15, n. 2; *NASS* February 2, 1867.

33. "Greeley's 'friendship' a casualty," *HWS* II, 269–270. Greeley "kept his word," they later wrote, to cut women out. "We have seen the negro enfranchised, and twenty long years pass away since the war, and still woman's turn has not yet come; her rights as a citizen of the United States are still unrecognized, the oft-repeated pledges of leading Republicans and Abolitionists have not been redeemed."

34. Ibid.

Chapter 14

1. *HWS* II, 151: "In the House, January 28, 1867, Mr. Noell, of Missouri, introduced a bill to amend the suffrage act of the District of Columbia, which, after the second reading, he moved should be referred to a select committee of five and on that motion demanded the previous question, and called for the yeas and nays, which resulted in 49 yeas to 74 nays, 68 not voting" (*CG*, 39th Congress, January 28, 1867, 806).

2. The Colorado Bill, December 10, 1866, S. 462, had no reference to suffrage. The Nebraska Bill, December 5, 1866, S. 456, also did not mention suffrage. For passage of the amendments to these Bills see *House Journal*, 39th Congress, January 16, 1867, 181; and *Senate Journal*, 39th Congress, January 16, 1867, 104. Congress received the presidential veto of the Colorado Bill on January 29, 1867. See *Senate Journal*, 39th Congress, January 29, 1867, 157–162.

3. *Senate Journal*, 39th Congress, January 30, 1867, 166–169.

4. *CG*, 39th Congress, February 4, 1867, 991.

5. *Noell Speech*, 104–108.

6. McPherson, *Struggle for Equality*, 373 and n. 12.

7. *CG*, 39th Congress, February 4, 1867, 991.

8. S. 564, introduced in the Senate on February 4, 1867. H.R.1143, introduced in the House, February 5, 1867.

9. Between late November and mid-March 1867, the AERA held more than 30 meetings promoting its full agenda (Dudden, *Fighting Chance*, 231, n. 26).

10. Ibid., 92.

11. Nebraska became a state on March 1, 1867.

12. Edward McPherson, "The Political History of the United States of America during the Period of Reconstruction, from April 15, 1865, to July 15, 1870" (Washington: Solomon & Chapman, 1875), 166, in *Making of America Books*, retrieved June 29, 2018, from http://quod.lib.umich.edu/m/moa/abz4761.0001.001/3?view=image&size=100.

13. Nebraska ratified on June 15, 1867.

14. *CG*, 39th Congress, February 11, 1867, 1127–1128.

15. *Noell Speech*, 104.

16. Ibid.

17. Ibid., 107.

18. Gordon, *Selected Papers*, II, 22, n. 8.

19. Judith Sargent Murray, aka Constantia, "On the Equality of the Sexes," originally published in *Massachusetts Magazine* (Boston: I. Thomas and E.T. Andrews, 1790), II, 132–135, transcript in Mary Mark Ockerbloom, "A Celebration of Women Writers," retrieved from http://digital.library.upenn.edu/women/murray/equality/equality.html April 9, 2018.

20. Poem by Thomas Hood, 1843.

Chapter 15

1. *House Journal of the Legislative Assembly of the State of Kansas, Begun and Held at Topeka, on Tuesday, January 8th, A.D. 1867* (Leavenworth, KS: Clarke, Emery, 1867), 62–64, hereinafter referred to as *Kansas House Journal*.

2. *Senate Journal of the Legislative Assembly of the State of Kansas, Begun and Held at Topeka, on Tuesday, January 8th, A.D. 1867* (Leavenworth, KS: Clarke, Emery, 1867), 76–77.

3. *Kansas House Journal*, 186. See also Horace Edgar Flack, *The Adoption of the Fourteenth Amendment*, vol. 26 (Baltimore: Johns Hopkins Press: 1908), 172–173, retrieved from https://books.google.com/books?id=1XdDAAAAIAAJ&printsec=frontcover&dq=Flack+the+adoption+of+the+Fourteenth+Amendment&hl=en&sa=X&ved=0ahUKEwiSot3MzK_KAhWCNSYKHbgiAXQQ6AEIHTAA#v=onepage&q=172&f=false April 9, 2018, hereinafter referred to as Flack, *Fourteenth Amendment* Vol. 26.

4. *Kansas House Journal*, 64.

5. Gordon, *Selected Papers*, II, 18, n. 6. See also Jessica Reyes, *A Mere Demagoguery: Leavenworth and Atchison County Newspaper Coverage of the Kansas Women's Suffrage Campaign of 1867*, Dept. of History, Kansas State University, 11 May 2011, accessed February 4, 2016, at http://hdl.handle.net/2097/12139, hereinafter cited as Reyes, *A Mere Demagoguery*.

6. "A Step Forward," *Emporia News*, February 8, 1867.

7. "Col. Wood's Amendment," *Emporia News*, February 2, 1867, 2; "The Legislature Is Acting the Fool," *Kansas Chief*, February 14, 1867.

8. "Concurrent Resolution No. 49 of February 18, 1867," retrieved March 8, 2018, from *Kansas Memory*, accessed at http://www.kansas memory.org/item/209676.

9. *Kansas House Journal*, 62–64.

10. "Manhood Suffrage," *Emporia News*, February 15, 1867.

11. "Suffrage," *Kansas Chief*, February 7, 1867.

12. "Col. Wood's Amendment," *Emporia News*, February 2, 1867.

13. "A Step Forward," *Emporia News*, February 8, 1867.

14. Barry, *Singular Feminist*, 174–5.

15. "The Legislature Is Acting the Fool," *Kansas Chief*, February 14, 1867.

16. The author's name is unclear ("Col. Wood's Amendment," *Emporia News*, February 2, 1867).

17. Ibid.

18. Ibid.

19. See the history of the founding of the woman's rights association in Kansas Territory on February 2, 1858, at *Moneka Woman's Rights Association*, "Kansapedia," accessed May 17, 2017, at https://www.kshs.org/kansapedia/moneka-woman-s-rights-association/15158; see also Bernadette Cahill, *Money, Politics and Equal Rights for Women*, History Blog, Women's History Network Conference, Women's Material Cultures/Women's Material Environments, Leeds Trinity University, England, September 16–17, 2016, retrieved July 7, 2019, from https://womenshistorynetwork.org/money-politics-and-equal-rights-for-women/.

20. "Manhood Suffrage," *Emporia News*, February 15, 1867.

21. "A Step Forward," *Emporia News*, February 8, 1867. Gordon, *Selected Papers*, II, at 18, n. 6, states, "Historians have concluded, without much evidence, that the entire project to place women's enfranchisement on the ballot in 1867 reflected an intention on the part of a few men to defeat black suffrage." Kerr, *Stone—Speaking Out*, 267, n. 15, said that Wood, "a friend of woman suffrage, had voted against black suffrage each year since 1862," the inference being that Wood was against black suffrage.

22. Gordon, *Selected Papers*, II, 18, n. 6.

23. *Kansas Chief*, February 28, 1867.

24. "Kansas Territory had been a battleground for pro- and antislavery forces, and Kansas was the first state to protect women's rights in its constitution." Gordon, *Selected Papers*, II, 18 n. 6.

25. Gordon, *Selected Papers*, II, 16.

Chapter 16

1. Anthony anticipated 60 such conventions (SBA to AED, December 2, 1866, Anna Dickenson Papers, Library of Congress, quoted in DuBois, *Feminism and Suffrage*, 66, n. 35).

2. Editorial note, Gordon, *Selected Papers*, II, 23. Dudden, *Fighting Chance*, 92; 231, n. 26, gives a list compiled from the *NASS* of towns canvassed, beginning on January 26 and extending to March 30, 1867. Gordon (*Selected Papers*, II, at 17, n.3; 22, n.9; 23; 43, n.2; 46, n.1; 53, n.1) also gives dates for meetings between January and March 1867. See Ibid., 4–5 for the AERA announcement of the December 1867 conventions.

3. *CG*, 39th Congress, March 2, 1867, 1969–1976 at 1976.

4. The House introduced H.R. 830, *An Act to Fix the Times for the Regular Meetings of Congress*, on December 3, 1866. On January 28, Congress recorded that the president had signed it.

5. Foner, *Reconstruction*, 274, citing *CG* 39th Congress, 1097, 1176–1182, 1211; Appendix 175.

6. Dudden, *Fighting Chance*, 95.

7. ECS to SBA, December 29, 1864, Stanton and Blatch, *Letters, Diaries and Reminiscences*, II, 103–104.

8. Judith Mesinger in "The Feminist Movement as Reflected in the Gerrit Smith Papers," *Courier* 10, no. 3 (Spring 1973) (Syracuse University Library Associates), dates the letter to March 3, 1867, which indicates that Phillips had notified Anthony of his withdrawal of AERA money immediately the Military Reconstruction Act was passed on March 2.

9. SBA to GS, March 6, 1867, Gordon, *Selected Papers*, II 42–43.

10. *HWS* I, 667; Dudden, *Fighting Chance*, 22–23; Gordon, *Selected Papers* II, 43–44, n. 5.

11. *HWS* I, 667. Phillips was equally vindictive with others: in 1864 he refused a request from Garrison for aid for freedmen. See James Brewer Stewart, *Wendell Phillips: Liberty's Hero* (Baton Rouge: Louisiana State University Press, 1986), 253.

12. Sterling, *Kelley*, 337.

13. "New York Legislature," *NYT*, March 7, 1867.

14. Lucy Stone, *Woman Suffrage in New Jersey: An Address Delivered by Lucy Stone, at a Hearing before the New Jersey Legislature, March 6th, 1867* (Boston: C.H. Simonds, 1867), 14, hereinafter referred to as Stone, *Woman Suffrage in New Jersey*, accessed at https://babel.hathitrust.org/cgi/pt?id=hvd.3204401363 5727;view=1up;seq=11, May 18, 2018.

15. Ibid., 22.
16. Ibid., 34.
17. Kerr, *Stone—Speaking Out*, 121.
18. Ibid., 121–122.
19. Ibid., 123.
20. SBA to AED, March 24, 1867, Gordon, *Selected Papers*, II, 45.
21. McPherson, *Struggle for Equality*, 372–375.
22. "Fourteenth Amendment to the United States Constitution," Wikipedia, accessed at https://en.wikipedia.org/wiki/Fourteenth_Amendment_to_the_United_States_Constitution June 11, 2018. See also Flack, *Fourteenth Amendment*, vol. 26, 186–188.
23. Harper, *Life and Work* I, 275. See also Dorr, 192; Anthony, *Anthony Era*, 202; Lutz, *Rebel Crusader*, 126; Barry, *Singular Feminist*, 174.
24. *New York Evening Post*, Tuesday, March 26, 1867, 4; hereinafter referred to as *EPNY*.

Chapter 17

1. LS to ECS April 10, 1867, *HWS* II, 234.
2. Ibid.
3. Ibid.
4. HBB to ECS et al., April 21, 1867, *HWS* II, 236.
5. Ibid.
6. HBB to ECS, April 5, 1867, *HWS* II, 233.
7. Ibid.
8. LS to ECS, May 1, 1867, *HWS* II, 238.
9. HBB to ECS, April 5, 1867, *HWS* II, 233.
10. HBB to ECS et al., April 21, 1867, *HWS* II, 236.
11. LS to ECS, April 10, 1867, *HWS* II, 234.
12. HBB to ECS, April 5, 1867, *HWS* II, 232.
13. Ibid.
14. HBB to ECS et al., April 21, 1867, *HWS* II, 236.
15. LS to ECS, April 10, 1867, *HWS* II, 234.
16. HBB to ECS et al., April 21, 1867, *HWS* II, 236.
17. Ibid.
18. Ibid.
19. Ibid.
20. Ibid.
21. LS to ECS, April 10, 1867, *HWS* II, 235.
22. Ibid., 234.
23. HBB to ECS et al., April 21, *HWS* II, 235–237.
24. Dudden, *Fighting Chance*, 109–110, 112.
25. "We Fear," *Kansas Chief*, April 19, 1867.
26. Dudden, *Fighting Chance,* 110–111.
27. Gordon, *Selected Papers*, II, 50–51, n. 6.
28. Dudden, *Fighting Chance*, 113.
29. "Impartial Suffrage Convention," *Kansas Chief*, April 4, 1867.
30. Dudden, *Fighting Chance*, 111.
31. Ibid., 114.
32. "We Object," *Emporia News*, April 12, 1867.
33. LC to ECS, April 20, 1867, *HWS* II, 235.
34. Ibid.
35. HBB to ECS, April 5, 1867, *HWS* II, 233.
36. HBB to ECS, April 21, 1867, *HWS* II, 236.
37. "We Fear," *Kansas Chief*, April 19, 1867.
38. HBB to ECS, April 21, 1867, *HWS* II, 236.
39. Gordon, *Selected Papers*, II, 50–51 n. 6.
40. HBB to ECS, April 21, 1867, *HWS* II, 236.
41. HBB to ECS, April 5, 1867, *HWS* II, 233.
42. LS to ECS, April 10, 1867, *HWS* II, 234.
43. Dudden (*Fighting Chance*, 94) writes that Anthony "kept the speakers in the field just long enough to fulfill engagements." The campaign ended in Buffalo on April 12 (Gordon, *Selected Papers*, II, 53, n.1; Dudden, *Fighting Chance*, 232, n. 31).
44. SBA to Samuel N. Wood, April 21, 1867, Gordon, *Selected Papers*, II, 53–54.
45. She said that the *NASS* had given a weak, "unofficial" endorsement. See Ibid., 53–54.
46. Gordon, *Selected Papers*, II, 54; 55, n.3, and 56, n.6. Some of the tracts Susan sent were by men—still active—now effectively opposing woman's rights: an 1851 speech by Phillips, and an 1860 one by Henry Ward Beecher, both used for the Ohio campaign in 1860.
47. SBA to Samuel N. Wood, April 21, 1867, Gordon, *Selected Papers*, II, 53–54.
48. LS to SBA, May 1, 1867, *HWS* II, 237.
49. Ibid.
50. Ibid., 237–238.
51. Ibid., 238.
52. "The following communication from S.N. Wood," *Emporia News*, May 3, 1867.
53. "A Woman's View of Lucy Stone," *Emporia News*, May 3, 1867, gives excellent insights into attitudes to women at the time.
54. Gordon, *Selected Papers*, II, 22, n. 9. See also, "Manhood Suffrage in Ohio," *NYT*, April 4, 1867.
55. The Democrats won 63 seats and the Republicans 97; the majority was 34. See Homer Adolph Stebbins, *A Political History of the State of New York, 1865–1869* (New York: Columbia University, 1913), 213.
56. Katherine T. Corbett, *In Her Place: A Guide to St. Louis Women's History* (St. Louis: Missouri Historical Society Press, 1999), 132–134. Minor wrote Senator Gratz Brown thanking him for his support in Congress of woman suffrage. In March 1867 she presented a petition of more than 350 names to the Missouri Legislature. It was unsuccessful. See also "Virginia Minor," *Historic Missourians*, State Historical Society of Missouri, accessed April

7, 2016, at http://shsmo.org/historicmissourians/
name/m/minor/.

Chapter 18

1. "The Anniversaries: Thirty-Fourth Annual Meeting of the Anti-Slavery Society,"
NYT, May 8, 1867.
2. A. Caperton Braxton, "The 15th Amendment: An Account of Its Enactment," in Eugene
C. Massie, ed., *Report of the Fifteenth Annual
Meeting of the Virginia State Bar Association,
Held at Hot Springs of Virginia, August 26, 27
and 28, 1903* (Richmond: Everett Waddey, 1903),
243–308, at 300.
3. "The Anniversaries: Thirty-Fourth Annual Meeting of the Anti-Slavery Society,"
NYT, May 8, 1867.
4. McPherson, *Struggle for Equality*, 323, 355.
5. *The Southern Loyalists' Convention: Call
for a Convention of Southern Unionists, to Meet
at Independence Hall, Philadelphia, on Monday,
the Third Day of September, 1866* (Tribune Tracts
No. 2, Philadelphia [?], 1866), accessed in Hathi
Trust Digital Library April 13, 2018, at https:
//babel.hathitrust.org/cgi/pt?id=loc.ark:/13960
/t3417359p;view=1up;seq=1; Goldsmith, *Other
Powers*, 122–125; McPherson, *Struggle for Equality*, 360–363.
6. Parker Pillsbury, "The Face of the Sky,"
NASS, April 27, 1867. He wrote that Phillips,
Greeley, and Theodore Tilton by the date of
his letter—April 20—were agitating for so-
called impartial or universal suffrage nationwide through a 15th amendment.
7. "The Anniversaries: Thirty-Fourth Annual Meeting of the Anti-Slavery Society,"
NYT, May 8, 1867.
8. See "Speech of Col. T.W. Higginson,"
NASS, May 18, 1867.
9. *AERA First Anniversary Proceedings*, 5–7.
10. Ibid.
11. *Cincinnati Daily Enquirer*, Tuesday, May
14, 1867. This news report came from the *New
York World*. Gage attacked Phillips on day two
over his analysis of the sources of intemper-
ance, for which he blamed "Saxon blood."
12. "The Anniversaries—Equal Rights Association Second Day," *NYT*, May 11, 1867.
13. Ibid. Wright's words here seem more
pointed than in the *AERA First Anniversary
Proceedings*, at 67, and *HWS* II, 220 versions,
where he appears as "Mr. Henry C. Wright."
The Newburyport, Massachusetts-based Garrisonian abolitionist had supported the Grimké
sisters in the 1830s and Lucy Stone in 1850 in
women's equality controversies. He was one of
the first postwar abolitionists to support true
universal suffrage. See "Henry Clarke Wright,"

https://en.wikipedia.org/wiki/Henry_Clarke_
Wright, accessed April 3, 2018. The *New York
Tribune* omits much detail on Wright, while
reporting Downing's criticism of Stanton in
depth. The *NASS* neglected to cover this debate.
14. "The Anniversaries—Equal Rights Association Second Day," *NYT*, May 11, 1867.
15. SBA to GS, March 6, 1867, Gordon, *Selected Papers* II, 42–43.
16. *AERA First Anniversary Proceedings*, 53;
HWS II, 214.
17. "The Anniversaries—Equal Rights Association Second Day," *NYT*, May 11, 1867. Her
reply does not appear in either the *Proceedings*,
53, or in *HWS* II, 214.
18. *AERA First Anniversary Proceedings*, 53;
HWS II, 214. Neither the *NYT* nor the *New
York Tribune* reported well what happened
next, but the *Proceedings* recorded it, which
HWS II repeated.
19. Ibid.
20. Dudden, *Fighting Chance*, 98, states
Downing made a habit of targeting equal rights
meetings to insist on enfranchising black males
first.
21. *AERA First Anniversary Proceedings*,
53–54; *HWS* II, 214–215.
22. "The Anniversaries—Equal Rights Association Second Day," *NYT*, May 11, 1867.
The exact terminology is unclear: *Proceedings*, 53, and *HWS* II, 214, say "colored" not
"black" men. Remond's statement does not appear in this manner in either. The *New York
Tribune* summarized considerable contention
in one small paragraph.
23. *AERA First Anniversary Proceedings*,
53–54.
24. Ibid.
25. Ibid. Note that women had voted in
New Jersey until 1807.
26. Ibid.
27. *AERA First Anniversary Proceedings*,
54–55; *HWS* II, 214–5. As recently as the Albany meeting in December 1866, Stanton had
rejected educated suffrage because blacks had
no schools.
28. *AERA First Anniversary Proceedings*,
53–55; Gordon, *Selected Papers*, II, 71 n. 12.
29. *AERA First Anniversary Proceedings*,
55–60.
30. Ibid., 58.
31. Ibid., 60.
32. Ibid., 61.
33. Stone to Anthony, May 9, 1867, *HWS* II,
238. Stone, in fact, had sent a letter on May 6,
1867, to Anthony. Arriving too late for the
meeting, it appeared for the record in the
AERA First Anniversary Proceedings, 71–72.
34. LS to SBA, May 9, 1867, *HWS* II, 238.

Chapter 19

1. "Call for the First Anniversary Meeting," dated March 12, 1867, in *AERA First Anniversary Proceedings*, 3–4.

2. While some northern and western states banned black male voting outright, in others they could vote, if they met hefty property qualifications. See Alexander Keyssar, *The Right to Vote: The Contested History of Democracy in the United States* (New York: Basic Books, 2000).

3. Nell Irvin Painter, *Sojourner Truth: A Life, A Symbol* (New York: W.W. Norton, 1996), 230.

4. *AERA First Anniversary Proceedings*, 55.

5. "The Anniversaries—Equal Rights Association Second Day," *NYT*, May 11, 1867. Galloway, *AERA, 1866–70*, at 201, gives her full name.

6. *AERA First Anniversary Proceedings*, 61–62.

7. See Appendix D.

8. Sojourner Truth, *AERA First Anniversary Proceedings*, AERA Convention, May 9, 1867, *HWS* II, 193.

9. Ibid.

10. FDG, *HWS* II, 197; *AERA First Anniversary Proceedings*, 27.

11. *HWS* II, 173.

12. ECS, "Pronunciamento," *The Revolution*, July 15, 1869.

13. "Political and Militant," *The Vote*, August 8, 1916. In 1918 Britain, all men were enfranchised but only half of all women.

Chapter 20

1. *AERA First Anniversary Proceedings*, 61.

2. LS to SBA, May 9, 1867, *HWS* II, 238. Stone was very angry with eastern men. See her letter to Anthony of May 6, 1867, *AERA First Anniversary Proceedings*, 71–72.

3. *AERA First Anniversary Proceedings*, 71–72.

4. LS to SBA, May 9, 1867, *HWS* II, 238.

5. Ibid.

6. Gordon, *Selected Papers*, II, 51, n. 10.

7. "Impartial Suffrage," *Emporia News*, May 10, 1867.

8. "Suffrage Canvass," *Emporia News*, May 3, 1867.

9. See also Reyes, *A Mere Demagoguery*.

10. LS to SBA, May 9, 1867, *HWS* II, 238.

11. Ibid.

12. "Republican State Central Committee," *Watertown (NY) Daily Reformer*, May 16, 1867; "Meeting of the Republican State Central Committee," *Watertown (NY) Patriot*, May 18, 1867.

13. "Republican State Central Committee," *Daily Reformer*, May 16, 1867.

14. "Address to the Republicans of the State of Kansas," *Emporia News*, May 24, 1867.

15. "Republican State Central Committee," *Atchison Champion*, May 23, 1867.

16. "Address to the Republicans of the State of Kansas," *Emporia News*, May 24, 1867.

17. HBB to ECS et al., April 21, 1867, *HWS*, II, 236.

18. LS to SBA, May 9, 1867, *HWS* II, 239. Already on April 25 Stone had written to the *Atchison Champion* denying its scurrilous lies. The *Kansas Chief* reproduced her letter on June 6, 1867.

19. "The Suffrage Meeting," *Emporia News*, May 17, 1867.

20. "Another 'Woman's View of Lucy Stone and Female Suffrage,'" *Emporia News*, May 17, 1867.

21. Joseph G. Gambone, "The Forgotten Feminist of Kansas: The Papers of Clarina I. H. Nichols, 1854–1885, IV, 515–563: The Papers, 1867–8," *Kansas Historical Quarterly*, Winter 1973 (Vol. 39, No. 4); hereinafter referred to as Gambone, *Forgotten Feminist*, retrieved from https://www.kshs.org/p/the-forgotten-feminist-of-kansas-4/13241 April 30, 2018. See also, "Diane Eickhoff," *Revolutionary Heart: The Life of Clarina Nichols and the Pioneering Crusade for Women's Rights* (Kansas City: Quindaro Press, 2006), and *Clarina Nichols: Frontier Crusader for Women's Rights* (Kansas City: Quindaro Press, 2016).

22. Clarina I.H. Nichols, *Wyandotte (KS) Commercial Gazette*, May 28, 1867.

23. "Hon. Sidney Clarke," *Emporia News*, May 24, 1867.

24. "Proceedings of the New England Anti-Slavery Convention," *NASS*, June 8 and 15, 1867. DuBois, *Feminism and Suffrage*, 72–73.

25. See "Speech of Col. T.W. Higginson," *NASS*, May 18, 1867.

26. "Proceedings of the New England Anti-Slavery Convention," *NASS*, June 15, 1867.

27. *New York Tribune*, May 29, 1867, quoted in Harper, *Life and Work* I, 281, 294, n. 42.

28. "Womanhood Suffrage," *EPNY*, Monday, June 3, 1867.

29. DuBois, *Feminism and Suffrage*, 74 points to a "naïve analysis" that allowed abolitionists to apply widely different standards to women and black men, even while calling for equality. The difference could just as well be ascribed to lack of principle.

Chapter 21

1. "Woman Suffrage," *Plain Dealer*, June 7, 1867. Note the numbers are population figures and not voting-age adults.

2. Ibid.

3. "Lucy Stone's Protest," *Kansas Chief*, June 6, 1867.

4. Charles Vernon Eskridge had lived in Kansas since 1855 and moved to Emporia, where he became one of the town's early leaders and was subsequently elected to many positions, including lieutenant-governor (1869–71). Robert Christopher Childers, "Charles Vernon Eskridge and Kansas politics, 1855–1900," master's thesis, Department of Social Sciences, Emporia State University (Emporia, Kansas: 2004), accessed April 3, 2018, at https://esirc.emporia.edu/handle/123456789/976; hereinafter referred to as Childers, *Eskridge*. See also "Kansas Lieutenant Governors," Kansas Historical Society, accessed April 3, 2018, at https://www.kshs.org/p/kansas-lieutenant-governors/10998#eskridge.

5. Charles V. Eskridge to *Emporia News*, June 7, 1867. For the relationship between C.V. Eskridge and Jacob Stotler, the *Emporia News* owner, see Childers, *Eskridge*, 11.

6. "Should Women Vote? Important Affirmative Authority," *Emporia News*, June 14, 1867.

7. William Frank Zornow, "'Bluff Ben' Wade in Lawrence, Kansas: The Issue of Class Conflict," *Ohio History Journal* 65, no. 1 (January 1956), 44–52, retrieved from http://resources.ohiohistory.org/ohj/browse/displaypages.php?display%5B%5D=0065&display%5B%5D=44&display%5B%5D=52 April 14, 2018, hereinafter referred to as Zornow, "'Bluff Ben' Wade."

8. "Senator Wade's Speech at Lawrence, Kansas," datelined June 13, *NYT*, June 20, 1867; "The Union Pacific Railroad," *NYT*, June 11, 1867, hereinafter referred to as "Wade's Speech, 1867."

9. Ibid.

10. Ibid.

11. Ibid.; "The Senatorial Excursion," datelined Fort Riley, Kansas, June 12, 1867, in *NYT*, June 23, 1867; Zornow, "'Bluff Ben' Wade."

12. "The Senatorial Excursion," datelined Fort Riley, Kansas, June 12, 1867, in *NYT*, June 23, 1867.

13. Zornow, "'Bluff Ben' Wade."

14. Edward F. Underhill, official stenographer, *Proceedings and Debates of the Constitutional Convention of the State of New York, Held in 1867 and 1868 in the City of Albany*, vol. I (Albany, New York: Weed, Parsons and Company, 1868), 38, retrieved from http://babel.hathitrust.org/cgi/pt?id=umn.31951p01104033t;view=1up;seq=7 June 23, 2016, hereinafter referred to as Underhill, *New York Constitution Proceedings*.

15. Flack, *Fourteenth Amendment*, Vol. 26, 189. See also "Fourteenth Amendment to the United States Constitution," Wikipedia, accessed April 11, 2018, at https://en.wikipedia. org/wiki/Fourteenth_Amendment_to_the_United_States_Constitution.

16. "Fourteenth Amendment to the United States Constitution," Wikipedia, accessed April 11, 2018, at https://en.wikipedia.org/wiki/Fourteenth_Amendment_to_the_United_States_Constitution.

17. Clarina I.H. Nichols from Quindaro, Kansas, February 24, 1867, to the *Vermont Brattleboro Phoenix*, Gambone, *The Forgotten Feminist*. The 19th Amendment in 1920 successfully concluded the first successful nonviolent civil rights campaign in U.S. history. See Bernadette Cahill, *Alice Paul and the National Woman's Party: The First Civil Rights Struggle of the 20th Century* (Jefferson, NC: McFarland, 2015), hereinafter cited as Cahill, *Alice Paul*.

18. "Thursday's Daily," *Atchison Champion*, May 30, 1867.

19. Clarina I.H. Nichols to *Western Home Journal*, June 18th, 1867," in Gambone, *Forgotten Feminist*.

20. Ibid.

21. A reception for the visitors was held in St. Louis on June 14. See "From St. Louis," *Indianapolis Daily Herald*, 17 June 1867.

22. "A Raid on the Doctors: George Francis Train on Hygiene and Other Things; Some Extracts from a Rambling Speech of His in New York," *Plain Dealer*, April 24, 1867.

23. "George Francis Train: His Speech on the Summit of Pilot Knob," datelined June 17, St. Louis Dispatch, *Memphis Daily Avalanche*, June 27, 1867.

24. George Francis Train, *The Great Epigram Campaign of Kansas*, 3–4, Kansas Historical Society, retrieved from http://www.kansasmemory.org/item/206263, April 3, 2016, hereinafter referred to as Train, *Epigram*.

25. Underhill, *New York Constitution Proceedings*, 82.

26. Ibid., 95; *Journal of the Convention of the State of New York Begun and Held at the Capitol in the City of Albany on the 4th day of June 1867*, 78, hereinafter referred to as *New York Constitution Journal*.

27. Goldsmith, *Other Powers*, 132.

28. Ibid., 132.

29. *HWS* II, 269–270.

30. Goldsmith, *Other Powers*, 132.

31. Harper, *Life and Work* I, 280.

32. Olympia Brown, *Acquaintances Old and New, Among Reformers* (Olympia Brown: 1911), 55, hereinafter referred to as Brown, *Acquaintances*.

Chapter 22

1. "The Term 'elm peeler,' according to the old masters of the Hoosier language, signifies

a slur," in "'Elm Peeler' No Slur: Man Who Gathers Slippery Bark Furnishes Basis for Patent Medicines," *Tribune* (Chicago), May 29, 1904. "Call an Indiana man an 'elm peeler' and you wreck his pride. Usually it draws from him a venomous retort." See also *Annual Iowa Year Book of Agriculture*, J. Simpson, Ed. (Des Moines, Iowa: 1904): "On the Ohio side [of the river] was shown a long-nosed, slab-sided, razor-backed elm-peeler, with starvation minutely pictured in his face."

2. No title, *Springfield Republican*, June 21, 1867.

3. "A Rich Mine," *Kansas Chief*, June 20, 1867.

4. Reyes, *A Mere Demagoguery*, 23.

5. "The Suffrage Meeting," *Weekly Free Press*, June 22, 1867, cited in Reyes, *A Mere Demagoguery*, 24 and 28, n. 53.

6. "Womanhood Suffrage," *EPNY*, Monday, June 3, 1867.

7. See, for example, "A correspondent of the *Boston Congregationalist,* in a letter from New York, tells us, 'A Constitutional Convention is to be held shortly in this State, and we expect to see universal suffrage adopted. The Strong-Minded Women aim to secure female voting, but they will fail, as they should'" (*HWS* II, 228). Editors used this pejorative regularly during the Kansas campaign.

8. *New York Constitution Proceedings*, 126–127.

9. *New York Constitution Journal*, 137–138.

10. Ibid., 180.

11. SBA to Lucy Read Anthony, June 28, 1867, referring to delegate Curtis's work of that day for women during the convention, Gordon, *Selected Papers*, II, 78.

12. "Female Suffrage," *New York Herald*, June 28, 1867;

13. "The Convention," *New York Tribune*, June 28, 1867.

14. *HWS* II, 284.

15. "Female Suffrage," *New York Herald*, June 28, 1867; *HWS* II, 284.

16. *HWS* II, 284. Harper (*Life and Work I*, at 278) wrote, "'Miss Anthony, you know the ballot and the bullet go together. If you vote, are you ready to fight?' Instantly she retorted: 'Yes, Mr. Greeley, just as you fought in the late war—at the point of a goose-quill!'" Harper reported that Anthony's answer produced "merriment." Whatever her words, Anthony pointed to Greeley's hypocrisies.

17. *HWS* II, at 284, notes the *Albany Evening Journal* of June 28, 1867, "said, editorially" that Anthony, "in response to queries … said she expected that women would … be drafted. Several hundred had fought in the late war, but when their sex was discovered they were dis-

missed in disgrace; and to the shame of the Government be it said, they were never paid for their services."

18. *HWS* II, 286.

19. *New York Tribune*, "The Convention," June 28, 1867.

20. SBA to Lucy Read Anthony, June 28, 1867, Gordon, *Selected Papers*, II, 78.

21. *The Revolution*, January 29, 1868.

22. *HWS* II, 286–287.

23. Ibid.

24. See Gordon, *Selected Papers*, II, 74, n. 2; Mabel Abbott, Compiler, *George William Curtis Papers* (New York: Staten Island Museum Archives and Library Special Collections), retrieved April 6, 2016 from http://www.staten islandmuseum.org/images/uploads/collections/ Curtis_(George_William)_Papers_Finding_ Aids.pdf.

25. *HWS* II, 286–287.

26. Ibid.

27. *New York Constitution Journal*, 82, 98; at 151, on June 26, Delegate Ezra Graves presented 37 petitions, making 40 petitions in all presented on that day.

28. *New York Constitution Journal*, 163.

29. Ibid., 172–173.

30. *New York Constitution Proceedings*, 176.

31. The story seems due less to faulty memories than to deliberate distortion to increase the story's impact. *HWS* II, 286 lists the petitions submitted to the New York Convention from July 1, 1867, until July 31, 1867, excluding mention of Mrs. Greeley's petition on July 16. Having created their narrative, they left out inconvenient facts.

32. *HWS* II, 285; *New York Constitution Proceedings*, 177–179, at 178–179.

33. Clarina I.H. Nichols of Kansas had written the previous February: "Each and every reason, yet given, why women, as a class, should not have and exercise the right of suffrage is equally conclusive against its possession by men" (Nichols, from Quindaro, Kansas, February 24, 1867, to the editor, *Brattleboro Vermont Phoenix*, Gambone, *Forgotten Feminist.*

34. *New York Constitution Proceedings*, 177–181 at 179.

35. Blackwell to Henry Wadsworth Longfellow, June 28, 1867 (Houghton Library, Harvard University, cited in DuBois, *Feminism and Suffrage*, 91 and n. 39).

36. "Lucy Stone—Again," *Emporia News*, June 28, 1867.

Chapter 23

1. *New York Constitution Proceedings*, 192.

2. Brown, *Acquaintances*, 55–56.

3. Dudden, *Fighting Chance*, 115–117.

4. SBA to AED, July 12, 1867, Gordon, *Selected Papers* II, 79–80.

5. For the colorful life of Milton Reynolds see Dan W. Peery, "Hon. Milton W. Reynolds (Kicking Bird)," *Chronicles of Oklahoma* 13, no. 1 (March 1935), accessed April 12, 2016, at http://digital.library.okstate.edu/Chronicles/v013/v013p046.html.

6. Brown, *Acquaintances*, 55–56.

7. Ibid., 57–58.

8. "Mrs. E. Cady Stanton on Mr. Greeley's Report Against Female Suffrage," *NYT*, July 4, 1867, reprinting letter from the *EPNY.*

9. "American Equal Rights Association," *New York Herald*, July 5, 1867.

10. "Sen. Ross on the Issues of the Hour," *Emporia News*, July 5, 1867.

11. *New York Constitution Proceedings*, 194.

12. Ibid., 199.

13. "A Despatch," *Daily National Intelligencer* (Washington, D.C.), July 11, 1867; "Equal Rights Association," *Washington (D.C.) Evening Star*, July 12, 1867. During the 1867 AERA anniversary meeting, Josephine Griffing advocated a campaign to win female suffrage in the nation's capital (see *AERA First Anniversary Proceedings*, 61–62). She formed a local branch of the AERA on July 11 in Washington, D.C.

14. Ibid., 215.

15. "The Convention," *New York Tribune*, July 11, 1867.

16. Gordon, *Selected Papers*, II, 80, n. 2.

17. *New York Constitution Proceedings*, 232.

18. *Washington (D.C.) Evening Star*, July 12, 1867.

19. *AERA First Anniversary Proceedings*, May 1867, 61.

20. *New York Constitution Proceedings*, 250–251.

21. "The Pernicious Proposition," *Emporia News*, July 12, 1867.

22. Dudden, *Fighting Chance*, 118–119.

23. "George Francis Train and Woman Suffrage," *New York Tribune*, letter of Train dated July 15, 1867, Train, *Epigram*, 3–4.

24. "George Francis Train and Woman Suffrage" (*New York Tribune*, August 1, 1867) first carried the story of Train's letter of July 15 sent to Mrs. W.T. Hazard of the St. Louis Woman Suffrage Association.

Chapter 24

1. SBA to AED, July 12, 1867, Gordon, *Selected Papers*, II, 79–80.

2. "Mass Convention in Westchester Co., New York," *NASS*, July 20, 1867.

3. "The Constitutional Convention," *NYT*, July 18, 1867.

4. *New York Constitution Proceedings*, 283.

5. Ibid.

6. *Springfield (MA) Republican*, July 20, 1867.

7. *Columbus (OH) Crisis*, July 31, 1867.

8. "Personal," *NASS*, July 20, 1867.

9. "Woman in Politics," *New York Tribune*, July 26, 1867.

10. Harper, *Life and Work* I, 281–282. See also, for example, Kerr, *Stone—Speaking Out*, 126, stating, "Greeley's support ended abruptly following a political miscalculation on the part of Stanton and Anthony...."

11. ECS to Emily Howland, September 1, 1867, Stanton and Blatch, *Letters, Diaries and Reminiscences*, II, 116–119.

12. Gordon, *Selected Papers*, II, 77 n. 3.

13. See "Horace Greeley, *Emporia News*, June 7, 1867.

14. "Jefferson Davis and His Friends," *Kansas Chief*, June 20, 1867.

15. "One Mrs. Miller," *St. Johnsbury (VT) Caledonian*, June 28, 1867.

16. "Raphael Semmes," *Kansas Chief*, July 25, 1867. Semmes was a former U.S. naval officer turned privateer for the Confederacy.

17. "Mrs. Swisshelm," *Kansas Chief*, July 4, 1867.

18. L.P. Brockett and Mary C. Vaughan, *Woman's Work in the Civil War: A Record of Heroism, Patriotism and Patience* (Boston: Zeigler, McCurdy, 1867), retrieved from https://archive.org/details/womansworkincivi5900broc, June 8, 2018.

19. *New York Constitution Proceedings*, 350.

20. Ibid., 356.

21. Ibid., 364. July 18 begins on page 349, the 4:00 P.M. session starting at 364.

22. Ibid., 364.

23. Speech of George Curtis, *New York Constitution Proceedings*, 364–372; *HWS* II, 288–304; "The Constitutional Convention," *NYT*, July 21, 1867.

24. Gordon, *Selected Papers*, II, 85.

25. Speech of George Curtis, *New York Constitution Proceedings*, 364–372; *HWS* II, 288–304; "The Constitutional Convention," *NYT*, July 21, 1867.

26. *New York Constitution Proceedings*, 391.

27. "The Suffrage Canvas," *Emporia News*, July 19, 1867.

28. *New York Constitution Proceedings*, 411.

29. "The Constitutional Convention," *NYT*, July 21, 1867.

30. "Suffrage Meeting," *Emporia News*, August 2, 1867.

31. *New York Constitution Proceedings*, 466.

32. Ibid., 468–469.

33. Ibid., 470.
34. "Constitutional Convention," *NYT*, July 24, 1867.
35. *New York Constitution Proceedings*, 493.
36. "A Canvass Needed," and "State Affairs," *Leavenworth Daily Conservative*, July 24 and 26, 1867, cited in Dudden, *Fighting Chance*, 120 and 240, n. 90.
37. *New York Constitution Proceedings*, 537–538.
38. Ibid., 540.
39. Ibid.
40. Ibid., 547.
41. "Impartial Suffrage," and "Lt. Gov. Green on Impartial Suffrage," *Emporia News*, July 26, 1867.
42. *New York Constitution Proceedings*, 624.

Chapter 25

1. Harper, *Life and Work* I, 282–283.
2. Bisbee had campaigned for the AERA in New York. See *HWS* II, 182.
3. Gambone, *Forgotten Feminist*.
4. Brown, *Acquaintances*, 72–73.
5. Ibid., 62–64.
6. "Olympia Brown," *Lowell (MA) Daily Citizen and News*, August 1, 1867.
7. "Suffrage Meeting," *Emporia News*, August 2, 1867.
8. "The Female Suffrage Meeting," *Emporia News*, August 9, 1867.
9. Ibid.
10. "Rev. Olympia Brown" and "Rev. Samuel E. McBurney," *Emporia News*, August 9, 1867. See also "The Bible on Female Suffrage," *Emporia News*, August 9, 1867.
11. "Proposed Amendments," *Emporia News*, August 9, 1867.
12. "Our Suffrage Imbroglio," *Emporia News*, August 9, 1867.
13. SBA to unnamed recipient, possibly Parker Pillsbury, from Salina, Kansas, September 12, 1867, *HWS* II, 242–243.
14. After a short sojourn in Martha's Vineyard that summer, Stone and Blackwell went to New York to work in the AERA office while Anthony hunted campaign funds for Kansas (Wheeler, *Loving Warriors*, 214).
15. SBA to Wood, August 9, 1867, Holland and Gordon, *ECS and SBA Papers*, reel 12, frames 344–349, cited in Dudden, *Fighting Chance*, 106 and 236, n. 118, and 120 and 240, n. 91.
16. Harper, *Life and Work* I, 282–283. Harper said Anthony and Stanton left for Kansas on August 28. SBA mentioned in a letter around August 21 that she was leaving "one week from today."

17. "SBA in a private note, dated Albany, N.Y., March 12," *NASS*, March 16, 1867.
18. "Purifying Politics," *Emporia News*, June 7, 1867.
19. See *AERA First Anniversary Proceedings*, 77–80, for the list of contributions for both 1866 and 1867. Most contributions were $1.00.
20. Francis Jackson died on November 14, 1861, his will dated January 28, 1861.
21. *Notes of Will of Francis Jackson, January 28, 1861*, retrieved from Boston Public Library Anti-Slavery Collection, April 14, 2018, at https://archive.org/stream/willoffrancisjac00mays/3 9999063811150#page/n0/mode/2up.
22. Dudden, *Fighting Chance*, 68 and 225, n. 39.
23. Samuel J. May, *Francis Jackson's Anti Slavery Bequest*, originally sent for publication on August 27, 1867, to Aaron A. Powell of the *NASS*; it was subsequently rejected and returned (Boston Public Library Anti-Slavery Collection, retrieved April 14, 2018 from https://archive.org/details/francisjacksonsa00mays). Neither Anthony nor Stone was included in this meeting. Case reporting dates the decision to January 1867 (see *Edmund Jackson vs. Wendell Phillips et al.*, 14 Allen 539, 96 Mass. 539, 571, January 1867, Suffolk County, Massachusetts, accessed April 14, 2018, at Commonwealth of Massachusetts, Trial Court Law Libraries, masscases.com at http://masscases.com/cases/sjc/96/96mass539.html).
24. "Concerning Wills," *Commonwealth*, February 16, 1867.
25. "The Diversion of Francis Jackson's Bequest," *Commonwealth*, August 17, 1867; "The Jackson Bequest," *Commonwealth*, September 7, 1867; "Francis Jackson's Will," *NASS*, August 10, 1867; "Mr. Garrison and the Jackson Bequest," *NASS*, August 24, 1867.
26. SBA to AED, August 1867, Holland and Gordon, *ECS and SBA Papers*, reel 12, frames 369–70, cited in Dudden, *Fighting Chance*, 106 and 236, n. 113.
27. In January 1866 he called the 51-year-old Stanton—a mother of seven—"child" (WP to ECS, January 14, 1866, Frost and Cullen-DuPont, *Eyewitness History*, 180).
28. "Concerning Wills," *Commonwealth*, February 16, 1867; "The Diversion of Francis Jackson's Bequest," *Commonwealth*, August 17, 1867; "The Jackson Bequest," *Commonwealth*, September 7, 1867; "Francis Jackson's Will," *NASS*, August 10, 1867; "Mr. Garrison and the Jackson Bequest," *NASS*, August 24, 1867.
29. SBA to AED, August (nd) 1867, Holland and Gordon, *ECS and SBA Papers*, reel 12, frames 369–370, cited in Dudden, *Fighting Chance*, 106 and 236, n. 115.
30. The only attorney at the trial, an S.E.

Sewell, representing "one of the trustees" argued, among other issues, for the Women's Rights Fund. Another attorney represented unspecified trustees. The heirs had their own representation. The women, per se, with their unique concerns and interests, were not represented (*Edmund Jackson vs. Wendell Phillips et al.*, 14 Allen 539, 96 Mass. 539, 571, January 1867, Suffolk County, Massachusetts, 545–546).

31. At the time, women could not be practicing attorneys.

32. Like so much of the dubious Jackson Fund episode, it is unknown why some of this money was not advanced for Olympia Brown and Bessie Bisbee.

33. SBA to Wood, August 9, 1867, Holland and Gordon, *ECS and SBA Papers*, reel 12, frames 344–349 cited in Dudden, *Fighting Chance*, 106 and 236, n. 118; 120 and 240, n. 91.

34. Barry, *Singular Feminist*, 174.

35. LS to HBB, October 13, 1867; HBB to LS, October 25, 1867, Wheeler, *Loving Warriors*, 220.

36. Wendell Phillips' conduct with the Jackson Fund is suspicious. Some accounting was made, but biographers of Anthony say only that Stone and Blackwell used up the $1,500. See Harper, *Life and Work* I, 275; Dorr, 192; Anthony, *Anthony Era*, 202.

Chapter 26

1. "A Protest Against Woman Suffrage in Kansas," *Flake's Weekly Galveston Bulletin*, September 28, 1867, reprinting an undated news story from the *Cincinnati Times*.

2. "Impartial Suffrage," *Kansas Chief*, August 15, 1867.

3. "Meeting of the Opponents of Female Suffrage," *Emporia News*, August 16, 1867.

4. HBB to LS, October 25, 1867, Wheeler, *Loving Warriors*, 221.

5. "If [Wood] should die next month I should consider the election lost" (HBB to ECS, April 21, 1867, *HWS* II, 236).

6. "What a Compliment," *Emporia News* August 16, 1867.

7. "Experimental Legislation," *Emporia News*, August 16, 1867.

8. All quotations in the next several paragraphs are from a letter of Mrs. W.T. Hazard to Samuel N. Wood, August 20, 1867 (Olympia Brown Willis Papers, ca. 1849–1963, digitized microfilm Series 3, correspondence folder number 142, other to other, 1863–1903 [scattered]; Schlesinger Library, Radcliffe Institute, Harvard University, Cambridge, Massachu-

setts). DuBois (*Feminism and Suffrage*, at 94. n. 47) cited the letter as Mrs. W.T. Hazard to SBA, August 20, 1867.

9. For the original disclosure of this document, see Barry, Singular Feminist, 179–187, at 181, and 391, n. 14, citing Isabella Beecher Hooker to Susan Howard, January 2, 1870, from notes taken during her meeting with Blackwell in late 1869 (Document 98/E5–10, Harriet Beecher Stowe Center, formerly the Stowe-Day Foundation). See also White, *The Beecher Sisters*, 137–138, and 351, n. 137.

10. LS to SBA, May 9, 1867, *HWS* II, 238.

11. Isabella Beecher Hooker to Susan Howard, January 2, 1870.

12. "Rev. S.E. McBurney and Hon. C.V. Eskridge," *Emporia News*, August 23, 1867.

13. "The Suffrage Question," *Kansas Chief*, August 22, 1867.

14. Dudden, *Fighting Chance*, 122.

15. "The Suffrage Question," *Kansas Chief*, August 22, 1867.

16. Ibid.

17. Letter to the editor from "Coeur de Leon," *Kansas Chief*, September 12, 1867.

18. Ibid.

19. Ibid.

20. LS to SBA, May 9, 1867, *HWS* II, 238.

21. Dudden, *Fighting Chance*, 122.

22. Ibid.

23. Ibid., 123.

24. Ibid., 124.

25. "Hon. Thaddeus H. Walker," *Emporia News*, August 23, 1867.

26. SBA to Lydia Maria Child, August 23, 1867; *HWS* II, 239–240.

27. Harper, *Life and Work* I, 283.

28. "Olympia Brown's Movements," *Emporia News*, August 30, 1867.

Chapter 27

1. "Sliding Off," *Kansas Chief*, August 29, 1867.

2. "Anti-female Suffrage in Emporia," *Emporia News*, September 6, 1867.

3. Ibid.; Gordon, *Selected Papers*, II, 93 n. 5.

4. "Anti-female Suffrage in Emporia," *Emporia News*, September 6, 1867; Gordon, *Selected Papers*, II, 93, n. 5.

5. Reyes, *A Mere Demagoguery*, 5.

6. "Impartial Suffrage Meeting at Atchison," *Leavenworth Bulletin*, September 3, 1867.

7. "Anti-Female Suffrage at Burlingame," *Emporia News,* September 6, 1867.

8. "Democratic," *Emporia News*, September 6, 1867.

9. "Impudent," *Emporia News*, September 6, 1867.

10. "Stand by the Party," *Emporia News*, September 6, 1867.

11. Kerr, *Stone—Speaking Out*, 126.

12. Ibid.

13. Harper, *Life and Work* I, 283.

14. See "Suffrage Meetings," *Leavenworth Bulletin*, September 5, 1867, for a sample of the meetings that Wood arranged.

15. "Suffrage Meeting at Wyandotte," *Leavenworth Bulletin*, September 6, 1867.

16. "Impartial Suffrage in Kansas," *Washington (D.C.) Evening Star*, September 21, 1867. This report omits a date for the Lawrence meeting. The dating here is based on Anthony's letter of September 15, 1867, to an unnamed recipient, in *HWS* II, in which she said the anti-women forces "held a meeting here [Lawrence, where she was staying] the day after ours." The distance between the two locations was about 30 miles.

17. "Manhood Suffrage," *Emporia News*, September 13, 1867.

18. "Why This Fluttering?" *Kansas Chief*, September 12, 1867.

19. "Letter from Lawrence," *Emporia News*, September 13, 1867.

20. *HWS* II, 243.

21. "Their Plan of Campaign," *Kansas Chief*, September 5, 1867. Bessie Bisbee appears to have left Kansas early in August because of illness.

22. "Suffrage Meetings," *Leavenworth Bulletin*, September 5, 1867.

23. Harper, *Life and Work* I, 283.

24. SBA to unnamed recipient, possibly Parker Pillsbury or Lucy Stone, September 15, 1867, from Lawrence, Kansas, *HWS* II, 242–243.

25. *HWS* II, 239.

26. SBA to unnamed recipient, possibly Parker Pillsbury or Lucy Stone (*HWS* II, 242–243).

27. LS to HBB, October 13, 1867, Wheeler, *Loving Warriors*, 220.

28. LS to HBB, October 11, 1867, Wheeler, *Loving Warriors*, 220.

29. Kerr, *Stone—Speaking Out*, 65–70.

30. "Kansas," *NASS*, September 14, 1867.

31. ECS to Theodore Tilton, September 15, 1867, Gordon, *Selected Papers*, II, 89–91.

32. *Pottawatomie Gazette*, September 18, 1867, quoted in Gordon, *Selected Papers*, II, 91 n. 2.

33. Gordon, *Selected Papers*, II, 91, n. 3.

34. Harper, *Life and Work* I, 286.

35. DuBois, *Feminism and Suffrage*, 92; Louise R. Noun, *Strong-Minded Women: The Emergence of the Woman-Suffrage Movement in Iowa* (Ames: Iowa State University Press, 1969), 70.

36. *HWS* II, 243. SBA to unnamed recipient, possibly Parker Pillsbury or Lucy Stone, September 15, 1867, from Lawrence, Kansas (*HWS* II, 242–243).

37. "Manhood Suffrage Tonight," *Leavenworth Bulletin*, September 17, 1867.

38. "The Right Sentiment," *Kansas Chief*, September 26, 1867.

39. Senator Phelps soon kidnapped Mrs. Phelps' child. As the law favored him, Mrs. Phelps lost her child permanently. See Barry, *Singular Feminist*, 51, for a similar incident in 1852 but with a happier ending (*HWS* I, 175–178).

40. Harper, *Life and Work* I, 286.

41. "The Right Sentiment," *Kansas Chief*, September 26, 1867.

42. "A Mystery," *Kansas Chief*, September 26, 1867. See "Advantage of Two Sides," *Kansas Chief*, October 3, 1867; "Kalloch Blowing," *Kansas Chief*, October 10, 1867; "Kalloch's Record," *Kansas Chief*, October 31, 1867, for the "two-sided" history of the Reverend Kalloch and sexual indiscretions with a member of his congregation in Boston.

43. *Wyandotte Commercial Gazette*, September 21, 1867, quoted in Dudden, *Fighting Chance*, 125; see also 242, n. 134.

44. "His Position," *Kansas Chief*, September 26, 1867.

45. "Another Position," *Kansas Chief*, October 3, 1867.

46. *Leavenworth Bulletin*, November 4, 1867. Appearing November 2, 4 and 5, it was obviously republished to tell Republicans how to vote.

47. William G. Cutler's *History of the State of Kansas*, Legislative and Political Annals, Part 2 (Chicago: A.T. Andreas, 1883), retrieved from Kansas Collection Books at http://www.kancoll.org/books/cutler/sthist/annals-p2.html, March 27, 2018.

48. "State and General News Items," *Emporia News*, September 20, 1867.

Chapter 28

1. "Grand United Suffrage Celebration," *Kansas Chief*, September 19, 1867. The September 26, 1867, edition lists further Brown meetings.

2. "The Right Sentiment," *Kansas Chief*, September 26, 1867.

3. Ibid.

4. Ibid. This event occurred the Saturday before Langston's convoluted attempt to downplay his appearance at the Leavenworth anti-woman suffrage meeting.

5. SBA to AED, September 23, 1867, Gordon, *Selected Papers*, II, 92–95.

6. The convention of Germans took place just ten days after the *NASS* editorial of September 14.

7. They would speak in Garnett, south of Lawrence, on September 26 (Gordon, *Selected Papers* II, 94 n. 7). "Impartial Suffrage Meetings" (*Emporia News*, September 20, 1867) said Stanton, Robinson, and others would canvass Eureka October 4; Eldorado October 5; Marion Center October 7; Cottonwood Falls October 8; Council Grove October 9; Americus October 10; and Emporia, October 11, all at 7:00 p.m.

8. SBA to AED, September 23, 1867, Gordon, *Selected Papers*, II, 92.

9. Gordon, *Selected Papers*, II, 92 and 94, n. 8.

10. SBA to AED, September 23, 1867, Gordon, *Selected Papers*, II, 93.

11. Gordon, *Selected Papers*, II, 94, n. 8.

12. "State and General News Items," *Emporia News*, September 20, 1867.

13. Gordon, *Selected Papers*, II, 94, n. 9.

14. Albert D. Richardson, quoted in Willis Thornton, *The Nine Lives of Citizen Train* (New York: Greenberg, 1948), 164, hereinafter cited as Thornton, *Nine Lives*.

15. Thornton, *Nine Lives*, 159.

16. "Geo. Francis Train at Junction City," *Topeka State Record*, Train, *Epigram*, 60–67, at 67.

17. Thornton, *Nine Lives*, 108–120, at 120.

18. "Geo. Francis Train at Junction City," *Topeka State Record*, Train, *Epigram*, 60–67, at 60.

19. Thornton, *Nine Lives*, 153.

20. "How Does This Look?" *Kansas Chief*, October 3, 1867.

21. SBA to AED, September 23, 1867, Gordon, *Selected Papers*, II, 94, n. 8.

22. Formed at meeting in Lawrence in early June. See *Kansas Tribune*, Lawrence, May 30, 1867.

23. Gordon, *Selected Papers*, II, 94, n. 6, citing the *Lawrence Kansas Daily Tribune*, September 25, 1867, and *Burlington Kansas Patriot*, October 5, 1867.

24. Gordon, *Selected Papers*, II, 94, n. 6.

25. "Address of the State Temperance Society" (held at Lawrence September 26, 1867), *Emporia News*, October 18, 1867.

26. "State Temperance Convention," *Emporia News*, October 4, 1867. The paper said the document would appear the next week "as it is … of importance in the history of the present struggle."

27. "To the Voters of Kansas," *Emporia News*, October 11, 1867. See also "Address to the Voters of Kansas," September 25, 1867, which "forty-five men signed [as] the result of a meeting in Lawrence," in *Kansas Memory*, Kansas

Historical Society, accessed at http://www.kshs.org/km/items/view/206171 May 17, 2018.

28. "To the Voters of Kansas," *Emporia News*, October 11, 1867.

29. SBA to AED, September 23, 1867, Gordon, *Selected Papers*, II, 92–95, at 94, n. 10.

30. "Kansas," *New York Tribune*, October 1, 1867.

31. "George Francis Train," letter from SBA and others to George Francis Train, dated Lawrence, Kansas, October 2, 1867, *Omaha Herald,* in Train, *Epigram*, 5–6, at 5.

Chapter 29

1. Barry, *Singular Feminist*, 179–187, at 181, and 391, n. 14; White, *The Beecher Sisters*, 137–138 and 351, n. 137.

2. "Kansas—Woman as a Voter," *New York Tribune*, October 1, 1867.

3. "Kansas," *NASS*, September 14, 1867.

4. *HWS* II, 247. For the states besides New York and Michigan, see Appendix A.

5. "A Significant Movement," *Kansas Chief*, September 26, 1867; "German Convention," *Kansas Chief*, October 3, 1867; "The German Question," *Kansas Chief*, October 10, 1867; "It is Working" and "Liberty," *Kansas Chief*, October 17, 1867.

6. Reports of female suffrage events did not equal wall-to-wall campaign coverage ("How the Papers Stand," *Emporia News*, October 4, 1867).

7. Different committees of the campaign sent out conflicting and constantly changing information about meetings ("A Hint," *Kansas Chief*, September 26, 1867).

8. "Politics in Kansas: The Struggle for Woman's Suffrage," *NYT*, October 12, 1867.

9. LS to ECS April 10, 1867, *HWS* II, 234.

10. HBB to ECS, SBA et al., April 21, 1867, *HWS* II, 237.

11. Hubbard signed the "Address to the Voters of Kansas" of September 25, 1867 (see "Address to the Voters of Kansas September 25, 1867," *Kansas Memory*, Kansas Historical Society, accessed at http://www.kshs.org/km/items/view/206171, March 27, 2018). For information on Hubbard see William G. Cutler, "History of Kansas," *Kansas Collection Books*, accessed April 3, 2018, at http://www.kancoll.org/books/cutler/atchison/atchison-co-p11.html.

12. "George Francis Train," *Omaha Herald*, letter from SBA and others to GFT, dated Lawrence, Kansas, October 2, 1867, Train, *Epigram*, 5–6, at 6.

13. This author's transcription.

14. "Right and Wrong in Kansas," *Independent*, October 3, 1867.

15. "The New York Independent," *Emporia News*, October 11, 1867.

16. "George Francis Train," *Omaha Herald*, letter from GFT to S. N. Wood and Committee [at] Woman's Suffrage, Lawrence, Kansas, dated October 9, 1867, Train, *Epigram*, 5–6 at 5.

17. SBA to GFT, October 9, 1867, "George Francis Train," *Omaha Herald*, Train, *Epigram*, 5–6 at 5.

18. Thornton, *Nine Lives*, 19–21.

19. "George Francis Train: His Speech on the Summit of Pilot Knob," *Memphis Daily Avalanche*, June 27, 1867; "A Raid on the Doctors. George Francis Train on Hygiene and Other Things," *Plain Dealer*, April 24, 1867.

20. "The Leavenworth Commercial," *Kansas Daily Tribune*, November 2, 1867.

21. "On the Plains: From the Editorial Railway Excursion—Geo. Francis Train in Charge of Two Hundred Newspaper Men," *Philadelphia Enquirer*, October 15, 1867.

22. "George Francis Train," *Kansas Chief*, October 10, 1867.

23. ECS to Henry B. Stanton October 9, 1867, Gordon, *Selected Papers*, II, 96.

24. For more on Reynolds, see Dan W. Peery, "Hon. Milton W. Reynolds (Kicking Bird)," *Chronicles of Oklahoma* 13, no. 1 (March 1935), accessed April 12, 2016, at http://digital.library. okstate.edu/Chronicles/v013/v013p046.html.

25. SBA to Samuel N. Wood, Lawrence, October 10, 1867, Gordon, *Selected Papers*, II, 97.

26. Ibid., 98.

27. Kerr, *Stone—Speaking Out* at 127, says Brown received "more than a thousand dollars … in a four-week period," and Anthony received $2,000 in September.

28. Ibid.; Dudden, *Fighting Chance*, 130 and 244 n. 174. He left around October 11, 1867 (see LS to HBB on October 11 after his departure, and letter saying, "I suppose you are in St. Louis today," LS to HBB October 13, 1867, Wheeler, *Loving Warriors*, 219–220).

29. LS to HBB October 11, 1867, Wheeler, *Loving Warriors*, 219–220.

30. Ibid. Kerr (*Stone—Speaking Out*, 126) says Stone "arranged to borrow the money."

31. Subsequently Stone would receive money from the Jackson Fund—a total of $3,728 between April 15, 1868, and November 13, 1871 (see "Accounts of Wendell Phillips with the Francis Jackson Fund," *NAWSA Papers*, Reel 11: 351–353, National American Woman Suffrage Association Records, Manuscript Division, Library of Congress, Washington, D.C., hereinafter referred to as *NAWSA Papers*, "Accounts of Wendell Phillips."

32. LS to HBB, October 13, 1867, Wheeler, *Loving Warriors*, 220–221.

33. Reyes, *A Mere Demagoguery*, 2.

34. "Miss Olympia Brown," *Kansas Chief*, October 17, 1867.

35. "George Francis Train," *Kansas Chief*, October 17, 1867.

36. See "Train and Reynolds," *Lawrence State Journal*, no date, Train, *Epigram*, 44. See also Gordon, *Selected Papers*, II, 98, notes 2, 3 and 4.

37. "Correction," *Emporia News*, October 18, 1867.

38. *Burlington (KS) Patriot*, October 19, 1867 (Gordon, *Selected Papers*, II, 100).

39. "Suffrage Meetings," *Emporia News*, October 18, 1867.

40. Both quotations from "Impartial Suffrage Meeting," *Kansas Daily Tribune*, October 23, 1867.

41. "Suffrage Meetings," *Emporia News*, October 18, 1867.

42. In the declaration, the word is "unalienable."

Chapter 30

1. HBB to LS, October 13, 1867, 220–221; HBB to LS, October 25, 1867, both in Wheeler, *Loving Warriors*, 221–222.

2. HBB to LS, October 25, 1867, Wheeler, *Loving Warriors*, 221.

3. *Wyandotte Commercial Gazette*, October 26, 1867.

4. "Train and Reynolds," *Leavenworth State Journal*, no date, Train, *Epigram*, 44.

5. White, *The Beecher Sisters*, 137–138 and 351, n. 137.

6. "Geo. Francis Train's First Great Speech," *Leavenworth Commercial*, no date, Train, *Epigram*, 6–15, at 6.

7. GFT, *Great Speech on the Withdrawal of McClennan and the Impeachment of Lincoln* (New York: American News, 1864).

8. *Leavenworth Bulletin*, October 22, 1867. See also the *Kansas Daily Tribune*, October 23, 1867, for equally negative commentary about Train's speech in Lawrence.

9. "Train," *Atchison Champion*, October 23, 1867.

10. "Geo. Francis Train's First Great Speech," *Leavenworth Commercial*, no date, Train, *Epigram*, 6–15, at 8.

11. "Train," *Atchison Champion*, October 23, 1867.

12. "Laing's Hall—Geo. Francis Train," *Leavenworth Commercial*, no date, Train, *Epigram*, 15–17, at 17.

13. "First 'Train' in Olathe!" *Olathe Mirror*, October 24, 1867.

14. Introductory page of Train, *Epigram,* Kansas Historical Society accessed May 5, 2016, at http://www.kansasmemory.org/item/206263. Train's plan was to appear in Atchison, but a last-minute travel hitch prevented his appearance. Anthony spoke briefly there just before the election.

15. "'Train,'" *Atchison Champion,* October 25, 1867.

16. Untitled, *Emporia News,* November 1, 1867, 2, col. 2, and "What they want," same date, same page.

Chapter 31

1. "Geo. Francis Train's First Great Speech," *Leavenworth Commercial,* no date, Train, *Epigram,* 6–15, at 6.

2. "Train[']s Speech at Ottawa," *Fort Scott Monitor [FSM],* October 30, 1867; Train, *Epigram,* 33–40 at 37.

3. SBA et al., telegram to Train, October 2, 1867, Train, *Epigram,* 5.

4. "What They Want," *St. Louis Democrat,* October 28, 1867, Train, *Epigram,* 47–48, at 48.

5. "Train at Paola," *Lawrence State Journal,* datelined October 24, 1867, midday, Train, *Epigram,* 29.

6. "Train in Johnson County," *Lawrence State Journal,* no date, Train, *Epigram,* 28–29.

7. Ibid.

8. "Junction City, Nov. 1," *Leavenworth Commercial,* Train, *Epigram,* 52–53.

9. "Train Attacks the Whole State," *Kansas State Journal,* no date, Train, *Epigram,* 27–28.

10. "Train Firing Hot Shot into Johnson County," *Leavenworth Commercial,* no date, Train, *Epigram,* 28.

11. "Geo. Francis Train's First Great Speech," *Leavenworth Commercial,* no date, Train, *Epigram,* 6–15, at 12.

12. "Geo. Francis Train at Fort Scott," *FSM,* October 26, 1867, Train, *Epigram,* 43.

13. "Geo. Francis Train's First Great Speech," *Leavenworth Commercial,* no date, Train, *Epigram,* 6–15, at 10.

14. "Geo. Francis Train's Valedictory to the People of Kansas," *Leavenworth Commercial,* November 5, 1867, Train, *Epigram,* 71–74, at 72.

15. "Junction City, Nov. 1," *Leavenworth Commercial,* Train, *Epigram,* 52–53, at 53.

16. "Geo. Francis Train at Junction City," *Topeka State Record,* no date, Train, *Epigram,* 60–68, at 66.

17. Ibid., 60–68, at 65.

18. "Train[']s Speech at Ottawa," *FSM,* October 30, 1867; Train, *Epigram,* 33–40, at 38.

19. "Train's Second Great Speech," *Lawrence State Journal,* no date, Train, *Epigram,* 17–24, at 24.

20. Ibid., at 20–22.

21. Ibid., 17–24, at 19. The source of Train's numbers is unknown. In 1859 during the Constitutional Convention at Wyandotte, the Moneka Women's Suffrage Association presented 250 petitions asking for female suffrage (see "Moneka Woman's Rights Association," *Kansapedia,* accessed May 16, 2016, at https://www.kshs.org/kansapedia/moneka-woman-s-rights-association/15158, and Gordon, *Selected Papers,* II, 49 and 51–52.

22. "George-Francis-Trainiana," *Leavenworth Commercial,* no date, Train, *Epigram,* 58.

23. Elizabeth Cady Stanton, "The Anniversaries: Equal Rights Association Second Day," *NYT,* May 11, 1867.

24. "Chain Lightning," *Leavenworth Commercial,* datelined Humbolt, October 28, 1867, Train, *Epigram,* 51.

25. "Chain Lightning," *Lawrence State Journal,* datelined Mound City, October 25, 1867, Train, *Epigram,* 32.

26. "The Proof," *Emporia News,* November 8, 1867.

27. "'Northern doughfaces' at the South, who seek more popularity than the Southerners themselves" (quote from the *Richmond Republic,* in *Independent,* May 10, 1866).

28. See "List of Ethnic Slurs," *Wikipedia* retrieved April 14, 2018, at https://en.wikipedia.org/wiki/List_of_ethnic_slurs#S.

29. "Chain Lightning," *Lawrence State Journal,* datelined Mound City, October 25, 1867, Train, *Epigram,* 32.

30. She had written that if black men got the vote before women "they will be just so much more dead weight to lift" (LS to SBA, May 9, 1867, *HWS* II, 238).

31. "Sparks from the Locomotive Geo. Francis Train," no citation, Train, *Epigram,* 31–32.

32. "Geo. Francis Train at Junction City," *Topeka State Record,* no date, Train, *Epigram,* 60–68, at 68.

33. See the political ditty at "Sparks from the Locomotive Geo. Francis Train," no citation, Train, *Epigram,* 31–32.

34. "Geo. Francis Train at Junction City," *Topeka State Record,* no date, Train, *Epigram,* 60–68, at 68.

35. "Geo. Francis Train's First Great Speech," *Leavenworth Commercial,* no date, Train, *Epigram,* 6–15, at 15.

36. "Geo. Francis Train at Junction City," *Topeka State Record,* no date, Train, *Epigram,* 60–68, at 68. A third referendum in Kansas, rarely mentioned, was to disfranchise former Confederates.

37. Ibid., 62.

38. Ibid., 61.

39. "Opinions of the Press," *Leavenworth Conservative*, Train, *Epigram*, 24–26, at 25.

40. "George-Francis-Trainiana," *Leavenworth Commercial*, no date, Train, *Epigram*, 58.

41. "Train Stopping Along the Line," *Leavenworth Commercial*, datelined Manhattan, November 1, 1867, 4 o'clock, Train, *Epigram*, 53.

42. "Train[']s Speech at Ottawa," *FSM*, October 30, 1867; Train, *Epigram*, 33–40 at 36.

43. "Geo. Francis Train at Junction City," *Topeka State Record*, no date, Train, *Epigram*, 60–68, at 62–63.

44. Ibid., 60–68, at 66.

45. Clara McDiarmid, the leading Little Rock, Arkansas, suffragist, by 1890 was pointing out the injustice of her own coachman having the vote while she did not.

46. "Trains Speech at Ottawa," *FSM*, October 30, 1867; Train, *Epigram*, 33–40, at 38.

47. Ibid., at 38.

48. "George Francis Train," *New York Times*, August 16, 1862.

49. "Train[']s Speech at Ottawa," *FSM*, October 30, 1867; Train, *Epigram*, 33–40, at 38.

50. "Geo. Francis Train at Junction City," *Topeka State Record*, no date, Train, *Epigram*, 60–68, at 67–68.

51. "Train[']s Speech at Ottawa," *FSM*, October 30, 1867; Train, *Epigram*, 33–40, at 39.

52. See, for example, Robert E. DiClarico, *Voting in America: A Reference Handbook* (Santa Barbara, CA: ABC–CLIO, 2004), 158; Stephanie Coontz, *The Social Origins of Private Life: A History of American Families, 1600–1900* (London and New York: Verso, 1988), 242.

53. "Geo. Francis Train at Junction City," *Topeka State Record*, no date, Train, *Epigram*, 60–68, at 66. Phillips stated his "one idea for a generation" at the AASS Meeting in May 1865, while Stanton later spelled it out in *The Revolution*, on January 15, 1868.

Chapter 32

1. *Wyandotte Commercial Gazette*, November 2, 1867.

2. "Geo. Francis Train at Junction City," *Topeka State Record*, no date, Train, *Epigram*, 60–68, at 60–61.

3. "Train's Second Great Speech," *Lawrence State Journal*, no date, Train, *Epigram*, 17.

4. Lutz, *Rebel Crusader*, 131.

5. "Chain Lightning," *Lawrence State Journal*, datelined October 24, 1867, Train, *Epigram*, 29–30, at 29; "Geo. Francis Train at Paola," *Leavenworth Commercial*, datelined October 29, 1867, Train, *Epigram*, 46–47, at 46.

6. Lutz, *Rebel Crusader*, 131.

7. "Train's Second Great Speech," *Lawrence State Journal*, no date, Train, *Epigram*, 17–24, at 17.

8. "Train[']s Speech at Ottawa," *FSM*, October 30, 1867; Train, *Epigram*, 33–40, at 40.

9. "Geo. Francis Train at Junction City," *Topeka State Record*, no date, Train, *Epigram*, 60–68, at 66.

10. Ibid., at 67.

11. "Train[']s Speech at Ottawa," *FSM*, October 30, 1867; Train, *Epigram*, 33–40, at 39.

12. Ibid., at 40.

13. Harper (*Life and Work* I, at 289) says that "from Ottawa they travelled, still in a lumber wagon, to Mound City and then to Fort Scott, where they had an immense audience. After the meeting Train went to the newspaper office and wrote out his speech, which filled two pages of the Monitor."

14. For a brief history of the start of this scurrilous campaign, see "Reminiscences of Helen Ekin Starrett, *HWS* II, 252–253.

15. "Meanness Boiled Down," *Wyandotte Commercial Gazette*, November 2, 1867.

16. "Another Ministerial Reprobate" and "Meanness Boiled Down," *Wyandotte Commercial Gazette*, November 2, 1867.

17. DuBois, *Feminism and Suffrage*, 89, n. 31.

18. "A Mystery," *Kansas Chief*, September 26, 1867. See "Advantage of Two Sides," *Kansas Chief*, October 3, 1867; "Kalloch Blowing," *Kansas Chief*, October 10, 1867; "Kalloch's Record," *Kansas Chief*, October 31, 1867, for the "two-sided" history of the Reverend Kalloch and sexual indiscretions with a member of his congregation in Boston.

19. "Kalloch and Walker in Emporia," *Emporia News*, November 1, 1867.

20. "Female Monstrosities," *Emporia News*, November 1, 1867.

21. "Train's Blowing," *Atchison Champion*, November 7, 1867.

22. "George Francis Train," *Kalloch's Home Journal*, no date, Train, *Epigram*, 45–6, at 45.

23. Ibid., at 46.

24. DuBois, *Feminism and Suffrage*, 89, n. 31.

25. "Train[']s Speech at Ottawa," *FSM*, October 30, 1867; Train, *Epigram*, 33–40, at 38.

26. All quotes from a letter from "Patsy's Husband" to *Kansas Chief*, October 24, 1867.

27. "Train[']s Speech at Ottawa," *FSM*, October 30, 1867; Train, *Epigram*, 33–40, at 34.

28. "General Blunt Gives One Yell of Agony," *Leavenworth Commercial*, no date, Train, *Epigram*, 41–42, at 42.

29. "Train," *Atchison Champion*, October 23, 1867.

30. "Train After Blunt with a Sharp Stick,"

Kansas State Journal, datelined Ottawa, October 24, 1867, Train, *Epigram,* 30–31, at 30.

31. "Geo. Francis Train at Junction City," *Topeka State Record,* no date, Train, *Epigram,* 60–68 at 63.

32. "Train attacks the whole State," *Kansas State Journal,* no date, Train, *Epigram,* 27–28.

33. "Train after Blunt with a Sharp Stick," *Kansas State Journal,* datelined Ottawa, October 24, 1867, Train, *Epigram,* 30–31, at 31.

34. "Laing's Hall—Geo. Francis Train," *Leavenworth Commercial,* no date, Train, *Epigram,* 15–17, at 16.

35. "Train Firing Hot Shot into Johnson County," *Leavenworth Commercial,* October 23, Train, *Epigram,* 28.

36. "Train[']s Speech at Ottawa," *FSM,* October 30, 1867; Train, *Epigram,* 33–40, at 40.

Chapter 33

1. Harper, *Life and Work* I, 288.

2. "Train and Reynolds," *Lawrence State Journal,* no date, Train, *Epigram,* 44.

3. Harper, *Life and Work* I, 288.

4. Ibid.

5. "Chain Lightning," *Lawrence State Journal,* datelined October 24, 1867, Train, *Epigram,* 29–30, at 29; "Geo. Francis Train at Paola," *Leavenworth Commercial,* datelined October 29, 1867, Train, *Epigram,* 46–47, at 46.

6. Harper, *Life and Work* I, 288–289.

7. "Train After Blunt with a Sharp Stick," *Kansas State Journal,* datelined Ottawa, October 24, 1867, Train, *Epigram,* 30–31, at 30.

8. *Buffalo Express,* December 2, 1867, Susan B. Anthony Scrapbook 2, Library of Congress, Rare Books Division, cited in Patricia G. Holland, "George Francis Train and the Woman Suffrage Movement, 1867–70," *Books at Iowa* 46 (April 1987), retrieved July 2, 2018, from http://www.lib.uiowa.edu/spec-coll/bai/holland.htm, 2, and n. 7, hereinafter referred to as Holland, *George Francis Train and Woman Suffrage.*

9. The first campaign stops were Leavenworth (October 21), Lawrence (October 22), Olathe (October 23), Paola, and Ottawa (October 24) (see Train, *Epigram,* 28–30). The two were lost in the woods between Paola and Ottawa.

10. Harper, *Life and Work* I, 288.

11. "George Francis Train at Ottawa: Kalloch's Headquarters," no attribution, no date, 1867, Train, *Epigram,* 33–40 at 37.

12. "Train's Second Great Speech," *Lawrence State Journal,* no date, Train, *Epigram,* 17–24, at 20.

13. Ibid., 22.

14. Ibid., 20.

15. "Train Firing Hot Shot into Johnson County," *Leavenworth Commercial,* October 23, Train, *Epigram,* 28.

16. Letter to the editor, dated Ottawa, Oct 25, 1867, *Wyandotte Commercial Gazette,* November 2, 1867.

17. "George Francis Train Storms Topeka," *Topeka Leader,* no date, Train, *Epigram,* 68–69, at 69.

18. "Train Bursts Up the Eskridge-Plumb-McBurney Clique," *Leavenworth Commercial,* October 30, 1867, Train, Epigram, 52.

19. "George Francis Train at Junction City," *Topeka State Record,* Train, *Epigram,* 60–68, at 68.

20. "Train After Blunt with a Sharp Stick," *Kansas State Journal,* datelined Oct. 24, Ottawa; Train, *Epigram,* 30–31, at 30.

21. "Train Follows Kalloch, and Pins Blunt on His Own Dung-Hill," *Leavenworth Commercial,* Train, *Epigram,* 47.

22. "Train in Coffey County—The Democracy, as Elsewhere, the Champions of Woman," datelined Burlington, October 30, 1867; Train, *Epigram,* 52.

23. Eldo B. Lane, Pueblo, Colorado, "Pioneer Days in Strawn and Ottumwa," retrieved from http://www.rootsweb.ancestry.com/~ks coffhp/history/pioneerdaysstrawnottumwa.html on August 28, 2016.

24. "Train in Coffey County—The Democracy, as Elsewhere, the Champions of Woman," datelined Burlington, October 30, 1867; Train, *Epigram,* 52.

25. "Train Stirring Up Coffey County," *Leavenworth Commercial,* datelined Leroy, October 29; Train, *Epigram,* 51.

26. No title, *Leavenworth Commercial,* datelined Junction City, November 1, 1867; Train, *Epigram,* 52–53, at 53.

27. "Train Stopping Along the Line—The Fever at Its Height—All the Towns Gather as the Train Passes for a Speech," *Leavenworth Commercial,* datelined Manhattan, November 1, 1867; Train, *Epigram,* 53.

28. "Train in Johnson County," from Olathe, no date, *Lawrence State Journal,* reprinted from *Kansas State Journal,* Train, *Epigram,* 28–29, at 29.

29. "Train After Blunt with a Sharp Stick," *Kansas State Journal,* datelined Oct 24, Ottawa; Train, *Epigram,* 30–31, at 31. Ottawa was "Kalloch's town."

30. "Geo. Francis Train at Fort Scott," *FSM,* October 26, 1867, Train, *Epigram,* 43–44, at 43.

31. "Geo. Francis Train's First Great Speech," *Leavenworth Commercial,* undated, Train, *Epigram,* 6–15, at 15.

32. "Train's Second Great Speech," *Lawrence State Journal,* no date, Train, *Epigram,* 17.

33. "Geo. Francis Train at Fort Scott," *FSM*, October 26, 1867, Train, *Epigram*, 44.

34. "Train at Olathe," *Lawrence State Journal*, no date, Train, *Epigram*, 45.

35. "Geo. Francis Train at Junction City," *Topeka State Record*, no date, Train, *Epigram*, 60–68, at 60.

36. Note datelined North Lawrence, October 25, 1867, *Leavenworth Commercial*, Train, *Epigram*, 54–55, at 55.

37. "Tremendous Gathering at Frazer's Hall," *Lawrence State Journal*, no date, *Epigram*, 26–27, at 27.

38. "Train attacks the whole State" *Kansas State Journal*, no date, Train, *Epigram*, 27–28, at 28.

39. "Geo. Francis Train at Ottawa" no citation, Train, *Epigram*, 33–40, at 39; "Train[']s Speech at Ottawa," *FSM*, October 30, 1867.

40. "Chain Lightning—Train at Humboldt," *Leavenworth Commercial*, October 28, 1867, Train, *Epigram*, 50–51, at 50.

41. Ibid., at 51.

42. "George Francis Train at Junction City," *Topeka State Record,* Train, *Epigram*, 60–68, at 67.

43. "George Francis Train, *Kalloch's Home Journal*, no date, Train, *Epigram*, 45.

44. "G.F.T.," *Topeka (KS) Leader,* no date, Train, *Epigram*, 49.

45. "Geo. Francis Train at Ottawa" no citation, Train, *Epigram,* 33–40, at 39; "Train[']s Speech at Ottawa," *FSM*, October 30, 1867.

46. "Chain Lightning—Train at Humboldt," *Leavenworth Commercial*, October 28, 1867, Train, *Epigram*, 50–51, at 51.

47. Ibid.

48. "Train Stopping Along the Line," *Leavenworth Commercial*, datelined Manhattan, November 1, 1867, Train, *Epigram*, 53.

49. "George Francis Train at Junction City," *Topeka State Record,* Train, *Epigram*, 60–68, at 67 and 68.

50. *HWS* II, 246–247.

51. Correspondent's report "to the Editor of the *Kansas State Journal*" on the Oskaloosa debate between Judge Sears and Brown, which the latter won handily (*HWS* II, 241).

52. "George Francis Train," *Kalloch's Home Journal*, no date, Train, *Epigram*, 45–6, at 45.

53. Ibid., at 46.

54. "Train[']s Speech at Ottawa," *FSM,* October 30, 1867; Train, *Epigram,* 33–40 at 39.

55. "Kalloch Proves Himself a Trump," *Western Home Journal*, reprinted in the *Leavenworth Commercial,* Train, *Epigram* 58–59, at 59.

56. Ibid.

57. "G.F.T.," *Topeka (KS) Leader,* no date, Train, *Epigram*, 49.

58. "Geo. Francis Train at Junction City," *Topeka State Record*, no date, Train, *Epigram*, 60–68, at 64.

59. Ibid., 67.

60. Ibid.

Chapter 34

1. *Kansas Chief*, October 24, 1867. For the text of the amendment see "Ohio Denial of Right to Vote, Amendment 1 (October 1867)," retrieved from *Ballotopedia* June 10, 2018, https://ballotpedia.org/Ohio_Denial_of_Right_to_Vote,_Amendment_1_(October_1867).

2. See Appendix A.

3. Octavia Williams Bates, "Municipal Suffrage for Women in Michigan," in Eagle, *Congress of Women*, 664–667.

4. *HWS* II, 247.

5. Author's italics. The measure failed to pass. Several other states allowed male noncitizens to vote. For Minnesota see "Minnesota Right to Vote, Amendment 1 (1867) accessed May 17, 2018, at https://ballotpedia.org/Minnesota_Right_to_Vote,_Amendment_1_(1867).

6. "Local Matters," *Lawrence Kansas Daily Tribune,* November 1, 1867; "Not Authorized," *Atchison Champion*, November 2, 1867.

7. Dudden (*Fighting Chance*, 129 and 243, n. 163 and 164) cites reports from *Leavenworth Daily Conservative*, October 27, 1867; *Leavenworth Evening Bulletin*, October 28, 1867; *Leavenworth Daily Conservative*, October 31, 1867; and *Leavenworth Daily Commercial*, November 1, 1867.

8. "Sparks from the Locomotive Geo. Francis Train," no citation, Train, *Epigram*, 31–32, at 32.

9. Dudden, *Fighting Chance*, 129 and 243, n. 163 and 164, citing reports from several Leavenworth newspapers.

10. HBB to LS, October 29, 1867, Dudden, *Fighting Chance*, 130 and 244, n. 174.

11. "The Vote in Leavenworth," *Lawrence Kansas Daily Tribune*, November 6, 1867; "State Items," *Junction City Weekly Union*, November 9, 1867.

12. Harper, *Life and Work* I, 291.

13. *HWS* II, 247.

14. Ibid.

15. Harper, *Life and Work* I, 291.

16. "Kalloch Proves Himself a Trump," *Western Home Journal*, reprinted from the *Leavenworth Commercial*, Train, *Epigram* 58–60 at 59.

17. All preceding quotes from "The Election in Lyon County," *Emporia News*, November 8, 1867.

18. See Gordon, *Selected Papers*, II, 644.

19. Dudden, *Fighting Chance*, 130 and 244, n. 178 and 180.

20. Gordon, *Selected Papers*, II, 643; Reyes, *A Mere Demagoguery*, 25.

21. Dudden, *Fighting Chance*, 130 and 244, notes 175–180.

22. HBB to LS, October 29, 1867, Dudden, *Fighting Chance*, 130 and 244, n. 174.

23. Charles Robinson to ECS, Lawrence, Kansas, November 20, 1867; see Gordon, *Selected Papers*, II, 102–104, 104 n. 8.

24. HBB to LS, October 13, 1867, 220–221; HBB to LS, October 25, 1867, Wheeler, *Loving Warriors*, 221–222.

25. "The Vote in Leavenworth," *Kansas Daily Tribune* (Lawrence), November 6, 1867; "State Items," *Junction City Weekly Union*, November 9, 1867.

26. Charles Robinson to ECS, Lawrence, Kansas, November 20, 1867; see Gordon, *Selected Papers*, II, 102.

27. *HWS* II, 247.

28. Dudden, *Fighting Chance*, 130.

29. "Train's Blowing," *Atchison Champion*, November 7, 1867.

30. Dudden, *Fighting Chance*, 130 and 244, n. 175–180.

31. Brown, *Acquaintances*, 73.

32. "The Late Elections—Negro and Woman Suffrage," *New York Herald*, November 9, 1867.

33. Ibid.

34. SBA to Olympia Brown, Leavenworth, November 7, 1867, Gordon, *Selected Papers*, II, 100–101.

35. Sex discrimination in voting rights in the Constitution would be annulled only in 1920 after a tumultuous campaign (see Cahill, *Alice Paul*).

36. See the reminisces of Kansas women in *HWS* II, 250–261.

37. SBA to Olympia Brown, Leavenworth, November 7, 1867, Gordon, *Selected Papers*, II, 100–101.

38. *Leavenworth Commercial*, November 14, 1867, *HWS* II, 262–263.

39. Ibid.

Chapter 35

1. "Geo. Francis Train at Junction City," *Topeka State Record*, Train, *Epigram*, 60–68, at 67.

2. Harper, *Life and Work* I, 290–291.

3. This writer saw his "fancy" fulfilled. Stanton died in 1902 and Anthony in 1906. The 19th Amendment abrogated sex discrimination in voting only in 1920–fifty-three years after the vicious Kansas campaign.

4. "The Irrepressible Females," *Daily Reformer*, November 12, 1867.

5. "Woman Suffrage—Large Meeting in St. Louis—Address by Elizabeth Cady Stanton," *Chicago Daily Inter Ocean*, November 16, 1867.

6. On November 10 Anthony released this list from Leavenworth: November: 19—Omaha; 21—Des Moines; 22—Chicago; 23—Milwaukee; 26—St. Louis; 27—Louisville; 28—Cincinnati; 29—Cleveland; 30—Buffalo. December: 2—Rochester; 3—Syracuse; 4—Albany; 6—Springfield; 7—Worcester; 9—Boston; 10—Hartford; 12—Philadelphia; 14—New York (see *Cincinnati Daily Gazette*, November 11, 1867).

7. Thornton, *Nine Lives*, 108–20, at 111 and 114.

8. See *New York Tribune*, November 21, 1866, Gordon, *Selected Papers* I, 600–601.

9. Holland, *George Francis Train and Woman Suffrage*, n. 18, referencing the letterhead of a letter from SBA to Olympia Brown, on January 1, 1868, in the Olympia Brown Papers, Schlesinger Library, Radcliffe Institute, Harvard University, Cambridge, Massachusetts.

10. For an example of his wide-ranging ideas delivered before the suffrage campaign, see GFT, *Great Speech on the Withdrawal of McClennan and the Impeachment of Lincoln* (New York: American News, 1864).

11. Tim O'Neil, "A Look Back: St. Louis Hosts Convention in 1869 in Pitch to Become Nation's Capital," *St. Louis Post-Dispatch*, October 20, 2012, accessed June 10, 2018, at http://www.stltoday.com/news/local/metro/a-look-back-st-louis-hosts-convention-in-in-pitch/article_965ad70c-2207-5406-a875-bd786bf6a20c.html. See also Richard W. Stephenson, Robert Grogg introduction, "Where Oh Where Should the Capital Be? The Seat of the Government in an Expanding Nation," *White House History*, accessed June 1, 2016, at https://www.whitehouse.org/where-oh-where-should-the-capital-be-white-house-history-number-34.

12. See ECS "Pronunciamento," *The Revolution*, July 15, 1869, 24.

13. "Wendell Phillips," Women's Rights National Historic Park, New York accessed April 17, 2018, at https://www.nps.gov/wori/learn/historyculture/wendell-phillips.htm.

14. Holland, *George Francis Train and Woman Suffrage*.

15. "To Our Radical Friends," *The Revolution*, May 14, 1868, 296.

16. ECS, "Pronunciamento," *The Revolution*, July 15, 1869, 24.

17. *HWS* II, 264.

18. DuBois, *Feminism and Suffrage*, 83 described it as "openly vengeful."

19. Sterling, *Kelley*, 275.

20. *HWS* II, 264.

21. "Address of Susan B. Anthony Delivered in Twenty-nine of the Post Office Districts of

Monroe, and Twenty-one of Ontario, in Her Canvass of Those Counties, Prior to Her Trial in June 1873," in *The Trial of Susan B. Anthony, Lynn Sherr*, ed. (New York: Humanity Books, 2003), 151–178, hereinafter referred to as Sherr, *Trial of Susan B. Anthony*.

22. *HWS* II, 264.

23. Elizabeth Cady Stanton to Clara Colby, June 16, 1890, quoted in Lori D. Ginzberg, *Elizabeth Cady Stanton: An American Life* (New York: Hill & Wang, 2009), 216, n. 53.

24. "To Our Radical Friends," *The Revolution*, May 14, 1868, 296.

Chapter 36

1. Kerr, *Stone—Speaking Out*, 127–130.

2. *New York World*, May 15, 1868, Gordon, *Selected Papers*, II, 137.

3. Payment made April 4, 1868, see NAWSA *Papers*, "Accounts of Wendell Phillips."

4. White, *The Beecher Sisters*, 137–138.

5. Ibid., 138.

6. Gordon, *Selected Papers*, II, 137–138, quoting the *New York World*, May 15, 1868. The *HWS* II source for the meeting, according to Gordon at 138, was the *New York Tribune*, May 15, 1868. *The Revolution* also covered it on May 20 and May 27, 1868.

7. Underhill, *New York Constitution Proceedings*, vol. II, 1237; *HWS* II, 284.

8. *HWS* II, 310–311.

9. This author's emphasis (*HWS* II, 311).

10. GS to ECS December 30, 1868, in *HWS* II, 317.

11. Gordon, *Selected Papers*, II, 247–248 and 248, n. 2.

12. See *Minor v. Happersett*, 88 U.S. 162 (1875), 177, retrieved June 11, 2018 from Cornell Law School, Legal Information Institute, https://www.law.cornell.edu/supremecourt/text/88/162.

13. May 10, 1867, first Annual Meeting of the AERA. British suffragists in 1916 echoed Stanton's position when politicians planned to enfranchise previously excluded men now serving at the front. The Woman's Freedom League objected "very strongly to more men being enfranchised until women are on the Parliamentary Register" (see "Political and Militant," *The Vote*, August 8, 1916). Race issues did not encumber the votes for women debate in Britain in 1916, so condemning the fundamental argument of justice with racial slurs was not an option. In 1918 Britain all men but only half of all women were enfranchised; the sex barrier, at least, was finally demolished. Class and single status barriers against women remained.

14. SBA to the editor, *NYT*, June 4, 1869, Gordon, *Selected Papers*, II, 247–248.

15. ECS to Congress re D.C. Suffrage Bill to enfranchise women in D.C., January 1870, *HWS* II, 413.

16. "Tyranny on a Southern plantation is far more easily seen by white men at the North than the wrongs [against] the women of their own households," *The Revolution*, January 14, 1869, quoted in *HWS* II, 317.

17. *Debates and Proceedings, Arkansas*, 699, 701, 703–724 (February 11, 12, 1868). The motion was thrown out amid much merriment (see Bernadette Cahill, "The Thin End of the Wedge: Miles Ledford Langley, Equal Voting Rights and the Constitutional Convention, Little Rock, 1868," *Pulaski County Historical Review* (forthcoming).

18. *HWS* II, 307–308.

19. Gordon, *Selected Papers*, II, 139, n. 3. This attempt at female suffrage by state reform Stone and Antoinette Blackwell may explain the $88 payment by Phillips from the Jackson Fund in April 1868.

20. Declaration of T.H. Mundine, July 8, 1868, *Texas State Library and Archives Commission*, retrieved from https://www.tsl.texas.gov/exhibits/suffrage/beginnings/1868-1.html June 13, 2018.

21. See Appendix A. Michigan women did win the right to vote for school trustees in 1867 (see Octavia Williams Bates, "Municipal Suffrage for Women in Michigan," in Eagle, *Congress of Women*, 664–667).

22. This was the latest step in an effort begun during the summer to enact this limited reform. S. No. 141, "Equal rights in the District of Columbia," *CG*, 40th Congress, 2nd Session, 38, 49, 51, 65, 96, 98, 100, 107, 384, 720. The original bill was S. No. 137. *CG*, 40th Congress, 1st Session, 660, 677, 695, 696, 725, 726, 732, 747, 753, 757. The bill passed the Senate that day and the House on December 9, but bureaucratic wrangling prevented its signature, so there was no presidential veto.

23. S. No. 228, *For the Further Security of Equal Rights in the District of Columbia* (Senator Charles Sumner, *CG*, 40th Congress, January 7, 1868, 344).

24. Gordon, *Selected Papers*, II, 134, n. 2.

25. "14th Amendment to the U.S. Constitution: Civil Rights (1868), Passed by Congress June 13, 1866, and ratified July 9, 1868, the 14th Amendment extended liberties and rights granted by the Bill of Rights to former slaves," *The People's Vote: The Most Influential Documents in American History*, accessed February 14, 2017, at https://www.ourdocuments.gov/doc.php?doc=43. For observations on the process of ratification of the 14th Amendment, see

David Lawrence, "There is No 'Fourteenth Amendment,'" *U.S. News and World Report*, September 27, 1957; Mike Scruggs, "The Unconstitutional Fruit of an Unconstitutional Amendment," in *Ratifying the Fourteenth Amendment*, June 7, 2015, accessed April 9, 2018, at thetribunepapers.com, http://www.thetribunepapers.com/2015/06/07/ratifying-the-fourteenth-amendment-2/.

26. See Thomas Hudnall affidavit in U.S. Congress, *Use of the Army in Certain of the Southern States*, House of Representatives Executive Document No 30, September 4, 1868, Ex. Doc. 44th Congress, 2nd Session, 1877 (reprinted in New York: Arno Press and New York Times, 1969), 351; Bernadette Cahill, "Thanksgiving Visitor Learns How the Woman Saved the Day," *Rayville (LA) Richland Beacon-News*, December 31, 2009. See also Frank J. Wetta, *The Louisiana Scalawags: Politics, Race, and Terrorism During the Civil War and Reconstruction* (Baton Rouge: Louisiana State University Press, 2013), 156–158.

27. Grant won the popular vote by 300,000. See "United States Presidential Election of 1868," accessed July 13, 2019, at https://www.britannica.com/event/United-States-presidential-election-of-1868. The electoral college vote was 214–80 for Grant. See National Archives and Records Administration, "Electoral College: 1868 Election For The Twenty-First Term, 1869–1873," accessed July 13, 2019, at https://www.archives.gov/federal-register/electoral-college/votes/1869_1873.html. *Journal of the House of Representatives of the United States*, 40th Congress, December 7, 1868, 10, H. Res 363, *CG*, 9.

28. "Manhood Suffrage," *The Revolution*, December 24, 1868, 392.

29. S. 180, *Journal of the Senate of the United States of America*, 40th Congress, December 7, 1868, 7; CG, December 7, 1868, 6; HWS II, 324, quoting *The Revolution*, December 10, 1868.

30. "Mr. [George Washington] Julian, by unanimous consent, introduced a joint resolution (H. Res. 371) proposing an amendment to the Constitution of the United States; which was read a first and second time, referred to the Committee on the Judiciary, and ordered to be printed," *Journal of the House of Representatives of the United States*, December 8, 1868, 23; *CG*, 40th Congress, December 8, 1868, 21. *The Revolution*, December 17, 1868.

31. *House Joint Resolution Proposing the 15th Amendment to the Constitution*, December 7, 1868, National Archives, America's Historical Documents; *Journal of the House of Representatives* of the United States: 40th Congress, December 7, 1868, 10, H. Res 363 (*CG*, 40th Congress, December 7, 1868, 9).

32. "What the People Say to Us," *The Revolution*, May 14, 1868.

33. "Manhood Suffrage," *The Revolution*, December 24, 1868, 392.

34. Ibid.

35. Bettye Collier-Thomas, "Frances Ellen Watkins Harper: Abolitionist and Feminist Reformer, 1825–1911," in Ann D. Gordon and Bettye Collier-Thomas, ed., *African American Women and the Vote, 1837–1965* (Amherst: University of Massachusetts Press, 1997), 41–65; Margaret Hope Bacon, "One Great Bundle of Humanity: Frances Ellen Watkins Harper (1825–1911)," *Pennsylvania Magazine of History and Biography* 113, no. 1 (January 1989), 35–37.

36. Margaret Hope Bacon, "One Great Bundle of Humanity: Frances Ellen Watkins Harper (1825–1911)," *Pennsylvania Magazine of History and Biography* 113, no. 1 (January 1989), 21–43, at 21, 33, 33–34.

37. In the 1869 meeting of the AERA ("Annual Meeting," *HWS* II, 391).

38. Frances Harper, "We Are All Bound Up Together": Proceedings of the Eleventh Woman's Rights Convention, May 1866, 45–48, excerpted in Frances Smith Foster, *A Brighter Coming Day: A Frances Ellen Watkins Harper Reader* (New York: Feminist Press at the City University of New York, 1990), 217–219.

39. Ibid., 163 and 255, n. 16.

40. LS to Brown, January 6, 1868, quoted in Dubois, *Feminism and Suffrage*, 99, n. 64.

41. Harper, *Life and Work*, I, 319.

42. Dudden, *Fighting Chance*, 162–4.

43. "Stones Holding Their Peace," *The Revolution*, February 4, 1869.

44. "Lucy Stone and the Negro's Hour," *The Revolution*, February 11, 1869.

45. An entry, second in a list of receipts by Lucy Stone, does not name her (see "Accounts of Wendell Phillips," *NAWSA Papers*).

46. ECS to Lucretia Mott, January 21, 1869, on hearing of Julian's plans, Stanton and Blatch, *Letters, Diaries and Reminiscences*, II, 121–122.

47. Livermore to SBA, April 4, 1869, Harper, *Life and Work*, 321.

48. GFT to SBA, May 1, 1869 in *The Revolution*, May 6, 1869.

49. *HWS* II, 370–400, at 381–382.

50. *New York Tribune*, May 13, 1869.

51. *HWS* II, 381–382; "Anniversary of the Equal Rights Association," *NYT*, May 13, 1869; "American Equal Rights Association," *Tribune*, May 13, 1869.

52. The Third AERA Annual Convention, May 12–14, 1869, New York, *HWS* II, 382.

53. Attitudes to legal marriage varied among freedwomen. Some protesters objected to marriage servitude; others submitted; others

fought for recognition of their marriages and households against whites who expected to continue to control the lives and labor of former slaves as employees. Freedwomen also fought for parental rights against court rulings controlling apprenticed-out offspring. Many blacks, like many poor whites, also recognized marriage dissolution, whether formally or not, diverging from prevailing standards. In this perspective, upper-class women of any race, despite wealth, were more restricted, for social status involved inheritances and restriction on divorce. See Laura F. Edwards' study of post–Civil War relationships, *Gendered Strife and Confusion: The Political Culture of Reconstruction* (Urbana and Chicago: University of Illinois Press, 1997), 24–65 and 145–183.

54. Sojourner Truth, AERA, May 9, 1867, *HWS* II, 193.

55. Ibid., 397.

56. Ibid., 383.

57. Ibid., 398.

58. Ibid., 396.

59. *HWS* I, 53–61; Barry, *Singular Feminist*, 66–71.

60. *HWS* II, 400.

Chapter 37

1. For a pen picture of Vineland two years before, see "Letter from Mrs. Frances D. Gage," *NASS*, July 21, 1866.

2. "On November 3, 1868, 172 women…" *Cumberland County, New Jersey*, home page, the American Local History Network, accessed March 28, 2018, at http://www.usgennet.org/usa/nj/county/cumberland/VineVote/Vote.html, hereinafter cited as "172 women," *Cumberland County, New Jersey.*

3. Gage's initiative reflected international activity. In its first issue, *The Revolution* reported the resistance by British women to the 1867 voting act, which rejected female suffrage. Some of the many women who registered to vote succeeded. Their resistance continued throughout 1868 but was thrown out of court. *The Revolution* reported the story throughout. See Bertha Mason, *The Story of the Women's Suffrage Movement* (London: Sherrat & Hughes, 1912), 35–40.

4. "Women Who voted," *The Elizabeth Cady Stanton and Susan B. Anthony Papers Project*, Rutgers University, sorted chronologically at http://ecssba.rutgers.edu/resources/voters.html and accessed March 28, 2018, hereinafter cited as ECS and SBA, *Women Who Voted.*

5. "172 women," *Cumberland County, New Jersey.*

6. Ibid.

7. "Why in Vineland?"—*Cumberland County, New Jersey*, The New Jersey home page, American Local History Network, accessed March 28, 2018, at http://www.usgennet.org/usa/nj/county/cumberland/VineVote/Why.html.

8. *The Revolution*, September 17, 1868. Anthony and Stanton had just visited Vineland. Stone long before had raised this point about the cancellation, purely by legislation in 1807, of a constitutional provision. See Stone, *Woman Suffrage in New Jersey*, 14.

9. "Virginia Minor," *Historic Missourians*, State Historical Society of Missouri, retrieved from http://shsmo.org/historicmissourians/name/m/minor/ March 28, 2018.

10. ART. 16: "The Right of Suffrage in the United States shall be based on citizenship, and shall be regulated by Congress; and all citizens of the United States, whether native or naturalized, shall enjoy this right equally without any distinction or discrimination whatever founded on sex" (*HWS* II, 333).

11. *HWS* II, 333.

12. *The Revolution*, April 29, 1869.

13. See extracts from *The Revolution*, other newspapers and letters in *HWS* II, 333–340.

14. *The Revolution*, June 3, 1869 in *HWS* II, 334.

15. Ibid., 335.

16. Sally G. McMillen, *Lucy Stone: An Unapologetic Life* (Oxford: Oxford University Press, 2015), 181–185.

17. Dudden, *Fighting Chance*, 162–166; "Woman Suffrage," *NASS*, October 10, 1868; "Woman's Rights," *NASS*, November 28, 1868.

18. "Be it enacted 'by the Senate and House of Representatives of the United States of America in Congress Assembled, That from and after the passage of this act the right of Suffrage in the Territory of Utah shall belong to, and may be exercised by, the people thereof, without any distinction or discrimination whatever founded on sex,'" introduced in Congress on March 25, 1869, by Mr. George W. Julian (*HWS* II, 325). Utah women would lose the vote under the Edmunds-Tucker Act of Congress in 1887.

19. This entry, though second in a list of receipts by Lucy Stone, does not name her—hence the uncertainty. See *NAWSA Papers*, "Accounts of Wendell Phillips."

20. ECS "Pronunciamento," *The Revolution*, July 15, 1869, 24.

21. "Virginia Minor," *Historic Missourians*, State Historical Society of Missouri, retrieved March 28, 2018 from http://shsmo.org/historic missourians/name/m/minor/.

22. *HWS* II, 407–411; see *The Revolution*, October 21, 1869.

23. See ECS and SBA, *Women Who Voted*.

24. ECS to Isabella Beecher Hooker, February 3, 1871, Gordon, *Selected Papers*, II, 411–413. Hooker's view of the McFarland-Richardson case was that Abby, because of her child, should never have divorced (despite the abuse) and that falling in love so soon afterwards was suspicious. See White, *The Beecher Sisters*, 149.

25. See George Cooper, *Lost Love: A True Story of Passion, Murder, and Justice in Old New York* (New York: Pantheon Books, 1994).

26. *HWS* I, 749.

27. ECS to Isabella Beecher Hooker, February 3, 1871, Gordon, *Selected Papers*, II, 411–413.

28. ECS and SBA, *Women Who Voted*.

29. "Virginia Minor and Women's Right to Vote," *National Park Service*, Gateway Arch National Park, Missouri, retrieved March 28, 2018 from https://www.nps.gov/jeff/learn/historyculture/the-virginia-minor-case.htm, hereinafter referred to as *National Park Service*, "Virginia Minor."

30. See Anthony's letter, "November 1, 1872: Susan B. Anthony Registers to Vote," retrieved from *On This Deity*, at http://www.onthisdeity.com/1st-november-1872-%E2%80%93-susan-b-anthony-registers-to-vote/ March 28, 2018.

31. Approximately fourteen other Rochester women voted that day (see Gordon, *Selected Papers* II, 527–529).

32. SBA to ECS, November 5, 1872, Gordon, *Selected Papers* II, 524.

33. Ann D. Gordon, "The Trial of Susan B. Anthony," in *Federal Trials and Great Debates in United States History*, Federal Judicial History Office, 2005, Federal Judicial Center, accessed at https://www.fjc.gov/history/famous-federal-trials/us-v-susan-b-anthony-fight-womens-suffrage March 28, 2018, hereinafter referred to as Gordon, *Susan B. Anthony Trial*.

34. Chronology from Gordon, *Susan B. Anthony Trial*, 11–14.

35. Sherr, *Trial of Susan B. Anthony*, 151–178.

36. Ibid.

37. Gordon, *Susan B. Anthony Trial*, 5–6.

38. *The Butchers' Benevolent Association of New Orleans v. The Crescent City Live-Stock Landing and Slaughter-House Company et al.* [*Slaughterhouse Cases*], 83 U.S. 36 (1872).

39. *Bradwell v. State of Illinois*, 83 U.S. 36 (1873).

40. *National Park Service*, "Virginia Minor." See also Minor, Virginia Louisa, "Statement, brief, and petition," (St. Louis: Industrial Age, 1873), Harvard Library, accessed March 28, 2018, at https://iiif.lib.harvard.edu/manifests/view/drs:2575110$1i; *Minor, Virginia L., and Minor, Francis vs. Happersett, Reese*, Supreme Court Case Files, Box 740, Folder 03, Missouri State Archives. See also Truman A. Post, ed.,

Reports of Cases Argued and Determined in the Supreme Court of the State of Missouri, vol. 53 (St. Louis: Gilbert, 1907), 58–63, retrieved April 6, 2018 from https://books.google.com/books?id=ENIaAAAAYAAJ&pg=PR3&source=gbs_selected_pages&cad=2#v=onepage&q&f=false.

41. *National Park Service*, "Virginia Minor" (phrase italicized by this author for clarity).

42. Gordon, *Susan B. Anthony Trial*, 5–7.

43. Sherr, *Trial of Susan. B. Anthony*, 84–85.

44. Gordon, *Susan B. Anthony Trial*, 8.

45. Sherr, *Trial of Susan. B. Anthony*, vii-xxix; Gordon, *Susan B. Anthony Trial*, 5.

46. *Minor v. Happersett*, 88 U.S. 162 (1875), Cornell Law School, Legal Information Institute, accessed March 28, 2018, at https://www.law.cornell.edu/supremecourt/text/88/162.

47. Ibid.

48. *United States v. Reese et al.*, 92 U.S. 214 (1876), Supreme Court, Justia.com, accessed at https://supreme.justia.com/cases/federal/us/92/214/case.html March 28, 2018.

Epigraphs

1. *The Revolution*, January 14, 1869; *HWS* II, 319.

2. Harper, *Life and Work* I, 286.

3. *HWS* II, 323.

4. *HWS* I, 60–61.

5. SBA to Anna Howard Shaw, c. March 11, 1906, on her deathbed. See "Obituary of Susan B. Anthony," *NYT*, March 13, 1906.

Appendix A

1. See Gordon, *Selected Papers*, II: 22, n. 9, 10; 69–70, n. 2, 5; 86–87; DuBois, *Feminism and Suffrage*, 64–66, n. 29, 31–36. Washington, D.C. is a jurisdiction under the control of Congress.

Appendix B

1. "14th Amendment," U.S. *Constitution*, accessed April 9, 2018, at https://www.usconstamrat.net/constamrat.html#Am14. Note there is a difference between the date of a state's ratification and the secretary of state's certification. The Kansas state legislature, for example, ratified January 9, 1867. For each state, see Flack, *Fourteenth Amendment*, vol. 26, 172–3.

2. Nebraska entered the Union on March 1, 1867, becoming the 37th state, increasing the required three-quarters of states for ratification from 27 to 28.

3. The 14th Amendment was certified in a manner as dubiously constitutional as it was ratified. With the July 9, 1868, ratification of South Carolina and Louisiana, Congress declared the 14th Amendment ratified, ignoring Ohio and New Jersey rescissions and a potential rescission in Oregon. Secretary of State William H. Seward, in charge of certification, proclaimed ratification on July 20, referring to the "questionable status of the Ohio and New Jersey ratifications." Discontented, Congress, on July 21, "assuming the function of the Secretary of State … proclaimed by joint resolution that the 14th Amendment was officially ratified." Seward followed up on July 28 with another proclamation of the amendment's ratification (see Mike Scruggs, "The Unconstitutional Fruit of an Unconstitutional Amendment," in *Ratifying the Fourteenth Amendment,* June 7, 2015, accessed April 9, 2018, at thetribunepapers.com, http://www.thetribunepapers.com/2015/06/07/ratifying-the-fourteenth-amendment-2/.

Appendix C

1. Columns 1 and 2: The Civil War home page, "Results of the 1860 Census," accessed May 16, 2018, at http://www.civil-war.net/pages/1860_census.html.

2. Columns 3 and 4: Kennedy, *1860 Census,* 594–595.

Appendix D

1. Derived from Kennedy, *1860 Census,* 592–595.

2. Totals are age 20 and up.

Bibliography

Abbot, Mabel. *George William Curtis Papers.* Staten Island, New York, Museum Archives and Library Special Collections. n.d. http://www.statenislandmuseum.org/images/uploads/collections/Curtis_(George_William)_Papers_Finding_Aids.pdf.

"Address to the Voters of Kansas, September 25, 1867." Kansas Memory, Kansas Historical Society. n.d. http://www.kshs.org/km/items/view/206171.

"Affidavit of Roda Ann Childs." September 26, 1866. Freedmen and Southern Society Project, History Department, University of Maryland. http://www.freedmen.umd.edu/Childs.html.

American Local History Network. "On November 3, 1868, 172 women (including 4 'colored' women) voted in Vineland, NJ." n.d. New Jersey home page, Cumberland County, New Jersey. http://www.usgennet.org/usa/nj/county/cumberland/VineVote/Vote.html.

Anthony, K. *Susan B. Anthony: Her Personal History and Her Era.* New York: Doubleday, 1954.

Anthony, S.B. "Address of Susan B. Anthony Delivered in Twenty-nine of the Post Office Districts of Monroe, and Twenty-one of Ontario, in Her Canvass of Those Counties, Prior to Her Trial in June 1873." In L. Sherr, *The Trial of Susan B. Anthony.* New York: Humanity Books, 2003.

Bacon, M.H. "One Great Bundle of Humanity: Frances Ellen Watkins Harper (1825–1911)." *Pennsylvania Magazine of History and Biography* 113, no. 1 (January 1989), 35–37.

Barry, K. *Susan B. Anthony: A Biography of a Singular Feminist.* New York: Ballantine, 1988.

Bates, O.W. "Municipal Suffrage for Women in Michigan." In M.K. Eagle, *The Congress of Women Held in the Woman's Building, World's Columbian Exposition, Chicago, U.S.A., 1893.* A Celebration of Woman Writers. Edited by Mary Mark Ockerbloom. Chicago, 1894. http://digital.library.upenn.edu/women/eagle/congress/bates.html.

Beard, R. "The Birth of the 13th Amendment." *New York Times,* April 18, 2014. Retrieved November 15, 2016. http://opinionator.blogs.nytimes.com/2014/04/08/the-birth-of-the-13th-amendment/.

A Bill Extending the Right of Suffrage in the District of Columbia. Library of Congress, U.S. Congressional Documents and Debates, 1774–1875, Bills and Resolutions, House, February 6, 1866. https://memory.loc.gov/cgi-bin/query/D?hlaw:1:./temp/~ammem_0t03.

Blackwell, A.S. *Lucy Stone: Pioneer of Woman's Rights.* Boston: Little, Brown, 1930.

Blackwell, H.B. *What the South Can Do: How the Southern States Can Make Themselves Masters of the Situation.* New York: Robert J. Johnston, January 15, 1867.

Bradwell v. The State of Illinois, 83 U.S. 130 (1872).

Braxton, A.C. *The 15th Amendment: An Account of Its Enactment; Report of the Fifteenth Annual Meeting of the Virginia State Bar Association, Held at Hot Springs of Virginia, August 26, 27 and 28, 1903.* Richmond: Everett Waddey, 1903.

Brockett, L.P., and M.C. Vaughan. *Woman's Work in the Civil War: A Record of Heroism, Patriotism and Patience.* Boston: Zeigler, McCurdy, 1867. https://archive.org/details/womansworkincivi5900broc.

Brown, I. *Mary Grew: Abolitionist and Feminist, 1813–1896.* Selinsgrove, PA: Susquehanna University Press, 1991.

Brown, O. *Acquaintances, Old and New, Among Reformers.* Olympia Brown, 1911.

Cahill, B. *Alice Paul, the National Woman's Party and the Vote: The First Civil Rights Struggle of the 20th Century.* Jefferson, NC: McFarland, 2015.

_____. "A Bulwark against Equality: The 1868 Constitutional Convention in Little Rock, Arkansas." *Pulaski County Historical Review* 67, no. 3 (Fall 2019), 84–89.

_____. "Campaign Poverty, Women's Equality and the Right to Vote." History Blog. Women's History Network Conference, July 2016. Women's Material Cultures/Women's Material Environments, Leeds Trinity University, UK. https://womenshistorynetwork.org/campaign-poverty-womens-equality-and-the-right-to-vote/

_____. George Francis Train addresses Leavenworth, 1867 https://www.visitleavenworthks.com/visitors/page/george-francis-train-addresses-leavenworth-1867.

_____. Leavenworth Hosts Pioneering Women's Election-Day Campaign https://www.visitleavenworthks.com/visitors/page/leavenworth-hosts-pioneering-womens-election-day-campaign

_____. Leavenworth Resident Starts Nationwide Civil Rights Campaign https://www.visitleavenworthks.com/visitors/page/leavenworth-resident-starts-nationwide-civil-rights-campaign

_____. "Money, Politics and Equal Rights for Women." History Blog. Women's History Network Conference, June 2016. Women's Material Cultures/Women's Material Environments, Leeds Trinity University, UK. https://womenshistorynetwork.org/money-politics-and-equal-rights-for-women/

_____. "The Perils of Prejudice: Misadventures with Susan B. Anthony, Elizabeth Cady Stanton and George Francis Train in Reconstruction America." 25th Anniversary BrANCH Conference, Madingley Hall, Cambridge, UK, October 7, 2018, unpublished.

_____. "Thanksgiving Visitor Learns How the Woman Saved the Day." *Richland Beacon-News*, December 31, 2009.

_____. "Where There's a Will, There's a Crowd of Greedy Relatives: Women's Rights and Men's Wrongs in the United States, 1848–1870." Powerpoint Presentation, Women's History Network Conference, September 16, 2016. Women's Material Cultures/Women's Material Environments, Leeds Trinity University, UK.

A Century of Lawmaking for a New Nation: U.S. Congressional Documents and Debates (1774–1875). Congress of the United States. https://memory.loc.gov/ammem/amlaw/lwcg.html.

Chaput, E.J. "The Reconstruction Wars Begin." *New York Times*, February 1, 2015. http://opinionator.blogs.nytimes.com/2015/02/01/the-reconstruction-wars-begin/?_r=0.

Childers, R.C. "Charles Vernon Eskridge and Kansas Politics, 1855–1900." Master's thesis, Emporia State University, Department of Social Sciences, 2004. https://esirc.emporia.edu/handle/123456789/976

Civil Rights Act of 1866. Wikipedia. https://en.wikipedia.org/wiki/Civil_Rights_Act_of_1866.

Clifford, D.P. *Crusader for Freedom: A Life of Lydia Maria Child*. Boston: Beacon Press, 1992.

Collier-Thomas, B. "Frances Ellen Watkins Harper: Abolitionist and Feminist Reformer, 1825–1911." In A.D. Gordon, and B. Collier-Thomas, *African American Women and the Vote, 1837–1965*. Amherst: University of Massachusetts Press, 1997.

Concurrent Resolution Amending the Constitution of the State of Kansas. February 1867. Kansas Memory. http://www.kansasmemory.org/item/209676.

Congressional Globe. 1865–70.

Coontz, S. *The Social Origins of Private Life: A History of American Families, 1600–1900*. London and New York: Verso, 1988.

Cooper, G. *Lost Love: A True Story of Passion, Murder, and Justice in Old New York*. New York: Pantheon Books, 1994.

Corbett, K.T. *In Her Place: A Guide to St. Louis Women's History*. St. Louis: Missouri Historical Society Press, 1999.

Covkin, S. "The American Civil War and Women's Citizenship: Susan B. Anthony, Elizabeth Cady Stanton, and the Women's Loyal National League." *Journal of the Cornell Historical Society* (2014). Retrieved May 7, 2017. http://creativecommons.org/licenses/by-nc-nd/4.0/.

Cutler, W.G. *History of the State of Kansas: Legislative and Political Annals*, Part 2. Kansas Collection Books, 1883. http://www.kancoll.org/books/cutler/sthist/annals-p2.html.

Debates and Proceedings of the Convention Which Assembled at Little Rock, January 7th, 1868, under the Provisions of the Act of Congress of March 2d, 1867, and the Acts of March 23rd and July 19th, 1867, Supplementary Thereto, to Form a Constitution. Little Rock: J.G. Price, 1868.

DiClerico, R.E. *Voting in America: A Reference Handbook*. Santa Barbara: ABC-Clio, 2004.

Dorr, R.C. *Susan B. Anthony: The Woman Who Changed the Mind of a Nation*. New York: Frederick A. Stokes, 1928.

Douglass, F. *The Anti-slavery Movement: A Lecture by Frederick Douglass Before the Rochester Ladies' Anti-Slavery Society*. Rochester, NY: Press of Lee, Mann, 1855.

_____. *The Mission of War*. 1864. blackpast.org, "An Online Reference Guide to African American History." http://www.blackpast.org/1864-frederick-douglass-mission-war.

_____. "Speech before the International Council of Women, in Washington, D.C." *Woman's Journal* (1888). http://www.blackpast.org/?q=1888-frederick-douglass-woman-suffrage.

_____. "Speech before the Massachusetts Anti-Slavery Society, January 26, 1864, and May 9, 1865." Library of Congress, Frederick Douglass Papers. http://hdl.loc.gov/loc.mss/mfd. 22010.

Dubois, E.C. *Feminism and Suffrage: The Emergence of an Independent Women's Movement in America, 1848–1869.* Ithaca and London: Cornell University Press, 1978.

Dudden, F.E. *Fighting Chance: The Struggle Over Woman Suffrage and Black Suffrage in Reconstruction America.* New York: Oxford University Press, 2011.

Edmund Jackson vs. Wendell Phillips et al., 14 Allen 539, 96 Mass. 539, 571. Suffolk County, Massachusetts (January 1867). http://mass cases.com/cases/sjc/96/96mass539.html.

Edwards, J. *Timeline of Personhood Rights and Powers.* Women's International League for Peace and Freedom, 2002. http://www.ratical. org/corporations/ToPRaP.html.

Edwards, L.F. *Gendered Strife and Confusion: The Political Culture of Reconstruction.* Urbana and Chicago: University of Illinois Press, 1997.

Eickhoff, D. *Clarina Nichols: Frontier Crusader for Women's Rights.* Kansas City: Quindaro Press, 2016.

_____. *Revolutionary Heart: The Life of Clarina Nichols and the Pioneering Crusade for Women's Rights.* Kansas City: Quindaro Press, 2006.

1860 Census. Civil War home page, "Dedicated to the participants, both North and South, in the great American Civil War." http:// www.civil-war.net/pages/1860_census.html.

Emporia News, "Female Suffrage," by Charles V. Eskridge, June 7, 1867.

Emporia News, "Stand by the Party," September 6, 1867.

Epps, G. *Democracy Reborn: The Fourteenth Amendment and the Fight for Equal Rights in Post Civil War America.* New York. Henry Holt, 2006.

Eskridge, Charles V., "Female Suffrage," *Emporia News,* June 7, 1867.

Finkelman, P. "*Scott v. Sandford*: The Court's Most Dreadful Case." *Chicago-Kent Law Review* 8, no. 3 (2007): 3–48.

Flack, H.E. *The Adoption of the Fourteenth Amendment.* Baltimore: Johns Hopkins Press, 1908.

Flexner, E. *Century of Struggle: The Woman's Rights Movement in the United States.* Massachusetts and London: Belknap Press of Harvard University Press, 1975.

Foner, E. *Reconstruction: America's Unfinished Revolution, 1863–1877.* New York. Harper & Row, 1988.

Foner, P.S. *Frederick Douglass on Women's Rights.* New York: Da Capo Press, 1992.

_____. *Frederick Douglass: Selected Speeches and Writings.* Edited by Y. Taylor. New York: Lawrence Hill Books, 1999.

Fort Scott Monitor, "One of the best misunderstood Statesmen..." (October 26, 1867), reprinted in George Francis Train, *The Great Epigram Campaign of Kansas,* (1867), 43–44.

Foster, F.S. *A Brighter Coming Day: A Frances Ellen Watkins Harper Reader.* New York: Feminist Press at the City University of New York, 1990.

14th Amendment, U.S. Constitution. https://www. usconstitution.net/constamrat.html#Am14.

Fourteenth Amendment to the United States Constitution. Wikipedia. https://en.wikipedia. org/wiki/Fourteenth_Amendment_to_the_ United_States_Constitution.

"14th Amendment to the U.S. Constitution: Civil Rights (1868)." In *The People's Vote: The Most Influential Documents in American History.* February 14, 2017. https://www.our documents.gov/doc.php?doc=43.

Free, L.E. "Gendering the Constitution: Manhood, Race, and Woman Suffrage, 1865–1866." PhD diss., Cornell University, 2009.

_____. *Suffrage Reconstructed: Gender, Race and Voting Rights in the Civil War Era.* New York: Cornell University Press, 2015.

Friedman, L.J. *Gregarious Saints: Self and Community in Antebellum American Abolitionism, 1830–1870.* Cambridge: Cambridge University Press, 1982.

Frost, E., and K. Cullen-DuPont. *Women's Suffrage in America: An Eyewitness History.* New York: Facts on File, 1992.

Galloway, S. *The American Equal Rights Association, 1866–1870: Gender, Race and Universal Suffrage.* School of Historical Studies. Leicester: University of Leicester, 2014. Retrieved May 10, 2017. https://core.ac.uk/ download/pdf/42014280.pdf.

Gambone, J.G. *The Forgotten Feminist of Kansas: The Papers of Clarina I.H. Nichols, 1854–1885.* Edited by B.J. Scott. Kansas Historical Society, May 9, 2017. https://www.kshs.org/ p/the-forgotten-feminist-of-kansas-4/13241.

Gilbreth, T. *The Freedmen's Bureau Report on the Memphis Race Riots of 1866.* Memphis: Bureau of Refugees, Freedmen, and Abandoned Lands, 1865–1869.

Ginzberg, L.D. *Elizabeth Cady Stanton: An American Life.* New York: Hill & Wang, 2009.

Goldsmith, B. *Other Powers: The Age of Suffrage, Spiritualism, and the Scandalous Victoria Woodhull.* New York: HarperCollins, 1999.

Goodheart, A. "The Census of Doom." *New York Times,* April 11, 2011. Retrieved March 22, 2018. https://opinionator.blogs.nytimes. com/2011/04/01/the-census-of-doom/.

Gordon, A.D. *The Selected Papers of Elizabeth*

Cady Stanton and Susan B. Anthony. Vol. 1: *In the School of Anti-Slavery, 1840–1866.* New Brunswick, NJ: Rutgers University Press, 1997.

_____. *The Selected Papers of Elizabeth Cady Stanton and Susan B. Anthony.* Vol. 2: *Against an Aristocracy of Sex, 1866–1873.* New Brunswick, NJ: Rutgers University Press, 1997.

_____. *The Trial of Susan B. Anthony.* Federal Judicial Center: Federal Trials and Great Debates in United States History, 2005. https://www.fjc.gov/history/famous-federal-trials/us-v-susan-b-anthony-fight-womens-suffrage.

A Great Thing for Our People: The Institute for Colored Youth in the Civil War Era, Classes of 1856 to 1864, the Equal Rights League and Voting Suffrage. Falvey Memorial Library, Villanova University. https://exhibits.library.villanova.edu/institute-colored-youth/community-moments/equal-rights-league-and-suffrage/.

Griffing, Josephine, "…the ballot, in the hands of the negro, was a talisman…"quoted in Faye E. Dudden, *Fighting Chance: The Struggle over Woman Suffrage and Black Suffrage in Reconstruction America* (New York: Oxford University Press) 2011, 86, citing *Papers of Elizabeth Cady Stanton and Susan B. Anthony,* Microfilm Edition, (1991).

Grogg, R. *Where Oh Where Should the Capital Be?: The Seat of the Government in an Expanding Nation.* White House History, n.d. https://www.whitehousehistory.org/where-oh-where-should-the-capital-be-white-house-history-number-34.

Hampson, W. *On Account of Color or Sex: A Historical Examination of the Split between Women's Rights in the American Equal Rights Association, 1866–1869.* May 9, 2017. https://www.iup.edu. https://www.iup.edu/WorkArea/DownloadAsset.aspx?id=37705.

Harlow, R.V. *Gerrit Smith, Philanthropist and Reformer.* New York. Henry Holt, 1939.

Harper, I.H. *The Life and Work of Susan B. Anthony.* Indianapolis and Kansas City: Bowen-Merrill, 1899.

Harrison, J. "Reconstructing the Privileges or Immunities Clause." *Yale Law Journal* 10 (1992): 1385.

Harrison, R. *Washington during Civil War and Reconstruction: Race and Radicalism.* New York: Cambridge University Press, 2011.

Henry Clarke Wright. Wikipedia. https://en.wikipedia.org/wiki/Henry_Clarke_Wright.

Holland, P.G., and A.D. Gordon. *Papers of Elizabeth Cady Stanton and Susan B. Anthony.* Microfilm ed. Wilmington, DE: Scholarly Resources, 1991.

Holland, P.G. *George Francis Train and the Woman Suffrage Movement, 1867–70.* April 1987. Books at Iowa 46. http://www.lib.uiowa.edu/spec-coll/bai/holland.htm.

Hosen, F.E. *Federal Laws of the Reconstruction: Principal Congressional Acts and Resolutions, Presidential Proclamations, Speeches and Orders, and Other Legislative and Military Documents, 1862–1875.* Jefferson, NC: McFarland, 2010.

House Joint Resolution Proposing the 15th Amendment to the Constitution. December 7, 1868. National Archives, America's Historical Documents. https://www.archives.gov/historical-docs/todays-doc/?dod-date=1210.

House Joint Resolution Proposing the 13th Amendment to the Constitution. January 31, 1865. National Archives: America's Historical Documents. https://www.archives.gov/historical-docs/13th-amendment.

House Journal of the Legislative Assembly of the State of Kansas, Begun and Held at Topeka. Leavenworth, KS: Clarke, 1867.

Howard, J. M. "Congress Debates the Fourteenth Amendment (1866)." n.d. Encyclopedia.com. http://www.encyclopMedia.com/doc/1G2–3401804785.html.

Hudnall, T. "Affidavit: Use of the Army in Certain of the Southern States." In *House of Representatives Executive Document No 30, September 4, 1868, Ex. Doc. 44th Cong. 2nd sess.* 1877. New York: Arno Press and New York Times, 1869.

Jackson, F. *Will of Francis Jackson.* Boston Public Library Anti-Slavery Collection. January 28, 1861. archive.org. https://archive.org/stream/willoffrancisjac00mays/39999063811150#page/n0/mode/2up.

Johnson, Senator Reverdy, "The whole female sex not only are not, but never have been, free women…" *Congressional Globe,* Senate, 39th Congress, 1st Session, February 9, 1866, 768.

Johnson, W.H. *Autobiography of Dr. William Henry Johnson.* n.d. Archive.org. https://archive.org/stream/tohisadoptedhome00johnrich/tohisadoptedhome00johnrich_djvu.txt.

Jolley, L.R. *Benjamin Gratz Brown.* Historic Missourians. http://shs.umsystem.edu/historicmissourians/name/b/brownb/index.html.

Jones, R. *Women's Right to Vote in Kentucky.* Notable Kentucky African Americans Database, University of Kentucky Libraries, 2017. http://nkaa.uky.edu/record.php?note_id=1621.

Journal of the Convention of the State of New York, Begun and Held at the Capitol in the City of Albany on the 4th day of June, 1867. n.d.

Journal of the House of Representatives of the United States. n.d.

Journal of the Senate of the United States of America. n.d.

Kalloch's *Home Journal,* "Success to Train in everything but Female Suffrage," (1867), reprinted in George Francis Train, *The Great Epigram Campaign of Kansas,* (1867), no specific date, at 46.

Kansas Chief, "New York Gazette," *Thingamyjigs* column, September 26, 1867.

Kansas Lieutenant Governors. Kansas Historical Society. April 3, 2018. https://www.kshs.org/p/kansas-lieutenant-governors/10998#eskridge.

Kendi, I.X. "The Promise and Peril of the Civil Rights Act of 1866." American Historical Association, AHA Historians Blog. October 11, 2016. http://blog.historians.org/2016/10/promise-peril-civil-rights-act-1866/.

Kendrick, B.B. "The *Journal of the Joint Committee of Fifteen on Reconstruction.*" PhD diss., University of Columbia, 1914. https://archive.org/texts/flipbook/flippy.php?id=journaljointcom00recogoog.

Kennedy, J. *Population of the United States in 1860: Compiled from the Original Returns of the Eighth Census.* Washington, D.C.: Secretary of the Interior, 1864.

Kerr, A.M. *Lucy Stone: Speaking Out for Equality.* New Brunswick, NJ: Rutgers University Press, 1992.

Keyssar, A. *The Right to Vote: The Contested History of Democracy in the United States.* New York: Basic Books, 2000.

Kolmerten, C.A. *The American Life of Ernestine L. Rose.* Syracuse, NY: Syracuse University Press, 1999.

Lane, E.B. *Pioneer Days in Strawn and Ottumwa.* Rootsweb, Ancestry.com. April 3, 2018. http://www.rootsweb.ancestry.com/~kscoffhp/history/pioneerdaysstrawnottumwa.html.

Lawrence, D. "There Is No 'Fourteenth Amendment.'" *U.S. News and World Report,* 1957.

Lincoln, C.Z. *Constitutional History of New York, 1822–1894.* Rochester, NY: Lawyers' Co-operative, 1905.

List of Ethnic Slurs. Wikipedia. https://en.wikipedia.org/wiki/List_of_ethnic_slurs#S.

Lutz, A. *Created Equal: A Biography of Elizabeth Cady Stanton, 1815–1902.* New York: Van Rees Press, 1940.

_____. *Susan B. Anthony: Rebel, Crusader, Humanitarian.* Washington, D.C.: Zenger, 1959.

Margolis, A.T. *The Isabella Beecher Hooker Project: A Microfiche Edition of Her Papers.* Millwood, NY: KTO Microform, 1979.

Married Women's Property Laws. Retrieved May 3, 2017, Law Library of Congress. https://memory.loc.gov/ammem/awhhtml/awlaw3/property_law.html.

Mason, B. *The Story of the Women's Suffrage Movement.* London: Sherrat & Hughes, 1912.

May, S.J. *Francis Jackson's Anti Slavery Bequest.* August 27, 1867. Boston Public Library anti–Slavery Collection, archive.org. https://archive.org/details/francisjacksonsa00mays.

McKitrick, E.L. *Andrew Johnson and Reconstruction.* Oxford: Oxford University Press, 1960.

McMillen, S.G. *Lucy Stone: An Unapologetic Life.* Oxford and New York: Oxford University Press, 2015.

McPherson, E. *The Political History of the United States of America During the Period of Reconstruction, from April 15, 1865, to July 15, 1870.* Washington: Soloman & Chapman, 1875. http://quod.lib.umich.edu/m/moa/abz4761.0001.001/3?view=image&size=100.

McPherson, J.M. "Abolitionism, Woman Suffrage and the Negro." *Mid-America* 47 (1965), 40–47.

_____. *The Struggle for Equality: Abolitionists and the Negro in the Civil War and Reconstruction,.* Princeton, NJ: Princeton University Press, 1995.

Meltzer, M., P.G. Holland and F. Krasno *Lydia Maria Child: Selected Letters, 1817–1880.* Amherst: University of Massachusetts Press, 1983.

Memorial of the American Equal Rights Association to the Congress of the United States. November 3, 1867. National Archives Catalogue: Records of the U.S. House of Representatives, 1789–2015. https://research.archives.gov/id/7452160.

Mesinger, J. "The Feminist Movement as Reflected in the Gerrit Smith Papers." *Courier* 10, no. 3 (1973).

Minneapolis & St. Louis Ry. Co. v. Beckwith, 129 U.S. 26, Supreme Court (January 7, 1889).

Minnesota Right to Vote, Amendment 1. 1867. Ballotopedia—Encyclopedia of American Politics. https://ballotpedia.org/Minnesota_Right_to_Vote,_Amendment_1_(1867).

Minor v. Happersett, 88 U.S. 162 (1875).

Minor, Virginia Louisa. *Statement, Brief, and Petition, St. Louis.* Industrial Age, 1873. Harvard Library. https://iiif.lib.harvard.edu/manifests/view/drs:2575110$1i.

Moneka Woman's Rights Association. 1858. Retrieved May 17, 2017. Kansapedia. https://www.kshs.org/kansapedia/moneka-womans-rights-association/15158.

Mundine, T.H. *Declaration of T.H. Mundine.* Texas State Library and Archives Commission. February 14, 2017. https://www.tsl.texas.gov/exhibits/suffrage/beginnings/1868-1.html.

Murfreesboro Monitor, "We would prefer to see women vote…" (October 7, 1865). Quotation displayed in the Visitor Center, Stones River

National Battlefield, 3501 Old Nashville Highway, Murfreesboro, TN 37129.

Murray, J.S. *On the Equality of the Sexes.* Edited by M.M. Ockerbloom. A Celebration of Women Writers. 1790. http://digital.library.upenn.edu/women/murray/equality/equality.html.

NAWSA Papers. Accounts of Wendell Phillips with the Francis Jackson Fund, Library of Congress. (1859–1871). Microfilm Edition, Reel 11, frames 351–353.

New York Tribune, May 10, 1866, "The Anniversaries," quoting Stephen S. Foster.

Nichols, C.I.H. Letter dated February 24, 1867, to the Editor, *Vermont Phoenix,* reprinted in Gambone, J.G., *The Forgotten Feminist of Kansas* IV, 515.

_____. "The present government of Kansas is 'bogus,'" "Female Suffrage," *Kansas Farmer,* April, 1867.

Newsum, Dani, *Lincoln Hills and Civil Rights in Colorado,* at https://www.google.com/search?q=https%3A%2F%2Fwww.historycolorado.org+%E2%80%BA+files+%E2%80%BA+lincoln_hills_primary_resource_set&rlz=1C1CHBF_enUS719US719&oq=https%3A%2F%2Fwww.historycolorado.org+%E2%80%BA+files+%E2%80%BA+lincoln_hills_primary_resource_set&aqs=chrome..69i57.1975j0j7&sourceid=chrome&ie=UTF-8.

Noell, Representative T.E. House of Representatives, 39th Congress, 2nd Session, *Congressional Globe,* Appendix (February 11 and 18, 1867), 108–116 at 114.

Noell, T.E. "Speech of Hon. T.E. Noell of Missouri in the House of Representatives." *Congressional Globe,* February 11 and 18, 1867.

"Noell, Thomas Estes (1839–1867)." Biographical Directory of the United States Congress. http://bioguide.congress.gov/scripts/biodisplay.pl?index=N000123.

"North Country Played a Role in the Women's Rights Movement." *Watertown (NY) Daily Times,* August 30, 2015. http://www.watertowndailytimes.com/opinion/a-moment-in-history-north-country-played-a-role-in-the-womens-rights-movement-20150830.

Noun, L.R. *Strong-Minded Women: The Emergence of the Woman-Suffrage Movement in Iowa.* Ames: Iowa State University Press, 1969.

Oberholtzer, E.P. *A History of the United States Since the Civil War.* New York: MacMillan, 1917.

Ohio Denial of Right to Vote, Amendment 1 (October 1867). Ballotpedia. https://ballotpedia.org/Ohio_Denial_of_Right_to_Vote,_Amendment_1_(October_1867).

O'Neil, T. "A Look Back: St. Louis Hosts Convention in 1869 in Pitch to Become Nation's Capital." *St. Louis Post-Dispatch,* October 20, 2012. http://www.stltoday.com/news/local/metro/a-look-back-st-louis-hosts-convention-in-in-pitch/article_965ad70c-2207-5406-a875-bd786bf6a20c.html.

An Ordinance for the Government of the Territory of the United States Northwest of the River Ohio (July 13, 1787). Avalon Project: Documents in Law, History and Diplomacy, Yale Law School, Lillian Goldman Law Library, Newhaven, Connecticut. http://avalon.law.yale.edu/18th_century/nworder.asp.

Painter, N.I. *Sojourner Truth: A Life, a Symbol.* New York and London: W.W. Norton, 1996.

Palmer, B.W. *Selected Letters of Lucretia Coffin Mott.* Champaign: University of Illinois Press, 2002.

_____. *The Selected Papers of Thaddeus Stevens.* Pittsburg: University of Pittsburg Press, 1998.

Peery, D.W. "Hon. Milton W. Reynolds (Kicking Bird)." *Chronicles of Oklahoma* 13, no. 1 (March 1935), 46–52. http://digital.library.okstate.edu/Chronicles/v013/v013p046.html.

Phillips, W. "Woman's Rights Tract No. 1." In W. Phillips, Mrs. Mill, T. Higginson, and C.I. Nichols, *Woman's Rights Tracts.* Boston: Robert F. Wallcut, 1854.

Phillips, W., and T.C. Pease. *Speeches, Lectures and Letters of Wendell Phillips,* vol. 2. Boston: Lee and Shepard, 1891. http://www.perseus.tufts.edu/hopper/text?doc=Perseus%3Atext%3A2001.05.0189%3Achapter%3D11.

Post, T.A. *Reports of Cases Argued and Determined in the Supreme Court of the State of Missouri.* Vol. 53. St. Louis, MO: Gilbert, 1907.

Proceedings of the Colored Convention of the State of Kansas Held at Leavenworth, October 13, 14, 15 and 16, 1863. http://coloredconventions.org/items/show/270.

Proceedings of the First Anniversary of the American Equal Rights Association Held at the Church of the Puritans, New York, May 9 and 10, 1867. New York, Robert J. Johnston.

Proceedings of the National Convention of Colored Men, Held in the City of Syracuse, N.Y., October 4, 5, 6 and 7, [1864] with the Bill of Wrongs and Rights, and Address to the American People. Boston: J.S. Rock and Geo. L. Ruffin, 1864. ColoredConventions.org. http://coloredconventions.org/items/show/282.

Proceedings of the National Convention of the Colored Men of America, Held in Washington, D.C., on January 13, 14, 15 and 16, 1869. Colored Conventions.org. http://coloredconventions.org/items/show/452

Report of the Committee on the Rights of Suffrage and Qualifications to Hold Office: Documents of the Convention of the State of New

York, 1867–1868. Vol. 1, 1 to 39. Albany: Weed, Parsons, 1868. http://quod.lib.umich.edu/m/moa/AEY0592.0001.001?rgn=main;view=fulltext.

The Revolution, "Women ... must not look to these men...," January 14, 1869, 24.

Reyes, J. "A Mere Demagoguery: Leavenworth and Atchison County Newspaper Coverage of the Kansas Women's Suffrage Campaign of 1867." Kansas State University Department of History, February 4, 2016. http://hdl.handle.net/2097/12139.

Robertson, S.M. *Parker Pillsbury: Radical Abolitionist, Male Feminist.* Ithica and London: Cornell University Press, 2007.

Rutherglen, G.A. *Civil Rights in the Shadow of Slavery: The Constitution, Common Law, and the Civil Rights Act of 1866.* New York: Oxford University Press, 2012.

San Mateo County v. Southern Pacific Railroad, 116 U.S. 138: 6 S. Ct. 317, 29 L. Ed. 589 (December 21, 1885).

Scruggs, M. *The Unconstitutional Fruit of an Unconstitutional Amendment.* Ratifying the Fourteenth Amendment. June 7, 2015. http://www.thetribunepapers.com/2015/06/07/ratifying-the-fourteenth-amendment-2/.

Senate Journal of the Legislative Assembly of the State of Kansas, Begun and Held at Topeka. Leavenworth: Clarke, Emery, 1867.

Sherr, Lynn. *The Trial of Susan B. Anthony.* New York. Humanity, 2003.

Simpson, J. *Annual Iowa Year Book of Agriculture.* Des Moines, 1904.

Stanley, A.D. *From Bondage to Contract: Wage Labor, Marriage and the Market in the Age of Slave Emancipation.* New York: Cambridge University Press, 1998.

Stanton, E.C. *Eighty Years and More: Reminiscences, 1815–1897.* New York: European, 1898.

Stanton, E.C., S.B. Anthony and M.J. Gage. *History of Woman Suffrage.* Vol. 1. New York: Fowler & Wells, 1882.

_____. *History of Woman Suffrage.* Vol. 2. Rochester, NY: Susan B. Anthony, 1887.

Stanton, Elizabeth Cady, "Build a New House," *National Anti-Slavery Standard,* July 21, 1866.

Stanton, T., and H.S. Blatch. *Elizabeth Cady Stanton as Revealed in Her Letters, Diaries and Reminiscences.* New York and London: Harper & Brothers, 1922.

Stebbins, H.A. *A Political History of the State of New York, 1865–1869.* New York: Columbia University, 1913.

Sterling, D. *Ahead of Her Time: Abby Kelley and the Politics of Antislavery.* New York: Norton, 1994.

Stewart, J.B. *Wendell Phillips: Liberty's Hero.* Baton Rouge: Louisiana State University Press, 1986.

Stone, L. *Woman Suffrage in New Jersey: An Address Delivered by Lucy Stone, at a Hearing before the New Jersey Legislature, March 6th, 1867.* Boston: C.H. Simonds, 1867.

Sumner, C. S.R. 1: *A Joint Resolution Proposing an Amendment to the Constitution of the United States* (December 4, 1865). U.S. Congressional Documents and Debates, 1774–1875—Bills and Resolutions, Senate. https://memory.loc.gov/cgi-bin/ampage?collId=llsr&fileName=039/llsr039.db&recNum=0.

"Susan B. Anthony Boldly Writes the Speaker of the House Asking for a Public Endorsement of Women's Suffrage" (c. October 1866). Equal Rights Convention for New York State, Raab Collection. http://www.raabcollection.com/american-history-autographs/anthony-susan-1866#sthash.uBtelNst.dpuf.

"Susan B. Anthony Registers to Vote" (November 1, 1872). On This Deity. http://www.onthisdeity.com/1st-november-1872-%E2%80%93-susan-b-anthony-registers-to-vote/.

Tarter, B. "Fourteenth Amendment to the U.S. Constitution." June and October 26, 2015. Encyclopedia of Virginia. http://www.encyclopediavirginia.org/Fourteenth_Amendment_to_the_U_S_Constitution#.

Testimonials to the Life and Character of the Late Francis Jackson. Boston: E.F. Wallcut, 1861. https://play.google.com/store/books/details/In_Memoriam?id=M8zweFva3ocC.

"The Anniversaries." *New York Tribune,* May 10, 1866. Women's Advocacy Collection, Women Writers Resource Project, Emory University. http://womenwriters.digitalscholarship.emory.edu/advocacy/content.php?level=div&id=suffragist_008&document=suffragist.

The Butchers' Benevolent Association of New Orleans v. The Crescent City Live-Stock Landing and Slaughter-House Company et al. [Slaughterhouse Cases], 83 U.S. 36 (1872). Cornell Law School, Legal Information Institute.

The Civil Rights Bill of 1866. History, Art and Archives, United States House of Representatives. http://history.house.gov/Historical-Highlights/1851–1900/The-Civil-Rights-Bill-of-1866/.

The House Gag Rule. May 26, 1836. History, Art and Archives, United States House of Representatives. http://history.house.gov/Historical-Highlights/1800-1850/The-House-of-Representatives-instituted-the-%E2%80%9Cgag-rule%E2%80%9D/.

"The New Orleans Massacre." *The Impeachment of Andrew Johnson.* http://www.impeach-andrewjohnson.com/06FirstImpeachmentDiscussions/iiib-8a.htm.

"The Southern Loyalists' Convention: Call for a Convention of Southern Unionists, to Meet at Independence Hall, Philadelphia, on Monday, the Third Day of September, 1866." Hathi Trust Digital Library. https://babel. hathitrust.org/cgi/pt?id=loc.ark:/13960/t341 7359p;view=1up;seq=1.

13th Amendment to the U.S. Constitution. Library of Congress, Primary Documents in American History. http://www.loc.gov/rr/program/bib/ourdocs/13thamendment.html.

"Thomas Estes Noell, 3 Apr 1839–3 Oct 1867." Find a Grave Memorial. April 3, 2018. Findagrave.com. http://www.findagrave.com/cgi-bin/fg.cgi?page=gr&GRid=6908141.

Thornton, W. *The Nine Lives of Citizen Train.* New York: Greenberg, 1948.

Train, G.F. *The Great Epigram Campaign of Kansas.* Leavenworth: Prescott & Hume, 1867. Retrieved April 3, 2016. http://www.kansasmemory.org/item/206263.

_____. *Great Speech on the Withdrawal of Mc-Clennan and the Impeachment of Lincoln.* New York: American News, 1864.

Train, George Francis. "His Speech on the Summit of Pilot Knob." *Memphis Daily Avalanche,* June 27, 1867.

Underhill, E.F. *Proceedings and Debates of the Constitutional Convention of the State of New York.* Albany: Weed, Parsons, 1868. http://babel.hathitrust.org/cgi/pt?id=umn.31951 p01104033t;view=1up;seq=7.

U.S. Congress House Select Committee. *Report of the Select Committee on the New Orleans Riots.* Washington, D.C.: U.S. Government Printing Office, 1867.

United States v. Reese et al, 92 U.S. 214 (1876). Justia.com, Supreme Court.

Venet, W.H. *Neither Ballots nor Bullets: Women Abolitionists and the Civil War.* Charlottesville: University Press of Virginia, 1991.

Virginia L. Minor and Francis Minor v. Reese Happersett. Appeal from the Supreme Court of Missouri (53 Mo. 58 1873).

Virginia L. Minor and Francis Minor v. Reese Happersett, Supreme Court Case Files, Box 740, Folder 03, Missouri State Archives.

Virginia L. Minor and Francis Minor vs. Reese Happersett, Supreme Court of Missouri, 53 Mo. 58 (1873).

"Virginia Minor." Historic Missourians: State Historical Society of Missouri. http://shsmo.org/historicmissourians/name/m/minor/.

"Virginia Minor and Women's Right to Vote." National Park Service, Gateway Arch National Park, Missouri. https://www.nps.gov/jeff/learn/historyculture/the-virginia-minor-case.htm.

"Wendell Phillips." Women's Rights National History Park, New York. https://www.nps.gov/wori/learn/historyculture/wendell-phillips.htm.

Wetta, F.J. *The Louisiana Scalawags: Politics, Race, and Terrorism During the Civil War and Reconstruction.* Baton Rouge: Louisiana State University Press, 2013.

Wheeler, L. (1981). *Loving Warriors: Selected Letters of Lucy Stone and Henry B. Blackwell, 1853–1893.* New York: Dial, 1981.

White, B.A. *The Beecher Sisters.* New Haven, CT, and London: Yale University Press, 2003.

"Why in Vineland?" New Jersey home page, American Local History Network, Cumberland County, New Jersey. http://www.usgen net.org/usa/nj/county/cumberland/Vine Vote/Why.html.

"Woman Suffrage: Why the Radicals Give Negroes the Suffrage—Why They Will Refuse It to Women. *Cleveland (OH) Plain Dealer,* June 7, 1867.

"Women Who Voted." The Elizabeth Cady Stanton and Susan B. Anthony Papers Project. http://ecssba.rutgers.edu/resources/voters.html.

Zornow, W.F. "'Bluff Ben'" Wade in Lawrence, Kansas: The Issue of Class Conflict." *Ohio History Journal* 65, no. 1 (January 1956), 44–52. http://resources.ohiohistory.org/ohj/browse/displaypages.php?display%5B%5D=0065&display%5B%5D=44&display%5B%5D=52.

Newspapers

Albany Evening Journal
Atchison Champion
Boston Commonwealth
The Boston Liberator
Boston National Anti-Slavery Standard
Burlington (KS) Patriot
Chicago Daily Inter Ocean
Chicago Tribune
Cincinnati Daily Enquirer
Cincinnati Daily Gazette
Cleveland (OH) Plain Dealer
Columbus (OH) Crisis
Dallas (TX) Herald
Emporia (VA) News
Flake's Weekly Galveston Bulletin
Fort Scott (KS) Monitor
Harrisburg (PA) Patriot
Indianapolis Daily Herald
Junction City (KS) Weekly Union
Kansas Farmer
Lawrence Daily Tribune
Leavenworth Daily Commercial
Leavenworth Daily Conservative
Leavenworth Evening Bulletin
The London Vote
Lowell (MA) Daily Citizen
Murfreesboro (TN) Monitor
New York Evening Post

New York Herald
New York Independent
New York Times
New York Tribune
New York World
Philadelphia Enquirer
Philadelphia Press
Rayville (LA) Richland Beacon-News
The Revolution
Sacramento Daily Union
Springfield (MA) Republican

St. Johnsbury (VT) Caledonian
St. Louis (MO) Democrat
St. Louis Dispatch
Vermont Phoenix, Brattleboro, Vermont.
Washington (D.C.) Daily National Intelligencer
Washington (D.C.) Evening Star
Watertown (NY) Daily Reformer
Weekly Free Press
White Cloud (KS) Kansas Chief
Wyandotte (KS) Commercial Gazette

Index